RESOLVING RESISTANCES IN PSYCHOTHERAPY

RESOLVING RESISTANCES IN PSYCHOTHERAPY

Herbert S. Strean, D.S.W.

Director, New York Center for Psychoanalytic Training
Professor Emeritus, Rutgers University

BRUNNER/MAZEL, *Publishers* • New York

Library of Congress Cataloging-in-Publication Data

Strean, Herbert S.
    Resolving resistances in psychotherapy / Herbert S. Strean.
        p.   cm.
    Reprint. Originally published: New York : Wiley, c1985.
    Includes bibliographical references.
    ISBN 0-87630-584-2
    1. Resistance (Psychoanalysis) 2. Psychotherapist and patient.
3. Countertransference (Psychology)   I. Title.
    [DNLM: 1. Patient Acceptance of Health Care. 2. Patient
Compliance. 3. Patients—psychology. 4. Physician-Patient
Relations. 5. Psychotherapy. 6. Transference (Psychology)   WM420
S914r 1985a]
RC489.R49S77   1990
616.89'14 — dc20
DNLM/DLC
for Library of Congress
                                                          90-1340
                                                          CIP

Published by
BRUNNER/MAZEL, INC.
19 Union Square West
New York, New York 10003

Manufactured in the United States of America

10 9 8 7 6 5 4 3 2

To Reuben Fine, Ph.D.

a brilliant theoretician and a sensitive clinician—
in honor of his 70th birthday

Preface

Ever since psychotherapy has been recognized as a legitimate form of occupational endeavor, clinicians have been preoccupied with their clients' resistances. Although individuals who are in psychotherapy invariably acknowledge that they are dissatisfied with the way they are coping with their interpersonal relationships, are disturbed by their neurotic symptoms (e.g., phobias, obsessions, insomnia, psychosomatic complaints), and are tortured by their low self-esteem, weak self-images, and ugly body images, therapists observe a universal paradox in psychotherapy—all clients unconsciously want to preserve the status quo no matter how dysfunctional it is. Regardless of the setting (e.g., in a social agency, a mental health clinic, or a consultation room of a private practitioner) and regardless of the modality (e.g., one-to-one long-term treatment, short-term therapy, group therapy, or family therapy), all clients present obstacles to their feeling and functioning better.

Because most psychotherapists subscribe to the notion that the client's behavior, attitudes, and functioning are molded by unconscious and irrational motives, they are not shocked when they observe a client arriving 45 minutes late for a 50-minute therapy session and without complaining pay $50–100 for the session. Nor are therapists dismayed when they observe a man or woman who is making a lot of therapeutic progress speak disparagingly of the therapist and the therapy. Therapists who accept resistance as a part of the therapeutic process are accustomed to hearing the impotent man extol the virtues of celibacy, the unhappily married couple insist that fighting and hating are inevitable features of married life, and the alcoholic or drug addict proclaim that dysfunctional ways of coping are superior.

Inasmuch as clients must protect themselves from real and fantasied dangers that therapy induces, resistance seems to be an inevitable form of behavior in psychotherapy. Consequently, many authors have written on the dynamics of resistance. Starting with the father of modern psychotherapy, Sigmund Freud, there has been much discussion in the literature on the enormous importance of resistance and the desperation from which it derives. Freud pointed out quite early in his career that clients protect themselves in therapy the same way they do in their life situations. If a man or a woman feels that the gratification or even the acknowledgment of sexual or aggressive wishes is taboo, he or she will defend against them by denial, repression, projection, or some other defense mechanism. In his or her therapy, as unconscious wishes become conscious, the client will fight their recognition and expression by seeking familiar forms of flight.

Over the years such people as Anna Freud, Ralph Greenson, Wilhelm Reich, Heinz Hartmann, Reuben Fine, and Edward Glover have attempted to identify and categorize the many resistances that clients manifest in therapy. These therapists have also attempted to explain the psychological advantages that resistances offer to the client. Consequently, when clients chronically come late to interviews, consistently do not pay their bill, frequently threaten to leave treatment, or complain that they are not getting better and may be getting worse, most therapists realize that the clients are trying to cope with real or imagined dangers that seem to derive from the therapeutic experience. Clients may be worried that they will be punished for their aggression, entrapped for their sexual wishes, demeaned for their dependency, or scoffed at for their childishness.

To a lesser extent, a few authors have attempted to provide some strategies for helping clients resolve certain kinds of resistances. Freud's advice to the therapist is still pertinent. He suggested that, in many instances, the client's resistive behavior can be explained by investigating his or her transference fantasies. When the client's forbidden aggressive or sexual feelings toward the therapist become more conscious, usually the client has less need to cling to self-destructive, resistive behavior.

Since Freud, such writers as Ralph Greenson, Reuben Fine, Roy Schafer, Robert Langs, Joseph Sandler, and Reuben and Gertrude Blanck have suggested various means to help clients gain insight into and eventually resolve their resistances. For example, Roy Schafer (1983) has discussed the importance of the therapist's neutral attitude; Robert Langs (1973) has emphasized the contribution of the therapist's neurotic problems to the maintenance of the client's resistive behavior; Blanck and Blanck (1979) have focused on the level of the client's maturity in determining which treatment techniques are appropriate in helping clients resolve resistances; and Reuben Fine (1982) has stressed the importance of the therapist's own personal therapy in equipping him or her to help clients overcome their resistive attitudes and behavior.

Although the term *counterresistance* is not foreign to most therapists, there have been few systematic attempts in the literature to discuss the therapist's contribution to the evolution, maintenance, and intractability of client resistances. From the moment the client calls on the phone for a consultation to the termination of the contact, the therapist has fantasies and feelings toward the client that strongly influence the client's activity and inactivity in the therapy. Often therapists play a role in clients' absences from interviews, clients' tardiness, clients' nonpayment of fees, and other negative therapeutic reactions of clients. Freud himself considered some of these issues and more recently such writers as Robert Langs (1981) and Reuben Fine (1982) have dealt with certain features of counterresistance.

The first two chapters of this book review the pertinent literature from Freud to the present on resistance, counterresistance, and those therapeutic techniques that are used to resolve client resistances. This will serve as a background for our major mission—a visit to the consultation room to acquaint the reader with client resistances from the first telephone contact through the initial interviews, into the middle phases of treatment and on to termination.

In each of the following chapters, we will identify the major forms of resistance pertinent to a specific phase of treatment, and present and analyze case vignettes that demonstrate particular resistive behavior or attitudes. For example, in the early chapters we will focus on such situations as the client who eagerly makes an appointment for an initial consultation but cancels it before he or she meets the therapist and the client who "feels great" after six interviews and wants to quit the therapy prematurely. In later chapters we will discuss such situations as the client who has "worked and worked for 2 years" but feels worse and the client who after a year or two is convinced that the therapist is either incompetent, stupid, or a charlatan. Toward the end of the book, we will present such situations as the client who feels and functions quite well after several years of therapy but does not want to quit.

Chapters 3–7 will:

1. Discuss the dynamics of specific resistances and attempt to explain why, for example, Mr. Jones arrives late for interviews or why Mrs. Smith does not want to talk to the therapist.

2. Evaluate the therapist's activity and counterresistances, if applicable. For example, what did the therapist say or do, or not say or do, that "helped" Mr. Jones arrive late for interviews? Or what did the therapist say or do, or not say or do, that prevented Mrs. Smith from talking in the therapy?

3. Recommend specific procedures that will help clients resolve specific resistances. For example, what can the therapist do that will help Mr. Jones want to arrive for his appointments on time, help Mrs. Smith want to talk, or help Mr. Davis want to give up some of his excessive compliance?

More specifically, in Chapter 1 we will review the literature on resistance starting with Freud and work our way up to the present. We will discuss the various definitions of resistance and how certain authors have categorized, explained, and evaluated resistances as a dimension of therapy. In Chapter 2, we will review the literature on therapeutic techniques used in resolving resistances and examine some of the literature on the therapist's counterresistance. Here, we will attempt to demonstrate how more and more writers are viewing client resistance as a dynamic that can never be divorced from the therapist's activity or inactivity or from his or her fantasies and feelings toward the client. Chapter 3 will discuss the resistances that emerge in the early phases of therapy, such as the client's reluctance to make an initial appointment, his or her resistance to revealing such information as symptoms and history, and his or her reluctance to pay a fee. In Chapter 4, we will discuss a phenomenon formulated by the psychoanalyst Reuben Fine, called "the first treatment crisis." Here, the client finds the treatment quite threatening, and resistances can take the form of wanting to quit treatment or wanting to express distress by some other dramatic gesture. Chapters 5 and 6 consist of a theoretical discussion supplemented by case illustrations that will help the reader become more sensitized to the meaning and resolution of some of the most common types of resistances during psychotherapy. In Chapter 7, we will discuss the resistances to termination and the therapist's contribution to the resolution or maintenance of these resistances.

In sum, this book will examine each phase of therapy—beginning, middle, and end—and discuss the various forms of resistance that clients exhibit at each phase. The case vignettes and their analyses I hope will sensitize the reader to the reasons clients resist the way they do, how therapists contribute toward the maintenance of certain resistances, and how therapists can help clients overcome resistive behaviors and attitudes.

Those readers familiar with my previous work will note that some of the case illustrations appearing in this book have appeared in part in *The Sexual Dimension, The Extramarital Affair,* and *Psychoanalytic Theory and Social Work Practice.*

I am grateful to the many students, colleagues, patients, clients, and teachers who have contributed ideas and case examples to this book. I am also grateful to Mark Tracten, President of Brunner/Mazel, and Natalie Gilman, Editorial Vice President, for their cooperation and generous support in making this book available to the many mental health practitioners who have requested it. Finally, I would like to thank my wife, Marcia, and our two sons, Richard and Billy, for their patience and forbearance while I was working on this book.

—HERBERT S. STREAN

Contents

RESOLVING RESISTANCES IN PSYCHOTHERAPY

CHAPTER 1

Defining Resistance:
A Review of the Literature

Although most individuals who enter psychotherapy welcome the idea of unburdening themselves and saying everything that comes into their minds, sooner or later this process becomes painful and creates anxiety. As clients discover parts of themselves that have been repressed, confront forbidden sexual and aggressive fantasies, and recover embarrassing memories, they invariably begin to feel guilt and shame. This sense of discomfort can occur in the first, tenth, or twentieth session of psychotherapy, but sooner or later all clients feel frightened of what they are revealing. Then they may become silent and evasive, or want to quit the therapy altogether. In discussing certain incidents from their pasts or current circumstances, many clients become annoyed at the therapist for not reassuring, praising, or admonishing them. It is at this point that they may question the wisdom of being in therapy or the therapist's competence.

When clients stop producing material and cease to examine themselves, we refer to this kind of behavior as *resistance*. Resistance is any action or attitude of the client's that impedes the course of therapeutic work. Inasmuch as every client, to some extent, wants unconsciously to preserve the status quo, all therapy must be carried on in the face of some resistance.

Resistance always implies that the client feels that some kind of danger is impending. Individuals in therapy worry that they may be abandoned for their wishes, unloved for their demands, attacked for their opinions, or punished for their actions. When clients feel anxious about some impending danger, they have to protect themselves. What are referred to as defenses in the client's daily life—for example, projection, denial, repression—are resistances in psychotherapy. If, for example, a male client has a tendency to project his anger onto his wife and other individuals, in therapy he will try to avoid examining his own angry thoughts and feelings and will report how his wife, friends, and relatives are hostile to him. From time to time, he will also accuse the therapist of being contemptuous of him.

1

It is important to keep in mind that resistance is not created by the therapy. The therapeutic situation activates anxiety, and the client then uses habitual mechanisms to oppose the therapist and the therapy (Greenson, 1967). To a greater or lesser degree, resistances are present from the beginning to the end of treatment (Freud, 1912a).

Defining a resistance is, of course, a function of the therapist's view of personality functioning, his* view of what is neurotic or maladaptive behavior, and his aims and goals for the client (Langs, 1981). For example, a Jungian therapist may view a client's fear of asserting himself in the therapy as "a clash between collective and individual loyalties" (G. Adler, 1967), whereas a Freudian therapist may view the resistance as emanating from the client's unresolved oedipal conflict (Fenichel, 1945). Similarly, an Adlerian therapist may take the position that "a decrease in resistance can only be brought about when a patient develops contact with people on a more friendly and equal basis" (K. Adler, 1967, pp. 326–327), whereas a mainstream psychoanalyst would stress the importance of the patient gaining insight into wishes, defenses, and superego commands, particularly as they emerge in the transference relationship with the therapist (Greenson, 1967).

In a case example, ego psychologists Gertrude and Reuben Blanck (1979) pointed out that sending a postcard to a client during the therapist's absence helped the client with her sense of despair and depression. Upon returning to therapy, the client began arriving late for her sessions. The authors suggested that to regard this lateness as a resistance would have been damaging; instead, the authors viewed it as an act of genuine and constructive independence. Psychoanalyst Robert Langs, in reflecting on the Blancks' material, states that "many analysts would suspect that this behavior reflected a maladaptive resolution of underlying conflicts and fantasies, rather than a sign of true growth and independence" (1981, p. 463).

A piece of behavior such as lateness to appointments has different meanings to different clients because it emanates from different sets of motives, and as the above discussion suggests, the same behavior has different meaning to different therapists. From the therapist's perspective, the identification of resistive behavior relies in many ways upon the therapist's clinical judgment, conception of maladaptive behavior, and notions regarding the dynamics of the therapeutic process.

Let us now turn to a review of what the major contributors to the literature on resistance have said about the subject.

---

* For convenience and economy of words, the pronoun *he* is used in this book to mean either he or she.

SIGMUND FREUD

No writer has contributed more to the psychotherapist's understanding of resistance than has Sigmund Freud. As early as the 1890s in *Studies on Hysteria* (1893–1895), which was written with Josef Breuer, Freud mentioned the term *resistance* for the first time. While treating a young woman, Elisabeth von R., Freud pointed out that the patient fended off some incompatible ideas. He pointed out that when patients in psychotherapy have to face unbearable ideas, they feel endangered. To avoid danger, the patients "cut off the unbearable ideas" from the rest of their ideational life and from their free associations as if these unbearable ideas were "foreign bodies" (Breuer & Freud, 1893–1895, p. 157).

At the time Freud was treating patients such as Elisabeth von R., he was using hypnosis and stressed that the resistance to being hypnotized was the patient's unwillingness to be hypnotized. He further asserted that the therapist had to help the patient overcome "a psychological force" that was opposed to unbearable ideas becoming conscious and that this force played a part in creating the patient's symptoms in the first place. Inasmuch as the patient's ideas were unbearably painful, his ego erected a defense to drive the painful ideas out of consciousness and opposed their return in memory. The patient's not knowing was really a not wanting to know.

Freud's notion that resistances are used to protect the client against the pain of recognizing unbearable ideas continues to be accepted by most practicing therapists. Furthermore, his realization that the client unconsciously arranges his resistances is also accepted by most practitioners. And most contemporary therapists agree with Freud that resistances are stubborn, return repeatedly, take many forms, and are frequently rationalized away.

In *The Interpretation of Dreams* (1900), Freud noted that if the therapist can help a patient overcome a resistance, the patient will be enabled to recall a forgotten dream. In considering the forgetting of dreams, Freud concluded: "Whatever interrupts the progress of analytic work is a resistance" (p. 517).

In 1905, while working on the case of Dora, Freud wrote that the analysand's feelings and fantasies about the therapist constitute the patient's major resistance. Freud wrote a great deal about this phenomenon—that is, the transference—and we will review his findings on transference later in this discussion. In the case of Dora, Freud (1905a) pointed out that Dora broke off the analysis because she could not tolerate facing her erotic feelings toward the analyst—that is, she resisted facing her erotic transference. In a later paper, "The Dynamics of Transference"

(1912a), Freud concluded that the battles in the sphere of transference resistance are often selected for the most bitter conflicts in the therapy. He compared such resistance to a combat situation:

> If in the course of the battle there is a particularly embittered struggle over the possession of some little church or some individual farm, there is no need to suppose that the church is a national shrine, perhaps, or that the house shelters the army's pay chest. The value of the object may be a purely tactical one and may perhaps emerge only in this one battle. (p 104)

In "Remembering, Repeating, and Working Through" (1914), Freud discussed the "repetition compulsion," a special type of resistance in which the analysand reenacts a past experience instead of remembering it. An example of this might be the client's constantly trying to provoke the therapist into arguments, rather than remembering how much he hated his father and would have loved to fight with him but felt too intimidated to do so.

Of the numerous attempts that have been made to classify resistances, the most thorough one and the one that has been most used by dynamically oriented therapists is Freud's 1926 classification in his book *Inhibitions, Symptoms, and Anxiety.*

1.   *Repression and other defenses (projection, denial).*   These are used by the ego to ward off unconscious material that would arouse anxiety. In order to avoid a painful emotion, such as guilt or shame, that has been aroused by a forbidden sexual or aggressive impulse, the individual in therapy blocks the impulse from consciousness (repression), denies that he feels anything, or projects the forbidden impulse onto the therapist or someone else, such as a spouse or colleague. For example, a client might begin to experience sexual or aggressive fantasies toward the therapist but feel that he will be rebuked or abandoned by the therapist if he verbalizes them. To ward off this danger, he may *repress* his fantasies and say to the therapist, "Whenever I'm in your office, I feel nothing!" Or he may consistently arrive late for his sessions, "forget" to pay his bill, have his checks bounce, talk about how his family and friends question the value of psychotherapy, but concomitantly *deny* that he has any angry feelings toward the therapist! Finally, the client may frequently accuse the therapist of trying to seduce him or of feeling angry toward him, thus *projecting* his forbidden wishes onto the therapist.

In psychoanalysis or psychotherapy, as the patient or client free associates, inevitably he will become aware of forbidden thoughts or wishes that create anxiety—for example, incestuous wishes or murderous impulses. It is these forbidden wishes that are being warded off by the client's neurotic symptomatology. Although the client would consciously like to get rid of his symptoms, when he is in therapy he uses his habitual defense mechanisms to avoid facing his wishes. He then unconsciously opposes the therapy and the therapist, and tells the therapist, "Every time I come to your office, you make me feel uncomfortable."

By 1926, Freud recognized that analysands needed resistances to protect themselves from pain and that defenses were like skin—they protected the person and should not be removed abruptly or prematurely. Actually, as early as 1914, in "Remembering, Repeating, and Working Through," Freud said:

> The working through of the resistances may in practice turn out to be an arduous task for the subject of the analysis and a trial of patience for the analyst. Nevertheless, it is a part of the work which effects the greatest changes in a patient and which distinguishes analytic treatment from any (other) kind of treatment. (p. 145)

2. *Transference resistance.* Although Freud and many of his followers have at times separated transference and resistance as two distinct concepts, transference must be viewed as a resistance because it preserves the status quo and protects the client against real or fantasied danger. When Freud initially conceptualized transference as a resistance, he pointed out that analysands wish to perceive the analyst as if he were a figure of the past so that they can avoid facing unpleasant emotions and memories in the present. Rather than recognize their own wishes to continue a fight with parents or other members of their family, analysands frequently ascribe parental qualities to the analyst and then feel that the analyst is provocative, rejecting, or manipulative.

Freud (1912a) singled out the notion of transference for much discussion. He pointed out that it is a universal phenomenon of the human mind and in fact dominates the whole of each person's relations to his environment. Freud further averred that transference exists in all relationships: in marriage, the classroom, business relations, and friendships. Because of our histories, ego functioning, superego mandates, values, and social circumstances, all of which are unique, each of us brings with us to every new relationship wishes, fears, anxieties, hopes, pressures, defenses, and many more subjective factors that have evolved from previous relationships and that may or may not be appropriate in the new situation. Inasmuch as these universal phenomena are largely unconscious, we cannot will them away or consciously modify them. They influence our perceptions of the people we meet, and very often the reasons we give for responding to people with love, hatred, or ambivalence are rationalizations—that is, excuses to justify our reactions.

We have all had emotionally charged experiences—positive, negative, and ambivalent—with parents, siblings, extended family, and others that have left indelible marks on us; consequently, our attitudes toward intimate relationships in the present are colored by these past transactions. We continue to seek in new relationships what was pleasant in the past and to resist what was unpleasant.

The intimate relationship of client and therapist is one in which the client depends on the therapist. This invariably reactivates feelings and ideas about the therapist that the client experienced with those on whom he depended in the past. If the client has experienced those who nurtured, advised, and educated him as essentially positive and well meaning, he will in all likelihood experience the therapist in the same way. However, usually there are residual mixtures of love, hate, and ambivalence toward parents and others in all individuals, and every therapist will be the recipient of all these feelings.

Freud's notions on transference (1914, 1926, 1912a) have had enormous impact on therapists of many different theoretical orientations. Freud pointed out that, if therapists do not understand how they are being experienced by their clients, they cannot be very helpful to them. All clients respond to their therapists' interpretations, clarifications, or environmental manipulations in terms of their transferences. If Mrs. Smith loves her therapist, she will be inclined to accept most of his therapeutic interventions; if she hates the therapist, even the most neutral question, such as "How do you feel?" will be suspect. Finally, if she has mixed feelings, she will respond to virtually all interventions ambivalently. Freud further pointed out (1914) that one of the tasks of the analyst is to help the analysand see how and why he experiences the analyst as he does. Why does one analysand act like a compliant child and accept everything the analyst says? Or why does another analysand argue with the analyst every time the latter says something? Why is the analyst's quietness experienced by one analysand as rejection and by another as love?

Although transference reactions are always traceable to childhood, there is not always a simple one-to-one correspondence between the past and present. While sometimes there is a direct repetition, such as when the analysand is quite convinced that the analyst is almost identical to his father, mother, or sibling, frequently there can be a "compensatory fantasy" (Fine, 1982) to make up for what was lacking in childhood. That is, the analysand fantasies that the therapist is somebody that his mother or father should have been.

When therapists recognize that transference always exists in all the relationships that clients have with them, they can look at their therapeutic results more objectively. If the client wants the therapist to be an omnipotent parent to whom he can cling, then the client will fight interventions that are aimed to help him become more autonomous. If the client wants the therapist to be a sibling rival, then the therapist's interventions will be used by the client to continue his sibling fight. Inasmuch as the client responds to all the therapist's interventions through the lens of his transference, the therapist must explore with the client, not just why he resists change, but more specifically, why he wants to perceive the therapist in a childish way (Freud, 1912a).

Freud pointed out that the analysand's overt statements toward the analyst might cover up opposite feelings (Freud, 1905a, 1912a). From the analysand's dreams and fantasies, it may be inferred that overt positive and loving feelings expressed toward the analyst might be covering up negative and hateful feelings. Similarly, proclamations of hatred might be defending against warm feelings toward the analyst.

A very common use of the transference is the client's projection onto the therapist of unacceptable parts of the client's psychic structure—id wishes, ego defenses, or superego mandates. Many therapists are perceived as "dirty old men" or "seductive women" because the client is resisting the treatment by projecting unacceptable id wishes onto the therapist. More often than not, the client projects his superego onto the therapist and expects punishment from him. Freud pointed out that in the process of socialization the child gives up various modes of instinctual gratification at the request of significant figures (Freud, 1905b). This process is crystallized in the superego, which induces guilt. Guilt is superego punishment (Freud, 1926). Inasmuch as the superego is formed in interaction with significant individuals, it can only be changed by interaction. The client projects his superego onto the therapist, and a consistent comparison of this projection with reality breaks down the superego in the course of time (Fine, 1982).

What distinguishes a therapeutic relationship from any other are not the dynamics of transference but its place in the relationship—that is, the therapist's attitude toward the transference and the use he makes of it. In contrast to a friend or relative, who will generally comply with the client's request for encouragement, advice, or punishment, the analytically oriented therapist wants to know why the client wants these responses and then helps the client try to discover the motives that propel his requests.

In sum, Freud pointed out that transference exists in all relationships (Freud, 1905a, 1912a, 1914, 1926). There is no such thing as a client who has no transference. As therapist and client accept transference as a fact of therapy and constantly study the client's transference responses, they gain an appreciation of the nature of the client's conflicts and the aspect of the client's history that is contributing to his dysfunctional behavior.

3. *Epinosic gain.*   A common form of resistance that Freud recognized quite early in his work with his analysands was their tendency to derive unconscious gratification and protection from their neurotic symptoms. He pointed out that, although there is much conscious pain when the analysand suffers from a phobia, compulsion, obsession, or psychosomatic disease, the analysand enjoys the benefit of being relieved from responsibilities in work, marriage, or other areas of interpersonal interaction and therefore clings to the illness.

Because a client can get considerable masochistic gratification from complaining about being the victim of a spouse's belittling, an employer's derision, a parent's criticism, or a bodily ache, the therapist may unconsciously be viewed by the client as an enemy who when trying to examine his client's motives is also trying to disrupt an important, albeit neurotic, balance. On viewing the therapist as an opponent, the client might then wish to leave treatment.

Freud's awareness that clients in many ways write their own psychological and interpersonal scripts has helped many therapists recognize that a common form of resisting therapy is to complain about one's sad plight in marriage, work, school, or elsewhere. Clients in their therapeutic sessions can indulge themselves by "injustice collecting" (Bergler, 1969) rather than mature by examining themselves. Freud's notion of epinosic gain, or what is sometimes referred to as "secondary gain" (Greenson, 1967), has stimulated the modern clinician to recognize that behind every chronic complaint is an unconscious wish. The man who chronically complains to his therapist that his wife is cold and unyielding unconsciously wants his wife to be ungiving; if the wife behaved otherwise, the man would become frightened. Similarly, the wife who chronically complains that her husband is weak and passive, unconsciously wants her husband to behave this way; if he became strong and assertive, she would become frightened. And the parent who chronically complains about his son or daughter achieves gratification from the dysfunctional behavior of the child (Strean, 1979, 1980).

The proof that the epinosic gain is a crucial variable in therapy is the common observation that the chronically complaining spouse rarely divorces and the perennial psychosomatic patient rarely tries to give up the habitual taking of medication. A valid proof that the chronic complaint is an unconscious wish is that clients seen in dynamically oriented therapy will invariably complain about their therapists in the same way that they complain about their spouses or their children. If the complaining wife views her husband as weak, eventually she experiences the therapist in this way, and if the complaining husband perceives his wife as unresponsive, sooner or later he will perceive the therapist in this way, too.

4. *Superego resistance.* In superego resistance, clients abuse themselves with guilt and self-punishment because of their unacceptable sexual and aggressive wishes.

Freud's discovery of superego resistance has helped many clinicians understand a very frequent occurrence in psychotherapy—namely, clients begin to understand their resistances and transference reactions, and to give up neurotic symptoms and maladaptive functioning, only later to function worse and feel horrible. As Freud noted this phenomenon repeatedly in his work, he began to realize that many individuals feel very guilty when they make progress in therapy and feel better; consequently, they punish themselves by feeling and functioning worse.

Superego resistance emerges when one or more of the following conditions is taking place: (1) the client is unconsciously obeying a parental mandate (e.g., "Do not have pleasure, and do not enjoy your life"); (2) the client is in an unconscious battle with his parents and significant others, and by getting better, he feels hostilely triumphant and then must punish himself by getting worse; (3) by feeling worse and functioning poorly, the client is unconsciously releasing anger toward the therapist and covertly trying to defeat the therapist.

Many clients in therapy have internalized images of parents who are constantly admonishing them that they will never amount to anything. These internalized images are part of the client's superego, and every time the client moves forward in life or in therapy, he feels obligated to acquiesce to the parents' commands.

By understanding that analysands carry their parents around with them, even if the parents are dead, Freud was able to demonstrate that a great deal of despair is built up in individuals who go into psychotherapy. It is as if these individuals were convinced very early in life that they become criminals when their lots in life become better. Consequently, they feel more comfortable when they are feeling miserable.

It is well known that, when children feel frustrated, restricted, or ungratified, they become revengeful. Often clients in treatment have many murderous fantasies toward their parents. These men and women experience their therapeutic progress as retaliation on their parents. Although they may gloat for a while, eventually they arrange for their superego to punish them for their "transgressions," and this is done by unconsciously arranging for more neurotic suffering and therapeutic impasses.

As we discussed in the section on transference resistance, all clients during a great part of the therapy turn the therapist into a parental figure. Many clients unconsciously try to take revenge on the therapist by not getting better, in the same way that they took revenge on parents by not functioning well in the outside world. As Fine has said:

This kind of revenge, paradoxical though it may seem, can become an enormously meaningful drive for some patients; in a few cases it has been driven as far as suicide, with the thought: "I'll show the world what a lousy psychiatrist (or psychologist) he is." When a human being becomes attached to a parent substitute in a masochistic way, the vicissitudes of his self-damaging activities may be, and often are, quite serious. (1971, p. 122)

5. *Id resistance.* Freud used the term *id resistance* in referring to individuals in psychotherapy who continue to seek gratification of unrealistic childish wishes, such as the wish to be omnipotent infants and have all demands met pronto. Id resistances are ubiquitous in psychotherapy. Many clients want to be the therapist's favorite child and make many demands on the therapist, such as making constant phone calls between sessions, pleading for advice in and out of sessions, and refusing to accept the frustrations and abstinence that are necessary for therapy to have a positive effect.

Freud recognized that many men and women can manufacture crises and appear quite despondent in order to gratify the wish to be the therapist's baby. He pointed out how tenacious the resistance to remain an omnipotent baby is and how tempting it is for the therapist to give in to the client's demands. That is probably why Freud (1912b, 1915, 1919) never abandoned the model of the abstinent, anonymous surgeon who is an opaque mirror for his analysand.

In his last paper on the dynamics of resistance, "Analysis Terminable and Interminable" (1937a), Freud gave more thought to the tenacity of resistances in psychotherapy and offered some new theories on the nature of resistance. He concluded that there are three factors that can serve as obstacles to helping a patient succeed in psychotherapy: (1) the influence of traumas; (2) the constitutional strength of the instincts; and (3) alterations of the ego.

A trauma, such as the premature and sudden death of a loved one, abandonment, or loss of the love of an important person, will make the client reluctant to trust the therapist because the client will constantly anticipate that the therapist will die, abandon him, or withhold love.

By "constitutional strength of the instincts," Freud was referring to those individuals who have strong drives and may find it very difficult to renounce or control the expression of certain childish id impulses. These individuals seem to have a "lack of mobility of their libido," and Freud felt that the reason for this was their "adhesiveness of the libido and psychical inertia," which he designated as "resistance from the id" (Freud, 1937a, p. 242).

When Freud discussed "alterations of the ego," he was referring to those alterations due to the individual's defense mechanisms. For example, if a person denies, projects, and represses a great deal, in the treatment he will deny many psychological truths, project his wishes and fantasies onto the therapist and others, and repress many of his affects and memories.

Freud ended "Analysis Terminable and Interminable" (1937a) with some thoughts about the greatest resistances in men and in women. Recognizing that most people believe that the grass is always greener on the other side, he concluded that the greatest resistance in men stems from their fear of their passive feminine wishes toward other men, whereas in women the greatest source of resistance seems to be connected to their wishes to be men (i.e., their penis envy).

In reviewing Freud's writings on the definitions and the dynamics of resistance, we can note how his thinking changed as he acquired more experience. At first, Freud viewed resistance essentially as an obstacle to therapeutic work; later, he realized it was an inevitable reality in all therapy. He began to recognize that, inasmuch as individuals defended themselves in life situations in order to protect themselves against real and imagined dangers, the therapeutic situation would emerge as a danger and they would have to resist it by using their habitual defense mechanisms. Furthermore, when Freud embarked on his career, most of his work involved helping the patient to abreact and recover memories. Later, he realized that the resistances themselves were important sources of knowledge about the analysand's character traits, symptoms, and adaptation. As we have also seen, Freud at first thought that resistances were exclusively ego operations (i.e., repressing, projecting, denying); later he showed that the concept of resistance can also involve the id and the superego. Freud never wavered from his position that the working through of the resistances "is a part of the (analytic) work which effects the greatest changes in a patient and which distinguishes analytic treatment from any other kind of treatment" (1914, p. 145).

ANNA FREUD

The daughter of Sigmund Freud, Anna Freud has contributed a great deal to our understanding of resistances. In her book *The Ego and the Mechanisms of Defense* (1946), she enlarged and systematized our understanding of the various mechanisms of defense and related them to the resistances that emerge in psychotherapy. In addition to repression, projection, and denial, she discussed several other defense mechanisms. By doing so, she was able to reaffirm that resistances are not only obstacles to treatment but also important sources of information about ego functions in general. Defenses that come to light as resistances during therapy, Anna Freud pointed out, carry out important protective functions for the client in his outside life as well as in the therapy. Furthermore, these defenses are repeated in transference reactions to the therapist.

In order for the individual to cope with the anxiety stimulated by instinctual wishes that are unacceptable, by commands from the superego, or by threats from external reality, Anna Freud suggested that the individual employs one or more of the following defense mechanisms (which can become resistances in the therapeutic situation): (1) repression; (2) regression; (3) reaction formation; (4) isolation; (5) undoing; (6) projection; (7) introjection; and (8) turning against the self.

Repression is considered to be the chief factor at work in the genesis of neuroses. The other defenses, even when they assume an acute form, remain more within the limits of the normal. They manifest themselves in transformations, distortions, and deformities of the ego, which are in part the accompaniment of and in part substitutes for neurosis (A. Freud, 1946).

Repression gets rid of instinctual derivatives, just as external stimuli are abolished by denial. In denial, the client refuses to acknowledge a painful truth (e.g., that the therapy session is over or the therapist is ill or on vacation). *Reaction formation* reverses the real impulse or thought (e.g., "I do not hate, I love"). And *projection* is ascribing to another person one's unacceptable thought (e.g., "*You* have dirty thoughts, not I.").

Regression involves going back to earlier forms of satisfaction when anxiety occurs in the present—for example, the man who finds sex with his wife frightening and so leaves her every night and goes out with the boys to drink. In treatment he avoids discussing sexuality and wants to talk exclusively about how the therapist should nourish him.

In *isolation,* the individual separates feelings (which would be anxiety provoking) from thoughts—for example, the very obsessive person who describes an affect-laden experience, such as an illness or injury, quite factually and without emotion. *Undoing* involves an action or thought that undermines the anxiety that would emanate from another thought or action—for example, the individual who washes himself after having sexual thoughts or sensations. *Introjection* may be viewed as the partner of projection, in that the individual takes in qualities that he has ascribed to another person. *Turning against the self* involves turning emotions, frequently hostile emotions, against oneself rather than directing them at the person who evoked them.

Anna Freud's creative work on defenses culminated in her excellent contribution, the concept of identification (Dyer, 1983). Identification, she pointed out, is very important in superego formation and hence to the mastery of internal drives. It is one of the ego's most powerful devices for combatting external anxiety. For this to be achieved, identification must operate with other defensive processes, particularly projection. In one example, Anna Freud (1946, p. 110) discussed the case of an elementary schoolboy who involuntarily grimaced at a pathetic caricature of the angry face of his teacher, whereby he both projected his anger on to the teacher and identified with her anger. In another case illustration, she described a little girl who, being afraid of crossing the hall in the dark because she feared meeting ghosts, decided to pretend to be a ghost. Anna Freud noted that, far from being idiosyncratic, this behavior was "one of the most and widespread modes on the part of the primitive ego (in all children)" (1946, p. 111). Exorcism of spirits, primitive religious ceremonies, and certain games of childhood are all examples supporting her view that "identification is a common mechanism by which objective anxiety is converted into a feeling of safety and pleasure" (Dyer, 1983, p. 110).

The case illustrations cited above may be classified under the defense mechanism called "identification with the aggressor." This defense has three stages: (1) introjection of the characteristics of the person or people who are experienced as threatening; (2) impersonation of and identification with the person or people who are threatening; and (3) projection of the threatening and aggressive aspects of the perception back into the outside world (A. Freud, 1946, pp. 111–112). Many therapists have noted that many clients, children and adults, form a transference in which the helping professional is experienced as the aggressor with whom the client identifies. In using this mechanism, they misinterpret their friends', family members', and therapist's behavior.

As a response to objective anxiety, Anna Freud considered the mechanism of identification with the aggressor quite normal. She considered it abnormal, however, in a relationship such as a marriage when one partner with a wish to be unfaithful projects the wish onto the other partner, attacks the other partner for infidelity, and then develops an acute jealous reaction.

Anna Freud agreed with her father that what provokes defenses in life or resistances in therapy is anxiety. However, she elaborated on different types of anxiety:

1. *Real* or *objective anxiety* coincides with events in the actual world. She gave as an example "air-raid anxiety," in which the person is frightened of something very real. Most children, she noted, "use denial in the face of real anxiety so that they can return apparently undisturbed to the pursuits and interests of their own childish world" (1942b, p. 166). An example of this would be the client who realistically perceives that the therapist has erred in the therapeutic work, but the client refuses to acknowledge this.

2. *Instinctual anxiety* arises from the activation of sexual or aggres-

sive impulses that the client feels are asocial or bad. In treatment, the client will use habitual mechanisms to block awareness of these impulses.

3. *Moral anxiety* is when someone has the uncomfortable feeling that he has done something immoral and then is constantly on the lookout against being attacked by a person, animal, or some other dreaded object. An example might be the client who has murderous fantasies toward the therapist and then dreams following a therapy session of being arrested by a policeman.

An increment to the therapist's diagnostic and therapeutic repertoire comes from Anna Freud's notion that ego strength is not a static condition but must always be evaluated not only in terms of the functions of the ego but in relation to the individual and the intensity of pressures on him (A. Freud, 1946, 1965). For example, a strong ego of a 4-year-old is unable to tolerate the same frustrations and pressures as that of a 10-, 16-, or 30-year-old (Garrett, 1958).

Perhaps the greatest contribution to therapeutic practice that comes from Anna Freud is the respect for the client's defenses. As we have noted, in the early days of psychotherapy, many analysts and therapists viewed resistances and defenses as obstacles to be overcome rather than as protective layers of psychological skin that bind anxiety. Particularly when therapists are engaged in work with clients who have fragile egos, they recognize that frequently they have to go along with defensive statements of the client; otherwise, unbearable anxiety erupts, and the client either regresses or drops out of treatment (Strean, 1979).

In addition to her extremely well-received writing, Anna Freud organized, developed, and directed the Hampstead Child Therapy Clinic in London, England. Numerous publications produced by Freud and her colleagues have concerned themselves with the maturation and treatment of children and adolescents. In all her work, there is a constant emphasis on the direct observation of children and the effect of this observational material on aspects of classical psychoanalytical theory (Dyer, 1983; Wolman, 1972). Always remaining loyal to classical Freudian psychoanalysis, Anna Freud has at no point in her research or treatment departed from Sigmund Freud's orientation to people and their problems.

WILHELM REICH

Wilhelm Reich, primarily in his book *Character Analysis* (1949), added some theoretical insights on resistance to those formulated by Sigmund Freud and Anna Freud. Reich's main thesis was that, among the various resistances to be resolved in psychotherapy, are *character resistances*.

Character resistances are character traits that the client uses in coping and that are not felt as ego-alien problems (e.g., compulsiveness, masochism, arrogance). Reich contended that the bearing and attitude of the client—that is, his characterological "armor"—was the crucial guiding thread to understanding his psychodynamics, particularly how his idiosyncratic past has influenced his modus vivendi in the present.

Character traits, like defense mechanisms, express themselves as resistances in treatment. Reich pointed out that character resistances are manifested, "not in the content of the material, but in the formal aspects of the general behavior, the manner of talking, of the gait, facial expression and typical attitudes such as smiling, deriding, haughtiness, over-correctness, the manner of the politeness or of the aggression, etc." (1949, p. 47). What is important about the character resistance is not what the client says or does, but *how* he talks and acts; not what he gives away in a dream, but *how* he censors and distorts.

Reich pointed out that the character trait in ordinary life and the character resistance in treatment both serve the function of avoiding unpleasure, of establishing and maintaining a psychic equilibrium, albeit neurotic, and of absorbing repressed energies. One of the cardinal functions of the character resistance is binding free-floating anxiety. Just as the historical, infantile elements are present and active in neurotic symptomology, they are also present in the character. "This is why a consistent dissolving of character resistance provides an infallible and immediate avenue of approach to the central infantile conflict" (1949, p. 48).

Reich, in virtually all of his writings (1945, 1946, 1948, 1949), emphasized the "sexual core" of neurosis. He maintained that only by a thorough analysis of "the sexual inhibitions in the character" can a person eventually mature and function well. He stated over and over, "If the patient is to get well and stay well he must become able to establish satisfactory genital sex life" (1949, p. 15). As the patient's "character armor is loosened," his sexual energies become available for gratification.

Like most analytically oriented therapists of his day (and of today), Reich contended that the patient's present-day conflicts must be viewed as emerging from his childhood. He was able to demonstrate from his clinical material that current sexual difficulties emerge because the patient is still trying to gratify infantile wishes that his superego rejects.

Notions of character analysis and of character resistance, although not always identified as coming from Wilhelm Reich, are accepted by many modern psychotherapists. Reich and his work, however, tend to be dismissed frequently because, during Reich's last few years of life, he became preoccupied with the orgone box as a cure for neuroses, particularly neurotic sexual problems, and was found guilty by federal authorities of fraudulent practices of advertising. Although he appeared confused and possibly paranoid in his last few years, his contributions to the therapeutic world, particularly his notions on character resistance, cannot be denied.

HEINZ HARTMANN

As one traces the development of dynamically oriented psychotherapy, one sees a movement from a preoccupation with the id and the sexual and aggressive drives to a concern with the ego and its functions. A theoretician very identified with the psychology of the ego is Heinz Hartmann. Although in his writings Hartmann tended to neglect clinical data, his concepts regarding the ego have profound implications for therapeutic work in helping clients resolve resistances.

Most of Hartmann's major contributions to ego psychology are in his volume *Ego Psychology and the Problem of Adaptation* (1958). Here Hartmann begins the study of ego functions by noting that, although the ego grows as a result of conflict (which is what Freud contended), this is not the only root of its development. Hartmann distinguished two groups of ego functions: those specifically involved in conflict and those that develop outside of conflict—perception, thinking, memory, language, walking, and learning processes. Hartmann introduced the concept of a "conflict-free ego sphere" for that "ensemble of functions" that at any given time exert their effects outside the region of mental conflicts.

In effect, conflict-free ego functions exist from birth and are not the result of drive modification. Their independence from drives is also characterized by their autonomous development, and for these reasons, Hartmann decided to call them "primary autonomous functions of the ego." The notion of autonomy is relative, for Hartmann has noted that one cannot think of an ego in isolation, without considering the influence of drives, the superego, and the external environment.

Development was viewed by Hartmann as the result of the complicated interaction between instinctual drives, ego defenses, and autonomous ego functions—as a gradual unfolding of the psychic structure under the impact of the processes of differentiation and integration. In discussing adaptability and the processes of adaptation, Hartmann emphasized that a therapist must consider not only a person's early childhood but also the person's ability to maintain his adaptation in later life.

In the life of the individual, the ego's autonomous functions are not limited to those present in infancy. During his socialization in childhood and his complex later adaptations to the exigencies of society, the human being forms various behavior patterns, character structures, ego apparatuses, and tendencies (Hartmann, 1958, 1964).

One of Hartmann's major concepts is that, in the process of development and socialization, parts of the ego that are initially involved in conflict may show a change of function (Hartmann, 1958). For example, a child may use part of the ego to defend himself against anal matters by being clean, orderly, punctilious, and so on. These character traits may eventually become part of the character and be conflict free.

Hartmann distinguished primary autonomous ego functions—that is, those present at birth or soon after—from "secondary autonomous ego functions," which mature subsequently as a result of change of function. The stability of secondary autonomous zones can be measured by their "resistivity to regression" (Hartmann, 1950).

One other well-known concept of Hartmann's is "regression in the service of the ego." By this concept, Hartmann (1958) meant that in certain instances regression (play, daydreaming, fantasy) can serve creative ends and contribute to adaptation.

Hartmann's contributions to ego psychology may be summarized in the following four propositions:

1. The human being is born adapted to an average expectable environment. From the beginning, the individual possesses the roots of primary autonomous ego functions belonging to the conflict-free sphere. These include mobility, language, memory, and perception. They serve the ends of adaptation and are not born out of conflict with the environment.

2. Adaptation is a reciprocal process between the individual and his environment.

3. Through change of function, many processes that were originally defensive become apparatuses of secondary ego autonomy.

4. Regression in the service of the ego can serve creative ends and contribute to adaptation.

In reviewing Hartmann's contributions, we find that several of his notions relate to the clinical situation and can be helpful to the therapist in assessing and trying to resolve a client's resistances.

Hartmann, much more than his predecessors, stressed the importance of the client's social context. He has taken the position that the clinician can never divorce human beings from their environment because they are always affecting and being affected by it. For example, certain types of defenses are favored by certain ethnic groups and shunned by others. Many Jews are encouraged to cope with distress by intellectualizing and philosophizing, whereas this would not be the favored defensive maneuver used by the majority of blacks. Consequently, the therapist's question, "What should we do about it?" might be welcomed by many black clients but shunned by many Jewish clients. However, the question, "What are your thoughts about your past?" might be welcomed by many Jews but shunned by many blacks.

A particularly helpful concept for the therapist who is interested in treatment resistances and their resolution is Hartmann's notion of conflict-free ego zones. When the therapist recognizes that certain character traits, such as orderliness, punctiliousness, or avid curiosity, might be secondarily autonomous, the therapist realizes that there is a limited need to explore these traits with the client in treatment; they are conflict free.

Hartmann's emphasis on the ego helps the therapist recognize that, if several of the client's ego functions are weak, the client will feel strong anxiety if too much dynamic material is probed too quickly or if interpretations are made that the client's ego cannot master. Therefore, by assessing ego functions, the therapist can plan differential treatment that will relate to the client's unique capacities to handle frustration, bear anxiety, and relate to the therapist. The therapeutic maxim "Begin where the client is" can be broadened to mean "Begin with an understanding of the client's ego functions" and offer the client the kind of therapeutic experience commensurate with his ego capacities (Stamm, 1959).

Another use of Hartmann's ego psychology is that it can serve as a guide for choosing an appropriate treatment modality for the client. For example, some clients' ego apparatuses are so weak and their capacity for an intensive treatment relationship so minimal that even the idea of long-term treatment is for them too anxiety provoking. In using ego psychology as an orientation in making a diagnostic evaluation of the strengths and weaknessses of primary and secondary autonomous functions, the therapist is in a better position to decide which clients can benefit from long-term treatment and which clients can benefit from briefer therapy. The same kind of appraisal can also serve as a guide in determining when family treatment is appropriate, when group treatment is called for, when advocacy may be indicated, and so on.

The concept of regression in the service of the ego (Hartmann, 1958) has been of enormous help to therapists. Many clients, children and adults, because of deficits in the nurturing process to which they have been exposed, are incapable of functioning in a manner appropriate to their chronological age. These clients need to communicate with the therapist, sometimes for long periods of time, as if they were really young children. It is as if the therapist, by tolerating long periods of regression from the client, can make restitution for what was frustrated early in life by the client's parents and significant others.

Heinz Hartmann, a brilliant theoretician and practicing psychoanalyst, died in New York City in 1970, where he had practiced since 1941. His many contributions to ego psychology and to the treatment of resistances are equally profound.

ERIK ERIKSON

As the complexity of the ego and its many functions began to be more appreciated by psychoanalysts, psychiatrists, psychologists, social workers, and other professionals, the role of the individual's reality became more important in assessing clients and planning treatment with and for them. As we suggested in our review of Hartmann's work, one example of this was Hartmann's implication that particular ethnic groups foster certain defensive operations while rejecting others when experiencing stress.

No writer has devoted more attention to the client's social orbit than has Erik Erikson. His notions have several implications for understanding resistances and for working toward their resolution.

In Erikson's conceptualizations, each phase of the life cycle is characterized by a specific developmental task that must be resolved before the individual proceeds to the next level. He points out that these tasks are never completely resolved but are worked out further in successive stages, each depending on the preceding stages (Pumpian-Mindlin, 1966). Erikson (1950) has formulated these stages in terms of psychological polarities that represent hypothetical extremes of successful and unsuccessful resolution. The actual outcome is always somewhere between the polarities that he has formulated. Erikson's eight stages are (1) trust versus mistrust (infancy); (2) autonomy versus shame and doubt (2 years); (3) initiative versus guilt (3–5 years); (4) industry versus inferiority (latency, 6–10 years); (5) identity versus identity diffusion (adolescence and youth, 11–18 years); (6) intimacy versus isolation (young adulthood, 19 to mid-twenties); (7) generativity versus self-absorption (adulthood, late twenties to forties); (8) integrity versus despair (senior years).

In examining the life cycle, Erikson saw his task as bridging the theories of infantile physical and social growth so that the contribution of the family and the social structure are always apparent. According to Erikson (1950), for every maturational stage or psychosocial crisis, there always appears a "radius of significant relations" who aid, abet, or hinder the person's coping with and resolving specific life tasks.

Erikson (1959) uses the term *crisis* to connote not a threat of catastrophe but a turning point and crucial period of increased vulnerability and heightened potential—that is, the maturing individual has a task to resolve. The crisis implies that there is a danger that the growing person can be stunted in its maturation if crucial biological, psychological, and social factors do not appropriately coalesce in the task's resolution. The task also presents the opportunity to enlarge the individual's repertoire of social, interpersonal, psychological, and intellectual skills.

Erikson, like Hartmann, has pointed out that the ego state emerging from a given stage should not be viewed as a final achievement that has been mastered solidly and hence is a closed issue. The dynamic interplay between the individual and his environment is such that the person can retreat to earlier ego states when more advanced tasks are too anxiety provoking.

Again similar to Hartmann, Erikson (1959) posited that there is an inborn coordination to the "average expectable environment" and therefore human beings can never be assessed without noting their interactions with their social milieus. The assumption of *mutuality*, a term that recurs throughout Erikson's work, presupposes that no human event can be evaluated without noting the constant interaction and vital coordination between person and situation. Erikson gave as an example that the infant who needs emotional nurturing in the first stage of life, in order to mature must be linked to an adult whose life stage is marked by a need to nurture emotionally.

In attempting to help an individual in a therapeutic situation, Erikson sees the encounter as characterized by "a human immediacy." The total person emerges as more than a diagnostic label, more than a unit in a system, and more than a statistic. For Erikson, the sphere of attention in therapy is life itself, with a particular concentration on the life tasks that the individual and his social orbit are not able to resolve. With this perspective, seemingly malignant disturbances appear to be more ably treated as aggravated life crises rather than as diseases subject to routine diagnosis (Erikson, 1964).

Erikson contends that clients in psychotherapy may be regarded as having some difficulty in coping with one or more of their life tasks. The human immediacy or crisis might be better understood if the therapist is able to specify which particular life task or tasks in the life cycle the client cannot confront either alone or with the aid of significant others.

If we apply Erikson's perspective to psychotherapy, it would appear that the practitioner can regard himself as one of the significant persons in the client's social radius who should be able to help the client cope with a specified life task. Parent–child dysfunctions, family pathology, marital stress, job conflicts, and all the other psychosocial problems brought to therapists by clients can then be viewed as a regression to, or a fixation at, one of the eight life tasks or stages.

In using Erikson's conceptualizations to understand better a client's specific resistance, the therapist can have a conversation with himself or a colleague that would go somewhat as follows:

> Is Mr. Jones' lateness to appointments a manifestation of his not being able to trust me? Or, does it have anything to do with the fact that we have been talking lately about his fear of independence? Maybe he is afraid to look at his anxiety concerning his growing *autonomy*? Yet, I wonder also about his *guilt* regarding his recently taking some sexual *initiative*. Maybe one or more of these issues are at work? (Strean, 1975)

As the therapist reviews the client's history, assesses the client's dynamics, and evaluates the current state of the transference, the therapist can determine where on the psychosocial ladder the client is fixated or why he has regressed to a particular rung. On listening to Mr. Smith's constant demands for reassurance and nurturance, his female therapist asks, "Is this id resistance showing itself because the client wants me to be different from his mother—a mother who never fed him or cuddled him and one whom he could not trust? Or is Mr. Smith so demanding with me now because he is acutely anxious about his fantasies to penetrate me sexually (i.e., take initiative) and therefore he has to regress to a trust–mistrust mode of interaction?"

Erikson, in addition to his contributions to therapists, wrote a series of prize-winning works. Among the better-known writings are *Childhood and Society* (1950); *Identity and the Life Cycle* (1959); *Insight and Responsibility* (1964), and *On the Generational Cycle* (1980). Erikson's biography by the Harvard psychiatrist Robert Coles (1970) reflects Erikson's brilliant insights into such personalities as Ghandi and Luther. Coles also shows that, in the course of a very productive career, Erikson has opened the boundaries of psychoanalysis to anthropology and sociology. He has expanded the domain of his field to include the study of people's strengths as well as their problems and difficulties. In addition to his work as a psychoanalyst, Erikson has responded to such significant contemporary issues as nonviolence, social reform, and the youth culture.

EDWARD GLOVER

As more therapists began to appreciate that, during the entire course of psychotherapy, the client will resist in one way or another, several writers began to categorize resistances so that practitioners could feel better organized in responding to their clients' defensive maneuvers. One of the first writers to develop such categories was the British psychiatrist and psychoanalyst Edward Glover. Recognizing that any mental state (id, ego, or superego) or any defense mechanism (repression, regression, projection, etc.) can be pressed into the service of resistance, Glover (1955) divided resistances into two groups: *obvious* kinds of resistances and those that are essentially *unobtrusive*.

Obvious resistances are "crass" and can scarcely be overlooked. The most obvious of all is when the client decides to terminate treatment. Other examples of obvious resistances are absences, lateness, lagging on the way to the therapist's office, and delaying the departure from the consultation room. In the therapy sessions themselves, Glover considers as obvious resistances prolonged silences, "pedantic circumstantiality," repetition, and "trivial garrulousness."

With regard to unobtrusive resistances, Glover refers to minor pauses, slips, inattentions, and circumlocutions in the sessions. Other examples are the excessive compliance of the "model patient," somatization, constant self-demeaning, and subtle attempts at seduction. Glover contends that unobtrusive resistances are frequently silent, "and it might be said that the sign of their existence is our unawareness of them" (1955, p. 54). Most of the time, we detect them in retrospect, and one of their major characteristics is that they are subtle, not explosive. They "do not break through or disrupt the superficies of the (therapeutic) situation, but rather infiltrate the situation, exude through it, or to vary the expression, move with the stream rather than against, snagwise" (1955, p. 54).

In addition to his categorization of resistances into obvious and unobtrusive types, Glover has examined how certain types of defenses manifest themselves as resistances in the therapeutic situation. Regression, because it is usually the precipitating cause of symptom formation and is the earliest form of defense, generally appears in treatment when the client feels frightened of the therapeutic situation. Forms that it can take are drowsiness or changing the subject—that is, avoiding an immediate conflict by concentrating on an earlier, and for the time being, less urgent conflict.

In repression, the client shows disturbances of memory. An example of this is the client who had been seduced at 4 years old but at 35 constantly told the therapist that she had never experienced any sexual interest and did not even know how babies were made.

Glover saw projection, reaction formation, and displacement as similar types of defenses, because almost always they are used to ward off id impulses. Furthermore, these defenses frequently emerge in the transference relationship with the therapist because the client often needs to protect himself from experiencing id wishes toward the therapist.

According to Glover, one of the most common causes of stalemates in treatment is the client's projection of his superego onto the therapist. Although the client is always ready for attack and criticism, he may become very disappointed when the therapist "sits on the fence on all ethical issues" (1955, p. 65) and does not punish him for real or imagined transgressions.

Edward Glover has also written about counterresistance and therapeutic technique. He is best known for his book *The Technique of Psychoanalysis* (1955).

OTTO FENICHEL

In his still popular book *The Psychoanalytic Theory of Neurosis* (1945), Otto Fenichel stressed the inevitability of resistance as an ever-present phenomenon in therapy and discussed several types of resistances. With regard to the inevitability of resistance, Fenichel states:

> To tell everything is much more difficult than one imagines. Even the individual who conscientiously tries to adhere to this basic rule fails to tell many things because he considers them too unimportant, too stupid, too indiscreet, and so on. There are many who never learn to apply the basic rule because their fear of losing control is too great, and before they can give expression to anything, they must examine it to see exactly what it is. . . . The strongest and deepest resistances—that is, those that originated in childhood and that are directed against unconscious instinctual outbursts—cannot be swept out of existence by a stipulation to tell everything. [The patient] is in a struggle between certain unconscious impulses and certain resistances of the ego which likewise are unconscious. (1945, p. 24)

In his discussion of types of resistances, Fenichel points out "that it is impossible to tabulate the various ways in which resistance can be expressed" (1945, p. 27). Yet he does go on to discuss several common types that appear in many psychotherapeutic encounters. The client may stop talking or may talk so much that a theme cannot be deduced from his productions. Another type of resistance that appears frequently is where the client talks only about the present because examining the past is too painful; in the converse form of this resistance, the client talks only about childhood memories and refuses to see their representations in reality because talking about the present is much too frightening.

Inasmuch as it is the aim of psychotherapy to confront the client's reasonable ego with his irrational emotions, the client can resist this by always being reasonable and refusing to understand his emotions. For example, the client may insist that it is ridiculous to want to be childishly dependent, stubbornly defiant, or insatiably starved for infantile sexual gratification. In the opposite type of resistance, the client basks in discharging affects without getting the necessary distance and freedom to look at them reasonably.

Fenichel talks about how certain resistances operate more secretively. One example is the client who seems very cooperative, talks freely, and accepts the therapist's interventions with ease, but never changes. The secret resistance is really a rebellious fantasy in which the client is quietly but defiantly saying, "That would be very fine if it were true, but I don't know if it is true." Or the client may have understood what his productions and the therapist's interpretations showed him, yet that knowledge remains entirely separated from his real life. It is as if the client is saying to himself, "This is only valid while I'm in this office. Outside of here, it means nothing." Or a client may accept everything the therapist says merely to be courteous. The courteous attitudes protect him from reliving his conflicts and also serve as a defense against hostile fantasies toward the therapist.

Intellectual resistances have been examined by Fenichel. These are maneuvers that clients use to try and refute the theoretical validity of their therapy instead of seeking to clarify their own lives. However, there are also intellectual resistances in which clients become enthusiastic supporters of psychotherapy to avoid applying it to themselves. Fenichel believes that this type of resistance is very prevalent among obsessive–compulsive clients.

Like most, if not all, dynamically oriented therapists, Fenichel believes that virtually all the client's resistances express themselves in the transference relationship with the therapist. He points out that previously acquired attitudes manifest themselves in feelings and attitudes toward the therapist, "the handling of which is the core of analysis, i.e., the transference resistance. Understanding the contents of the patient's unconscious from his utterances is, relatively, the simplest part of the analyst's task. Handling the transference is the most difficult" (1945, p. 29).

One of the reasons that handling the transference is difficult is that clients often feel convinced that their perceptions of the therapist are accurate, and therefore they do not see any need to examine their feelings about the therapist. They are sure the therapist is either cold, rejecting, and harsh, or seductive, overstimulating, and not sufficiently neutral. Instead of examining themselves, they want their therapists to go for supervision or more therapy.

Otto Fenichel, an early pioneer in psychoanalysis, also provided many insights into the diagnosis and treatment of neuroses. In addition to his text *The Psychoanalytic Theory of Neurosis* (1945), many papers on diagnosis and intervention can be found in the two-volume set, *The Collected Papers of Otto Fenichel* (1953).

KARL MENNINGER

Karl Menninger, a renowned psychiatrist and psychoanalyst who has written such interesting works as *Love against Hate* (1942) and *The Vital Balance* (1963), has also increased our understanding of resistances. In his *Theory of Psychoanalytic Technique* (1973), he insightfully discussed two common resistances: acting out and the erotization resistance.

Acting out is the tendency to substitute an act or series of acts for issues that the client is too frightened to discuss with the therapist. Although in the early days of psychotherapy it was assumed that this type of resistance occurred more often with severely disturbed clients, it is now recognized that acting out can occur with almost any client and usually happens quite unconsciously. Many clients with varying degrees of maturity would rather have an affair than deal with sexual fantasies toward the therapist. Many clients would rather provoke a fight with a boss than deal with sadistic fantasies toward the practitioner, and many clients would rather rescue other people than face their own dependency wishes in the therapy.

Acting out can occur in the therapist's office as well as outside of it. A client might unconsciously arrange to arrive late for an interview, or prematurely leave the consultation room on some pretext, rather than face uncomfortable sexual or aggressive feelings.

In discussing the erotization resistance, Menninger (1973) refers to the phenomenon of clients talking about memories, fantasies, dreams, and experiences, not so much to understand or relieve themselves, but to please the therapist. It is as if these clients are saying, "I want you to want me to get well, and to make me well; therefore I will try to please you, in order that you will do so."

Usually when clients are using this resistance, they are entertaining a fantasy that the therapist is an omnipotent parent who can bring them to a paradise that has been lost or a Garden of Eden not yet discovered. By ingratiation, seduction, and manipulation of the therapist, they hope to gratify their infantile wishes.

In his observations of clients who have made use of the erotization resistance, Menninger has noted that the client's feeling that he is doing something to please the therapist develops into a feeling that the therapist is getting pleasure from treating the client. "To give pleasure affords pleasure and the patient begins to enjoy pleasing, a pleasurable emotion quite aside from his lessened tension" (1973, p. 115).

Very often the client wants to have sexual contact with the therapist. In other words, he sexualizes the therapeutic situation and wants the therapist to directly gratify infantile wishes, which may be oral (e.g., kissing, hugging), anal (e.g., giving gifts), or phallic (e.g., sexual intercourse). Menninger's recognition that the client's wish for physical contact is always infantile and always a resistance has important implications for the therapist. Many clients mask their infantile wishes by sounding like mature, loving adults, and the therapist may be manipulated into believing that this is "true love" rather than helping these clients get in touch with why they want infantile gratification. Also, when the therapist recognizes that the client's seductive attempts are a resistance, the therapist can begin to consider what currently dangerous or dreaded elements in the therapy the client's seductive attempts are trying to protect.

Menninger reminds us that there is usually an aggressive component involved in the erotization resistance and that "the erotic wish and display act as a disguise for the hidden aggression underlying them" (1973, p. 119). Often the client secretly wants to weaken or belittle the therapist. In addition, what the client wants is often self-destructive, and the client usually knows this.

Besides his discussion of the two common clinical forms of resistance, acting out and erotization, Menninger categorizes resistances by dividing them into "consciously felt opposition" and "opposition occurring with the best of intentions." For some clients, it is necessary to pretend to be skeptical or independent. Other clients will cling to the notion that it is their tempermental makeup that leads them to dawdle or delay (i.e., what W. Reich, 1949, would call a character resistance). Some clients will insist that they cannot talk spontaneously and then use this "limitation" as a rationalization for not communicating their thoughts and feelings to the therapist.

Menninger's categories in effect divide resistances into conscious and unconscious means of opposing the therapy. Recognizing that resistance always connotes danger and dread, Menninger concludes: "The important thing to see is that resistance is something that exists, that operates, that opposes change, that is aggressive, and that is self-defeating" (1973, p. 121).

LEO STONE

Almost every writer who has discussed resistance has agreed with Freud's statement that everything said in the therapeutic situation is a message to the therapist and that virtually every resistance will be expressed in the transference (Freud, 1926). An id resistance that has been elaborated on by the well-known psychiatrist and psychoanalyst Leo Stone is what he calls "the irredentist drive to reunion with the primal mother" (1973, p. 57). This wish, according to Stone, is seen in all clients; it opposes therapeutic progress, healthy maturation, and appropriate individuation; and may be viewed as a "primordial transference" that expresses a striving toward physical approximation and merger. Much of therapy involves a conflict between seeing the therapist as he is and wanting him to be the primordial mother. Stone views this regressive wish for merger with the mother as the most formidable resistance in therapy.

Another resistance that Stone discusses, which has been elaborated on by Gill (1982), is resistance to the awareness of transference. Here clients want to repress and deny any feelings or fantasies toward the therapist because they feel the material might be self-damaging or fear what the analyst will feel or do. One of the first examples in the psychotherapeutic literature of a client consciously withholding material from the therapist is Freud's case of the "Rat Man" (1909). The "Rat Man" concealed for some time his suspicion that Sigmund Freud was related to another man named Freud in Budapest who had committed one of the most notorious crimes of that day. Here the "Rat Man's" hostility to Freud was being held back because he was frightened of Freud's possible retaliation.

Stone (1973) sees three broad aspects of the relationship between resistance and transference, and he contends that the proportional importance of each will vary with the individual client: (1) resistance to awareness of the transference; (2) resistance to the dynamic and genetic reductions of the transference—that is, reluctance of the client to see that transference feelings and fantasies are based on his idiosyncratic dynamics and unique history; and (3) resistance to giving up the transference attachment itself.

Stone has categorized resistances into two types: (1) "tactical resistances," which deal with "manifest process phenomena of ego resistances" (i.e., overt signs of resistance—lateness, absence, and refusal to pay fees) and (2) "strategic resistances," "those largely subsumed in the 'silent' group (for example, delays or failure of expectable symptomatic change, omission of decisive conflict material . . . inability to accept termination). [They] relate to the depths of the patient's psychopathology and personality structure and to his total reactions to the psychoanalytic situation, process, and the person of the analyst" (1973, p. 46).

In commenting further about these two types of resistances, Stone says:

> These are, I believe ultimately and fundamentally related and exist in varying degree in all (therapy). However, one or the other is usually of preponderant importance; and they are, in a practical and prognostic sense, quite different: (a) Those manifested largely in discernible impediments of the psychoanalytic process in its immediate operational sense. These are usual in the neuroses, in persons who have achieved relatively satisfactory separation of the "self" from the primary object, but whose lives are disturbed by the residues of instinctual and other intrapsychic conflicts in relation to the unconscious representations of early objects, and thus to transference objects. (b) Those which may be similarly manifested at

times, but may indeed be relatively or even exaggeratedly free of them, where the essential avoidance is of the genuine and effective biphasic involvement in the transference neurosis, with regard to fundamental and critical conflicts, and thus of the potential relinquishment of symptomatic solutions and the ultimate satisfactory separation from the analyst (1973, p. 52).

Stone has also discussed how certain special factors, sometimes extrinsic to the therapeutic situation, may prolong the therapy indefinitely. In some clients, real guilt may not be faced. With other clients, emotional distress based on real-life problems (e.g., illness) may not be confronted or accepted. Then there are those clients who have been described by Freud (1916) as exceptions. These individuals feel that they have been abused by Fate. As Fenichel (1945) noted, Stone, too, has observed that certain clients exploit the rules of psychotherapy and, in obedience to a traditional rule, delay certain decisions to the point of absurdity, invoking "the therapy" in support of their neuroses and sometimes in contempt of important obligations in real life. Financial support of the therapy by someone other than the client can provide a basis for resisting facing infantile dependency and rage. Finally, where resistance is an expression of sustained rebellion against the authority and methods of the therapist, "we are dealing with a special category of resistance, based on early disorders of object relationships and germane character problems, which may require long-term preanalytic preparatory work, or may, indeed, make actual analytic work impossible" (Stone, 1973, p. 66).

Leo Stone, in addition to his lucid expositions on resistance, has written *The Psychoanalytic Situation* (1961), a classic that describes many facets of the therapeutic process. He also has written interesting papers on aggression (1971), transference (1966), and brief psychotherapy (1951).

RALPH GREENSON

In his book *The Technique and Practice of Psychoanalysis* (1967), Ralph Greenson has provided the most comprehensive classification on resistance that currently exists in the psychotherapeutic literature. In pointing out that we have to distinguish between the fact that the client is resisting, how he does it, what he is warding off, and why he does so, Greenson believes that all resistances should be classified according to their sources, their fixation points, their types of defenses, their diagnostic categories, and whether they are ego alien or ego syntonic.

Source of Resistance

All psychic structures (i.e., id, ego, superego) participate in all psychic events to varying degrees, and therefore a resistance may take the form of the client's constantly (1) seeking infantile gratification (id resistance); (2) protecting himself against the awareness of a dreaded idea or unacceptable impulse (ego resistance); or (3) insisting that he must be punished for real or imagined transgressions (superego resistance). Freud referred to all these ways of resisting in *Inhibitions, Symptoms, and Anxiety* (1926). While Greenson repeats Freud's formulation, he adds that, although the stimulus that triggers the resistance may originate in any of the psychic structures—ego, id, or superego—the perception of danger is always an ego function: "I believe that the activity of avoiding pain, no matter what the evocative stimulus is, is always initiated by the ego" (1967, p. 86).

Fixation Points

Greenson points out that it is important for the therapist to determine which aspect of psychosexual development is being resisted at a particular phase of the therapy. Is the client now fighting dependency wishes? This might be an oral problem. Or is the client trying to ward off the wish to defecate and urinate all over the therapist? Obviously, this is an anal resistance. Possibly the client fears his phallic wishes? In describing resistances as oral, anal, phallic, latency, and adolescent types, Greenson's formulation is similar to Erikson's, who asked, "Where on the psychosocial ladder is the client stuck?"

Types of Defense

Another fruitful approach to the study of resistances is to ascertain the type of defense that is being used. This refers to distinguishing the mechanisms of defense that Anna Freud (1946) described, and noting how the resistances employ them in opposing the therapy. As was mentioned earlier in this chapter when we discussed the work of Anna Freud, particularly her *The Ego and the Mechanisms of Defense* (1946), as well as Glover's (1955) contribution, we showed how *repression* can enter into the therapeutic situation when the client forgets his appointment or his mind goes blank concerning certain experiences or people. *Isolation* enters the therapeutic situation when clients split off emotions from ideas. Clients may, for example, describe a death of a loved one in great detail but show no emotion—no grief, no sadness, no anger.

In addition to describing how the various mechanisms of defense can be used in the service of resistance, Greenson states: "By far the most important types of resistance met with in (therapeutic work) are the *transference resistances*" (1967, p. 91). Transference resistances, Greenson avers, refer to two different sets of resistances: (1) those developed by clients because they have transference reactions—for example, the client resists discussing an argument with a spouse because the client fears the loss of the therapist's love; (2) those developed by clients to avoid transference reactions—for example the client comes late for appointments to avoid feeling sexual feelings toward the therapist.

Like Menninger (1973), Greenson sees acting out as a type of defense that always serves as a resistance. Acting out, as was pointed out in our review of Menninger's work, is replacing the examination of feelings, thoughts, and memories with action. According to Greenson, all clients engage in some acting out during treatment, and in constricted and inhibited clients, this may even be a welcomed sign. However, he also points out that, when clients are prone to repeated and protracted acting out, they become difficult if not impossible to treat. In order to be helped, the client must have some capacity to bind stimuli sufficiently so that he can express impulses in words and feelings.

Greenson also describes *screen defenses*. These are defensive maneuvers used in treatment whereby the client recalls certain memories (i.e., screen memories, affects, or identity) to ward off an underlying more painful memory, affect, or identity. For example, the client might repeat how frightened he was playing doctor at age 4 in order to ward off the painful memory that also at age 4 he overheard his parents having sexual intercourse.

Diagnostic Category

Although many different forms of resistance come to light in all therapies, according to Greenson, certain diagnostic entities (e.g., the hysterias and obsessional neuroses) make use of special types of defenses. Therefore, it follows from this point of view that certain types of resistances will be expressed by certain diagnostic categories.

Although the usefulness of diagnostic categories has been questioned by some writers (Fine, 1982; Strean, 1979), and although Greenson himself acknowledges that clinical entities are rarely seen in pure form because most clients have some admixture of different pathologies along with the clinical label given to them, Greenson believes that, within certain diagnostic categories, certain resistances do predominate. His diagnostic categories (Greenson, 1967, pp. 93–94) are as follows:

The hysterias. Repression and isolated formations. Regression to phallic characteristics. Emotionality, somatizations, conversions, and genitalizations. Identifications with lost love objects and guilt-producing objects.

The obsessional neuroses. Isolation, undoing, projections, and massive reaction formations. Regression to anality with reaction formation of the character traits: orderliness, cleanliness, and stinginess becoming important resistances. Intellectualization as a resistance to feelings. Magical thinking, omnipotence of thought, rumination. Internalization of hostility and sadistic superego reactions.

The neurotic depressions. Introjections, identifications, acting out, impulsivity, and screen defenses. Oral and phallic instinctuality regressively distorted. Emotionality, counterphobic behavior and attitudes, addictiveness, and masochism.

Ego-Alien Resistances versus Ego-Syntonic Resistances

Classifications, as we have noted, overlap with one another and have their advantages and also their limitations. One practical classification is the distinction between ego-alien and ego-syntonic resistances. Ego-alien resistances appear foreign, extraneous, and strange to the client's reasonable ego. An example would be when a client, for no apparent reason, feels that the therapist hates him and is about to throw him out of treatment.

Ego-syntonic resistances are felt as familiar, rational, and purposeful. These resistances are usually well-established, habitual patterns of behavior. Because the client does not sense the resistance function of the activity (e.g., excessive compliance, extreme punctuality, marked orderliness), such resistances are more difficult to recognize.

Ralph Greenson was a prolific writer who introduced a number of concepts that have been very helpful to many therapists. In his two books, *The Technique and Practice of Psychoanalysis* (1967) and *Explorations in Psychoanalysis* (1978), he has discussed "the working alliance" and "the real relationship" between therapist and client. He also wrote articles on boredom (1953), screen defenses (1958a), variations in technique (1958b), empathy (1960), silence (1961), and many other topics.

REUBEN FINE

One of the most prolific writers on the current psychotherapeutic scene is Reuben Fine. Author of numerous books, such as *Psychoanalytic Psychology* (1975), *The History of Psychoanalysis* (1979a), *The Psycho-*

analytic Vision (1981), and *The Healing of the Mind* (1982), Fine has introduced a philosophical dimension into psychotherapy that has tremendous implications for understanding resistances and helping clients resolve them. Fine's "analytic ideal" (1982) takes the position that a human being can attain happiness through a reasonable way of living, which involves the following: He must learn to love rather than to hate and seek pleasure, have sexual gratification, have a feeling for life that is guided by reason, have an adequate role in the family, have a sense of identity, be creative, have a role in the social order, be able to communicate, and be reasonably free of psychiatric symptoms.

Of the various components of the analytic ideal, the most central is the attainment of love. According to Fine, nothing is more important in the growth process and in the resolution of neurotic conflicts because it is apparent that most of the difficulties that individuals suffer from involve some disappointment in love.

In contrast to the analytic ideal, with its emphasis on love, pleasure, creativity, and so on, what is frequently found in our culture is hate, suffering, lack of feeling, absence of family roles. Therefore, the gap between the analytic ideal and the social reality is immense, and the consequence of this gap is that virtually every member in our society can use psychotherapeutic help.

Fine's analytic ideal provides the practitioner in psychotherapy with specific goals by which therapeutic progress can be assessed and resistance can be determined. If the client is examining his hatred and moving toward feeling more love of others, including the therapist, he is in all probability making progress. However, if the client constantly expresses contempt toward the therapist and others, avoids experiencing love and intimacy, and is not examining the why's and wherefore's of the hatred, then strong resistance is probably at work. The same could be said regarding other features of the analytic ideal as it pertains to the therapeutic situation. As another example, a client who is progressing would be talking about his sexual fantasies toward the therapist and others, whereas a client in resistance would be avoiding the subject of sex.

Although Fine is a philosopher, he is also a realistic therapist who has come up with a classification of resistances that is both clear and practical. Fine divides resistances into those in which the client simply refuses, for one reason or another, to comply with basic requests and those in which the resistance is of a more subtle nature. The therapist asks the client to do three things: to come at a certain time, to say everything that comes to mind, and to pay a certain fee. Later, if the individual is in psychoanalytic treatment, a fourth request is made: The analysand is asked to lie on the couch. Although these requests appear quite simple, many people will defy them in a variety of ways. Lateness, not talking, refusing to pay fees, and refusing to take the couch are all examples of the first category of resistances—refusal to comply with basic requests (Fine, 1982). More subtle are those resistances where the client seems to be complying with basic requests but fights the therapy in one way or another. Examples of subtle resistances are an overemphasis on reality, a demand for gratification, a sense of hopelessness, excessive regression, acting out, absence of feeling, and somatization (Fine, 1982).

Fine's approach to therapy, in which the therapist must have a clear image of how the client might achieve happiness, together with his practical classification is an example of what Fine prescribes for the competent therapist—to be a visionary with technique and a technician with vision (1981).

CHARLES BRENNER

Most dynamically oriented therapists subscribe to the notion that anxiety is what evokes a resistance. The client experiences danger in reaction to an id wish, superego command, or external stimulus. The danger may be one of several possibilities: abandonment, loss of love, guilt feelings, or social censure. Not wanting to face these disastrous consequences, the client opposes the recognition of id wishes, superego commands, or external stimuli by erecting defenses. These defenses become resistances in treatment (Freud, 1926).

Charles Brenner in his books *The Mind in Conflict* (1982) and *Psychoanalytic Technique and Psychic Conflict* (1976) has introduced some new ideas about what sets defenses in motion. His major notion is that "unpleasure" in our clients is responsible for their erecting defenses, and unpleasure is of two kinds: anxiety and what Brenner (1976) refers to as "depressive affect."

Brenner views anxiety as an emotion evoked in the ego when the individual anticipates danger. It is always experienced as if something unpleasurable is going to happen and is accompanied by ideas that in one way or another have to do with danger. If the danger is perceived as acute or imminent, we speak of fear; if the unpleasure is intense, we speak of panic; and if the unpleasure is mild and the danger is perceived as slight, uncertain, or distant, we may speak of worry or uneasiness. The unpleasure may be unconscious even though the ideational content is conscious. Conversely, unpleasure can be conscious in large measure, but the ideational content of the affect unconscious (Brenner, 1976). Here, Brenner is referring to the defense mechanism of isolation (A. Freud, 1946).

Brenner has introduced a new notion into the study of defenses and resistances by noting that not all unpleasure is concerned with thoughts of an impending calamity. Unpleasure may be associated with thoughts of a calamity that has already happened, and Brenner calls this "depressive affect" in order to distinguish it from anxiety. Depending on the intensity of the unpleasure, one may speak of misery, sadness, or discontent. If the emphasis is on longing for a lost object, wishing it were back, we may speak of loneliness. If there is no relief in sight, we speak of despair, and if the emphasis is on being scolded or ridiculed, we speak of shame or humiliation (Brenner, 1976, 1982).

Brenner's notion of depressive affect has important therapeutic implications. Many clients resist the therapy, not because of an impending danger, but because they dread revealing experiences where they felt humiliated, lost love, or experienced guilt. Therefore, it behooves the therapist to be alert to why the client is resisting.

Brenner gives an example of a client who showed both anxiety and depressive affect, as most clients do. When the client withdrew from competitive situations and became passive and withdrawn, anxiety was clearly playing its role and induced the client to cope with the anxiety by reaction formation. However, when the client ached and begged to be coddled, he no longer *feared* he would be unloved; he was sure he *was* unloved. His yearning to be coddled, which unconsciously meant to be forgiven, stemmed from his depressive affect.

In sum, according to Brenner, either anxiety or depressive affect can play a role in mobilizing defenses, which Freud assigned exclusively to anxiety. Whenever satisfaction of a childhood drive derivative gives rise to unpleasure, the unpleasure is either anxiety, depressive affect, or a combination of the two. By anxiety is meant unpleasure plus thoughts of an impending calamity. By depressive affect is meant unpleasure plus thoughts of a past calamity.

Brenner, in addition to the two books cited earlier, has written the popular *An Elementary Textbook on Psychoanalysis* (1973) as well as numerous articles on such subjects as masochism (1959), repression (1966), depression (1979), and mourning (1974a). With Jacob Arlow, he has written *Psychoanalytic Concepts and the Structural Theory* (1964).

JOSEPH SANDLER

As the reader, no doubt, is aware by now, the way Sigmund Freud conceptualized resistances remains central to the psychodynamic theory of resistances. However, his categorization (repression resistance, transference resistance, epinosic gain, id resistance, and superego resistance), as the reader is also aware, has been embellished and extended by the contributors whose work we have been reviewing. A classification by Joseph Sandler and his colleagues, Christopher Dare and Alex Holder (1973), may serve as a partial summary, with additions from some of the literature we have reviewed to this point. The following is an edited summary of Sandler and his colleagues' classification of resistances that appears in their book *The Patient and the Analyst: The Basis of the Psychoanalytic Process* (1973).

1. Resistances due to the threat posed by the therapy to the particular adaptations made by the client. This refers to the client's adaptations to forces both from the external world and from within the client. Repression resistance can be included here, being a specific example of what might be termed *defense resistance* inasmuch as defenses other than repression can give rise to resistance. As we will recall from our review of Anna Freud's work (1946), mechanisms of defense can be regarded as mechanisms of adaptation, since they are essential for both normal functioning as well as being involved in pathological processes.

2. Transference resistances, essentially as described by Freud and discussed earlier in this chapter.

3. Resistances derived from secondary gains—that is, what Freud described as the epinosic gain discussed earlier in this chapter.

4. Superego resistances as described by Freud and discussed earlier in this chapter.

5. Resistances that we will discuss more in Chapter 2 are those that arise from faulty procedures and inappropriate technical measures adopted by the therapist. Here it can be pointed out that such resistances may be dealt with during the normal course of therapy if their sources are realized and acknowledged by both therapist and client. If this does not occur, these resistances may lead to a breakdown of treatment or to poor therapeutic results (Glover, 1955; Greenson, 1967; Langs, 1981).

6. Resistances because changes in the client brought about by the therapy may lead to difficulties in the client's relationships with important individuals in the client's environment. For example, a submissive masochistic husband or wife may resist insight and change because such insight and change may threaten the marriage.

7. Resistances prompted by the danger of recovery and the loss of the therapist. Many clients remain in treatment because of gratifications from the therapeutic relationship—for example, when the client wishes to sustain a transference fantasy that the therapist is a protective, nurturing parent. If the therapist continues to be experienced in this way, termination

of treatment is perceived as the disruption of a very much needed relationship.

8.   Resistances due to the threat that the therapy will injure the client's self-esteem. Abraham (1919), a contemporary of Freud, noted this resistance particularly in those analysands in whom the arousal of shame is a major motive for defensive activity. Such individuals may have difficulties in tolerating infantile aspects of themselves that emerge in treatment (e.g., wishes to be fed, cuddled, touched, or sexually fondled) because they regard these desires as shameful.

9.   Resistances to the giving up of past adaptive yet dysfunctional solutions (including neurotic symptoms). For example, in response to unacceptable passive wishes, the client might cope with anxiety by becoming a workaholic. Even when the client recognizes and accepts the passive wishes, it might still be difficult to relinquish old work habits.

10.   Character resistances, of the sort described by Wilhelm Reich (1949), due to the fixed nature of character traits.

11.   A resistance that Sandler et al. (1973) discuss that occurs fairly frequently is the "flight into health." For some clients, the threat that the therapeutic work may constitute to the particular equilibrium that they have established may be so great that they can justify their wish to terminate treatment by pointing out that, for the time being at least, their conflicts have disappeared. For these clients, the worry that their therapy may lead to a divorce from their spouses, a reevaluation of their job situations, or some other disruption to their current modus vivendi can motivate them to relinquish the primary and secondary gains that they derive from their symptoms and from other neurotic conflicts. This, of course, is usually done on an unconscious basis. For example, some spouses who have sought treatment for sexual conflicts might find themselves free of these conflicts after a few sessions. What has occurred here is not the working through of conflicts, but the giving up of epinosic gains from their neurotic adaptation because the terror of marital separation is much too difficult to face.

12.   Intellectual resistances that are used to prevent experiencing frightening emotions in the therapy. These resistances may be found in highly intellectual as well as in obsessional clients. The intellectual resistances are part of a threefold classification prepared by Helene Deutsch (1939): (1) the intellectual resistances, found in clients with blocked or disturbed affects who, having repressed the affective side of their lives, have retained the intellectual side as the main means of expressing themselves; (2) the transference resistances; and (3) those resistances that emerge as a consequence of the client's need to defend against the recollecting of childhood material.

Sandler et al. point out that the concept of resistance can be extended from psychoanalysis and psychotherapy to all forms of treatment, "and we can see the manifestations of resistance even in ordinary medical practice, in the form of forgotten appointments, misunderstandings of the doctor's instructions, rationalizations for breaking off treatment, and the like" (1973, pp. 82–83).

Joseph Sandler currently is a psychoanalyst in Israel. From 1956 until recently, he was associated with Anna Freud in her work at the Hampstead Child Therapy Clinic in England.

ROBERT LANGS

Robert Langs, whose major contributions to resistance theory pertain mainly to the role of the therapist, particularly how the therapist's countertransference interferes with the therapeutic process (see Chapter 2), has categorized resistances into two types: *gross behavioral resistances* and *communicative resistances*. Gross behavioral resistances refer to such blatant resistances as lateness, absence, or refusal to pay the fee. The more subtle resistances (e.g., a latent negative transference) are communicative resistances (Langs, 1981).

From the communicative approach, three interrelated categories have been developed that pertain to the protective and adaptive aspects of resistance. As Langs says:

> A resistance may, by design, protect the patient—and often the therapist— from: (1) threatening perceptions of the therapist; (2) threatening fantasies about the therapist; or (3) threatening perceptions and fantasies related to persons outside of the therapeutic relationship, but which usually have a significant bearing on the therapeutic interaction (1981, p. 536).

It is in the sphere of communicative resistances that the therapist's counterresistances contribute significantly to the client's own resistances. According to Langs (1976), the most effective resistance a patient can use is one that is offered or sanctioned by the therapist. As Langs has reiterated on numerous occasions, "Patients are exquisitely, though unconsciously, sensitive to such offers, and will characteristically exploit their presence" (1981, p. 537).

Langs' major thesis, which we will discuss further in Chapter 2, is that a study of unconscious communication between therapist and client always demonstrates the presence of some element of countertransference in every intervention by the therapist (Langs & Stone, 1980, Langs, 1981). Therefore, Langs concludes that the therapist "is always contributing in some meaningful way to the presence of resistances in the client, and it is incumbent upon the therapist to ascertain his own contribution to each resistance before dealing with those sources which arise primarily from within the patient" (1981, p. 540).

Langs has emphasized that there are many resistances used by clients that, upon careful analysis, turn out to be nonpathological and reflect appropriate defensive efforts. He avers that many nontransference resistances are well founded and sensible. "After all, it is hardly inappropriate to protect yourself against overly aggressive or seductive therapists, or against a therapist who unconsciously is exploiting you for his own needs" (Langs, 1981, p. 123).

In sum, Langs's perspective on resistances is an interpersonal or interactional one. He strongly believes that one cannot discuss a client's resistance without taking the therapist and the therapeutic relationship into consideration. He has enlarged on this perspective in several books, among them *Resistances and Interventions* (1981), *The Technique of Psychoanalytic Psychotherapy* (Vol. 1, 1973; Vol. 2, 1974), *The Bipersonal Field* (1976a), and *The Therapeutic Environment* (1979).

NEO-FREUDIAN AND NON-FREUDIAN APPROACHES TO RESISTANCE

As was suggested earlier in this chapter, therapists' views of resistance will be predicated on their theoretical orientations to the human being, their notions about the psychotherapeutic process, their clinical judgments, and a host of other variables, including their own countertransference. For example, if a therapist is an Adlerian and working with the client to enhance his social productivity, then he would consider as a resistance the client's opposition to moving toward constructive social relationships. Similarly, if the therapist is guided by Reuben Fine's notion of the analytic ideal, attitudes and behavior of the client that are opposed to mature love would be considered resistance.

As Sandler et al. (1973) suggested, resistance takes place in all professional relationships. However, the concept of resistance is used mainly by Freudian psychotherapists and psychoanalysts, and is only occasionally mentioned by neo-Freudians and non-Freudian therapists. In this section we briefly review some neo-Freudian and non-Freudian views of resistance.

The Object-Relations or Developmental Orientation

The object-relations or developmental orientation tends to deemphasize the sexual and aggressive drives and instead to emphasize the clients' interpersonal relationships and their maturity or lack of maturity. This school is composed of such people as Gertrude Blanck and Reuben Blanck (1974),

Otto Kernberg (1976), Margaret Mahler (1968), and Heinz Kohut (1977). In their assessment and treatment of clients, these writers view resistances to treatment, not so much as an expression of the clients' anxiety regarding forbidden thoughts and frightening impulses, but as an expression of their developmental lags. Developmental lags refers to "internalized objects" that intimidate the clients. These internalized objects are really images of parents, often called "parental introjects," who stand in the clients' way of freely interacting and liking themselves. In the treatment situation, the therapist is frequently experienced as the internalized object.

Adapting some of Mahler's notions about the relationship between development and resistance, the therapist would bear in mind her (1968) proposition that there are three phases of maturation, leading at approximately age 4 to the establishment of identity. These phases are the autistic, symbiotic, and separation–individuation phases. As an illustration, a client who has not been able to resolve symbiotic wishes would probably resist ending most therapeutic hours, would strongly oppose the therapist taking vacations, and would constantly attempt to get in touch with the therapist between treatment sessions. Another client, fixated at the autistic stage, would probably resist emotional involvement with the therapist and would cancel sessions and oppose other requirements of the therapeutic process.

Kernberg's (1976) position is that varying types of pathologies are determined by an abnormal development of internalized object relations. The abnormality in the internalization of object relations impedes such ego functions as thinking, judgment, and frustration tolerance. Some examples of disturbed developments in object relations would be extreme narcissism or lack of "basic trust" (Erikson, 1950). A client who is fixated at the level of primary narcissism would probably make many childish demands on the therapist, and a client who was mistrustful would doubt the therapist's goodwill.

Kohut's (1977) perspective rests on his formulation that there are two separate and independent developmental lines: (1) from autoerotism to narcissism to object love, and (2) from autoerotism to narcissism to higher forms of narcissism. Resistance in treatment would be viewed in terms of how the client's narcissism manifests itself.

Resistance is not stressed very much by developmental therapists. When it is, these writers are concerned primarily with the client's ego functioning and immature ways of relating to other human beings.

Neo-Freudians

As one examines the theoretical formulations and clinical work of such neo-Freudians as Adler, Jung, Horney, and Sullivan, there is limited discussion of resistance. It would appear that when the unconscious is not considered as crucial in determining the why's and wherefore's of the client's attitudes, symptoms, and behavior, resistance is not considered a crucial dimension of therapy. Particularly if sexual and aggressive drives are not considered consequential, the notion of resistance is played down. However, there is some passing reference to resistance in the work of some neo-Freudians, and it is conceptualized in terms of the theoretician's or clinician's view of the human being.

Alfred Adler

Alfred Adler (1927) took the position that people coped with their real and imagined inferiorities by adopting an air of contemptuous superiority and a life-style of furthering the quest of attaining superiority. Consequently, when resistance is discussed among Adlerians (K. Adler, 1967; Loevinger, 1976), it is formulated in terms of the way the client shows his superiority over and depreciation of the therapist. It is considered an expression of the neurotic client's mistaken life-style.

Carl Jung

Carl Jung (1956) believed that each individual has a "persona," which is a facade or mask. The persona covers up the client's "shadow," or negative personal traits, which are essentially unknown to and unaccepted by his conscious ego. Although the concept of resistance (and transference) is blurred in Jung's theory (Loevinger, 1976), it would appear that resistance in Jungian therapy would be efforts by the client to keep the shadow hidden by using the persona, or mask. (Persona, in many ways, appears similar to Wilhelm Reich's character resistance.)

In contrast to Freud, Jung took the position that many conflicts of human beings can have their roots in the present and the client's past is inconsequential in understanding his present struggle. For example, Jungian therapists see many conflicts of clients as a clash between collective and individual loyalties, or a reluctance to give up adjustments and attitudes that once were necessary and useful but have now become antiquated (Jung, 1971). As the Jungian therapist Gerhard Adler (1967) stated: "More often than not, these two aspects of resistance are closely connected. If, for example, a man has for most of his life worked for his social adjustment and has climbed to the top of the ladder after considerable effort, it will produce a violent resistance if he sees himself forced to abandon this pattern" (p. 352). Gerhard Adler has given other examples, such as struggles of introversion versus extraversion and of rationality versus artistry, to demonstrate the Jungian conviction that "resistance has to be analyzed not so much as arising from infantile conflicts as against the background of the need of the moment" (pp. 352–353).

Karen Horney

Karen Horney used the concept of resistance to mean "the energy with which an individual protects repressed feelings or thoughts against their integration into conscious awareness" (1939, p. 34). As her theory evolved, she replaced the concept of resistance with the term *blockage* (Horney, 1945).

Blockages are those mechanisms used by the client that seek to maintain deeply embedded neurotic solutions. The client may move toward, away, or against the therapist to protect himself from feeling lonely in a hostile world. The forms that blockages can take are many. In the therapeutic situation, the client may become argumentative, sarcastic, assaultive, polite, compliant, or evasive. He may talk in theoretical terms or treat issues in the therapy as if they did not concern him (Kelman & Vollmerhausen, 1967). In addition, Horney points out

> because his pride is bound to be hurt in the process, he tends easily to feel humiliated. Because of his expectations and claims, he often feels frustrated and abused. The mobilization of his self-accusations and self-contempt makes him feel accused and despised . . . also patients regularly overrate the analyst's significance. . . . He is not simply a human being who may help him. . . . He is the magician who has the power to plunge them into hell or lift them into heaven. (1950, p. 339)

Although blockages are definite obstructions to growth and progress, they also point to what needs to be worked on in analysis. They aid in the process of working through and act as a protection against the potential damage from premature interpretation (Kelman & Vollmerhausen, 1967).

Harry Stack Sullivan

Harry Stack Sullivan was influenced by Freud but found many parts of Freud's theory of the personality untenable. For example, he found the use of the terms *id*, *ego*, and *superego* unacceptable and used the term *self-esteem* instead. The idea of human instinct is preposterous according to Sullivan, and he said, "Personality is the relatively enduring pattern of recurrent interpersonal situations which characterize a human life" (1953, pp. 110–111).

Sullivan was impressed with how much more similar than different human beings are to each other. He made anxiety a key element in his theory, viewing it as the most unpleasant experience that a human organism can have and as the opposite of euphoria. The way the individual copes with anxiety, according to Sullivan (1953), is through *dissociation*, *substitution*, and *selective inattention*. In the therapeutic situation, the client will cope with anxiety by removing himself from feelings, thoughts, or memories (dissociation); changing the subject to avoid anxiety (substitution); or not paying attention to aspects of his life or the therapist's remarks about them (selective inattention).

Sullivan emphasized the interpersonal dimension of life and believed that virtually all anxiety is induced by dysfunctional interpersonal interactions. Consequently, he believed that the interpersonal relationship of client and therapist was the essential ingredient in effective psychotherapy.

Non-Freudians

If the neo-Freudians use the concept of resistance sparsely, it can be said that, in the non-Freudian schools, it is hardly used at all. Learning theorists, particularly those who use behavior modification, have contended that there is little to gain from the concept (Sundel, 1982). In the client-centered therapy of Rogers (1954), although the notion of defense is used to mean "the behavioral response of the organism to threat, the goal of which is the maintenance of the current structure of the self" (Meador & Rogers, 1973, p. 135), there is no mention of resistance. In the rational-emotive therapy (RET) of Albert Ellis (1962, 1973a, 1973b), the notion of resistance is entirely bypassed. RET holds that virtually all serious emotional problems with which humans are beset stem from magic, superstitious beliefs. Consequently, the rational-emotive practitioner mainly

> employs a fairly rapid-fire active directive–persuasive–philosophic methodology. In most instances, he quickly pins the client down to a few basic irrational ideas which motivate much of his disturbed behavior; he challenges the client to validate these ideas, he shows him that they are extra-logical premises which cannot be validated. (Ellis, 1973a, p. 185)

Gestalt therapy (Kempler, 1973) can be located in the field of existential thought alongside many other disciplines that urge awareness to the immediate. Some mention of resistance in the writings of existentialists can be noted occasionally. In their description of existential therapy, Boss and Condrau point out that "the patient is tirelessly confronted with the limitations of his life and wherein these limitations are incessantly questioned so that the possibility of a richer existence is implied" (1967, p. 450). In Gestalt therapy, it is believed that symptoms are created and maintained by one part of the personality refusing to accept another. This refusal seems to be similar to what many therapists call resistance.

Reality therapy, introduced by William Glasser (1965), is similar to Ellis' rational-emotive therapy in that "it is a *system of ideas* which can help anyone gain a successful identity" (Glasser & Zunin, 1973, p. 292).

It views mental disturbance as irresponsibility, ignores the person's past, disregards transference, and takes the position that the client has to learn to apply values and moral principles in his daily life. The unconscious is discarded, and the client is implored to commit himself to executing plans to get better. The closest the reality therapists get to resistance is when they point out that clients are "not permitted to make excuses" when they do not change their behavior; that is, they are not permitted to resist.

The concept of resistance has been used in other modalities besides one-to-one psychotherapy, the modality that will be our major frame of reference in this book. Certain family and group processes have come to be understood as manifesting collective resistance to change. Communication processes, such as double binds, and relationship processes, such as scapegoating, have been viewed as resistance phenomena (Ackerman, 1958; Germain, 1982; Germain & Gitterman, 1980). As Sandler et al. (1973) have suggested, the concept can be used in many human interactions besides psychotherapy.

Most writers, particularly those with a psychodynamic orientation, agree that resistance occurs in all therapy and is more than an obstacle to be overcome. It is a vital part of the client's psyche that is complex and stubborn, has many possible sources and forms, and should be well understood. In Chapter 2, we review the literature on the therapist's role in resolving resistances.

The Therapist's Role in Resolving Resistances— Techniques and Counter-Resistances: A Review of the Literature

In Chapter 1, it was our intent to establish that no psychotherapeutic endeavor is ever carried out without resistance; resistance is par for the entire course of treatment. From the very first session to the very last, every client to some extent fights therapeutic progress. As our review of the literature in Chapter 1 attests, all clients enter therapy with a wish to feel and function better, but concomitantly they oppose change by using the habitual but dysfunctional mechanisms that made them feel bad before they came into therapy.

It is one thing to recognize resistances in clients; it is quite another to help them resolve their resistances. In this chapter we discuss the role of the therapist in helping clients overcome resistances. As the title of this chapter suggests, techniques that the therapist uses to aid clients in resolving resistances can never be divorced from the therapist's own personality and countertransference. Most experienced practitioners accept as a truism that a therapist can help a client grow only as much as the therapist himself has grown. If the therapist has problems with sex, aggression, dependency, or any other dimension of life, these problems will interfere with the practitioner's capacity to be objective, feel empathetic, and render effective therapeutic help.

As early as 1891, in a paper on aphasia, Freud wrote that the competent therapist must be able to put himself in the patient's shoes. Freud stated that it gave him an "uncanny feeling" whenever he was unable to gauge someone's emotions through his own.

In contrast to the plethora of literature on definitions of resistances, their sources, types, and so on, there is a limited literature on the techniques used in resolving them, and an even smaller literature on the role of countertransferences. In a review and evaluation of Freud's writings, Reuben Fine (1962) pointed out that, although Freud's observations of transference and resistance are of the most profound made about psychotherapy and frequently explain many of the baffling phenomena in the treatment situation, Freud never gave a systematic account of resistance and transference, basic as these concepts are to the whole theory and practice of psychotherapy. In all of Freud's writings, there is not a single paper devoted exclusively to resistance, and when we read his papers that mention transference and resistance, we note that the subjects are handled quite casually and rather sketchily. This is in rather sharp contrast to Freud's thorough and meticulous discussion of such issues as sexuality, aggression, and dreams. Fine (1962) has also noted that, just as Freud never wrote a full-length paper on resolving resistances, subsequent writers have not tackled the problem thoroughly and systematically either. Perhaps it can be hypothesized that there is a resistance on the part of therapists to face the many difficulties inherent in helping clients resolve resistances and to face the many countertransference problems that it can induce. Be that as it may, before embarking on a visit to the therapist's consultation room to observe how the therapist tries to help clients overcome their resistances (Chapters 3–7), we first will review the work of those writers who have made major contributions to the literature on technical procedures involved in resolving resistances. We will also review in this chapter the work of writers who have figured prominently in conceptualizing countertransference problems.

SIGMUND FREUD

Freud credits Josef Breuer as the first practitioner to discover a means of helping a patient resolve a resistance in psychotherapy (Breuer & Freud, 1893–1895). Breuer used hypnosis in treating hysterical patients and enabled them to find relief by reenacting under hypnosis an original traumatic situation. He called his approach the "cathartic method."

Between December 1880 and June 1882, Breuer treated a 21-year-old woman who had a severe paralysis and suffered from other symptoms, including hallucinations. The patient, Anna O., was able to rid herself of her symptoms when she followed Breuer's injunction to say whatever was on her mind, regardless of what her thoughts were. She was particularly encouraged "to cathart" whenever she felt hesitant to speak spontaneously. Thus, the first technical procedure to be used in psychotherapy to help a client resolve a resistance was direct suggestion and persuasion within the context of a hypnotic trance.

Anna O. referred to her successful treatment as "a talking cure," and her therapy also introduced what was to become known as the most powerful of all resistances in psychotherapy—the transference. As Anna O. continued to work with Breuer, she developed an intense sexual transference that was in part manifested by a false pregnancy. Breuer felt helpless in the face of Anna O's adoration, broke off treatment with her, and went off on a vacation with his wife to have a baby with her. Here, Breuer's countertransference difficulties interfered with his helping his patient overcome her resistance to explore her infantile sexual wishes (Freeman & Strean, 1981).

Freud learned many of the essential facts about hysteria from Breuer. He learned that catharsis and making the unconscious conscious had therapeutic effects. However, Freud found that many patients were resistive to hypnosis, and he himself did not feel particularly adept at performing it (Breuer & Freud, 1893–1895). In 1892 Freud developed a "concentration technique." At first he put his hand upon the patient's head and enjoined his patient to dwell on some part of his illness. However, Freud soon realized that physical contact with the patient was unnecessary, and he became convinced that the best way to help patients explore their conflicts was to grant them the freedom to say whatever came to their minds. Thus evolved the concept of free association, which has been the basic rule of psychoanalytic technique ever since.

When Freud formally established the basic rule (1904), he introduced a therapeutic procedure that has many advantages, has stood the test of time, and is still being used by many therapists. The rationale for the basic rule is as follows:

1. As he tells an unintrusive and empathetic listener what comes into his mind, the client begins to see for himself just how much he is writing his own script—that is, arranging for his own successes and failures. For example, if the client finds himself in a chaotic marriage, in an unrewarding job situation, or in a tense parent–child relationship, by listening to his own associations he slowly becomes aware of his fantasies of doing battle, his desires to seduce, his fears of interacting, and his urges to be mistreated.

2. If the therapist assumes a neutral posture during this process, the client's self-esteem usually rises and his anxiety lessens. When the therapist neither champions nor repudiates the client's productions, the client begins to feel like a child who has confessed a misdeed to an understanding and empathetic parent. Like the well-understood child who is not disliked nor criticized for what he has reported, the client begins to like himself more.

3. Free association usually induces the client to regress, and he begins to recall memories and distorted notions from the past that influence his functioning in the present. He may begin to see, for example, how the battle with a colleague that is causing his present psychosomatic symptoms may be part of an unresolved problem with a sibling. He may learn that his oversensitivity to his wife's demands is due to his wish that she become the punitive mother of his past.

4. Free association with an unintrusive listener usually, if not always, activates the client's major resistance, the transference. As the client studies his transference reactions, he begins to see how he distorts other relationships.

5. Free association with a benign and quiet listener usually activates other resistances (e.g., compliance, intellectualization, acting out). As client and therapist see what the client is doing to sabotage the therapy, they may learn how and why the client is behaving self-destructively in his day-to-day adaptation. For example, if the client freely associates to his passivity, dependence, hostility, or sexuality in one session and then finds himself coming late to the following sessions, missing them entirely, or feeling uncomfortable with the therapist, the reasons for the client's resistive behavior become clearer as therapist and client review the associations of the previous sessions.

In the years following the *Studies on Hysteria* (1893–1895), a slow alteration in Freud's technique of resolving resistances took place. He began to abandon the use of cathartic techniques of suggestion and concentration, and became more committed to the basic rule of free association. Coltrera and Ross (1967) note that as early as 1889, in his treatment of Frau Emmy von N., Freud took the position that no longer was the patient to be dominated by imperatives of word and act. Instead, the analyst was enjoined to assume a neutral and unintrusive position of relaxed attention, to listen mainly, and to be alert to the unconscious meanings behind the analysand's associations. To help the analysand examine his resistances, analysts were advised to do their work with tact, seriousness, and discretion.

Ernest Jones (1953), Freud's biographer, believed that the essential shape of the basic rule was known to Freud ever since he was 14 years of age, when he had been given the works of Ludwig Borne. In Borne's essay "The Art of Becoming an Original Writer in Three Days," Borne advised writers to free associate for three days and then to begin to write.

Almost as soon as Freud discovered the basic rule, he saw how it could be used as a resistance. In the *Studies on Hysteria* (Breuer & Freud, 1893–

1895), he described the resistance of "false connections." By "false connections" Freud was referring to the defense of isolation, often found in obsessive personalities who are frightened by their emotions or thoughts and protect themselves by keeping thoughts and feelings separated (A. Freud, 1946).

As Freud (1896) further reflected on the reactions of his patients to free association and hypnosis, he began to realize that some patients could be hypnotized and some could not, some could free associate spontaneously and others could not. At first, Freud felt that what was being resisted were memories; a little later he concluded that any unbearable idea was resisted. When Freud realized that suggestion and persuasion had limited effects and therefore concentrated more on helping the patient to free associate, he called attention to the importance of the analyst's silence (Freud, 1896). The silence, far from being an expression of passivity, should be considered an expression of what Reuben Fine (1982) has called "dynamic inactivity." Because the therapist is silent, the client is freer to associate and report memories, fantasies, transference reactions, and dreams, and to demonstrate resistances. Eventually, the therapist, and frequently the client, can interpret what is hidden—that is, unconscious (Freud, 1904). Although Freud explicitly restricted the role of interpretation to material that is unconscious, he used the concept to mean unconscious derivatives (i.e., repressed material that is near consciousness).

From 1895 to 1899, Freud embarked on his own self-analysis. His self-analysis served many lasting purposes for the psychotherapeutic movement: It established a precedent for all therapists—namely, that self-understanding is an absolute prerequisite for helping others therapeutically; it demonstrated that all human beings regardless of diagnostic label have an unconscious that is replete with sexual and aggressive fantasies, and that the differences between "the normal," the neurotic, and the psychotic are only a matter of degree; and it helped psychoanalysts and therapists realize that, to understand a client, practitioners have to experience their clients' emotions within themselves. In addition, the value of the dream as a means of resolving resistances was another positive outcome of Freud's self-analysis inasmuch as it was through an analysis of his own dreams that Freud gained an understanding of his own resistances and conflicts.

In *The Interpretation of Dreams* (1900) Freud was able to demonstrate that, in every dream, there is an unconscious wish seeking discharge. By associating to his own dreams, Freud was able to demonstrate that "the dream is the royal road to the unconscious." The introduction of dream analysis, therefore, was one of Freud's major contributions to the therapist's repertoire of technical procedures for resolving resistances.

The dream has a distinct advantage in sensitizing clients to their resistances and in helping them gain an inner conviction about them. Inasmuch as it is the clients, and only the clients, who write the scripts of their dreams, this realization sooner or later moves most of them to take responsibility for their thoughts and wishes when they dream, for example, that the therapist is being maimed, is initiating sex with them, or is torturing them. Associations to dreams inevitably bring to the surface, not only hidden transference fantasies, but also repressed childish desires, rigid superego mandates, and strong hopes for epinosic gains. As the therapist helps the client to free associate to each part of the dream, the client can slowly give up dysfunctional resistances, as unconscious material that the resistances oppose rises to consciousness. Then, energy that had been previously used to defend against repressed material is liberated and can be used in the service of constructive and pleasureful activity.

In his paper "The Handling of Dream Interpretation in Psychoanalysis," Freud (1911) was concerned with the two ways in which dreams can be used as a resistance. In the first instance, the analysand, knowing that the dream is critical for the treatment, may out of spite, revenge, or a negativistic character trait bring no dreams at all to the therapy. Here the analysand is unconsciously trying to defeat the therapist and may also have a latent wish for the practitioner to say that the treatment cannot proceed any further. Freud pointed out that the way to resolve this resistance is to show the analysand that the analysis will go on if necessary without dreams. Frequently, when the analysand realizes that the analyst will not insist on dreams being brought to treatment, he starts to remember dreams and begins to use them in the therapy.

The other way that dreams can be used as a resistance, Freud noted, is that the analysand can overwhelm the analyst with many dreams or produce a single dream of convoluted length, neither of which can be analyzed in any given session. Here it is important for the therapist to point out to the patient that his manner of presenting dreams is being used as a resistance and that the content of the dream should be considered as less crucial than the why's and wherefore's of the resistance.

The notion that the dynamics of resistance should precede the analysis of content is very much accepted by most contemporary therapists (Fine, 1982; Greenson, 1967; Langs, 1981). If the client is frightened to relate to the therapist, this fact is more important than the content of the client's dream (or the content of the client's fantasy, memory, or any other association). As Fenichel (1945) said, "Resistance always comes before content."

In the 1911 paper on dream interpretation, Freud warned that the interest of the analyst in the dream as a psychic phenomenon should not intrude on the analytic work. If the analysand associates to material that seems removed from the dream content, the analyst should not try to pressure the analysand to come back to the dream. An obvious research interest on the part of the analyst toward the dream will interfere with spontaneous transference responses.

Freud's self-analysis helped him become much more sensitive to his analysands' conflicts and much more secure in helping them resolve their resistances. In 1910, he said:

> We have noticed that no psychoanalyst goes further than his own complexes and internal resistances permit, and we consequently require that he shall begin his activity with a self-analysis and continually carry it deeper while he is making his observations on his patients. Anyone who fails to produce results in a self-analysis of this kind may at once give up any idea of being able to treat patients by analysis. (p. 145)

Freud modified his position about self-analysis and felt that it was difficult to be therapist and client simultaneously. Contemporary therapists often joke and say, "Self-analysis is impossible because the countertransference gets in the way!" In 1897, Freud, writing to his father-confessor Dr. Wilhelm Fliess about self-analysis said, "My self-analysis is still interrupted and I have realized the reason. I can only analyze myself with the help of knowledge obtained objectively (like an outsider). Genuine self-analysis is impossible; otherwise there would be no illness" (pp. 234–235). Later, in 1936, Freud wrote, "In self-analysis the danger of incompleteness is particularly great. One is too easily satisfied with a part explanation, behind which resistance can easily keep back something that may perhaps be more important" (p. 314).

After a prolonged discussion of therapeutic technique in *Studies on Hysteria* (1895), Freud did not write on the subject until 1904, when he published "Freud's Psychoanalytic Procedure." Here Freud pointed out that, by the study of free associations, dreams, and the patient's life history, the major objective of treatment was to lift the amnesias of childhood. The therapeutic role of abreaction was relegated to the background, and making the unconscious conscious became the major technical tool. Freud emphasized the importance of the analyst's neutrality so that associations of the patient would not be contaminated. To foster a regression so that the analysand could become more aware of memories and fantasies that his resistances opposed, the couch was recommended. Freud again emphasized the importance of the analyst being quiet and not "intruding" on the patient so that his "consciousness" could be "widened."

In the 1904 paper, Freud continued to talk about how interpretation helps to resolve resistances. When analysands are directed to see how they are experiencing the present as if it were the past (in the transference as well as outside of it), their observing egos can begin to perceive distortions better so that they can slowly begin to give up pathological resistances.

Freud made the observation in the *Three Essays on the Theory of Sexuality* (1905b) that the sexual life of children usually emerges in a form that can be observed around the third or fourth year of life. Inasmuch as it is at this time of life that many neurotic problems evolve (the oedipal complex), analysis should remove the amnesia of this period. The ideal of reconstructing the infantile amnesias led to a new concept, that of analyzability. In 1904, the first descriptive criteria of analyzability were stated:

> To begin with, he (the analysand) must be capable of a psychically normal condition, during periods of confusion or melancholic depression nothing can be accomplished even in cases of hysteria. Furthermore, a certain measure of natural intelligence and ethical development are to be required of him; if the physician has to deal with a worthless character, he soon loses the interest which makes it possible for him to enter profoundly into the patient's mental life. Deep-rooted malformations of character, traits of an actually degenerate constitution, show themselves during treatment as sources of a resistance that scarcely can be overcome. In this respect the constitution of the patient sets a general limit to the curative effect of psychotherapy. If the patient's age is in the neighborhood of the fifties the conditions for psychoanalysis become unfavorable. The mass of psychical material is then no longer manageable; the time required for recovery is too long, and the ability to undo psychical processes begins to grow weaker. (p. 254)

The criteria of analyzability that Freud discussed in 1904 have been modified over the years. Psychotics can be treated by the psychoanalytic method, people in their 60s or older have been successfully helped, and even the mentally retarded have been assisted through psychoanalytically oriented psychotherapy (Dickerson, 1981; Fine, 1962, 1981; Strean, 1982; Szasz, 1957).

In 1910 Freud published "On Wild Psychoanalysis." Here he warned against the indiscriminate applications of his theories without understanding them. He took a strong stand against psychoanalytic technique as pedagogy, stating that technique cannot be learned didactically from books, but only in a learning situation with those who have mastered it.

As Freud began to research his failures he became more and more impressed with the role of transference in psychotherapy. In the case of Dora (Freud, 1905a), he had already asked himself why the expected success was not forthcoming and answered:

If the theory of psychoanalytic technique is gone into, it becomes evident that transference is an inevitable necessity. Practical experience, at all events, shows conclusively that there is no means of avoiding it, and that this latest creation of the disease must be combatted like all the earlier ones. This happens, however, to be by far the hardest part of the whole task. (p. 116)

In the case of Dora, Freud was critical of himself for missing some of the transference manifestations that led to a premature termination of the therapy. He placed too much emphasis, he later realized, on lifting amnesias and did not pay enough attention to the transference. He also was unaware of his countertransference problems with this attractive teen-aged girl (Freeman & Strean, 1981). But by 1912, in "The Dynamics of Transference," Freud said, "Every conflict has to be fought out in the sphere of transference" (p. 104).

"The Dynamics of Transference" is considered to be one of his most important papers on techniques for resolving resistances. Here he points out that the transference emerges as the most powerful resistance to treatment. If the analysand is resisting reporting associations, "the stoppage can be invariably removed," Freud averred "by an assurance that (the analysand) is being dominated at the moment by an association which is concerned with the doctor himself or with something connected with him. As soon as this explanation is given, the stoppage is removed, or the situation is changed from one in which the associations fail into one in which they are being kept back" (1912a, p. 101). Although Freud was overoptimistic and oversimplistic here, his notion that "stoppage" is invariably connected with transference fantasies has proven to be valid to this day.

Freud also pointed out that the individual in therapy can select almost any aspect of the therapist's behavior or personality to satisfy the resistance. If the client is frightened to experience and express sexual or aggressive fantasies or to reveal frightening memories, he can resist doing so by objecting to virtually anything, from the analyst's silence to his verbosity, from objects in the therapist's office to where his office is located. Young therapists often fail to recognize that, regardless of whether there is some, a little, or a lot of validity to the client's objections about the therapist, changes in the therapist's decorum will serve no useful purpose because the client's objections are being used in the service of resistance.

Just as criticisms of the therapist can be used to ward off uncomfortable thoughts, feelings, or memories, so can admiration and praise of the therapist be used to defend against uncomfortable associations. Many positive transferences need to be carefully examined so that client and therapist can see what uncomfortable feelings the client is protecting (Strean, 1983).

Freud's position that the transference is the strongest weapon of resistance is a point of view with which most contemporary therapists still concur. Clients, through their transference relationship with the therapist, try to gratify childish id wishes, to receive superego admonishments, and to procure ego support. The transference wards off reality and blocks the maturation process. It inhibits therapeutic progress but is clung to tenaciously by virtually every client in psychotherapy.

In "Recommendations to Physicians Practising Psychoanalysis," Freud (1912b) developed a series of technical rules for therapists. He cautioned the therapist against taking notes and suggested that the practitioner try to maintain evenly suspended attention in the face of all that he hears. This is necessary in order to avoid selecting certain material and disregarding other associations of the analysand. If the therapist is too selective, he will be in danger of "never finding anything but what he already knows; and if he follows his inclinations he will certainly falsify what he may perceive. It must not be forgotten that the things one hears are for the most part things whose meaning is only recognized later on" (1912b, p. 112).

Freud advised therapists to model themselves after the surgeon "who puts aside all of his feelings, even his human sympathy, and concentrates his mental forces on the single aim of performing the operation as skillfully as possible" (1912b, p. 115). The justification for requiring this emotional coldness in the analyst, according to Freud, is that it creates the most advantageous conditions for both parties: It is a desirable protection for the doctor's own emotional life, and it ensures the patient available help.

Freud's model of the cold, unsympathetic surgeon who "should be opaque to his patients and, like a mirror, should show them nothing but what is shown to him" was not always carried out by him in practice. In the 1890s, he invited patients to have meals with his family, and in 1909 in the case of the "Rat Man" ("Notes upon a Case of Obsessional Neuroses") (Freud, 1909), he had refreshments brought in for both himself and his patient. In World War I, he collected funds to help "The Wolf Man," who was cut off from his estates in Russia. Therefore, the "newer" familiar relationships between client and therapist, advocated by some of the non-Freudian schools, can be seen as historical phases in Freud's evolving technique (Coltera & Ross, 1967).

Freud cautioned that too much "therapeutic ambition" will put the therapist into a state of mind that is unfavorable for doing therapeutic work. When the therapist is too ambitious, "this will make him helpless against certain resistances of the patient, whose recovery, as we know, primarily depends on the interplay of forces in him" (Freud, 1912b, p. 115).

Freud's recommendations to physicians practicing psychoanalysis were all intended to create for the therapist a counterpart to the fundamental rule that is laid down for the patient:

> Just as the patient must relate everything that his self-observation can detect and keep back all the logical and affective objections that seek to induce him to make a selection from among them, so the doctor must put himself in a position to make use of everything he is told for the purposes of interpretation and of recognizing the concealed unconscious material without substituting a censorship of his own for the selection that the patient has forgone. To put it in a formula, he must turn his own unconscious like a receptive organ towards the transmitting unconscious of the patient. (1912b, p. 115)

Freud felt that the therapist may not tolerate any resistances in himself that have been perceived by his unconscious. It is not enough, Freud felt, for the analyst to be a "normal person." "It may be insisted, rather, that he should have undergone a psychoanalytic purification and have become aware of those complexes of his own which would be apt to interfere with his grasp of what his patient tells him" (1912b, p. 116).

Although Freud was very explicit in pointing out that anyone who does therapy should be in therapy himself, he was equally forceful in pointing out that it is inadvisable for the therapist to reveal his own defects to the patient.

> But this technique achieves nothing towards the uncovering of what is unconscious to the patient. It makes him even more incapable of overcoming his deeper resistances, and in severer cases it invariably fails by encouraging the patient to be insatiable: he would like to reverse the situation and finds the analysis of the doctor more interesting than his own. The resolution of the transference, too—one of the main tasks of treatment—is made more difficult by an intimate attitude on the doctor's part, so that any gain there may be at the beginning is more than outweighed at the end. I have no hesitation, therefore, in condemning this kind of technique as incorrect. (1912b, p. 118)

Although Freud was very forceful in prescribing certain techniques and condemning others, he took the position that the therapist's style should be constant and true to his own "autonomous ego gifts." Nevertheless, the six papers on technique that Freud wrote between December 1911 and July 1914 all have one unifying theme: They all focus on resistance in general and on the most important resistance, the transference. The avoidance of social contact between therapist and patient and of replies to personal questions about the therapist, the handling of appointments and fees, the principle of abstinence, and many other matters that have become part of standard technique, all derive from Freud's need to keep the transference uncontaminated and therefore subject to examination (Fine, 1962).

The stress on transference led Freud to the recognition of the transference neurosis. Here the patient recapitulates with the therapist the pathological aspects of his relationship with his parents. Transference neuroses appear in all kinds of interpersonal situations, but it is only in intensive therapy that they are fully understood.

By 1914, Freud felt that resolving the resistances was the most important dimension of psychotherapy. In "Remembering, Repeating and Working Through" (Freud, 1914), he pointed out that a person does not overcome resistances by just taking note of them. They continue to reappear and must be analyzed every time they do. To this process, Freud gave the name of "working through." Working through does not differ essentially from any other learning procedure wherein the learner must go over the material time and again until it sinks in (Fine, 1962).

In spite of his many contributions to the technique of resolving resistances and to therapeutic technique in general, Freud was not satisfied and looked forward to a thorough revision of his theories. In a letter to Ferenczi in 1928, he wrote:

> The "Recommendations on Technique" I wrote long ago were essentially of a negative nature. I considered the most important thing was to emphasize what one should *not* do, and to point out the temptations in directions contrary to analysis. Almost everything positive that one should do I have left to "tact," the discussion of which you are introducing. The result was that the docile analysts did not perceive the elasticity of the rules I had laid down and submitted to them as if they were taboos. Some time all that must be revised, without, it is true, doing away with the obligations I had mentioned. (Jones, 1957, p. 241)

Freud occasionally apologized for his not being able to be more specific about the technical procedures involved in conducting an analysis and in helping a patient resolve resistances. Employing the metaphor of a game of chess, he said:

> Anyone who hopes to learn the noble game of chess from books will soon discover that only the opening and end-games admit of an exhaustive systematic presentation and that the infinite variety of moves which develop after the opening defy any description. This gap in instruction can only be filled by a diligent study of games fought out by masters. The rules which can be laid down for the practice of psychoanalytic treatment are subject to similar limitations. (1913, p. 123)

Freud's metaphor of chess was mentioned in his paper "On Beginning the Treatment" (1913). Here he also stated that it was his custom to accept a new patient for a trial period of several weeks during which the patient followed the analytic rules and the analyst did not make any interpretations. This was done not only to test the patient's suitability but to see if there was a psychotic process underneath the patient's neurosis. Freud felt that psychotics were not treatable with his method.

Advising against lengthy discussions about treatment before beginning it, Freud felt that too much verbal activity on the part of the analyst at any time would jeopardize the development of a true transference neurosis. He warned against the patient who postponed beginning treatment, contending that this patient would be very oppositional to therapy. He pointed out that if the analyst treated the children or wife of a friend, he would have to be prepared to lose the friendship. Freud took the position that seeing a patient for no fee had many hazards because it could gratify many transference fantasies (e.g., to be an indulged child). Psychoanalytic treatment, Freud averred, is always long, not only because of the complexity of the neurotic process, but also because of the timelessness of the unconscious and the slowness of deep changes. Further, Freud felt that it was unreasonable to ask for a selective analysis of certain symptoms while leaving others alone. Freud closed his paper "On Beginning the Treatment" (1913) with the complaint that he was helpless in dealing with the patient's relatives and that their hostility and dissatisfaction were to be expected.

Many of Freud's statements that appear in his 1913 paper have been challenged by subsequent generations of therapists. Sometimes an interpretation, if the data are available, can be made early in treatment. A client's fear of intimacy or of revealing himself can be interpreted early in therapy and may help the client continue in the treatment. We now know that psychotic clients can be helped therapeutically (Bychowski, 1952; Fine, 1979a; Frosch, 1983). Individuals who postpone treatment are not necessarily hopeless and may be able to be engaged in it if their resistances are well understood by the therapist and communicated to them with empathy (Blanck & Blanck, 1974). Finally, if it is understood by the therapist that the client can use the relatives' hostility toward the treatment as a resistance to ward off his own discomfort with the therapeutic situation, and if the therapist is not dominated by countertransference problems, the client's resistances can be interpreted, sometimes with successful results.

Freud believed that his paper "Observations on Transference Love" (1915) was one of his best. Here he recognized that, although transference love is a resistance, it can also help the therapy in that the patient in transference love will be receptive to influence. Although the patient's feeling of being in love cannot be denied, transference love must be worked through to expose its infantile, magical determinants. Eventually, when transference love is resolved, the patient will feel respect and affection for the analyst as a real person. Reluctance to resolve the transference love constitutes a resistance to ending the analysis, and sometimes it is more the therapist than the patient who resists the termination.

In "Lines of Advance in Psychoanalytic Therapy" (1919), Freud observed that an unhappy marriage and physical disease were the most common ways of keeping a neurosis alive, because both can satisfy the patient's masochistic wish to suffer and be punished. It is also because of the desire to be punished that many clients who "get well" begin to "get sick" again.

In his 1919 paper, Freud spoke out against the tendency he was observing in several analysts to guide their patients' lives in particular directions, to instruct them in the aim of life, and to induce them to adopt the analyst's personality as a model. He also objected to any attempts to foist a particular philosophy on patients. In the same paper, Freud suggested that at a certain point in the treatment of phobic patients, the therapist should urge them to endure the anxiety evoked by the dreaded situation rather than wait until the final resolution of the symptom.

The essential principles of psychoanalytic technique had thus been formulated before 1920. Freud had advanced from hypnosis and the cathartic method, to free association. From an emphasis upon the revival of memories of traumatic events, he moved to the stance that only by a careful analysis of the patient's resistances, particularly transference reactions, could the patient learn to work and love maturely and enjoyably.

After 1920, Freud did not write very much about technique or countertransference problems. He did point out in "The Psychogenesis of a Case of Homosexuality in Woman" (1920) that the ideal situation for therapy is when someone who is otherwise his own master is suffering from an inner conflict that he is unable to resolve alone and brings his trouble to a therapist for help. Then the therapist can form a pact with the healthy portion of the client's ego, and both parties can work together to rid the client of his pathology. Freud also pointed out in this paper that it is no more promising a prospect to convert a fully developed homosexual into a heterosexual than the reverse would be, and that a favorable prognosis is to be envisioned only when the homosexuality is not too strong or when there are considerable rudiments of a heterosexual object choice. Today, many therapists are not as pessimistic as Freud was regarding the prognosis of a homosexual client (Bieber, 1962; Socarides, 1978).

In the paper about his work with a homosexual woman, Freud wondered if his analysand would have done better with a female therapist, because of the patient's strong negative transference toward him. Many contemporary therapists contend that the sex of the therapist is quite crucial in effecting a positive therapeutic outcome. It is certainly true that many clients feel more comfortable with one sex over another, and their wishes for either a female or a male therapist should be honored, if possible. However, many clients, particularly those who have more or less stable ego functions, are able to establish transferences regardless of the sex of the therapist (Lipton, 1967).

In "Two Encyclopedia Articles," Freud (1923b) once more reaffirmed his view that the task of the analyst is to acquaint the patient with the resistances of which he is unaware and to help him overcome them. He pointed out again that the essential part of the process of cure lay in overcoming these resistances; unless this was achieved, no permanent mental change could take place. He added in these papers that, with the recognition that the psychoanalyst's efforts should be directed toward the patient's resistances, analytic technique had attained a certainty and delicacy rivaling surgery.

By 1923, Freud viewed psychoanalytic psychotherapy as much more than a therapy that provided symptom relief. In *The Ego and the Id* (1923a), it becomes clear that Freud was putting the central emphasis of therapy on analyzing resistances that, by reducing anxiety, would build the patient's ego. The removal of symptoms became a by-product of the therapy if the therapy was properly administered. This point of view has become one of the central differences between psychodynamic and other forms of therapy. Psychodynamic therapy, by trying to help the client resolve resistances, aims to help the client modify character, build ego functions, and grow toward optimum maturity. This would be in marked contrast to many current and popular therapies, such as behavior modification, in which the aim is to remove symptoms and reinforce or extinguish certain behaviors.

It was in *The Ego and the Id* (1923a) that Freud wrote that the most powerful impediment to recovery is an unconscious sense of guilt, which leads to a negative therapeutic reaction. Freud felt that one can attempt to make the sense of guilt conscious only by interpreting its derivatives as they emerge in the treatment. As we noted in Chapter 1, Freud did not discuss what contemporary therapists now know about the negative therapeutic reaction—namely, that it is the client's way, usually quite unconscious, of expressing hatred toward the therapist and subtly trying to defeat him.

In "Negation" (1925a), Freud drew attention to his old observation that an association that is a negation can also be a confirmation inasmuch as the content of the association has reached consciousness. He pointed out that a convenient method of reaching repressed material is to ask the patient, "What would you consider the most unlikely thing imaginable in that situation?" If the patient falls into the trap and says what he thinks is most unlikely to occur, he almost always makes the right admission. Freud's means of resolving the resistance in the above instance would probably be considered by contemporary therapists as an intrusion on free association and therefore not too helpful in the long run.

In Freud's preface to August Aichorn's *Wayward Youth* (1925b), he pointed out that psychoanalysis is not the treatment of choice for psychopaths, impulsive youngsters, psychotics, and other individuals who do not have relatively intact egos. However, experience with these individuals, including the work of Aichorn with delinquents, has demonstrated that, with much preparation of the client and some optimism from the therapist, these individuals can be helped (Fine, 1982; Strean, 1982).

In *Analysis Terminable and Interminable* (1937a), Freud again discussed the limitations of psychoanalytic treatment; we alluded to some of these limitations in Chapter 1. It has been suggested that when Freud wrote this paper, he was concerned about the faster treatment that was being advocated by the proponents of other therapies (Lipton, 1967). Freud warned that conflict cannot be activated in analysis, nor is psychoanalytic treatment suitable in crisis situations. Although Freud always pointed out that psychoanalytic therapy requires the collaboration of the "normal" ego, he also implied that normality is an ideal and that the ego of the normal person approaches that of the psychotic person's in many ways. It is somewhat surprising that Freud, who saw the differences between the psychotic and neurotic as a matter of degree, was so pessimistic about psychotherapy with the psychotic.

In "Constructions in Analysis" (1937b), Freud emphasized that the work of the analyst is to *construct* from the patient's associations, dreams, and fantasies. He defined an *interpretation* as an intervention that relates to a single element of the material (e.g., "You withdraw from me because you are afraid of your sexual fantasies toward me"), whereas a *construction* is more complex (e.g., "You withdraw from me because you are afraid of your sexual fantasies toward me. You feel toward me the same way you felt toward your mother when you were six. At that time you expected retaliation for your sexual wishes toward mother and your competitive fantasies toward father").

Freud emphasized that confirmation of the correctness of constructions comes from the many associations of the patient that follow the therapist's interventions. Agreement or disagreement on the part of the analysand can come out of a wish to comply with or to oppose the therapist. Consequently, Freud advocated and most contemporary therapists would agree that to test the accuracy of a therapeutic intervention, the therapist should examine carefully the client's productions and determine if he has an internal conviction regarding what the therapist has constructed or interpreted. This can, in some instances, take several sessions before the therapist is certain of the accuracy of the interpretation.

While Freud did not write a great deal about technique from 1920 until his death in 1939, this period can be described as one in which he enlarged on and refined the theory of resistances as an important part of the therapeutic process. The conceptualization of the ego allowed for more complete recognition of resistances and led Freud to characterize analytic work as veering from ego analysis to id analysis and back, allowing equal importance for both (Lipton, 1967).

By the time of his death (1939), Freud had established many principles for helping clients resolve resistances in therapeutic work: the necessity of starting from the current surface of the material (i.e., beginning where the client is); the juxtaposition of free association by the client and evenly hovering attention, interpretation, and construction by the therapist; the crucial importance of interpreting resistances before content; the development and resolution of the transference; the genetic reconstruction of disturbing experiences; the importance of dream interpretation; the futility of attacking symptoms; and the tremendous importance of countertransference (Fine, 1962, 1979a; Lipton, 1967). All these principles have stood the test of time and have been incorporated into the repertoire of most Freudian therapists, many neo-Freudian therapists, and some non-Freudian practitioners.

SANDOR FERENCZI

A contemporary of Freud's, Sandor Ferenczi is best known for his "active technique." Though always considering himself a Freudian, and in fact psychoanalyzed by Freud, Ferenczi discovered a number of clinical phenomena and technical procedures for resolving resistances that have been used by both Freudians and non-Freudians.

Ferenczi was one of the first clinicians to appreciate the value of regression in the therapeutic situation. He contended that, if the analysand could permit himself to regress and feel childish wishes and fantasies, particularly toward the therapist, then many of the patient's resistances would dissolve. He was also able to influence others regarding the overriding importance of transference interpretations as compared with anything else the analyst may say or do. Ferenczi also had strong convictions about the use of countertransference reactions in therapy. He felt that, if the analysand thought that the analyst was sleepy, irritable, or excited and the analyst really was, the analyst should confirm the correctness of the patient's perception. The therapist's sincerity, according to Ferenczi, was an absolute necessity for helping the patient resolve resistances. He also felt that, for some patients, the traditionally passive and quiet stance of the analyst could induce deleterious effects (Ferenczi, 1950).

Ferenczi, like Wilhelm Reich (1949), demonstrated that changes in the patient's body during a therapeutic session show a psychological structure that can be observed, understood, and interpreted by the therapist in the same manner as a neurotic symptom is dealt with by the practitioner. He called attention to the many possible types of bodily changes that can occur during a therapeutic hour, some of which are a change in the patient's breathing rhythm or in the pitch of the patient's voice; a sudden urge to urinate or defecate; a sudden feeling of coldness; or a feeling of drowsiness. Ferenczi reasoned that, because the analytic process stirs up repressed wishes that conflict with superego mandates, the patient copes with the resultant anxiety by showing many bodily symptoms right in the therapist's office. (Balint, 1967; Ferenczi, 1950).

An important aspect of the bodily changes that occur in the patient during a therapeutic session is that they are all, according to Ferenczi (1950), expressions of the transference. When the analyst interprets the patient's bodily changes as an expression of the transference, the patient acquires an unshakable conviction of the truth of analytic interpretations because he has been helped to feel their effects literally in his own body (Balint, 1967).

From the point of view of technique, Ferenczi's findings meant that analysts had to extend their field of observations so that bodily changes would be part of what was interpreted to their analysands. He contended that most analysts viewed transitory bodily changes as nuisances, and he advocated that instead they be welcomed by the analyst as if they were free associations. Ferenczi reasoned that, if by understanding and interpreting transitory symptoms, therapeutic changes can take place, then perhaps it is the analyst's obligation to facilitate their emergence. This idea paved the way for Ferenczi's (1950) theory of the break-through of an instinctual drive and later for his experiments with active techniques.

Whereas Freud, in his analysis of symptomatic acts, restricted himself to pointing out the relationship between the patient's instinctual drives on the one hand and the repressive forces on the other, Ferenczi investigated the changes brought about by the analytic process, chiefly by transference (Balint, 1967).

In his paper "On the Technique of Psychoanalysis" (Ferenczi, 1950) written in 1919, Ferenczi stated that the analyst, in addition to being aware of the verbal contents of the patient's free associations, must also be sensitive to the pervading mood of these associations and to the interplay between the patient's transference and the therapist's countertransference. What Ferenczi demonstrated in this paper is that patients, prompted by their resistances, do not really associate freely. If the analyst focuses on how the patient associates—with his hesitations, circumlocutions, and bodily movements—the analyst and eventually the patient can learn a great deal about the patient's prevailing mood of the day toward the analysis in general and toward the treatment that he has been receiving from the analyst in particular. Therefore, the study of the ways patients free associate (e.g., alterations in voice, breathing, etc.) is, in effect, a study of the interaction between transference and countertransference.

In the 1919 paper, Ferenczi contended that every transference in the therapeutic situation is directed either toward "the indulgent mother" or "the stern father." The corollary of this observation is that every patient wants to be treated as a child by the analyst. Therefore, Ferenczi prescribed that every analyst learn how to adapt his sternness, indulgence, or sympathy as the case dictates. The analyst must, on the one hand, listen sympathetically and accept everything the patient presents so as to be able to reconstruct the unconscious meaning of the patient's productions and actual behavior. On the other hand, the analyst must be in full control of his countertransference. Ferenczi felt that many therapeutic impasses occur because the patient is aware of the analyst's unrecognized countertransference feelings—the patient is dimly aware of the analyst's unrecognized hostility or sexual fantasies toward the patient.

Ferenczi warned therapists against being too rigid and too controlling with their patients, which may make the therapist appear as much too distant and unapproachable. This attitude on the part of the therapist would squelch the development of any natural transference. Ferenczi viewed this rigid demeanor of the analyst as a resistance against the countertransference. He stated that the analyst must "let himself go during the treatment as psychoanalysis requires of him" (Ferenczi, 1950, p. 188) and follow the patient's associations and fantasies. Then, after associating to the patient's associations, the analyst should stop himself and subject both the patient's material and his own to a searching scrutiny in order to see whether any interpretation should be given and, if so, what. In sum, according to Ferenczi, the analyst should try to keep a happy medium between responding too readily to the patient's emotions and being overcautious and rigid in his own emotional responses.

Based on Ferenczi's findings that the patient's bodily expressions were important manifestations of unconscious conflicts stirred up by the analytic process, and based further on his wish to free the drives from repression, Ferenczi (1950) embarked formally on his active technique. The underlying rationale behind the active technique was that, in many cases, the flow of free associations had become stagnant and this was caused by the disappearance of libido into unconscious bodily gratifications and fantasies. The patient then formed "habits," which were like neurotic symptoms, to ward off the drives that caused anxiety. Habits could be any bodily activity (e.g., picking one's nose) or any unconscious fantasy (e.g., sucking at the breast).

The analyst's active technique can take two forms. He can propose that the patient cease to indulge in a particular habit, or he can encourage the patient to enjoy it openly and freely. Ferenczi hoped that a successful intervention by the analyst would cause an increase of tension in the patient and produce a breakthrough into consciousness of repressed instinctual drive, changing an unpleasurable symptom into a pleasurable satisfaction, thereby strengthening the ego and further, by removing resistances, stimulating the flow of the patient's associations again (Balint, 1967). The titles of two papers "On Forced Fantasies," written in 1924, and "Psychoanalysis of Sexual Habits," written in 1925, suggest what Ferenczi did with his active techniques (Ferenczi, 1950). He often forced his patients to bring out sexual or aggressive fantasies that he was convinced were the latent content of the patient's manifest bodily symptoms, and he would from time to time encourage or forbid patients to masturbate or have sexual intercourse.

From Ferenczi's papers, he appears to be commanding his patients by using rules and prohibitions in a forceful manner. However, Ferenczi saw himself as merely giving "friendly advice" and "friendly suggestion." He also took the position that the term *active technique* meant that the patient should do or refrain from doing something and that it is the patient, not the analyst, who is active.

As was stated at the beginning of this section, Ferenczi's active technique has been used by Freudians and non-Freudians, alike. Many therapists, including Freud, have suggested to clients that, rather than persist in an analysis of a phobia, they should face the dreaded situation and then see what they feel. Also, many clients can flounder in therapy in self-destructive ways until a termination date is set. The setting of a date can motivate many clients to face their difficulties more constructively, and then they can terminate treatment with less apprehension. Facing the phobic situation and setting a termination date are therapeutic interventions that are directly attributable to Ferenczi (Balint, 1967).

Many of the popular forms of behavior modification therapy, which involve reinforcement, aversion conditioning, and punishment, seem to be very similar to the frustration and gratification inherent in the active technique. Although behaviorists rarely, if ever, invoke Ferenczi's name when they describe their work, many of their techniques are very reminiscent of what Ferenczi described.

One of the limitations of Ferenczi's active technique is that, by making suggestions and advising clients, therapists can inadvertently make themselves appear as superego figures. Then clients can legitimately contend that they must "obey orders" in order to be loved, which is often one of the cardinal factors in the etiology of their neuroses. Consequently, one of the hazards of the active technique is that it can induce unnecessary compliance in many clients. It can also provoke in other clients a wish to spite and take revenge against the therapist who reminds them of their punitive parents. These are clients who wish to defeat the therapist anyway, and suggestions and advice from the therapist can exacerbate their negative therapeutic reaction (Freud, 1923a).

Ferenczi's emphasis on the role of the therapist's countertransference is an extremely important contribution. By realizing that clients are frequently sensitive to the therapist's underlying moods and attitudes toward them, therapists are forced to keep in mind that, to help a client resolve resistances, the practitioner must be relatively free from hostility, overambitiousness, or unrecognized sexual fantasies in the therapeutic situation.

What Ferenczi may not have been sufficiently aware of is that the use of active techniques can evolve from countertransference problems. Many therapists, out of discouragement with the therapy and irritation with the client, change therapeutic plans and impatiently rush the client to get better quickly. When therapists want to advise or suggest, they should examine their own motives first. Sometimes the suggestion or advice that the therapist would like to offer may not, in the long run, be helpful to the client and to the therapy.

Ferenczi's emphasis on the therapist's sincerity, although seemingly a simple notion, has its complications. Although no client can make any progress if he thinks the therapist is not truthful, Ferenczi's idea that it is an absolute necessity for the therapist to confirm the client's correct perceptions of the therapist's moods may be questioned, at least in certain instances. Even if a therapist is tired, much more pertinent to helping a client resolve resistances is to help him ascertain why the therapist's tiredness is in the center of his attention and what unique meaning it has for him. If the client has a strong wish to be rejected or to make the therapist impotent, this may be of more importance than whether or not the therapist is really sleepy. It may yield many more therapeutic gains for the client if he finds out that he has wishes to put the therapist to sleep than if he finds out that the therapist is sleepy.

Sandor Ferenczi, who was born in 1873 and died in 1933, must be considered one of the leading psychoanalytic pioneers. Freud described Ferenczi's theoretical and clinical contributions as "pure gold." Ferenczi's many papers have been combined into three volumes: *First Contributions to Psychoanalysis* (1952), *Further Contributions to the Theory and Technique of Psychoanalysis* (1950), and *Final Contributions to the Problems and Methods of Psychoanalysis* (1955).

KARL ABRAHAM

Referred to by Sigmund Freud as the first German psychoanalyst, Karl Abraham was born in Bremen, Germany, in 1887 and died 48 eventful years later in Berlin. Despite his short life, he contributed a great deal to the therapist's understanding of many clinical subjects, including depression, sexual conflicts, drug addiction, and the psychotherapeutic process (Grotjahn, 1967).

Abraham's classic paper on resolving resistance, written in 1919, was entitled "A Particular Form of Neurotic Resistance against the Psychoanalytic Method." It appears in Volume 1 of his two-volume series entitled *Selected Papers on Psychoanalysis* (1960). The type of analysand that Abraham describes in this paper is familiar to most therapists, and Abraham's prescription for resolving the resistances of this client is instructive.

Abraham refers to a group of clients who tend to speak in a continuous and unbroken manner, and many of them refuse to be interrupted by a single remark of the therapist. They arrange what they have to say before their sessions and try to make sure that they will never be criticized, admonished, or corrected. To the therapist who is not experienced in recognizing this particular form of resistance, these clients seem to show an eager readiness to be treated. However, their resistance is hidden behind a show of willingness.

Under these clients' facades of compliance, there is an unconscious but a real attitude of defiance toward the therapist. Rather than really participating in therapy, these clients use their abundant communications to defend against being humiliated. They talk a great deal to keep the therapist silent. They carefully analyze their dreams to block the therapist from interpreting anything.

What Abraham discovered about these clients is their high degree of narcissism. They want to get pleasure, and only pleasure, from their therapy. They believe that, by being in therapy, they will become great novelists, superior intellectuals, or outstanding athletes. Furthermore, they want admiration and attention from the therapist and nothing else. Although they superficially recognize that they are in therapy, these men and women strongly resist taking on the role of client or patient. Often they attempt to manipulate the therapist into an intellecual discussion or a debate, and they are particularly eager to prove that the therapist is incorrect, weak, deficient, or stupid. Abraham states:

> The presence of an element of envy is unmistakable in all this. Neurotics of the type under consideration grudge the physician any remark that refers to the external progress of their psychoanalysis or to its data. In their opinion he ought not to have supplied any contribution to the treatment; they want to do everything by themselves. (1960, p. 307)

Although Abraham stated that therapy with such clients presents many difficulties because their pretended compliance cloaks their defiant resistance, he did effect an improvement of some practical value in many of them. Abraham found that the most expedient method of helping these clients resolve their resistances was to point out to them their extreme narcissism at the very beginning of treatment: "I lay the greatest stress on making an exhaustive analysis of the narcissism of such patients in all the forms it takes" (Abraham, 1960, p. 311), especially in relation to their competition with the therapist. Abraham contended that when these clients are robbed of their major resistance they are more able to free associate and get on with the work of treatment.

Many individuals in treatment who want to be omnipotent, narcissistic infants welcome the therapist's interpretation that they are striving for something unrealistic because it frees them of the enormous and impossible task of trying to become supermen or superwomen. It is as if they experience the therapist as a loving parent who is showing them how to cope more efficiently and more effectively with reality. This therapeutic stance, according to Abraham, can "bring about a positive transference (so that) they will one day unexpectedly produce free associations, even in the presence of the physician" (1960, p. 311).

The modern-day therapist might be able to answer why Abraham's approach with these individuals did not yield "a complete cure" (1960, p. 310). For very narcissistic individuals, it can also be very humiliating to be told that they want to be kings or queens and that their wishes are unrealistic. For some, the therapist's approach can intensify their rage, and then they may wish to defy the therapist even more. It may be more helpful for these individuals to get a quiet, accepting but nonindulgent ear from the therapist so that they can slowly begin to feel safe in the therapist's presence. As they feel less threatened, they may begin slowly to reveal their unrealistic ambitions and to accept, with less reluctance, the therapist's focus on their narcissism. Be that as it may, the contemporary therapist can gain a great deal from Abraham's assessment and prescription for resolving resistances of the very narcissistic client.

OTTO RANK

Otto Rank joined the original circle around Freud in 1906, and until 1924, he was one of the most creative and loyal men among the original pioneers (Eisenstein, 1966). Although at the time of his death in 1939 at the age of 55, he was repudiated by mainstream analysts, Rank must be considered the innovator of short-term therapy.

In *The Trauma of Birth* (1924), Rank introduced a new approach to the genesis of mental development, based on the separation anxiety that every infant is alleged to experience at birth. This "primal anxiety," Rank contended, is the most important element for the future development of the individual and also the major source of neurosis. He averred that all events that occur in the individual's life after separation from the mother are expressions of primal anxiety.

Rank argued that the organism is not merely a passive, helpless tool of inner drives and external forces, but it is or can become an initiating power that selects, organizes, modifies, and recreates what it assimilates. He formulated the concept of "the will," which is the guiding organization of the self that controls instinctual drives and uses them creatively. The will gives, receives, and transforms while it is being transformed. Conflict arises between the will of the individual and the coercive forces of society (Rank, 1945).

The will serves the process of individualization. The child makes its first acquaintance with the will in the form of the "counter-will." Only when children are able to say "no" and oppose the demands of grown-ups do they grasp the notion that they have wills of their own.

Rank's view of neuroses derives from his concept of will. In contrast to the average person, both neurotics and creative individuals, such as artists, have broken with the mandates of society. The average person, by contrast, continues to live his life within the deceptive unity of the collective social order and refuses to accept himself as an individual. The average person thinks he is being himself, but he is "appearing to be" and is never actually "being" (Rank, 1945; Wyss, 1973).

The neurotic, while recognizing the necessity for self-realization, isolation, and individualization, has broken down on the way and can neither move back to the level of the average person nor move toward creative productivity (Rank, 1932, 1945). Neuroses, then, according to Rank represent the individual's will to be individuated and separate, but this healthy wish runs into conflict with his fear of society's restraint. The average person submits to society's will, whereas the artist is able to disregard it.

The primary aim of Rank's psychotherapy is to enable the neurotic, who is vacillating between the bonds of the average person and the individualization and freedom of the artist, to accept his own will and individuality without feeling guilty or anxious about it. In Rank's therapy, uncovering the past is less important than emancipating the individual ego from ties to the collectivity—parents, teachers, and other authority figures.

When the neurotic enters treatment, he often feels that he is being subjected to the therapist's will. The success of the treatment depends on whether the client can acquire the courage to assert his own desires vis-à-vis the therapist. Rank contended that resistance, particularly in the form of aggression toward the therapist, is an extremely positive therapeutic force inasmuch as it is an expression of the client's aroused self-will.

Rank felt that the major resistance that all clients show in treatment is their fear of asserting themselves toward the therapist. He attempted to strengthen the client's will by encouraging assertiveness toward the therapist and advocated that the therapist adapt his will to the client's by encouraging an active inner participation in the client's fate. The knowledge that the client acquires from encounters with the therapist helps the client fight his way through to his own will, to himself, and to his own individuality.

In Rank's psychotherapy, a great deal of emphasis is placed on the client's day-to-day events, particularly those in which the client failed to assert his will. Furthermore, corresponding to the birth trauma and the necessity of separation–individuation, a time is set in advance for ending the therapy. The time period usually, although not always, corresponds to the gestation period of 9 months (Wyss, 1973).

Rank contended that to resolve the client's resistance to autonomy and help him relinquish dependent symbiotic ties, it is necessary to keep the treatment short. Because a termination date is set at the beginning of the therapy, clients are motivated to give up their resistance to individuate and untie themselves from their infantile pasts.

Rank's major contribution to the therapist's repertoire of skills in resolving resistances is his recognition that many clients who unrealistically fantasy a blissful symbiotic merger often need strong limits and clear structure in the therapeutic relationship. Furthermore, for some of these clients, a termination date can help them rely more on their own autonomous ego functions rather than on the therapist's. As they become more self-reliant in the therapy, they may be able to continue to do so in their day-to-day life.

Another of Rank's contributions is his identification of a major resistance of many clients—the wish to make the therapist an omnipotent parent and concomitantly renounce one's own will. Rank's suggestion that the therapist constantly demonstrate that he is convinced that the client's will is strong enough for him to function independently is an appropriate therapeutic attitude to have with most clients, particularly with those who strive for symbiotic mergers.

Rank's therapy, nonetheless, has several limitations. When a therapist abdicates his benign neutral attitude and fosters independence, he is inadvertently promoting a dependency on the therapist. He is in effect sending a double-bind message: "Take my advice—depend on my attitude, which is 'be independent'."

Perhaps a more serious limitation of Rank's therapy is his failure to recognize that psychotherapy is a learning experience, which like any other learning experience takes time. The learning process is hardly ever smooth. As we noted earlier in this chapter, there are impasses between teacher and student, fears of change, and the need for time to work through and to change maladaptive habits.

Rank's therapy rests on a limited view of the human being. There are many other anxieties besides separation anxiety, and the human being is far more complex than Rank has suggested. When a therapy rests on a limited view of the human organism, the therapist will have a tendency to bypass the many complicated resistances that all clients pose in therapy.

Freud, in "Analysis Terminable and Interminable" (1937a) refers to Rank's determined attempt to shorten treatment by assuming that the cardinal source of neurosis is the birth experience and that overcoming this primal trauma by therapy clears up the whole neurosis. Freud felt that Rank's argument was certainly "bold and ingenious," but it did not stand the test of critical examination. He thought that short-term therapy was a child of its time, conceived under the stress of the contrast between the postwar misery of Europe and the prosperity of America, and designed to accelerate the tempo of analytic therapy to suit the rush of American life.

Despite the limitations of Rank's methods of resolving resistances, some of his ideas regarding short-term work have influenced thousands of therapists. His notions regarding the birth trauma, separation–individuation, time, and end setting became the major theoretical underpinning of the functional school in social work. Schools of social work at the University of Pennsylvania, the University of North Carolina, and elsewhere were called Rankian schools for many years.

Rank was a prolific writer. *The Artist* (1907) is a brilliant book on the creative powers and psychology of the artist. His second book was *The Myth of the Birth of the Hero* (1909), to which Freud contributed the part on the "family romance." Rank discussed myths as products of people's wishes and fantasies. In *The Incest Motif in Poetry and Saga* (1912), Rank demonstrated how the artist derives unconscious gratification for his forbidden wishes through his artistic creations. In 1924, Rank coauthored a book with Ferenczi, entitled *The Development of Psychoanalysis* (Rank & Ferenczi, 1924). Here acting out is mentioned for the first time in the psychoanalytic literature. Rank and Ferenczi expressed the view that analyzing the acting out of the unconscious material should become the primary aim of the therapy and the reconstruction of the patient's past should be secondary.

In a biographical essay on Otto Rank, Samuel Eisenstein (1966) concluded:

> Had Rank continued within the framework of psychoanalysis, his idea about birth anxiety would probably have found some acceptance in psychoanalytic circles. The importance of the mother in modern psychoanalytic theory may have had a pioneer in Rank with his concepts of "primal fixation" "primal regression" and "primal anxiety." The modern concepts of "good and bad mother," "primal love" and "return to womb fantasies," and "fusion with the mother" may owe their origins in part to Rank. His idea of "end setting" is now employed in specific cases, and "separation anxiety" in analysis is a successor to Rank's primal anxiety. Shortening the therapeutic process and working on dependency in analysis are also used in specific cases; the "active-therapy" postulated by Rank and Ferenczi has followers today both within and outside of the psychoanalytic field—particularly in work with borderline and psychotic cases. (p. 47)

ANNA FREUD

Although Anna Freud's principal interest throughout her lifetime was in the diagnosis and treatment of children, as we saw in Chapter 1 some of her writings have direct applicability to therapeutic work with adults. In this section, we review the research of Anna Freud that has particular relevance to the resolution of resistances in psychotherapy with adults.

It has been said that psychoanalytic psychotherapy was born when resistances were taken into consideration—that is, when symptoms were recognized to be a result of conflict between instinctual drives, superego mandates, and the ego's defenses. The resistances, a manifestation of this conflict, had to be taken into active consideration if therapy was to be effective (Freud, 1926). The person who inspired countless numbers of therapists to relate objectively, empathetically, and rigorously to resistances in therapy and to help clients resolve them was Anna Freud (Sterba, 1953).

Anna Freud was the first writer to recognize that a crucial implication of ego psychology—the requirement that the analysand free associate from the beginning to the end of the therapy—was unrealistic and the demand had to be relaxed. She understood that the way the client resists free association may be as informative as the associations themselves. This point of view has helped many analysts and therapists avoid disappointments when their clients are not reporting fantasies and memories. It has also reduced some of the intensity of the angry countertransference responses that were part of the relationships between the early therapists and their resisting clients (Bergmann & Hartman, 1976).

In *The Ego and the Mechanisms of Defense,* Anna Freud (1946) stated:

> Even today many beginners in analysis have an idea that it is essential to succeed in inducing their patients really and invariably to give all their associations without modification or inhibition, i.e., to obey implicitly the fundamental rule of analysis. But, even if this ideal were realized, it would not represent an advance, for after all, it would simply mean the conjuring-up again of the now obsolete situation of hypnosis, with its one-sided concentration on the part of the physician upon the id. Fortunately for analysis such docility in the patient is in practice impossible. The fundamental rule can never be followed beyond a certain point. (p. 13)

The therapist's position, as Anna Freud (1946) formulated it, is "equidistant" from the various psychic structures that oppose each other. In his neutrality, the therapist does not crusade for or against the id, the ego, or the superego; the therapist has no favorites and is nonjudgmental. He remains neutral in relation to every aspect of the material presented by the client—verbal and nonverbal; conscious, preconscious, and unconscious; and material presented in great distress as well as productions presented blandly (Schafer, 1983).

While it is not a departure from the equidistant stance to call a spade a spade, the therapist who imposes his values on the client's productions will prevent the client from feeling safe to be himself and the therapy will suffer. Anna Freud rejected the notion that the therapist should champion good or bad ways to live. She deplored those therapists who worked in terms of saints and sinners, and victims and victimizers (Schafer, 1983), and pointed out that this attitude can only encourage the client to fixate on some form of pathological orientation to living.

Anna Freud constantly cautioned therapists against trying to break through resistances. She pointed out that the therapist's job is to sensitize clients to the role of resistances in their internal lives and to how they express themselves in their day-to-day functioning. In therapeutic situations, if practitioners are to be successfully equidistant from the id, ego, and superego, they do not encourage the client who is on the verge of crying, laughing, aggressing, or expressing sexual fantasies to go ahead and do so. If the client is inhibiting himself and is not expressing these affects, the helpful therapist who wants to acquaint the client with his conflicts instead points out to the client that he wishes to emote but is frightened to do so. It is the exposure of the conflict that is the decisive factor, avers

Anna Freud (1946), rather than the championing of a prescribed form of behavior.

As clients, uncontaminated and uninfluenced by their therapist's values and ambitions, study their own wishes and defenses in their therapy, they begin to see how and why they get into trouble in their daily lives. It is only through a careful review of all parts of their psyches that can enable clients to decide eventually how they may relinquish maladaptive and unproductive ways of coping (A. Freud, 1971).

A major implication of Anna Freud's position on resistances is that therapists do not take positions about their "goodness" or "badness." If clients are struggling not to reveal emotions or ideas, therapists must always sensitize themselves to the struggle, not just to what is being warded off.

In "Psychoanalytic Technique and the Ego's Capacity for Viewing Intrapsychic Activity," Paul Gray (1973) pointed out that psychodynamic therapy is basically a study of conflict and not primarily a cathartic method. When a therapist bypasses the client's inner struggle and encourages the pouring out of affect, memories, or ideas, the client is likely to feel seduced, violated, or coerced by the therapist who has taken sides unempathically, albeit unwittingly (Schafer, 1983).

In her book *Normality and Pathology in Childhood* (1965), Anna Freud stated that many therapists in recent decades interpret transference phenomena from the start of the therapy; the transferences "crowd out most other sources of material" and become "the royal road to the unconscious," a title that had in the past been reserved for dreams (p. 39). Anna Freud warned therapists against becoming so involved with transference phenomena that they forget that "transference is a means to an end, not a therapeutic measure in itself" (p. 39). As Raymond Dyer (1983), author of *Her Father's Daughter: The Work of Anna Freud,* stated: "Though this view is described as orthodox—that the treatment situation as starting from a real relationship, becoming increasingly distorted through transference manifestations, and ultimately returning to the dominance of a real relationship—such a description is also well suited to other more interpersonal and object relations oriented theories and models, as well as to common human experience" (p. 200).

In the paper "Anna Freud's Legacy," Peter Neubauer (1983) pointed out that, when we review Anna Freud's work, we can see her forever widening the scope of psychotherapy:

As a teacher, she asked from the student full dedication and independent thinking. As a clinician she examined and re-examined propositions of psychoanalysis proper and of its application to prevention, to education, and to the alleviation of a wide variety of emotional disorders. As a researcher, she opened up new fields of investigation and offered us outlines and new concepts as guides to the future of psychotherapy. (p. 513)

WILHELM REICH

As will be recalled from our discussion of Wilhelm Reich's work in Chapter 1, Reich saw character as a layer of resistances, where the ego defends against id impulses. The term *superego* hardly appears in his writings.

Reich added to the therapist's understanding of resolving resistances by sensitizing the practitioner to the crucial importance of how the client speaks, smiles, moves, sits, or lies on the couch.

Like Anna Freud (1946), Reich concluded that most analysands are incapable of following the fundamental rule and associating freely. Said Reich:

> They cannot immediately have full confidence in a strange person; more importantly, years of illness, constant influencing by a neurotic milieu, bad experiences with physicians, in brief, the whole secondary warping of the personality have created a situation unfavorable to analysis. The elimination of this difficulty would not be so hard were it not supported by the character of the patient which is part and parcel of his neurosis. (1949, p. 40)

Reich referred to the analysand's fear of free associating as his "narcissistic barrier" and suggested that there are, in principle, only two ways of resolving this difficulty. One way is by giving the patient information, reassurance, and admonition—that is, educating the patient to behave in a certain manner. The other way is to replace educational measures by analytic interpretation.

One of Reich's major and lasting contributions to the therapeutic world is his recognition that clients' resistances cannot be easily dissolved by exhortation or advice but that clients need to understand their resistances and their motives for them before they can even consider giving them up. Reich pointed out that "instead of inducing the patient into analysis by advice, admonitions, and transference maneuvers, one focuses one's attention on the actual behavior of the patient and its meaning: *why* he doubts, or is late, or talks in a haughty or confused fashion, or communicates only every other or third thought, *why* he criticizes the analysis or produces exceptionally much material from exceptional depths" (1949, pp. 40–41).

Reich cited the hypothetical case of a patient talking in a haughty manner. The therapist may try to convince him that this haughty manner is not helpful to the therapy. Or the therapist may wait until he understands why the patient behaves in this way. If the therapist waits, he may find out that the patient's behavior is an attempt to compensate for inferiority feelings in relation to the therapist. Then the therapist may be able to help the patient resolve his "haughty resistance." When the patient understands through the therapist's interpretations that the haughtiness is a protection (i.e., "character armor") used to ward off uncomfortable feelings of inferiority when with the therapist, he may be able to consider giving up the haughty behavior.

The emphasis of manner over content is repeatedly mentioned in Reich's writings:

> Apart from the dreams, associations, slips and other communications of the patients, their attitude, that is, *the manner* in which they relate their dreams, commit slips, produce their associations and their communications deserves special attention. . . . The manner in which the patient talks, in which he greets the analyst or looks at him, . . . all these things are valuable criteria for judging the latent resistances against the fundamental rule, and understanding them makes it possible to alter or eliminate them by interpretation. The *how* of saying things is as important material for interpretation as is *what* the patient says. One often hears analysts complain that the analysis does not go well, that the patient does not produce any material. By that is usually meant the content of associations and communications. But the manner in which the patient, say, keeps quiet, or has sterile repetitions, are also material which can and must be put to use. There is hardly any situation in which the patient brings no material; it is our fault if we are unable to utilize the patient's behavior as material. (1949, p. 45)

Reich (1949) had some ideas on working with "the cooperative patient" that were similar to Abraham's (1960). Reich pointed out that this patient camouflages a secret spitefulness and hatred that he unconsciously feels toward the therapist. What Reich's character analysis offers the contemporary therapist who works with the cooperative client is a procedure to resolve the resistances of this client. The therapist, Reich has suggested, should pay attention not only to what material the client produces but also, and this is of equal if not more importance, to the way he produces it. When the therapist consistently interprets to the client his wish to conceal hatred by acting compliantly and cooperatively, the client eventually feels his hostility toward the therapist, and then the maladaptive resistance slowly dissolves.

Character analysis, as formulated by Reich, consists of repeatedly confronting clients with their character resistances until they begin to look at them objectively and to experience them as if they were painful symptoms. Then resistances begin to be experienced like foreign bodies from which clients want to release themselves.

In working with character resistances, the therapist should first help the client see through the present-day meaning of the character resistance; this is usually possible without addressing the client's history. After the client is repeatedly presented with the meaning of his present-day behavior (e.g., that his compliance with the therapist defends against his spite), the historical material that initially gave rise to the resistance usually emerges spontaneously in the therapy.

Reich's character analysis is in consonance with a very much accepted tenet in modern psychotherapy—namely, that the therapist should work with the client's defenses first and then later help him see what id impulses are being covered up. Reich has presented an example of a patient of his whose silence covered up homosexual fantasies that were unacceptable to the patient. In the therapy, Reich did not interpret his patient's loving feelings toward the therapist, because he thought it would induce the patient to quit therapy. Instead, he worked with "the defense of the ego," which was more related to the patient's consciousness. Reich told his patient that his silence defended against feelings toward the therapist, without specifying what id impulses were being repressed. As the patient associated to his discomfort with the therapist, in due time he was able to face his homosexual fantasies.

One of the implications of Reich's approach that he himself did not discuss is that clients must feel that the therapist recognizes that their resistances are necessary because they are mobilized to ward off danger. Only when clients feel that it is permissible to resist and only when they feel that the therapist is sensitive to the fact that they feel in danger, will clients feel free enough to explore what id impulses are being defended against.

Another implication of Reich's prescription to work with the defense first is that an interpretation of an id impulse will fall on deaf ears unless the client feels safe with the therapist and has some conviction himself about the existence of a particular id impulse. For example, to tell a silent patient that he is warding off homosexual fantasies will not have much effect; in fact, as Reich advised, it may provoke the client to take flight. But if the client knows that the therapist realizes that he feels in danger and that that is why he is silent, he may then begin to associate to forbidden feelings toward the therapist. It may take many sessions of associating to derivatives of homosexual fantasies before the client is ready to give them frank expression. Usually the client will begin with feelings of admiration toward the therapist, then express feelings of affection toward him, and only much later will he discuss his erotic fantasies.

Reich pointed out that many clients who do not get better, who flee treatment, or who are labeled narcissistic and therefore untreatable are often clients whose character resistances were overlooked by the therapist. With these clients, the practitioner often interpreted id material without relating to resistances, and this way of intervening often exacerbated the clients' anxiety. Here Reich was being quite sensitive to a common counter-transference problem. When the client's progress is slow, when his transference reactions are essentially negative, and when his responses to interpretations are evasive, the therapist responding to his own injured narcissism with anger can label the client "borderline," "psychopathic," "preoedipal," "unmotivated," or some other label that only thinly disguises his contempt toward the client.

Reich has made some enduring contributions to the therapist who wants to help clients resolve resistances. His notion that interpretation of resistance should always precede interpretation of content is a rule that most psychodynamically oriented therapists follow to this day. Another therapeutic axiom "Analyze always from the surface" (i.e., work with the defense first) is also used by many therapists. Reich's point that it is necessary to recognize not only what is fended off but also the fending force itself is another formulation that is used by many contemporary therapists. One of his admonitions could be well heeded by those therapists who want to cut therapy short or to advise their clients how to behave. Reich stated that, when an analysand does not follow the basic rule of free association, the analyst should not lose patience and try to influence the analysand pedagogically or punish the analysand by depriving him of treatment; he must try to understand why the analysand behaves the way he does and why he does it in his own idiosyncratic manner.

Objections have been made to Reich's character analysis. Fenichel (1938) criticized Reich on several grounds: for not collecting enough material before making present-day interpretations; for shattering the patient's defensive armor too aggressively; for not realizing that responses to aggressive acts of the analyst are not, properly speaking, negative transferences but are understandable responses to manipulation; for preferring "crises," "eruptions," and theatrical emotions; for not recognizing that shattering the defense armor is masochistically enjoyable to many patients and that specific transferences can hide behind such enjoyment and escape discovery.

Sterba (1953) has pointed out that Reich seems to have conceptualized transference and resistance as identical and that this is an error inasmuch as transference is only one type of resistance. This stance makes Reich seem as if he is much too suspicious of every positive transference manifestation, particularly the appearance of a positive transference at the beginning of treatment. Sterba has also questioned Reich's notion that the initial transference is exclusively a means of resistance and quotes Freud, who said:

> The part taken by resistance in the transference-love is unquestionable and very considerable. But this love was not created by the resistance; the latter finds it ready to hand, exploits it and aggravates the manifestation of it. Nor is its genuineness impugned by the resistance. . . . it is true that the transference-love consists of new editions of old traces and that it repeats infantile reactions. But this is the essential character of every love. There is no love that does not produce infantile prototypes. . . . The transference love is characterized, nevertheless, by certain features which ensure it a special position. In the first place, it is provoked by the analytic situation; second, it is greatly intensified by the resistance which dominates this situation, and third, it is to a high degree lacking in regard for reality, is less sensible, less concerned about consequences, more blind in its estimation of the person loved, than we are willing to admit of normal love. (1915, p. 157)

Concerning the handling of the initial transference, Freud further states: "One must wait until the transference, which is the most delicate matter of all to deal with, comes to be employed as a resistance" (1913, p. 139). Here it is again clear that initial transference and resistance are not identical, but that the transference becomes employed by the resistance sooner or later. Apparently, it is one of Reich's basic errors that he denies the genuine character of positive transference (Sterba, 1953).

Anna Freud (1946) seemed to have Reich's technique in mind when she pointed out that we do our clients an injustice when we describe defense reactions as "camouflage" or say that clients are "pulling the analyst's leg." Anna Freud, as was pointed out earlier in this chapter, always took the position that the client is in fact candid when he expresses impulses or affects in the only way open to him—namely, in a distorted, defensive manner.

As we suggested in Chapter 1, although Reich eventually disassociated himself from acceptable psychoanalytic theory and practice, opinion is unanimous that his thinking and earlier works have earned him a permanent place in the archives of analytic literature (Briehl, 1966).

HELLMUTH KAISER

Hellmuth Kaiser, a disciple of Wilhelm Reich's, extolled character analysis in his paper "Problems of Technique" (1976) and essentially endorsed

Reich's formulations. However, his contribution to the modern therapist is his view of the role of transference in resolving resistances.

Kaiser took the position that the nature of the client's resistances can become clearer to the therapist if the therapist is vigilant to how and when the client rationalizes reality. Although most therapists would question the narrowness of this perspective, Kaiser's point that "the rationalizations of the patient are brought into the focus of (his) attention through the transference attachment, more exactly (through) his tender, reasonable attachment to the analyst" (1976, p. 390) is an interesting view that bears some attention.

Many beginning therapists are shocked when almost everything they say or do is rejected and refuted by a client; they are equally amazed when everything they say or do is admired and accepted by another client. What beginners often fail to appreciate is the power of the transference. As we suggested in Chapter 1, if the client is in a positive transference, then even the therapist's incorrect statements will tend to be viewed as gospel. And if the client is in a negative transference, the most brilliant and exact interpretations will be rejected or refuted. Finally, if the client is in an ambivalent transference, most of the therapist's statements will be responded to with: "Yes, but there's something you are saying that is wrong."

When Kaiser demonstrated to his patients how they were rationalizing their behavior and his patients accepted Kaiser's interpretations, he illuminated what is plausible when the patients are heavily influenced by a positive transference. Although this is a limited way of viewing the complexity of therapeutic interaction, many clients do benefit a great deal from a therapist's interpretations when they experience the therapist as different from their introjected parents, who are the voices of their punitive superegos. Kaiser gave an excellent illustration of this phenomenon:

> The destruction of the resistance is frequently brought about not by words but by actions or attitudes of the analyst. If, for instance, the resistance-thought of the patient is that the analyst will despise him because of his sexual fantasies (which are therefore kept out of the analysis), then the mere calmness and frankness of the analyst in regard to sexual topics may suffice to make this resistance-thought untenable. (1976, p. 392)

One of the major implications of Kaiser's position is that, because the client's responses are so heavily dictated by his current transference, resolving resistances inevitably involves helping the client to express continually his feelings toward the therapist, with the therapist constantly maintaining an empathetic, neutral posture. Because the therapist does not oppose, advise, or sympathize, the client usually feels more and more ready to examine his distortions and rationalizations, particularly his transference reactions, which almost always contain some irrationality.

Kaiser's "Problems of Technique," initially written in 1934 and not translated into English until 1976, is one of his very few pieces of writing. Although he never achieved prominence in the psychoanalytic or psychotherapeutic communities, his notions on the role of transference in resolving resistances and his ideas on how the therapist should conduct himself in helping the client give up resistances have proven very valuable to succeeding generations of therapists.

OTTO FENICHEL

Otto Fenichel, in his *Collected Papers* (1953, 1954) and in his classic text, *The Psychoanalytic Theory of Neuroses* (1945), provided some guidelines for resolving resistances. Fenichel consistently took the position

> that the effect which we desire to produce upon the ego will be lasting and profound in proportion (to how) we succeed in using no other means of overcoming resistances than that of confronting the reasonable ego with the fact of its resistances and the history of their origin. This enables the ego to recognize the unconscious element in them and at the same time renders them superfluous. (Fenichel, 1954, p. 21)

One of Fenichel's formulas was, "Work always where the patient's affect lies at the moment." This is an extremely important axiom that is often neglected in practice. What Fenichel has implied here is that the therapist should begin where the client is. For example, if the client is suffering from sexual impotence but wishes to discuss his business or recreational problems with the practitioner, the wise therapist will stay with the client's chosen topic and see what impulses are causing anxiety and what defenses are at work as the client talks about his business or recreational interests. The therapist will not impose the subject of sexuality on the client but will wait until the client gives some indication of readiness to talk about it.

Fenichel, like other writers, consistently advocated that interpretation of resistance goes before interpretation of content. He also prescribed that the therapist must continuously seek out and work on the momentarily acute resistances; (1) by separating the client's critical ego from his resistance-determined behavior; (2) by trying to help the client experience the latter as arising from his resistance; (3) by finding the occasions of the resistance being shown; (4) by explaining why the resistance takes the precise form it does; and (5) by telling the client what he is resisting (Fenichel, 1953, 1954).

Although most psychodynamically oriented therapists would concur with the procedures that Fenichel has outlined with regard to confronting the client's conscious rational ego with his resistances, they might also point out that Fenichel at times neglects the crucial role of transference in this process. As we have suggested repeatedly, if the client, for whatever reason, is feeling antagonistic toward the therapist, he will reject any explanation or interpretation of the therapist. At these times, helping the client to express his negative feelings toward the therapist will have to be a No. 1 priority in the therapy. As the client is given the opportunity to discharge his hostile feelings in an atmosphere of acceptance, he will be more able to cooperate with the therapist and work on understanding other resistances.

Fenichel believed, as did Freud (1912b), that the therapist should respond to the patient's unconscious with his own unconscious and wait until a structural plan arises of itself. He used Freud's analogy of the jigsaw puzzle (1896), in which one piece after another is observed at random until one finds how they fit together.

After having spoken of formulas, Fenichel (1954) reminded us that the use of psychotherapeutic techniques in resolving resistances is a living art in which rules never have more than a relative validity. The practitioner, Fenichel pointed out, should guard against two extremes, both equally incorrect: On the one hand, the clinician should not analyze too much according to a rational plan, by intellect alone, and on the other hand, the clinician should not be too irrational, because to analyze implies subjecting the irrational to reason. If this were not so, technique would be unteachable.

In interpreting a resistance, Fenichel has taken a position similar to what has been reiterated by several other psychotherapeutic experts— namely, that unless the client has some inner conviction about the validity of the therapist's observation, the interpretation of the therapist will be of limited value to the client. Fenichel has also advised that, when giving an interpretation about a resistance, the therapist should word it so that it does not appear to be a reproach against the client. Again, it is important to keep in mind that Fenichel had a tendency to overlook the role of transference in the client's perception of an interpretation. Many interpretations are experienced by the client as reproaches even when they are made benignly by the therapist, simply because the client unconsciously has projected his punitive superego onto the therapist and perceives the therapist as reproachful no matter what he says or does.

Fenichel pointed out that clients inevitably find dealing with resistances disagreeable. To motivate the client to face what is disagreeable, he suggested that the client be told that dealing with resistances is useful and will help the client feel better. This approach, modern therapists realize, has limited utility. It is like telling a fearful and angry child to swallow bitter medicine. Out of fear of the parent and a wish to please, the child may take the medicine. Of more importance for therapy would be to help the client discuss what is disagreeable rather than force an interpretation on the client.

Fenichel (1945) has discussed giving in to resistances. By this he was referring to such issues as gratifying the client's request for another therapist or making a home visit to a client who is too frightened to leave the home. Although in general Fenichel has taken the position that it is better to analyze resistances than to give in to them, he believed that this rule can be followed only up to a point. For example, sometimes a resistance is too intense (e.g., a resistance against verbalizing hatred) and "its analysis must be postponed and first be prepared by some other analytic work. If an agoraphobic is unable to leave his home, the analyst, at the beginning of the analysis, must go to the patient. In a similar way, the analysis of an intense father complex may be conducted better if the man with whom the patient has to talk does not actually resemble his father" (Fenichel, 1945, p. 579).

It should be borne in mind that giving in to a resistance is often a function of countertransference. Many therapists find it difficult not to gratify clients' requests because they fear becoming the recipient of their clients' hostility, disapproval, or possible abandonment. In deciding whether to go along with a client's request, it is important for the therapist to differentiate between the client's conflict and the therapist's anxieties and wishes.

Fenichel pointed out at the end of his encyclopedic book, *The Psychoanalytic Theory of Neurosis* (1945), that any honest therapist will admit that, even though he is very thoroughly analyzed, he does better work with certain types of clients than with others. Fenichel cautioned, however, that "this difference should never reach a degree at which work with certain personalities becomes entirely impossible" (1945, p. 580). Fenichel contended that a therapist has to have "the width of empathy" to work with a variety of individuals, and if he does not, the problem may be the therapist's, in which case he should receive more personal therapy.

JAMES STRACHEY

James Strachey, who practiced psychoanalysis in England, also translated from the German *The Standard Edition of the Complete Psychological Works of Sigmund Freud*. Although he did very little writing of his own, his paper "The Nature of the Therapeutic Action of Psychoanalysis"

(Strachey, 1934) is considered among the most influential works on resolving resistances in the history of psychoanalytic technique (Bergmann
& Hartman, 1976).

Strachey considered several factors that motivate a client to abandon
resistances: the will to recover; understanding the structure of his symptom and the motives for his repudiation of the objectionable trends; recognizing that current infantile motives are no longer valid; realizing that his
original solutions to difficulties have not been effective, whereas the new
one that the therapist proposes may be; and finally, through the resolution
of the transference, many of the client's other resistances are resolved.

It was Strachey's belief that the major factor in helping a client abandon
his resistances is having an "auxiliary superego" in the form of the therapist. As the client discharges impulses toward the therapist and notes the
therapist's reactions, he gradually becomes aware of the contrast between
the aggressive character of his own feelings and the real nature of the
therapist, who does not behave like the client's "bad archaic objects" (i.e.,
the punitive voices of the client's parents). As the client becomes aware
of the distinction between his archaic fantasy object and the real external
object (i.e., the therapist), there is a breach in the neurotic vicious cycle.
The client, having become aware of the lack of hostility in the real external object, will diminish his own hostility. Feeling less hated, the client will
hate less. The "new object" (i.e., the client's image of the therapist), which
the client has introjected, will be less hostile, and the client's punitive
superego will be replaced by a more benign one.

Strachey contended that the sine qua non of effective therapy was the
client's growing awareness of the difference between the therapist's attitudes and his own introjects. Consequently, he took the position that transference interpretations induced the most change in the client. He also believed that only transference interpretations were mutative interpretations
and, for mutative interpretations to work, they had to be governed by the
"principle of minimal doses." Interpretations have to be made in small
doses. The reason for this is that, if too much id material is activated, this
sharply conflicts with the voices of the superego, and therefore a great deal
of anxiety will be generated in the client. If the client feels too much anxiety,
he will cling to his resistances all the more. On the other hand, if anxiety is
bearable to the ego, resistances can slowly be dissolved.

Similar to Fenichel, Reich, and other analysts, Strachey felt that every
mutative interpretation should be emotionally immediate; the client should
experience it as something actual. The mutative interpretation must also
be specific, detailed, and concrete.

Most contemporary therapists accept Strachey's contention that, as the
client experiences a more benign auxiliary superego, he will become more

accepting of his own id wishes as he introjects the image of his benign and accepting therapist. Most contemporary therapists would also accept the corollary of this view that, as the superego becomes more tolerant of id wishes, anxiety diminishes and the need for maladaptive resistances becomes less. Furthermore, most modern therapists would also concur with Strachey that, to be effective, interpretations should be immediate and specific. Where many would disagree is with his firm belief that only transference interpretations can reduce the necessity for resistances.

Anybody who does therapeutic work recognizes that it is frequently through understanding their transference reactions, and how and why they are distorted, that clients can eventually abandon their resistances. This is not the same as what Strachey contends, which is that transference interpretations "are *the essence* of psychoanalytic therapy." It is quite possible, for example, that a client can become aware that his intense hostility toward his boss is sustained because of a childish id resistance to hold on to hatred toward his father. Without noting his transference reactions toward the therapist, the client may be able to modify his relationship with the boss on recognizing that he is perpetuating an old battle from his childhood that seems inappropriate for the present. In the above example, if the client saw that his feelings and reactions in the here and now were the same toward father, boss, and therapist, the client would probably gain even more conviction about his id resistance, but extratransference interpretations could be helpful in resolving his id resistance with the boss.

In his paper "The Position and Value of Extratransference Interpretation," Harold Blum (1983) points out that transference fantasy cannot be clarified without understanding the grains of truth to which it may be anchored in reality inside and outside the therapeutic situation. He also states that, although interpretation of the transference is the central area of psychodynamic psychotherapy,

> transference is not the sole or whole focus of interpretation, or the only effective mutative interpretation, or always the most significant interpretation. Extratransference interpretation has a position and value which is not simply ancillary, preparatory, and supplementary to transference interpretation. Transference analysis is essential, but extratransference interpretation, including genetic interpretation and reconstruction, is also necessary, complementary, and synergistic. (p. 615)

One also gets the impression from Strachey's paper that interpretation is the only procedure that can help a client resolve a resistance. He seems to idealize interpretation and overlook the fact that a question, clarification, confrontation, or even repetition of a client's statement can at times motivate a client to look at his resistances and consider what they protect.

Strachey died in 1967 at the age of 80. In addition to being a translator and practitioner, he was a leader in the British psychoanalytic movement.

EDWARD GLOVER

One of the first writers to consider seriously the role of counterresistance in therapy was Edward Glover. He pointed out that, just as the client can obstruct the therapy in a variety of ways, so too is the therapist capable of interfering with the treatment's progress in many ways. Glover constantly reiterated that the idea that experienced therapists invariably know what they are doing and invariably give accurate interpretations concerning the client's transference distortions and other resistances is part of the myth of the perfect therapist:

> There is no possible doubt that the professional psychotherapist is, in the sense of emotional and intellectual stability, just as vulnerable to current mental stresses as members of any other profession [and] it is manifestly absurd to attribute to him or indeed to demand from him, personal adaptability beyond the level that should be expected from persons of his type. (1955, p. 90)

Glover has provided the therapist with an appropriate therapeutic attitude when he points out that, allowing for differences in character, temperament, and symptom type between therapist and client, the counterresistances of the therapist in any given situation are similar and equal in intensity to the resistances of the client in that situation. Just as it is possible for a client to project sexual or hostile fantasies onto the therapist and call him "a dirty old man" or "a provocative therapist," it is equally possible for a therapist to project his own unacceptable fantasies onto the client and, under the guise of "helping" the client, show him his "repressed sexuality" or his "repressed aggression." Furthermore, the therapist might be able to project his own problems onto the client with more comfort and more impunity than the client can project feelings onto the therapist, because the client, after all, is the "neurotic" one.

Glover has pointed out that, just as resistances of clients have been classified (see Chapter 1), counterresistances of therapists can also be classified. However, no writer has ever attempted to do so in the same rigorous way that resistances have been classified. Yet, for every example of clients resisting that one can give, an example of therapists counterresisting can also be given. Glover (1955) cites an interesting parallel between a client resisting and a therapist resisting:

When an obsessional case constantly insists on making involved explanations, ostensibly embarked on "to make things clear," and at the same time
hates to leave a subject "in the air" and must "round it off," we may
reasonably regard this as evidence of an accentuated infantile anal characteristic, one which is being exploited in the interests of his analytic
resistances. Incidentally, when the analyst experiences a similar compulsion, e.g. to do a neat bit of work each day, to round off each analytic
session with a complete explanation, we may suspect a similar interest.
(p. 94)

Glover believed that psychotherapists have a great deal of difficulty
coping with their sadistic fantasies toward their clients. Being in a helping
profession in which they are expected to be understanding and empathetic
makes it difficult for them to acknowledge their sadism. Glover (1955)
has contended that when therapists find themselves unclear about their
clients' dynamics, unsure about how the treatment is progressing, and un-
decided about their feelings toward their clients, they should think first of
their own repressed sadism.

Glover has suggested that the client's resistances often frustrate the
therapist's wish to heal, and thereby weaken the therapist's reaction formation defense against infantile sadism. He further pointed out that nowhere is psychological viewing more complete than in the therapeutic situation, and nothing is more calculated to arouse the therapist's sadism than
the exasperating frustration of his curiosity induced by the client's resistance.

Examples of the therapist acting out his sadism are many: browbeating
the client into accepting an interpretation; arguing with the client about
the veracity of an interpretation; siding with the client against one of his
real or imagined enemies; siding with a real or imagined enemy against the
client; obstinately trying to cap a consciously rejected interpretation with
another of the same kind; and using pejorative diagnostic labels, such as
"psychopath" or "borderline," to describe the client.

Perhaps more common among therapists are counterresistances used to
defend against their sadism. The possible forms this can take include oversolicitousness; unnecessary reassurances; assisting the client out of a difficulty before the client has realized that there is any difficulty; postponing
confrontations, questions, or interpretations regarding a client's tardiness
or absence; glossing over interpretations of the negative transference; and
denying the existence of pathology, conflict, or resistance in the client.

The therapist should suspect counterresistances when he finds that one
or more of the following phenomena are at work: He is consistently acting
in a stereotyped way; he is consistently being silent but cannot justify this
behavior; or he cannot explain to himself why a particular client is still in
difficulty (Glover, 1955).

Glover (1955) has pointed out that, just as the client can resist facing oral, anal, phallic–oedipal, or homosexual wishes or fantasies, the therapist can also defend against facing these impulses in his client or in himself. A corollary of this perspective is that, if there is a consistent absence of oral, anal, phallic–oedipal, or homosexual material in the client's productions, then the therapist should consider whether or not he is doing something in the treatment to prevent its expression. Similarly, if a client's transference is always in one direction—always positive, always negative, or always ambivalent, the therapist should ask what he may possibly be doing to prevent certain transference feelings from being expressed.

While Glover essentially endorsed all of Freud's notions regarding techniques of resolving resistances, he had some independent notions on the therapeutic effects of inexact interpretation (1931, 1955). Glover took the position that when an interpretation was inexact or incorrect but the client improved as a result of the interpretation, the interpretation was being used as a defense. For example, a husband may be defending against his own sadism by saying that his impotency is caused by the fact that he is intimidated by his wife's aggression. The therapist may agree with the client and even tell him that his wife reminds him of his mother, who was also aggressive. None of the client's incestuous fantasies are touched, but the client feels better and functions better. Glover would explain this sequence of events as a function of repression. The inexact interpretation was used as a defense to repress the client's incestuous fantasies. This reduced some of the client's anxiety, and together with the positive transference that had been aroused, made the client feel stronger and function more ably.

Glover felt that many of the non-Freudian therapies could help clients by using a sequence of events similar to those described in the above case. Often telling clients to embark on a holiday, to take up a recreation, or to do a certain kind of reading can help them feel better. Glover would say that here the therapist unwittingly has reinforced the mechanism of repression and has encouraged the client by demonstrating his own capacity for repression. It is as if he were saying, "You see, I am blind; I don't know what is the matter with you, go and be likewise."

In reflecting further on nonanalytic therapies, Glover took the position that what made them work up to a point was that they were backed by strong transference authority and "by virtue of their complete opposition to the psychological truth and the stress they put on modifications of conduct and thought, might be regarded as 'obsessional systems of suggestion'" (1931, p. 411).

Throughout his whole career, Glover was a rigorous scholar. He always advocated that the therapist strive "to resolve as completely as possible the affective analytic bond" (i.e., the transference) and to make interpretations "to the existing maximum of objective understanding."

FRANZ ALEXANDER

Franz Alexander, a psychiatrist and psychoanalyst, founded the Chicago Institute for Psychoanalysis, which became a leading center for the teaching of psychoanalysis. Alexander directed this institute for over 25 years. In 1956, he left Chicago to become head of the department of psychiatry and director of research at Mt. Sinai Hospital in Los Angeles. He was a prolific writer, and among his contributions are *The Scope of Psychoanalysis* (1961), *Psychosomatic Medicine: Its Principles and Application* (1965), *Fundamentals of Psychoanalysis* (1948), *Psychoanalysis and Psychotherapy* (1956), and *The Western Mind in Transition* (1960).

Alexander is well known for his concept of "the corrective emotional experience." By this, Alexander meant that the client's view of parental figures whose voices have been internalized could be altered by an experience with the therapist that would be dramatically different from the one the client had experienced with his parents and significant others.

Like Strachey (1934), Alexander (1961) felt that the fundamental task of the therapist in helping the client resolve resistances is to weaken the impact of the punitive superego. Alexander prescribed a form of therapeutic role-playing in which the therapist enacts a form of behavior that is diametrically opposed to what the client anticipates from the voices of his superego. For example, if a male client has introjected an authoritarian father and anticipates rejection and punishment on asserting himself, the therapist will try to act very benignly. As the client repeatedly asserts himself and finds that the response he had anticipated from the therapist is not forthcoming, the client learns to feel freer to assert himself. Similarly, if a female client experienced her mother as symbiotic and engulfing, the therapist would try to be cool and distant in order to lessen the client's fear of engulfment.

Influenced by Rank (1924), Alexander contended that resistances could be resolved in a short period of time through the corrective emotional experience, and therefore Alexander was a staunch advocate of brief therapy. He did not believe that working through resistances and analyzing the transference fantasies were as crucial as was the corrective and unique experience that the therapist could provide.

Many therapists, if not most, would agree that the therapist's responses must not be similar to the client's parental introjects; otherwise the client will receive a reinforcement of his neurotic views. Many therapists would also concur with Alexander that, if resistances are to be resolved, clients must feel that they will not be punished, seduced, or overwhelmed in the same manner that their parents dealt with them. However, many therapists question the advisability of both role-playing and short-term therapy for a number of reasons.

To understand how the superego works, it is necessary to comprehend its relationship to the id. Whenever the superego is punitive, there are strong id wishes at work that create anxiety, and under the impact of anxiety, resistances are formed. In order to abandon resistances, the client has to feel sufficiently free in the therapy to express his id wishes. As the client verbalizes his sadistic thoughts, incestuous fantasies, homosexual urges, oedipal strivings, oral cravings, and anal spite and over time sees that the therapist does not punish or criticize, then he will begin to think of abandoning resistances.

Alexander's perspective does not permit the client to give full vent to his id impulses. In the above example of the man who is afraid to assert himself, one of the dangers of the therapist acting benignly is that the therapist's oversolicitousness can squelch the expression of the client's sadism. When the therapist departs from his neutral position, equidistant from id, ego, and superego (A. Freud, 1946), the client's id wishes may be repressed. When that happens, the client never gets to see just what his punitive superego is opposing, and many of the client's neurotic problems go unaddressed.

As we stated earlier in the chapter, short-term therapy tends to lose sight of the fact that it takes considerable time for a client to unlearn old patterns and learn new ones. Short-term therapists sometimes overlook that there are inevitable impasses between teacher and student. They also seem to forget that most clients need a patient listener in order to resolve resistances and that short-term treatment often can intensify an internal superego injunction "to hurry up and get well."

Despite these criticisms, Alexander's notion of the corrective emotional experience is applicable to all therapy, and his remarks regarding the role of the superego in treatment are very instructive.

RALPH GREENSON

Ralph Greenson (1967) has formulated a comprehensive and systematic perspective on technical procedures, similar to his comprehensive classification of resistances, that can be used in helping clients resolve resistances in therapy. According to Greenson, the therapist has to use four distinct procedures to help a client resolve a resistance: confrontation, clarification, interpretation, and working through.

The first step in helping a client with a resistance is to *confront* the client with it. The phenomenon in question has to be made evident to the client's conscious ego. For example, if Mr. Jones arrives 5 minutes late for every appointment, first the therapist has to make sure that Mr. Jones knows that he has been coming late and that this piece of behavior has psychological significance to him.

Confrontation leads to the next step, *clarification,* which refers to those activities that aim at placing the resistive behavior in sharp focus and examining the issues that motivate it. As the therapist asks Mr. Jones to associate to his tardiness—that is, to see what comes to his mind as he thinks about it—it may turn out that the client resents taking the subway trip to the therapist's office, feels controlled by the therapist as he does so, and has fantasies of rebelling against the therapist, whom Mr. Jones experiences as authoritarian.

The third step is *interpretation.* To interpret means to make an unconscious phenomenon (e.g., a defense, a wish) conscious. More specifically, it means to make conscious the unconscious meaning, source, history, mode, or cause of a given psychic event. By interpreting, the therapist goes beyond what is readily observable and assigns meaning and causality to a psychological event. In the example of Mr. Jones, the therapist in making an interpretation might say: "You are coming late to appointments because you experience me as your father who you felt was authoritarian and always made you submit to him. You handle your anger at me in the same way you handled your anger toward your father." As we have suggested earlier in this chapter, we need the client's responses in order to determine the validity of an interpretation (Fenichel, 1945).

The procedures of clarification and interpretation are intimately connected. Very frequently, clarification leads to an interpretation, which leads to a further clarification (Kris, 1951).

Working through refers to the repetitive, progressive, and elaborate explorations of the resistances that prevent an insight from leading to change. A variety of processes are set in motion by working through, in which insight, memory, and behavior change influence each other. As Mr. Jones works through his problem of submissiveness with his father, he will recall memories, feel the problem in the transference, and have dreams and fantasies involving this theme. Eventually this will lead to insight and change.

In addition to the client's associations, transference reactions, and resistances, and the therapist's confrontation, clarification, interpretation, and working through, there is, according to Greenson (1967), one other therapeutic ingredient that is vital for the success or failure of resolving resistances. This is the *working alliance.* By the working alliance, Greenson is referring to the relatively nonconflicted, nonneurotic, rational relationship between client and therapist that makes it possible for the client to work purposefully in the therapy. The clinical manifestations of the working alliance are the client's willingness to carry out the various required procedures; report feelings, thoughts, and memories; keep appointments; pay fees; and so on. The alliance, as Greenson sees it, is formed between the client's reasonable ego and the therapist's working ego. The client makes an identification with the therapist's attitude and method of work that he experiences in the treatment sessions.

The working alliance, in effect, is that part of the client's relationship to the therapist that makes it possible for the client to cooperate with the therapist. The therapist contributes toward the formation of the working alliance "by his consistent emphasis on understanding and insight, by his continual analysis of the resistances, and by his compassionate, empathic, straightforward and nonjudgmental attitudes" (Greenson, 1967, p. 46).

Although many therapists have endorsed Greenson's presentation regarding the appropriateness of the procedures of confrontation, clarification, interpretation, and working through, the concept of the working alliance may be open to some question. If one endorses the notion that behavior by itself does not tell us very much, it would follow that a working alliance may exist for reasons that range all the way from healthy flexibility to neurotic compliance. Ms. Armstrong may free associate, present her feelings and memories, pay her fees, and arrive on time because she genuinely sees these actions as helping her feel and function better. Mr. Baines, on the other hand, may manifest the same behavior because he feels intimidated by the therapist, thinks that he must comply with everything he believes that the therapist wants, and is worried that if he does not conform to the therapist's requirements he will be hated or abandoned.

It would appear that, although a working alliance exists in most therapeutic relationships, for most clients it is an expression of both mature and immature motives. Perhaps a more realistic way to view the working alliance is to regard it as part of the positive transference, with some of its elements serving as resistances that have to be confronted, clarified, interpreted, and worked through.

Greenson emphasizes what most therapists realize—that in order for resistances to emerge and eventually be worked through, the therapist must do a lot of listening. With regard to listening, Greenson suggests that the therapist not make a conscious attempt to remember. The therapist will remember significant data if he pays attention and if the client is not stirring up the therapist's own problems. Nonselective, nondirected attention will tend to rule out biases and allow the therapist to follow the client's lead. In order for the therapist to listen effectively, he must also pay attention to his own emotional responses inasmuch as these responses may lead to important clues. For example, if the therapist feels angry or experiences erotic fantasies in the therapy sessions, it may very well be that this is what the client unconsciously wants the therapist to experience.

In recapitulating the general procedures in working with resistances, Greenson outlines them as follows:

1. Recognize the resistance.
2. Demonstrate the resistance to the patient.
   (a) Allow the resistance to become demonstrable by waiting for several instances.
   (b) Intervene in such a way so as to help the patient become aware of the resistance.
3. Clarify the motives and modes of resistance.
   (a) What specific painful affect is making this patient resistant?
   (b) What particular instinctual impulse is causing the painful affect at this moment?
   (c) What precise mode and method does the patient use to express his resistance?
4. Interpret the resistance.
   (a) What fantasies or memories are causing the affects and impulses behind the resistance?
   (b) Pursue the history and unconscious purposes of these affects, impulses, or events in and outside the analysis, and in the past.
5. Interpret the mode of resistance.
   (a) Pursue this and similar modes of activity in and outside of the analysis.
   (b) Trace the history and unconscious purposes of this activity in the patient's present and past.
6. Working through
   Repetitions and elaborations of steps 4(a), (b) and 5(a), (b) (Greenson, 1967, pp. 121–122).

In agreement with such other writers as Anna Freud (1946), Otto Fenichel (1945), and Wilhelm Reich (1949), Greenson has pointed out that resistance should always be dealt with before content and that the therapist should begin at the surface rather than overwhelming the client with id interpretations. He also stressed what several authors have cautioned and has been reiterated in this chapter, that in order for an interpretation or confrontation to be effective, the therapist must make sure that the client can perceive the interpretation or confrontation correctly.

REUBEN FINE

In several of his books (Fine, 1979a, 1981, 1982) but particularly in *The Healing of the Mind: The Technique of Psychoanalytic Psychotherapy* (1982), Reuben Fine has presented several notions that can be of enormous assistance to the therapist who is trying to help clients resolve resistances.

Fine points out that, in learning techniques, the emphasis must be on goals rather than on specific procedures. Unless therapists have some theoretical background to back up their belief that the procedures being used make sense, they are apt to fail in their work: "A mechanical approach will never go far in therapy; the human situations involved are too varied; the emotions too powerful, and the need for sincerity too great. The beginning therapist should be encouraged to question the value of every procedure until its underlying rationale becomes second nature to him or her" (1982, p. 15).

Fine's goals for his patients can be subsumed under the rubric of "the analytic ideal" to which we referred in Chapter 1—to love, communicate, have a role in the family, have a sex life, be free of symptoms, and so on. He also points out that candidates for therapy are more treatable if they can assume some responsibility for their plights (i.e., be able to feel some guilt) and in addition be able to fantasize.

In providing an atmosphere that will help clients present their problems and observe their resistances, the role of the therapist, particularly at the outset of therapy, may be thought of as one of *dynamic inactivity*.

Fine's notion of dynamic inactivity is extremely pertinent. Many therapists, particularly beginning therapists, fail to realize that what helps clients feel their safest when examining their resistances is to have a benign listener. Because the helpfulness of listening is not sufficiently appreciated by many therapists, they feel obligated to present to their clients, often very prematurely, all kinds of clever confrontations, profound clarifications, and deep interpretations. In most instances, this alienates clients, who feel overwhelmed, pressured, and inadequate next to the seemingly sophisticated therapist.

Usually when clients are in the presence of a quiet but attentive listener, they begin to feel quite positively toward the therapist and eventually engage in what Fine has called "the analytic honeymoon." As a result of unburdening themselves (catharsis) and feeling uncriticized and accepted, they begin to feel more hopeful and can examine their defenses more easily because their egos have been strengthened.

Inasmuch as a honeymoon in therapy is similar to a honeymoon in marriage, it is always short lived. Sooner or later, the clients' unreal expectations become punctured, and the therapist, instead of emerging as a loving partner, starts to appear as a tough taskmaster. What evolves then is what Fine has labeled the "first treatment crisis." The client, now beginning to view the therapist as his own punitive superego, begins to feel unappreciated, unloved, and ungratified.

The first treatment crisis may be conceptualized as the first major resistance in therapy. It is usually, if not always, accompanied by a negative transference, with wishes to terminate the therapy. To resolve this resistance, the client should be helped to discharge his hostility toward the therapist, without censure from the therapist. Although the client's hostility can take many forms—criticism of the therapist's office, dress, voice, diction, fee schedule, appointment time, and so on—if the client is helped to verbalize his negative feelings, he usually feels relieved and more able to explore the genetic and dynamic roots of his resistances.

As we will discuss in more detail in Chapter 4, many clients leave treatment prematurely because the therapist did not make use of the negative transference that usually is a strong component of the first treatment crisis. Because the hostility is not discharged in the therapist's consultation room, the client acts it out by leaving treatment and satisfies an urge to defeat the therapist.

According to Fine, three major reasons account for the first treatment crisis (i.e., the sudden shift from a positive to a negative transference), and these reasons may be used as interpretations at the appropriate time:

1. The superego reasserts itself. Things have been going too well, and the client unconsciously is looking for punishment.
2. The id becomes too threatening. Sexual and aggressive fantasies create considerable anxiety.
3. The relationship becomes too close. The client feels frightened of warm, positive, and intimate feelings toward the therapist.

One of the major ways of helping a client resolve resistances is through the therapeutic relationship. As several writers whose work we have reviewed in this chapter have pointed out, as the client sees that the responses of the therapist are different from his own punitive superego, anxiety lessens, impulses are more acknowledged, and the need for resistances are less urgent. Fine's stance is in consonance with this perspective:

The patient produces material that contains forbidden impulses. True to his or her past, the patient punishes himself or herself for these impulses. The therapist—(the) new superego, does not give any punishment but merely understands the impulse. As this continues, the patient feels less and less threatened by his or her impulses. Eventually, the patient can talk about them freely, which gives him or her the possibility of rational choice; that is, the patient can now choose those impulses that can be given reality gratification and discard those that cannot. In either case, he or she makes choices on a conscious rational basis whereas before the patient was driven compulsively to act in certain ways that were too often self-destructive. (1982, p. 240)

Fine has pointed out that the goal of dynamic psychotherapy can be expressed as expanding the id, strengthening the ego, and weakening the superego. However, he has stressed that the expansion of the libido has proven to be of enormous use to many therapists in helping clients resolve resistances. Inasmuch as so many resistances are really protective devices to disown libidinal wishes and fantasies, when the client sees that the therapist is never against libido (i.e., never against sexual fantasies, erotic longings, or romantic cravings), the client slowly identifies with this orientation, feels freer to express and examine his libidinal wishes and fantasies, and experiences a decreasing need to hold on to resistances.

In making interpretations, confrontations, or clarifications, Fine believes that the sine qua non is the client's response. If, for example, the therapist says, "You seem to be silent because you are afraid of loving feelings toward me," what is crucial in helping the client resolve his resistances is for the therapist to observe what the client does with the interpretation. Did the client listen to the interpretation? If not, the therapist's job will be to examine what the client was feeling that made him reluctant to listen. Did the client reject or accept the interpretation? If the client accepted it, was it just a compliant act or was it a genuine acceptance? If it was a compliant act, then the compliance, which is a resistance, should be investigated. Does the client produce more material in response to the interpretation? This would be a good sign of the validity of the interpretation. However, a client might have listened to an interpretation, accepted its veracity, but become silent. Here, he was probably threatened by id wishes or transference fantasies, and this then will have to become the priority in the treatment situation.

Further observations of how a client reacts to an intervention involve whether the client talks or acts in response to it. Often actions are a response to a feeling that the therapist is commanding the client to behave in a certain way, and this is a resistance that needs exploration. Other clients verbalize insights and can "talk a good game," but isolate their insights from life; this, too, is a resistance to therapy that needs to be examined further.

Fine has pursued the subject of countertransference in several of his writings (1979a, 1979b, 1981, 1982). His major contention is that, as the therapist contributes to the growth of another human being, he should also experience some growth: "It becomes desirable for therapists to reformulate their conception of their role so that they look upon the entire therapeutic process as something that contributes to their growth as well as to that of the patient" (1982, p. 212). Like Freud, he believes that the therapist cannot get the client beyond the point that the therapist has reached.

In examining various countertransference problems, Fine points out that, just as a client's positive transference can mask resistances, so too a strong positive countertransference can interfere with the therapist's objectivity. When the therapist is in love with the client, he can join with the client against real or imagined enemies, deflect the client's hostility, and interfere with the client's producing a wide variety of emotions, memories, and thoughts in the treatment.

Fine views having sex with the client as one of the more serious expressions of the positive countertransference. Eschewing a moralist stance, he points out that, if the client is given too much gratification, then the opportunity to examine the fantasies connected with his action is lost. "Furthermore," Fine avers:

> the wish for gratification may be so overwhelming that further talking therapy is precluded. At times, therapist and patient have a love affair that runs its course like any other, but like love affairs in general this arrangement does not satisfy the needs of the patient and merely results in one more frustration. The therapist, because of his or her own conflicts, disregards the fact that what the patient needs is an uncovering of the unconscious, not physical sex as such. (1982, p. 224)

The positive countertransference, if too intense, can also interfere with helping the client get in touch with his childhood sexual fantasies—the root of many neuroses. If the therapist feels that the positive transference–countertransference relationship is "true love," fantasies of the client are blocked, memories are repressed, and genuine therapy is disturbed. Sometimes a too strong positive countertransference can be expressed by encouraging the client to act out sexually, and the therapist in his overzealousness can receive vicarious gratification for his own sexual fantasies.

Negative countertransference can take many forms: annoyance at the client for not getting better; bombarding the client with many interpretations; referring the client for drugs or hospitalization; and ascribing pejorative labels to the client, such as "psychopathic," "borderline," and "excessively narcissistic."

Fine's technical recommendations together with his optimistic philosophical stance (see Chapter 1) have helped many therapists feel quite secure and confident in helping clients resolve resistances.

CHARLES BRENNER

Although Charles Brenner's contribution to psychotherapy lies mainly in helping us better understand the dynamic evolution of resistances (see Chapter 1), several of his comments on technique are pertinent (1973, 1976).

Regarding a proper therapeutic attitude, Brenner points out that being "natural," therapeutic, and compassionate means something different from being a sociable, friendly, sympathetic "good doctor" or "good parent." It means acting toward one's clients in accordance with one's obligation to them, which is to understand and communicate to them the nature and origins of their conflicts and resistances. Brenner would see any other behavior on the part of the therapist as inappropriate and untherapeutic.

> The addition of a dash of encouragement or a measure of scolding or admonition, however tactful and well intended, may seem to hasten the process. It can, at times, produce symptomatic improvement. But it is no substitute for analysis of *why* the patient wants encouragement, admonition, or any other nonanalytic behavior from his analyst and in the long run it cannot fail to interfere to a greater or lesser degree with analytic progress and with the achievement of an optimal end result. (1976, p. 109)

Regarding interpretation, Brenner has pointed out that the principal purpose of interpretation is to convey to clients what the therapist has learned about their psychic conflict. In agreement with many other writers whose work we have reviewed in this chapter, Brenner has stated that learning about oneself is not always the main thing that happens when the therapist makes an interpretation, and it is never the only thing that happens. The effect on clients of a particular interpretation is never limited to increasing their knowledge of their conflicts, and in some cases, an increase in knowledge is only a small part of the effect an interpretation makes:

> Its chief effect may be that the patient feels discovered, accused, humiliated, praised, encouraged, rewarded, seduced, or rejected. Nevertheless, the intended effect is to increase a patient's knowledge of himself, and even if one's every single effort in that direction is not successful, the sum of one's efforts—the net effect of one's many interpretations—must be successful if there is to be any analysis worthy of the name. (1976, p. 49)

Many therapists have noted what Brenner has reaffirmed—namely, that interpretations can exert their full effect only gradually and after many repetitions. When one reads a clinical example in which a single interpretation seems to have resulted in a striking change in a client, one is justified in assuming that much preparatory work has preceded it.

Brenner has pointed out that, in helping clients resolve resistances, the dictum that defenses should be analyzed before one interprets the instinctual wishes (the id) can at times be held too rigidly. As defenses soften, it is quite appropriate, Brenner suggests, to interpret defense and drive derivative at the same time. An interpretation such as "You are attacking yourself, because you are frightened of your anger toward me" demonstrates an interpretation of the defense (projection) as well as an interpretation of the id (anger) at the same time.

Although most therapists have done what Brenner has suggested on many occasions (i.e., interpret drive and derivative at the same time), they also have noticed with many clients that, if sufficient preparatory work has not been done and if defenses have not been sufficiently soothed and empathically respected, interpretations of clients' anger or sexuality can create too much anxiety in them and they can then be driven out of treatment.

What Brenner is really trying to suggest is not a fundamental disagreement with the dictum "Resistance before content," but that no matter what the therapist is trying to help a client understand better—a dream, a fantasy, or a symptom—the therapist must pay attention to the defenses that are always part of its formation, but the therapist should not do so in an isolated way.

Regarding countertransference problems, Brenner has stated that the therapist's desire to understand his client's unconscious conflicts must itself have unconscious, infantile roots—roots he learns about in his own analysis or therapy—and so must his reaction to whatever his client's conflicts may be, and these vary from client to client, as most therapists know. Some clients' resistances and conflicts will be closer to the wishes, fears, joys, and disasters of the therapist's own childhood, while others will be more distant. If, as a result of his own therapy, the therapist is not too disturbed by being reminded of his own conflicts, he will be able to understand and interpret those of his clients. His countertransference will not interfere unduly with his ability to function as a therapist.

Like transference, countertransference is ubiquitous, Brenner has averred, since derivatives of infantile instinctual conflicts play a part in every adult relationship. "One cannot, therefore, distinguish sharply between countertransference that deserves to be called normal and that which deserves to be called pathological" (1976, p. 130).

ROBERT LANGS

As was stated in Chapter 1, Robert Langs' major thesis is that a study of unconscious communication between therapist and client always demonstrates the presence of some element of countertransference in every intervention of the therapist. Furthermore, according to Langs, the therapist is always contributing in some meaningful way to the presence of resistances in the client. All resistances are both interactional and intrapsychic, and it always behooves the therapist to investigate his contribution to the evolution and maintenance of the client's resistances.

Langs' many writings (e.g., 1973, 1974, 1975, 1976a, 1976b, 1979, 1981) all reflect a strong quarrel with classical, mainstream psychoanalysis and psychotherapy. He believes that classical analysts and therapists have given only lip service to the possibility of resistances within the client that arise primarily from the therapist's inappropriate attitudes and interventions. It is Langs' contention that countertransference contributions are underplayed by most therapists.

> There is little indication that classical analysts would accept the thesis that every resistance within the patient receives some input, however small, from the analyst, and that such inputs are part of the continuing spiraling, conscious and unconscious communicative interaction. Further, there are many types of resistance—evoking errors, especially those which involve mismanagement of the ground rules and framework, which are totally unrecognized in present-day classical writings. Little effort has been made to develop a listening process through which this particular source of resistances could be identified, and thereby rectified and interpreted. (1981, p. 489)

In studying clients' resistances and helping clients to resolve them, Langs has contended (1973, 1979, 1981) that maintaining ground rules in the treatment is extremely crucial. This includes the establishment of set hours, length of sessions, and frequency of visits; fixed fees; set positions for client and therapist, with the client either on the couch or sitting opposite the therapist; the client's commitment to say everything that comes to mind; the therapist's neutrality, anonymity, and use of neutral interventions geared toward interpretations; total privacy and confidentiality; and the rule of abstinence as it applies to both participants.

It is Langs' belief that many resistances of the client that evolve in the therapeutic situation emerge because the therapist in one way or another violated the ground rules (e.g., changed an appointment; raised fees; made a supportive, noninterpretive remark; or revealed something personal to the client). Disruption of the ground rules, according to Langs, always compounds resistances and disrupts the therapy.

Langs advises that any effort on the part of the client to modify the basic framework (e.g., a wish to change an hour) should be met with the basic response of silence, permitting the client to continue to free associate. The client's subsequent material will serve as a commentary on his proposal and will reveal in derivative form its unconscious meanings; it also will suggest ways and means for the therapist to intervene. According to Langs, as the therapist listens to the client's associations after the client makes a proposal, the therapist will realize that adherence to the basic frame is always the answer.

There is a strong tendency among therapists to respond to requests related to the ground rules with direct answers rather than permitting the client to free associate so that derivatives may guide the response of the therapist. There is also a related tendency to fail to recognize the extensive implications of such requests and the critical role played by the therapist's responses. Langs has strongly contended that "without exception, deviations gratify pathological symbiotic needs in both participants, while maintaining the boundaries and setting involves healthy symbiosis, and fosters individuation and autonomy" (1981, p. 616).

When Langs examines clinical material, his major focus from a theoretical point of view appears to be an interactional one—that is, he wants to observe the interaction of client and therapist and how they influence each other. In actuality, he emphasizes the therapist's countertransference and tries to demonstrate over and over again how the client is in many ways adapting to, or introjecting, the therapist's countertransference problems. He believes that the client is unconsciously perceptive of the therapist's countertransference problems and is expressing his awareness of them through dreams, fantasies and other associations.

Langs tends to view the many regressions and symptomatic relapses of the client that occur in treatment as provoked by the therapist's countertransference problems. When a client is not improving, Langs always wonders whether there is a mutually supportive resistance existing between client and therapist.

Langs' adherence to ground rules, his focus on the interaction between therapist and client, and his consistent stress on the countertransference are all excellent contributions to the therapist's repertoire of skills and attitudes that can be used in assisting clients to overcome resistances. However, Langs' approach has many limitations. He has overemphasized the importance of ground rules and countertransference and, as a result, fails to appreciate the crucial roles of other variables. By overstressing the countertransference, he fails at times to help the clinician realize that associations can be free and that transference reactions can arise spontaneously. If the therapist becomes too preoccupied with his countertransference problems, which Langs implicitly advocates, he can overlook the genetic and dynamic variables that help form transference reactions and other resistive behavior.

Langs' rigid adherence to ground rules, if emulated by therapists, would tend to make them insensitive to crises and other human departures from routine. Sometimes therapeutic movement can be enhanced and resistances more easily resolved if "scholarship, skill, and classical conviction (can) be accompanied by manifest human warmth and interest" (Langs & Stone, 1980, p. 17). This might necessitate offering a client an extra hour, a lowered fee, or an expression of sympathy.

Occasionally Langs' ground rules sound like rules and regulations devoid of empathy. This was the reaction of Leo Stone in his clinical dialogue with Langs, which appeared in their coauthored book, *The Therapeutic Experience and Its Setting* (Langs & Stone, 1980). In the dialogue, Langs goes so far as to say: "Even a suicidal patient, with whom you make life-saving special interventions will eventually express hostility toward you for invading his autonomy" (1980, p. 66).

Stone's sentiments would probably be shared by most contemporary therapists when he states:

> And I persist in the (quaint?) notion that considerations of equity and humanity must often be given priority over a geometrical neatness of the frame. . . . The idea, for example, if you permit me to resort to a reductio ad absurdum, that to maintain the integrity of the analytic situation you should let the patient jump out of a window, instead of pulling him back and later risking some recriminations, I don't hold with (Langs & Stone, 1980, pp. 66–67).

While acknowledging Langs' erudite scholarship and his pinpointing of variables that are often neglected or dismissed by therapists when they discuss working with resistances, most clinicians would object to a stance that often appears to subordinate human needs to routines. They also might wonder about a practitioner's own countertransference problems when he rigidly adheres to such rules as never providing tissues for clients who are crying, never offering supportive remarks to clients who are in real crises, and never discussing his own clients with colleagues (Langs, 1981).

ROY SCHAFER

Roy Schafer, a psychologist and psychoanalyst, is a professor in psychiatry at Cornell University Medical College and a training analyst at the Columbia University Center for Psychoanalytic Training and Research. He is also a prolific writer whose books and articles provide guidelines for the clinician who is interested in the art and science of resolving resistances. Two of Schafer's books, *The Analytic Attitude* (1983) and *A New Language for Psychoanalysis* (1976), are particularly pertinent to our discussion of the treatment of resistances.

Schafer has very much endorsed Anna Freud's (1946) idea that the therapist's position should be equidistant from the various forces in the client that are at war with one another—that is, the client's id wishes, defenses, and superego admonitions. This implies a total repudiation of any adversarial notion of the therapeutic relationship. Rather, it involves conceptualizing the client's resistance in an affirmative manner, approaching it, not as if the client is in a state of opposition, but as if he manifests behavior that seems puzzling or unintelligible and that requires the therapist's understanding.

Schafer, in discussing further the notion of equidistance, cautions therapists not to respond to their clients' productions in kind. This means not meeting anger with retaliation or appeasement, and not meeting confessionals with gratitude or self-revelations. Responses in kind impede therapeutic work because they are really the acting out of countertransference problems. In order to relate empathically to clients' resistances, therapists have to accept the fact that clients can abide by the ground rules and free associate in only compromised ways. When therapists respond in kind, they are like punitive parents, attacking their children for their transgressions rather than understanding and interpreting their conflicts.

In considering various forms of resistance, Schafer draws our attention to one that is infrequently mentioned—namely, that many clients fear being empathized with and so attack the very thing they long for, the empathetic therapist. Many individuals in psychotherapy need a therapist who is secure enough to tell them that they are afraid of being loved by the therapist. When this resistance is further explored, it usually turns out that clients who resist being empathized with are frightened of their erotic fantasies toward the therapist, which may be of an oedipal or homosexual nature (Schafer, 1976, 1983).

Schafer also points out that there is no way that the therapist can avoid being hated. The neutral equidistant stance frustrates infantile wishes and thereby activates rage. Beginning therapists who may need to be loved by their clients often find it difficult to assume a neutral position simply because it frequently does activate the client's disappointment and anger with the therapy and the therapist. Neutrality often can be experienced by clients as provocation and manipulation.

Schafer believes that much of the resistance to the uncovering of resistances stems from the therapist. Although not as adamant as Robert Langs

(1973, 1981), he believes that many therapists fear their own erotic and hostile feelings toward their clients and worry that these feelings will get out of hand. He believes that too many therapists secretly prefer an atmosphere of strained distance where sexuality and aggression are subdued. Although it is difficult to be sure how common counterresistances toward sexual and aggressive material are, when they appear the therapist needs to seek out more supervision and more personal therapy.

In all of his writings, Schafer has emphasized that resistance should be viewed as no different from any other clinical data that have to be understood and eventually interpreted. He has further averred that resistance is material from which a great deal can be extracted concerning the history and current status of the client's problems. In agreement with Freud, Schafer believes that the greatest therapeutic gains will be made through the analysis of resistances.

NEO-FREUDIAN AND NON-FREUDIAN APPROACHES TO THE RESOLUTION OF RESISTANCES

As was stated several times in Chapter 1, therapists' views of resistance will be predicated on their theoretical orientations to human functioning, their notions about the psychotherapeutic process, and a host of other variables, including their countertransference responses. It was also pointed out in Chapter 1 that the more the therapeutic perspective rejects one or more of the following variables—the unconscious; the sexual and aggressive drives; the tripartite system of id, ego, and superego; and history—the less it will be concerned with the assessment and treatment of resistances. Consequently, the following section in which we review the available material on resistances from the non-Freudian and neo-Freudian schools will be brief.

Object-Relations or Developmental Orientation

It was mentioned in Chapter 1 that the object-relations or developmental orientation tends to deemphasize the importance of the sexual and aggressive drives as motivators of behavior, and instead focuses on the client's interpersonal relationships and their maturity or lack of maturity. Such writers as Blanck and Blanck (1974), Kernberg (1976), Kohut (1977), and Mahler (1968) view resistances to treatment, not so much as an expression of anxiety regarding forbidden thoughts and frightening impulses, but more as expressions of developmental lags. The aforementioned writers rarely use the term *resistance,* but rather they discuss their clients' difficulties in coping with the therapy, particularly with the therapeutic relationship. Most of these difficulties are alleged to evolve because of the client's internalized objects or parental introjects.

Much of the treatment of the object-relations therapists appears to be very similar to Alexander's use of the corrective emotional experience, noted earlier in this chapter. In one way or another, the object-relations therapist is trying to provide the client with a new object who will help the client feel more individuated, less symbiotic, or less pathologically narcissistic.

Although it is doubtful that such writers as Blanck and Blanck (1974) would view themselves as espousers of Alexander's corrective emotional experience, as one reviews their clinical material it appears that their approaches are quite similar. In discussing the treatment of a client in their book *Ego Psychology: Theory and Practice,* Blanck and Blanck (1974) refer to the therapist in the case as one "who provided optimal symbiotic gratification at the phase-specific time" (p. 110). Later, they state: "Disagreement with the therapist was welcomed also as occasion to discuss employment of aggression in the service of separation and to further neutralization" (p. 111). Still later, they write, "When memories of incestuous wishes were presented, the therapist explained that this is a welcome sign of masculinity" (p. 112). Finally, they conclude, "All aspects of the patient's attempts at independence were examined, encouraged in the present, and in the transference" (p. 113).

Similar ideas are expressed in the work of other object-relations writers. This is particularly true in the approach of Kohut (1971, 1977), who eschewed such issues as homosexuality, sadism, orality, anality, and oedipal conflicts, and concentrated much of his work on trying to avoid puncturing the client's fragility and narcissism.

As we review the above statements of the Blancks, it may be reasonably inferred that the therapist was frightened of the client's incestuous wishes and, instead of helping the client discuss and examine his fantasies, the therapist prohibited this by being too reassuring. Futher sexual material did not emerge because the client received the message that the therapist was consciously or unconsciously against explorations of id material. The therapist, by encouraging disagreement, was actually fostering a neurotic dependency by rewarding a certain type of behavior. This was also true earlier in the treatment when symbiotic gratification was promoted.

The object-relations therapist, by encouraging certain behavior, actually interferes with the client's spontaneity and growing maturity. Because examination of id material is essentially rejected, the punitive superego cannot be altered, and in the final analysis, the growth of the ego can be realized in only very limited ways.

HYMAN SPOTNITZ AND MODERN PSYCHOANALYSIS

Psychiatrist Hyman Spotnitz has written several books and articles on the management of resistances. Among his better known books are *Psychotherapy of Preoedipal Disorders* (1976); *Treatment of the Narcissistic Neuroses,* with Phyllis Meadow (1976); and *Modern Psychoanalysis of the Schizophrenic Patient* (1969). Initially designed for the treatment of schizophrenic clients and individuals suffering from pre-oedipal disorders, Spotnitz's formulations are now used in the treatment of resistances with clients who demonstrate neurotic and characterological difficulties as well as with those who have psychotic reactions.

One of Spotnitz's major notions is that the individual in psychotherapy, particularly at its inception, should be shown that he has the right to resist (Spotnitz, 1969). The procedure employed to give the client this right has been called "joining the resistance." An example of this technique would be when a client is late for an appointment or reluctant to free associate, the therapist tells the client, "You have a right to come late" or "You should feel free not to talk." Joining the resistance is a procedure designed to help the client feel protected against unwanted feeling states. In addition, the technique is an attempt to relate to the client's negative suggestibility. Many clients try to defeat the therapist out of spite (Kesten, 1970); consequently, when they are instructed not to talk they may speak, and when they are told that coming late for appointments is quite permissible, they may come on time.

Spotnitz and his followers have formulated their therapeutic techniques out of a conviction that clients, particularly very disturbed clients, have difficulty coping with their hostile and murderous impulses. They view much of resistive behavior as an attempt to ward off hostility. Hence, when clients depreciate themselves in order to defend against their negative transference feelings, several procedures have been formulated to help them discharge their anger in treatment. For example, if a client says, "I'm disgusted with myself," the therapist might respond, "You are disgusting!" Or when the client says, "I am a confused person, please help me," the therapist might say, "I am a confused therapist, please help me" (Spotnitz, 1969, 1976; Spotnitz & Meadow, 1976). These comments of the therapist often do release aggression in the client.

One very popular procedure among Spotnitz and his followers is "mirroring." To demonstrate to the client how latently provocative he is, the therapist often behaves the way the client does. If, for example, the client says, "I'd like to stop coming to see you" or "I'm not getting much out of seeing you," the therapist might retort with what Schafer (1983) has termed a "response in kind" and say, "I'd like to stop treating you" or "I'm not getting much out of working with you."

Some of the above procedures have been incorporated into the work of other therapists. Haley (1963), responding to the client's negative suggestibility joins the resistance or mirrors the client and refers to his work as "paradoxical therapy." Nelson (1968) uses these procedures in what has been called "paradigmatic psychotherapy" or role-playing.

The reader who has reviewed our discussion on resistances in Chapters 1 and 2 may be able to anticipate some of our criticisms of Spotnitz's procedures. If a therapist joins clients and reinforces any of their behaviors, whether it is a resistance, a verbalized fantasy, or a piece of action, they abdicate their neutral, equidistant position (A. Freud, 1946). This abdication leads to several therapeutic problems. When clients experience the therapist as joining them in anything, the rest of their psychic apparatus may be silenced. If lateness or absence from an interview is joined by the therapist, there is the strong likelihood that the client will not get in touch with the id wishes and superego admonitions that are contributing to his lateness or absenteeism. Psychic conflict, as we know, is a compromise formation of instinctual wishes, ego defenses, and superego pressures. When a therapist joins a resistance, many parts of the psychic apparatus go unaddressed.

Joining the resistance, mirroring, and the other procedures advocated by Spotnitz interfere with the development of a spontaneous transference. Transference reactions become muddied because the therapist has taken a stand, rather than remaining neutral. As a result, the client is forced to comply, rebel, feel seduced, or feel attacked. The opportunity for therapist and client to examine the client's major resistance objectively is forfeited.

The procedures mentioned above do not permit the client's observing ego sufficient opportunity to examine spontaneous associations, such as transference fantasies, memories, and superego commands, because the client has to cope with the therapist's joining and mirroring, rather than just being himself and freely associating with the therapist.

Those who use Spotnitz's procedures tend to overemphasize the importance of hostility and underestimate the crucial role that libidinal wishes play in the etiology of all psychological conflicts. Most clients, neurotic, psychotic, and character disorders, are suffering a great deal because their infantile sexual fantasies create in them anxiety, terror, and despair; many of their resistances are ways of coping with their forbidden sexual thoughts and wishes. Aggression, hostility, and murder are often used as defenses to ward off infantile sexuality; consequently, the release of anger for many clients is antitherapeutic.

In consonance with their overlooking the place of infantile sexuality in psychic life, Spotnitz and his followers assign too much importance to pre-oedipal problems and give insufficient attention to oedipal difficulties. Although they repeatedly assert that schizophrenia is a pre-oedipal problem, many therapists who have worked with schizophrenic clients have noted that these individuals often have several problems with incestuous fantasies, phallic competition, and homosexual urges. They respond very well to a neutral, equidistant empathic therapist, and function and feel better when their oedipal fantasies and conflicts are aired with the practitioner (Strean, 1982).

Perhaps the most serious objection that can be made to Spotnitz's techniques is that the therapist can use them in the service of his own countertransference problems. Joining and mirroring are designed to liberate the client's hostility, but more often than not their use can gratify the therapist's sadism, which very frequently he seems to be projecting onto the client. The therapist's acting out of his sadism is often rationalized by terming it "induced feeling," emanating from the client's resistances (Spotnitz, 1969). What is disregarded here is that when therapists are *feeling* hostile toward their clients they are obligated to examine their own anxieties and vulnerabilities so that they can then empathically help their clients understand what their transference reactions are all about, rather than responding to resistive behavior in kind (Schafer, 1983).

NEO-FREUDIAN SCHOOLS

As we discussed in Chapter 1, the Neo-Freudian schools of Adler, Horney, Sullivan, and Jung make very limited use of the concept of resistance. Consequently, they offer few ideas regarding resolution. However, some of their notions that verge on the issue bear brief review.

Adler

The Adlerian perspective avers that the main issue in therapy is to help the client abandon a neurotic life-style by giving up faulty "fictions" and a defensive air of superiority. The major means of helping the client resolve a neurotic resistance (i.e., a false superiority) is to provide a setting of equality in the treatment situation. Consequently, Adler prescribed that therapists should sit face to face with their clients and engage them in free discussion. Sessions should be few per week, and the length of treatment short. According to Adler (1927), the intent of the therapist is to interpret to clients how they are deceiving themselves in not really furthering their own creative life-styles.

Because of the interest, warmth, and activity of the therapist in Adlerian therapy, the client's feelings of being attacked or criticized are minimized. Client and therapist spend much of their time discussing the manner in which early life experiences have led to the client's feelings of inadequacy and his neurotic life plan. Adler did not consider a person as successfully terminated with treatment until he had redirected his life-style and established social interests.

Adler's short-term treatment with its emphasis on equality is very reminiscent of Alexander's corrective emotional experience. Therefore, it contains all the limitations that have been discussed earlier in this chapter when we reviewed Alexander's theories.

Horney

Like Adler, Horney regarded treatment as a human collaborative adventure. Dogma, rules, and technique are eschewed, and emphasis is on the client and the therapist's equal partnership (Horney, 1945). She categorized the behavior of the therapist into five groupings: (1) observation; (2) understanding significant patterns; (3) interpretation; (4) general human help (i.e., concern, sympathy, and praise); and (5) help in resistance (Horney, 1950).

Help in resistance referred to those times in the therapy when the client feels hurt, frightened, or angry by the therapist's comments. A follower of Horney offers the client reassurance and points out that the therapist is genuinely interested in the client's welfare and means well (Ford & Urban, 1965). In contrast, a psychodynamically oriented therapist attempts to examine the client's anger, hurt, or fear by viewing these emotions as expressions of the client's fantasies, history, id wishes, superego commands, and so on.

The concern, sympathy, and praise that a therapist offers during times of resistance, according to Horney, reduces the client's feeling of hurt and anger. There is no doubt that this can be the effect for some clients. Other clients, however, might feel seduced and manipulated, and wonder if they are being talked out of their distress. Of more importance is that, when a client is reassured, the variables that have created the resistance are bypassed and bound to come up again in a disguised form later in the therapy or later in the client's daily life.

Sullivan

In consonance with the here-and-now orientation of neo-Freudians, Harry Stack Sullivan also emphasized the importance of the interpersonal relationship of therapist and client. However, in contrast to a Freudian approach, where the client's transference is examined and the therapist's countertransference is silently observed by the therapist alone, Sullivan prescribed a transactional process between client and therapist in which both study what they induce in each other. Sullivan (1954) felt that the therapist should be a participating observer and share with the client his own apprehensions inasmuch as these always impede or facilitate therapeutic communication.

Although Sullivan's emphasis on reciprocity is a helpful one inasmuch as the therapist's presence and activity are always affecting the client's productions, his prescription that the therapist share his feelings with the client has dubious value. It is difficult enough for clients to work on their own resistances. To have to cope with the therapist's as well compounds the task. As we suggested earlier in this chapter, when clients have to cope with the therapist's fantasies and countertransference problems, they cannot freely associate because their own spontaneous transference fantasies are squelched.

Jung

Jung was a profound psychologist whose main contribution to therapists lies in his elucidation of a variety of symbols (Fine, 1973). As seems to be true of all neo-Freudian therapies, the treatment encounter in a Jungian setting involves an active interchange between therapist and client. Here, too, the therapist will share personal thoughts with the client, exchange feelings, experiences, and even dreams (Jung, 1956).

Although resolving resistances is hardly mentioned in Jung's writings, he does point out that when the client is not getting in touch with his problems, the therapist "may teach, suggest, cajole, give advice, reflect feelings or give support" (Whitmont & Kaufmann, 1973, p. 101). Interpretation is used occasionally in Jungian therapy, particularly the interpretation of dreams. This is done with much of the emphasis on symbolism. While the notion of transference is not rejected in Jungian therapy, it is minimized (Jung, 1954).

NON-FREUDIANS

As we suggested in Chapter 1, the concept of resistance is hardly used at all among the non-Freudians. As its name implies, behavior therapy, one of the most popular treatments today, places its emphasis exclusively on the client's behavior. The client's inner life is completely bypassed, and the therapist concentrates his activity on reinforcing, rewarding, or punishing the client. Punishing is often referred to as aversive conditioning (Wolpe, 1958). Behavior therapy dispenses with the notion of transference but does believe that a positive working relationship is necessary for the treatment to be effective (Goldstein, 1973).

In client-centered therapy, although the notion of resistance is also by-passed, Rogers (1954) believes that the client must be treated with unconditional positive regard. As Rogers himself has said:

> The theory does not stress the technical skills or knowledge of the therapist. It asks him to be genuine or congruent, to be empathic or understanding, and to be unpossessively caring or confirming. The presence of these attitudes in the person of the therapist is the catalytic agent in the client-centered therapeutic relationship. (Meador & Rogers, 1973, p. 137)

The rational-emotive therapy of Ellis (1973b), as we discussed in Chapter 1, involves a forceful attack on the client's superego. The therapist quickly pins the client down and shows him that his dysfunctional behavior is irrational. If the client resists accepting the attack, the therapist again tries to persuade the client that he is not being logical or rational. This is essentially the approach in reality therapy (Glasser, 1965) also.

In Gestalt therapy, there is an emphasis on here and now, with limited concern about the client's history. Transference and resistances are by-passed, but the therapist must "act with sincerity, confidence, basic trust, inspiration, and many other things. It corresponds with the patient's hope that he will change" (Kempler, 1973, p. 269).

Having defined resistance and reviewed the literature on the subject, we are now ready to enter the consultation room and get a glimpse of how resistances manifest themselves and how the therapist deals with them.

CHAPTER 3

On Beginning the Treatment: Initial Resistances

A dimension of psychotherapy that has received limited attention in the literature is the tremendous ambivalence most prospective clients feel about beginning treatment. Although candidates for psychotherapy can acknowledge dissatisfactions in their interpersonal lives and do experience pain in their intrapsychic lives, the idea of entering psychotherapy is extremely frightening for most of them.

As soon as a person thinks of starting treatment, or as soon as it is suggested, inevitably resistances are formed. Particularly when one lives in a Western culture, such as the United States, where independence is championed and omnipotence is admired, entering therapy can puncture one's narcissism and be a blow to one's self-esteem. The idea of relying on an expert for help forces the candidate for psychotherapy to realize that he needs somebody else's assistance in coping with life, and being in this position can feel humiliating.

Depending on a professional for assistance with psychological problems conjures up associations to when the person was a child and needed help from others in order to survive. Consequently, many individuals shun psychotherapy and say, "I will not be reduced to a child. I don't need a daddy or mommy to take care of me." Their repudiation of the dependent role of client is a defense against strong dependency wishes that terrify them.

The idea of psychotherapy also arouses fears of being placed in a submissive position inasmuch as the prospective client is aware that he will be asked to keep regular appointments, pay a fee, and talk about feelings, fantasies, dreams, and memories. Many a prospective client perceives cooperating with a therapist as submitting to a parental figure, and it is as if he were on the toilet seat having to produce what mother or father insists should be produced. Stated one man whose physician suggested that he consider psychotherapy, "I will not be put on the hot seat." A woman whose clergyman advised that she consider counseling responded, "I will not show anyone my dirty linen. My dirt is my own business and it is not for anybody to gape at."

Inasmuch as most people who experience interpersonal and intrapsychic stress have conflicts in their love lives, anxieties about their sexual competency often contribute in a major way to their reluctance to enter psychotherapy. Therapists are often viewed by clients as "dirty old men" (or as "dirty old women"), who will seduce, rape, or expose them. Many individuals resist the idea of starting therapy because they feel that they will be ordered to psychologically undress. Remarked a man whose wife suggested that he consider treatment for his depression, "I'll be damned if I'm going to pull down my trousers for a stranger! Who does he think he is?" A woman whose husband thought that she needed psychotherapy for her insomnia and her sexual inhibitions exclaimed, "Those god-damn therapists are voyeurs. They just want to pry into your sex life. I want to keep as far away from those bastards as I can."

What frightens many prospective clients about therapy is the possibility that their secret sexual fantasies will be dissected and condemned. Inasmuch as most clients project their own punitive superegos onto the practitioner, they are convinced that they will be demeaned for their homosexual fantasies, ridiculed for their incestuous desires, castigated for their masturbatory practices, chastised for their real or fantasied extramarital affairs, and rejected for their past or present romantic interests. Individuals who resist beginning therapy often point out, "It is an invasion of my privacy" and view the therapist as a sadistic voyeur rather than as an enabling helper.

The mental health of people in psychotherapy is the same or possibly a little better than those who are not in treatment because individuals in psychotherapy are not as plagued by denial and have enough ego strength and courage to face themselves (Fine, 1982). It is still the rare individual, however, who does not experience going into treatment as some kind of failure. "When I think of depending on a therapist, I feel like a fool for not being able to take care of myself," stated an applicant at her initial consultation in a social agency. "If I were a mature parent, I would not have to come to this child guidance center for help," said a dejected father at intake. A married couple who disagreed about everything—child rearing, handling the in-laws, sex, and vacations—at their first appointment were able to agree completely with the therapist, who remarked, "You both resent it when you have to turn to me for help with your marital problems."

The fact that entering psychotherapy is experienced as a blow to one's narcissism and to one's feelings of omnipotence is best revealed by therapists when they become clients. Helping professionals often rationalize their being clients by saying, "It is important for my training" or "It is required by my analytic institute." Although they will overtly avow that only the strong, courageous, and mature can ask for help, many therapists view being in therapy as a sign of either weakness, timidity, or immaturity. Many of the early followers of Freud, such as Otto Rank, bragged that they did not need personal analysis (Jones, 1953). As the life of Otto Rank attests (Novey, 1983), those who repudiate the need for psychotherapy the loudest, often seem to need it the most.

Inasmuch as the idea of beginning psychotherapy stimulates anxiety about id wishes, activates punitive voices of the superego, and mobilizes many different ego defenses, it should not surprise us that the decision to enter psychotherapy is often delayed, postponed, or even rejected completely. In clinics and social agencies, only about one-third of those applying for counseling and psychotherapy remain in treatment (Strean, 1978), and the dropout rates in private practice are probably quite high as well. Although many prospective clients are so frightened of the idea of entering psychotherapy that even the most astute, sensitive, and empathetic therapist could not help them resolve their initial resistances, there are large numbers of prospective clients who can be helped to remain in treatment. Very often a client drops out of therapy after a phone contact or after one or two interviews because the therapist was not aware of the client's resistances, was inept in responding to them, or was too influenced by countertransference problems.

In this chapter we examine some of the common resistances that clients demonstrate early in treatment, try to understand the dynamics of these resistances, and suggest procedures that the therapist can use in helping clients resolve their initial resistances.

THE FIRST TELEPHONE CALL

Because the prospective client is so frequently ambivalent about receiving professional help and inasmuch as he has probably delayed making the first phone call to the therapist (sometimes for weeks or even months and years), the practitioner should be alert to the many possible manifestations of resistance during the first telephone call. Some candidates for psychotherapy, because of their dread of being entrapped in a situation that appears so ominous, secretly hope that the therapist will say or do something over the phone that will make entering treatment appear to be a foolish idea. They may fantasy that the therapist has no convenient time available for them, charges too high a fee, or has a perspective on psychotherapy that appears too incompatible with their own values.

One way that the client may reveal over the phone his resistance to beginning psychotherapy is by asking questions about the therapist's fee policy, time schedule, or theoretical biases. Inasmuch as these questions usually emanate from the client's dread of involvement in treatment, any answer by the therapist can compound the client's resistance. For example, if a prospective client has fears of intimacy and asks over the phone what the practitioner's orientation is (e.g., Freudian, Jungian, etc.) and if the therapist then states his orientation, the client's resistance to treatment can be exacerbated. If the client wants a Jungian therapist, and the therapist says over the phone that he is indeed a Jungian, the client who is afraid of intimacy will certainly have to find some other reason to avoid the therapy. On the other hand, if the therapist says that he is not a Jungian, then the prospective client has a good reason to resist the therapy and the therapist, because as far as the client is concerned, his needs are not being met. Consequently, it is best for the therapist to tell the client that the questions being asked over the phone are important ones but that the therapist would prefer to deal with them in person.

Joe A., a young man in his twenties, called a therapist for a consultation. Over the phone Joe said, "I'm looking for a therapist who will be active and give me some feedback." The therapist, Dr. Z., responded, "Well, you've called the right guy. I believe in getting involved in the treatment, and I try not to be a blank screen." Joe told the therapist that he liked the therapist's attitude and made an appointment to see him. However, he never kept the appointment.

Several months later, Joe called another therapist. This time when he asked if the therapist would be active and provide some feedback, the practitioner, Ms. Y., suggested that Joe might consider coming in for a consultation with her and discuss his concerns about the therapist's activity. Joe kept his appointment with Ms. Y. and stayed in treatment.

A few weeks after Joe had been in treatment with Ms. Y., he explained why he responded so negatively to Dr. Z.: "He seemed too eager to have me as a patient. I became suspicious of a therapist who was so eager. I wondered if he was hard up and needed patients. I worried that he'd want too much from me. In some ways I felt raped by Dr. Z."

Very few prospective clients are put off when they are told over the phone that it might be a good idea to make an appointment with the therapist to discuss their questions about such matters as therapeutic orientation, fee policy, and schedule. If the prospective client cannot cope with the delay, in all probability his motivation for therapy is quite weak and his terror of it is quite strong.

Many candidates for psychotherapy handle their resistance to treatment by insisting on making an appointment at a specific time, with the unconscious wish that the therapist will not have that time available. Although it is desirable if the practitioner can give the applicant the time and date he prefers, when the applicant insists on a specific time and shows limited flexibility, then the therapist should begin to wonder about the candidate's strong fear of being involved in treatment.

Barbara B. called Dr. X. for a consultation. She was having problems on the job, difficulties with men, somatic reactions, and a host of other difficulties. However, the only time she had for an appointment was Friday evenings at 8 o'clock. When Dr. X pointed out that he did not have office hours at that time, Barbara refused to consider other possibilities and told Dr. X. she was sorry that his schedule "was so rigid."

A few weeks after her phone conversation with Dr. X., Barbara called Dr. W. and again asked for an appointment on Friday evenings at 8 P.M. Recognizing that Barbara's request was a possible manifestation of her resistance, Dr. W. said to Barbara, "I'd like to meet your request, but I'm having my difficulties." Barbara laughed at this but said that she "could reserve no other time for therapy other than Fridays at 8 P.M." Here, Dr. W. said, "You know, Ms. B., I'm getting the feeling that maybe having treatment right now is inconvenient and possibly quite difficult for you." Barbara responded, "Gee, I never thought about it that way. I guess it is a bit scary. Could I call you back and let you know if I can make it at another time?"

Barbara did call back 2 days later and made an appointment for a time different from Friday evenings at 8. During her second phone call and in more detail in her consultation interview, she thanked Dr. W. "for being so sensitive to my fears." As she explored her fears of therapy, what frightened her the most was the possibility that she would be rejected by the therapist. By not permitting the therapist too much opportunity to be with her, Barbara could defend herself from possible rejection and abandonment.

In the case of Barbara B., not only did the therapist respond helpfully to the client's resistance by verbalizing her fear of getting involved in treatment, but Dr. W. also intuitively responded to another fear of Barbara's that exists in most prospective clients—namely, the fear that the therapist will emerge as a cold, rigid, omnipotent automaton. When Dr. W. talked about "having my difficulties," he emerged as a humane person with limitations and vulnerabilities, somebody who seemed more inviting than Dr. X., whom Barbara with some justification labeled "rigid."

Candidates for psychotherapy often project their own fantasies of omnipotence onto the therapist and unrealistically expect him to read their minds. When the therapist demonstrates imperfections on the phone or in the therapeutic situation, this can be quite reassuring for many individuals. Stated one client, "When I saw you weren't God, I could like myself better because *I* didn't have to be perfect."

An individual may manifest resistance to treatment by making requests or demands over the phone that seem bizarre to the therapist because they conflict with the therapist's habitual routines in conducting treatment. For example, a prospective client can call an agency, clinic, or private practitioner and ask for monthly therapy, nude marathons, sexual encounter groups, vocational advice, divorce mediation, or some other kind of therapeutic intervention that is beyond the scope of the therapist's expertise, theoretical predilections, or ethical values. What is sometimes overlooked, particularly by inexperienced therapists, is that seemingly irrational requests and provocative demands often mask complex resistances. Consequently, these requests and demands should not be dismissed quickly but instead should be explored in the therapist's consultation room or the intake office of the agency or clinic.

Arthur C., a man in his forties, called a social agency because he wanted some help in finding a mate. He wasn't particularly interested in marrying the companion, but he wanted somebody with whom he could "fool around." When the social worker who was on intake at the agency told Arthur over the phone that the agency did not provide the service he was looking for and, furthermore, that all therapeutic work was done on a weekly basis, Arthur told the intake worker, "I can see by your officious attitude that your place doesn't want to help people."

Several months after the above telephone contact, Arthur called Dr. V., a private practitioner. When Arthur repeated the requests he made of the agency, Dr. V. asked him if he would like to come in and see her at her office and discuss his requests further. Arthur responded positively to Dr. V.'s suggestion that he make an appointment.

During his initial consultation, Arthur told Dr. V. that he was an extremely lonely man who had not had a date with a woman in years. He confessed how socially inept he felt and how prone he was to anticipate rejection from people, particularly from women. He revealed a long and painful history of "never making it with anybody—at school, on the job, or anywhere." On Dr. V.'s suggesting that Arthur come in to see her for another appointment in a few days, Arthur readily complied.

When the therapist recognizes that resistance is part of the therapeutic relationship from the very first phone call, he does not respond to requests literally or to demands impulsively. Each demand and request of a client has to be studied carefully by the therapist because it is a complex expression of the client's resistances. A client's request to be seen monthly or his demand to be provided with a girl friend is a manifestation of intense dependency yearnings, strong superego prohibitions, and a cluster of defenses. When clients call therapists and make unusual requests, therapists must remember that clients are handling themselves in the best possible way they know, and need understanding and empathy from the therapist. All too often, therapists do not sufficiently respect a client's resistance and try to bypass it by telling the client over the phone to modify his behavior immediately.

Sandra D., a married woman in her forties, at the urging of her husband called a therapist for therapy. When the therapist, Mr. T., heard that Sandra wanted once-a-week treatment, he told her over the phone, "If you want to get something out of it, you should come more often." Although Sandra made an appointment with Mr. T., she never kept it. She told the person who ended up being her therapist that she felt too pressured by Mr. T.

All clients who consider psychotherapy must protect themselves from real or imaginary danger. If practitioners sensitize themselves to this notion, they can better meet prospective clients where they are (Hamilton, 1951) and will not impose their own ways of coping on them. Many candidates for psychotherapy are very distrustful of their potential helpers, and their distrust must be honored, not refuted. Their distrust may take the form of not wanting to give the therapist information over the phone.

Herman E., a married man in his thirties, wanted job counseling and needed treatment for a variety of problems—depression, anxiety attacks, and physical symptoms. However, over the phone he would not give the prospective therapist his name. When the therapist did not insist that Herman give his name but did make an appointment with him, Herman sounded very relieved. He kept his appointment but did continue to be very skeptical of the therapist and of the therapy for some time. He refused to give his name to the therapist for over a year and withheld other information for some time as well. (See Chapter 5 for a fuller explication of Herman's resistances to treatment (where he is identified as Mr. A.) and for a discussion of the therapist's attempt to resolve them.)

A difficult phone call for the therapist to cope with is from the individual who is calling on behalf of a prospective client. Often a husband phones a therapist to arrange treatment for his wife, and just as frequently, a wife may call to arrange therapy for her husband. If the therapist asks the person who makes the phone call to arrange for the spouse to contact the therapist, often the therapist never hears from that person. And just as frequently, when an appointment is made by one person for another, the appointment is broken by the prospective client. What is the therapist to do?

Very frequently when one person calls a therapist for another, the person calling is unconsciously asking for help for himself. Most of the time the parent, spouse, or friend who calls for someone else does not feel free to ask directly for therapy and finds it easier to ask for help for someone else (Strean & Blatt, 1976). However, if the caller's unconscious wish is interpreted over the phone and he is told that he wants treatment, the caller will probably deny it. Therefore, to respect the caller's latent wish for help and concomitantly respond to his resistance to treatment, the sensitive therapist will ask the person making the call to come in and discuss his child's, spouse's, or friend's problem. Many parents, spouses, and friends welcome the possibility of an appointment for such purposes, and if empathically responded to by the therapist, they often become clients in their own right.

Sadie F. called a mental health clinic to arrange treatment for her 12-year-old niece, Maxine. Over the phone she pointed out that Maxine had difficulty forming relationships with peers, had sexual difficulties, and had low self-esteem. "She needs to talk to someone right away," stated Sadie with a sound of urgency in her voice. The attentive social worker told Sadie that she would like to discuss her concerns about Maxine, and suggested that Sadie come in for an appointment.

For two sessions Sadie talked about Maxine—Maxine's parents, Maxine's history, and Maxine's sexual problems. Later the discussion turned to how Sadie had been a "mother-figure" for Maxine because Sadie was "much more maternal and nourishing than was my sister, Lillian, Maxine's mother." From her competition with her sister, Sadie slowly moved to a discussion of her own identification with Maxine, and eventually became a client in her own right.

Frequently in psychotherapy the prospective client makes an appointment for a consultation but cancels it. Sometimes this individual does not even call to cancel but just does not show up. In many, if not most, cases, a canceled appointment is a sign of resistance and a warning to the therapist that the person is frightened of what he believes will take place in the interview.

Inasmuch as the nature of the prospective client's resistance is usually very vague to the therapist, it is difficult for most clinicians to relate to it. Sometimes the prospective client just wants to feel wanted, and a telephone call rearranging the missed interview will suffice. In other instances, the reasons for the resistance are more complicated and more baffling. In almost every situation, however, the therapist should make an attempt to discuss with the prospective client just what is troubling the person about getting involved in treatment.

Usually applicants for psychotherapy who cancel appointments are not aware of the anxiety that propels their resistances. Other commitments stand in their way—illnesses intervene, accidents take place, traffic snarls occur, or alarm clocks do not work. Although it would compound their distress and intensify their fears of treatment if the therapist interpreted the nature of their resistances to them, the practitioner should try to respond to the client's feeling of vulnerability and attempt to help him recognize that the interview is not so dangerous.

Most prospective clients respond positively when a therapist is not critical of the client for not showing up for the initial interview. The client's manifest statement, even if it appears to the therapist to be a rationalization, should be respected. Sometimes accidents do occur, and traffic snarls do take place. What is crucial for the prospective client who is frightened and reluctant is a therapist who is accepting and not critical, understanding and nonjudgmental. Consequently, when a client cancels an appointment, first he should be told by the therapist that it was regrettable that the interview could not take place and that another interview can be arranged.

Those clients who call the therapist after they cancel an appointment are usually less resistive than those who do not, and many of them do keep their second appointments. However, those clients who do not call after failing to show up for an appointment are often very terrified people who need considerable assistance before they can approach the therapist's office. It is these people who need to hear from the therapist that the idea of psychotherapy can be very upsetting and that in many ways it feels like something to be avoided. When clients realize that the therapist understands their resistance and empathizes with it, they feel more accepted and usually become more motivated to arrange another appointment. Neophyte therapists often overlook this fact.

All too often therapists try to convince reluctant clients to come in for an interview. On doing this, they overlook that this stance exacerbates the person's mistrust and compounds his resistances. Resistive clients need to feel that they have the right to resist treatment. When the therapist com-passionately notes that beginning treatment might be something that the person would prefer to avoid right now, this attitude often frees the reluc-tant applicant to view therapy more favorably.

Therapists need to allow themselves and their reluctant clients several phone calls, often with much time intervening between the calls, before frightened clients can keep their appointments.

George G., a young man in his early twenties, had been referred by his college advisor for therapy. He did not show up for three appointments and did not call to cancel them. When the therapist phoned George, George agreed to make other appointments but he either "forgot" about them, overslept, or did "not feel well."

After his third cancellation, the therapist told George that she got the impression that therapy was something he might find easier to postpone right now. When George vigorously denied this, the therapist pointed out that it was her experience that when appointments were forgotten, the person, without being aware of it, was feeling that the interview might con-tain something that could be irritating or frightening. After a pause, George said, "You know, I avoid going to class and I've never figured out why. Do you think that I'm irritated, there?" The therapist responded, "Perhaps." George, after another silence, said he thought it might be a good idea to keep his next appointment so that he could find out "what I feel when I avoid things."

George kept his next appointment and was on time for succeeding ones. As he and his therapist examined what feelings he experienced when he canceled his appointments, they learned that the reasons were the same for his cutting classes. George had a lot of repressed rage toward parental authorities and was unconsciously trying to defeat them. As he himself said in his fifteenth interview with the therapist, "I'm telling all of you—teachers, parents, and therapists—to leave me alone and go to hell."

Many forms of resistance emerge when the prospective client telephones for the first appointment. The therapist, from the moment the call is answered to the end of the conversation, realizes that the applicant has many mixed feelings about calling, fears future contacts, and in many ways would rather not be on the phone seeking a consultation. The sensitive, empathic therapist recognizes that virtually no human being is fully com-mitted to therapy. Consequently, he tries to make it as safe as possible for the reluctant client to resist, and to show this person that apprehension about the first interview is par for the course of treatment.

THE FIRST INTERVIEW

As we have suggested several times in this book, although candidates for psychotherapy experience all kinds of conflicts and although they wish that they felt more pleasure from living, it is usually a frightening prospect to face the truth about oneself. Therefore, the first interview is often replete with various forms of resistance. If resistances are not dealt with empathically by the therapist, in all likelihood the client will not return for succeeding interviews.

The Involuntary Client

While it is difficult enough for individuals who voluntarily seek psychotherapeutic help to reveal themselves to a stranger, this becomes all the more of an issue when the client enters therapy against his will. Many individuals are forced into therapy by court mandate or some other form of legal authority. It is many a judge who has declared to a man or woman who has been found guilty of some infraction, "Go into psychotherapy, or else go to jail!" It is many a college dean who has said to a failing student, "Get yourself into psychotherapy, or you'll have to leave school!" And it is many a spouse or lover who has told the partner, "See a shrink, or I'll leave you!"

At first, the adjudicated criminal, the troubled student, or the criticized spouse or lover may welcome the idea of psychotherapy because it is better than the alternative. However, most people placed in this position resent it on some level. They may not feel free to express their vindictiveness about being forced into treatment, but it is difficult for them, as it is for anybody, to accept a situation they have been coerced into. Because the involuntary client hates the idea of treatment but often cannot tell anybody this, the skillful therapist knows that, unless the client's resentment is faced and discharged, treatment will have a limited effect or none at all (Blanck & Blanck, 1974). This is a difficult process for both client and therapist to confront, because to the client, the therapist often appears similar to the coercive judge, the authoritarian school official, or the threatening lover or spouse.

With an involuntary client, two important issues must be considered before therapy can get off the ground: (1) The practitioner must try to help the client discharge his hostility about being in the therapeutic situation; and (2) the practitioner must try to help the client eventually see that the helping person is not the same as the individual who referred the client for treatment.

Ruth H., a woman in her twenties, was involved in a romance with a man 10 years her senior. Her lover, Ronald, a psychologist, told Ruth that her neurotic problems were interfering with their relationship and that, if she wanted Ronald to stay around, she would have to go into treatment. Inasmuch as Ruth was deeply in love with Ronald and desperately wanted to maintain her relationship with him, she called a therapist immediately.

On seeing Dr. U., a male therapist, Ruth had a long list that she brought with her to the interview. She told Dr. U., "I'm dependent, needy, hysterical, symbiotic, infantile, and demanding." When Dr. U. asked Ruth what gave her the impression that she had all these characteristics, with surprise, Ruth uttered, "Well, Ronald told me these things, and he ought to know because he's a psychologist!" After a long silence, Ruth volunteered the information that she would not have considered beginning psychotherapy if Ronald had not "made me do it." When the therapist asked, "Made you?", Ruth said that she felt somewhat like a naughty girl who was ordered to the school principal's office. With some help from Dr. U., Ruth was able to say that the therapist bore a physical resemblance to her school principal and that "both of you look like Ronald."

When Dr. U. empathized with Ruth's plight and recognized with her how much she resented being in his office, Ruth then asked, "Well, don't you agree with Ronald? Haven't you already observed all of my neurotic characteristics?" Here Dr. U. pointed out that it took a long time to understand another person's psychodynamics, so he could not really say very much about Ronald's comments.

Near the end of her interview, Ruth realized that she felt forced into treatment and repeated the therapist's remark made earlier in the interview that "treatment never works if you feel compelled to be in it." She asked Dr. U. if she could defer the decision to begin treatment, and he told her it would be entirely up to her. If she wanted to discuss the idea further, he would be available for another consultation.

Ruth got in touch with Dr. U. 2 weeks later to make another appointment with him. At her second appointment, she reviewed with Dr. U. what transpired between Ronald and herself since her consultation. She said, "I told Ronald that I would not be coerced into treatment and that, if he couldn't accept me with my neuroses, we would have to split. Somehow it didn't feel like such a horrendous idea because I knew I could come to you and discuss my feelings—I wasn't so alone." Ronald accepted Ruth's decision but wished to continue his relationship with her whether she did or did not go into therapy. Ruth was then able to decide on her own that she wanted therapy from Dr. U. because, as she stated, "I think you can help me with my readiness to become too easily intimidated by men."

It is extremely important for the involuntary client to hear from the practitioner that therapy never works when the client feels under legal, moral, or psychological coercion. This attitude of the therapist's often helps the client evaluate the idea of therapy more objectively because he feels less shackled and freer to make a decision. Sometimes, as in the above case, the client moves toward a conviction that therapy will be in his best interest.

In many situations, even after involuntary clients recognize that they abhor the idea of therapy, they still find themselves in a horrible dilemma. If they quit therapy, they will be in jail, out of college, or in jeopardy with a lover or spouse. Here it is important for the therapist not to try to talk the client into treatment. Rather the clinician should empathize with the client's plight and wonder out loud if there is anything that client and therapist might talk about that would make it worthwhile for the client to visit the therapist on a regular basis. This attitude is frequently enabling to the client who feels coerced and on the verge of being rejected. Sensing that the therapist will accept him on whatever terms the client wishes to arrange, the client can slowly move into treatment.

Ian I., a 15-year-old high school student, was referred for treatment because he was failing all of his courses, was belligerent toward both peers and teachers, and seemed to be involved in delinquent acts, such as stealing. The principal who referred Ian to the therapist, Dr. S., pointed out that, if Ian did not go to his therapy sessions on a regular basis, he would have to go to a reformatory for incorrigible students.

Although Ian welcomed Dr. S.'s recognition that Ian didn't want to be in therapy "no how," nonetheless, Ian continued to feel in a conflict. "I can't stand people like you, but if I don't come here, they'll put me in the looney bin," lamented Ian. When Dr. S. asked Ian what he couldn't stand about him and people like him, Ian replied, "You know god-damn well you wouldn't have anything to do with me unless it was your job. You are really like a truant officer who forces kids to do things that they don't want to do. So why should I want to be here, and how can I possibly like it?"

Dr. S. responded to Ian's conviction that Dr. S. was not genuine and did not really care about Ian and Ian's own wishes. He wondered if there was something that he and Ian could do that would make it worthwhile for Ian to come and see him. Ian tried many ploys to test the therapist. First, he told the therapist that the best way Dr. S. could be of assistance was to say as little as possible. When the therapist complied, Ian tired of this arrangement and tried something else. He went on to discuss his major interest, electricity. As he saw that Dr. S. did not reject him for setting his own therapeutic agenda, Ian became more involved in the therapy.

Inasmuch as the involuntary client frequently appears very belligerent toward the therapist and very rejecting of any attempt of the therapist to offer help, this client is very capable of inducing strong countertransference reactions in the practitioner. Clinicians, in response to the involuntary client's hostility and contempt, have been known to react with their own hostility and contempt. This reaction of the therapist only convinces the involuntary client that helping professionals cannot be trusted and that they cannot deal with what really concerns the client. It is only when the therapist relates to what forms the involuntary client's resistances—his feelings of being unwanted, rejected, and vulnerable, which are often masked by a belligerent demeanor—that the involuntary client can come to treatment with more inner directedness.

Clinicians can come to feel less attacked and less threatened by the involuntary client by reminding themselves periodically that this client's belligerence masks feelings of desperation, terror, and weakness. To defend against the anxiety and panic that evolves from deep feelings of unworthiness, the client attacks the therapist so that the latter will feel what the client is trying to deny—the unpleasant feelings of inadequacy and despair.

Requests for Information about the Therapist and the Therapy

Inasmuch as many clients are very suspicious of therapists and worried about what they are being led into, they often have many questions about the nature of the therapeutic process and the adequacy of the therapist's professional qualifications. There are at least two schools of thought regarding how a clinician should respond to such questions. One position states that, inasmuch as clients are going to spend much time discussing with the therapist such personal issues as their pains, embarrassments, anxieties, fantasies, memories, and dreams, they should have some idea about the therapist's professional background and orientation. Without such knowledge, clients have every right to feel some caution about the therapy and the therapist and some concern about whether they are paying their money to a qualified practitioner.

In addition, many professionals and lay people have pointed out that it is important for prospective clients to know about the therapist's preferences for particular therapeutic modalities. For example, many clients prefer to be seen in therapy once a week and for a period of no more than 6 months. Should not these individuals be told in their first interview whether or not the therapist subscribes to their therapeutic preferences? Would it not be unethical for a Freudian therapist who believes in long-term intensive therapy to remain silent while the prospective client asks for brief therapy of once a week or less? Similarly, if the prospective client would like to participate in marital counseling or family therapy, would it not be appropriate for the therapist to inform the client in the first interview that he does not have expertise in these areas?

With so many unqualified, poorly trained, unsupervised, and unanalyzed people calling themselves therapists, prospective clients should certainly heed the adage: "Caveat emptor" (buyer beware). It behooves every prospective client to check out a therapist before having a consultation, and there are many ways to get information. If the referral source is a physician, clergyman, attorney, school official, therapist, or client or former client of the therapist, these individuals can usually provide the pertinent information about the therapist's training and background. Furthermore, such organizations as the American Psychological Association and the American Psychoanalytic Association can also supply needed data.

The second position regarding the client's queries about the practitioner's training and background suggests that almost every question about the therapist's person or qualifications that is asked in the interview is a disguised expression of anxiety and apprehension about being in treatment. Often when clients have many uncertainties about being in therapy, they have many questions to ask the therapist. Consequently, queries of the therapist about most issues, particularly about training or professional qualifications, should be considered manifestations of resistance and responded to by the therapist as such.

Very frequently when a prospective client asks questions about the therapist's qualifications, he is unconsciously trying to prove that the clinician is not the appropriate person with whom he should be in treatment. It is much easier for most clients to discuss their doubts about the therapist's qualifications than it is to face their own doubts about themselves and their own uncertainties about being in treatment.

If the therapist answers the client's questions about his background, the client's resistances are not confronted and his anxieties go underground. This frequently can lead to client dropout.

Jill J., a married woman in her thirties, sought a therapist because she was experiencing difficulties in her marriage, had acute sexual problems, and was very depressed. Although Dr. R. was highly recommended to her by her personal physician, Jill had many questions to ask her.

When Jill asked Dr. R. about her training, Dr. R. told her where she attended graduate school, who her supervisors were, and where she had her training in psychotherapy. Jill responded by saying that Dr. R. had "an impressive list of credentials" and was "sure you are a very competent therapist." She agreed to see Dr. R. for ongoing therapy but never returned for further appointments.

A few weeks later, Jill saw Ms. Q., a therapist who was about the same age as Dr. R. and had similar training and background. When Jill asked Ms. Q. about her qualifications, Ms. Q. did not answer her but asked, "What are you feeling and thinking right now that makes you ask me?" After a moment of silence, Jill said with some irritation in her voice, "I'm evaluating you and wondering whether you are qualified to be my therapist." Ms. Q. responded, "Apparently you have your doubts about me?" Here, Jill smiled and said, "You were highly recommended by my internist, but I do have a lot of nervousness when it comes to talking about my problems. I have a lot of sexual problems too, and I'm embarrassed to talk about them with someone who is as knowledgeable as you are. I feel very inadequate and very inferior when I'm in a therapist's office."

Ms. Q. empathized with Jill's plight and said that Jill seemed to feel like a second-class citizen next to a superior human being like the therapist. On hearing this Jill was able to laugh and say that was the way she felt in most of her interpersonal relationships and particularly in her marriage. She went on to describe her earlier contact with Dr. R. who, according to Jill, "made me feel so inadequate and so incompetent when she told me about her impressive list of credentials. I felt that I could never work with somebody who had accomplished so much more than I have."

Jill left her consultation with Ms. Q. feeling that she had "been very much understood." She returned to Ms. Q. for therapy and was able to use it very well.

The above case demonstrates that the best way a therapist can deal with a client's questions about the practitioner's qualifications is to view the questions as a sign of resistance and an expression of feeling vulnerable in the therapeutic situation. When clients are shown that behind their queries are concerns and doubts about treatment, usually they are able to explore these doubts and concerns with the therapist. A therapist can best attest to his qualifications by demonstrating skill and tact when a client asks about his qualifications. This is most expeditiously and sensitively done when the therapist can feel free to explore with the client the motives that propel the client's questions.

Just as the client's queries about the clinician's training and background usually mask fears, anxieties, and uncertainties, questions about the therapist's theoretical biases and therapeutic predilections often cover the client's latent fears and resentments. Therefore, when a candidate for psychotherapy asks the therapist if he does marital, short-term, or long-term therapy, these queries should be investigated and examined by client and therapist. The same can be said when the prospective client asks if the therapist is a classical Freudian, a neo-Freudian, or a behaviorist. Often such questions serve as a resistance, covering up the client's fear that he will have to expose his infantile sexuality, primitive aggression, latent homosexuality, or hidden feelings of competition. Whether a prospective client is looking for a short-term behaviorist or a long-term Freudian, it will be in the client's best interests to understand the dynamics of his preferences. This can be realized when the therapist investigates with the client what motivates his queries.

Norman K., a married man in his forties, sought treatment because he was very conflicted about being involved in an extramarital affair. Despite his constant agony and indecision about his affair, Norman postponed going into therapy for over a year. On seeing a therapist who specialized in behavior modification, the treatment that Norman was seeking, he asked the therapist, Dr. P., if behavior modification was indeed Dr. P.'s specialty and if it really was the best treatment for him. Dr. P. acknowledged that he was a behaviorist and explained how behavior modification worked. Norman said that he was fascinated by the discussion with Dr. P. and made another appointment to begin treatment with him.

Norman did not return to see Dr. P., but a few months later, he made an appointment to see Dr. O., a Freudian analyst. After Norman described his conflict to Dr. O., he asked him if he was a Freudian analyst. Dr. O. replied by asking, "What really concerns you about my orientation?" Norman replied that he was worried about making a long-term commitment to a therapy that would cost him a fortune and would not guide him enough. He wanted to make a decision about his extramarital affair as soon as possible.

As Dr. O. explored Norman's requests for short-term therapy, for advice, and for a treatment that did not require too much emotional or financial investment, client and therapist learned a great deal about Norman. They learned that, just as Norman feared making a commitment to therapy, he also feared making a commitment to his wife and his mistress. His request for quick advice seemed to emanate from the pain and agony that he experienced because of his chronic indecision, particularly his indecision about his marital status. Norman also was able to learn that the reason short-term therapy appealed to him so much was that he derived his greatest pleasure from relationships that were short term. "I feel dominated and controlled if someone wants too much of me."

Alert to Norman's statement that he felt "dominated and controlled" if too much was asked of him, Dr. O. was very careful in responding to Norman's subsequent remarks and questions. "I see you are a Freudian," observed Norman, "because you have a couch here and you also have a picture of Sigmund on your wall! I guess you only work with people if they see you often and if they lie on the couch?" Dr. O. told Norman that the use of the couch was not necessary and he would be glad to see him face to face and as infrequently as Norman wanted to be seen. Surprised, Norman then asked, "Are all Freudians as flexible as you are? I always thought that they were rigid, pompous, and authoritarian bastards. Are you different?" Dr. O. replied, "I baffle you, don't I? I don't conform to your image of a Freudian?" Norman laughed and said, "In a peculiar way I like it that you don't answer my questions. It helps me figure out my own answers." He then went on to discuss his experience with Dr. P., whom he called a "learning theorist." "That guy explained too much. He made me feel dumb."

While many clients handle their anxieties about starting treatment by asking questions of the therapist, others express their resistances by telling the therapist directly that he is unqualified. Young therapists are often disparaged for their youth, while older therapists are demeaned for their senescence. Women therapists are told that they are biased against men, and men therapists are told that they discriminate against women. Every mannerism of the therapist's is open to ridicule by the client, and everything that he possesses or is identified with—clothes, furniture, diplomas, pictures on the wall, etc.—is subject to scrutiny.

Certainly therapists are not exempt from biases or from poor taste, and they can be legitimately criticized for many things. However, when a prospective client is critical of the therapist's youth, old age, gender, or taste in clothes or furniture, it is important for both client and therapist to study what is really upsetting the client. In most cases, derisive remarks about the therapist conceal the client's own fear of being exposed and criticized. That is why it is very important for therapists not to be defensive when they are criticized or to be attacking when they are provoked. If the client's critical statements are neutrally and empathically subjected to examination by the therapist, eventually the client may be stimulated to learn more about himself and feel motivated to begin treatment.

Joan L., a woman in her early twenties, sought therapy because she was having difficulties in her relationships with men and was also having problems with peers at the elementary school, where she was a teacher. On meeting the male therapist who was assigned to her at the mental health clinic where she was being seen, she blurted out: "Oh my God! I didn't expect a therapist to be as young as you are! How many years of experience do you have?" The therapist, Mr. N., replied that he had 3 years of

clinical experience and that he would not have been assigned to Joan unless he had sufficient expertise and experience. Joan, feeling rebuked,
asked more questions of Mr. N., but implied in all of them was a tone of
disdain. When Mr. N. pointed out to Joan that she was very attacking and
castrating, she left the therapist's office, exclaiming, "You are a male
chauvinist pig! I wouldn't let you treat a dog."

It was obvious that Mr. N. was unable to cope with a powerful countertransference problem. Feeling that his youth and inexperience were therapeutic liabilities, he had to try to convince his client that he could help
her. Whenever therapists find themselves arguing with clients or trying to
convince them of something, they should tell themselves that they have
stopped relating to their clients empathically and are no longer dealing with
their clients' resistances and the anxiety that propels them. If a clinician
is arguing with a client, he has ceased being a therapist and in many ways
has become like an attorney arguing a case.

When a client siezes on some feature of the therapist's personality (training, age, etc.) and criticizes it, the therapist must keep in mind that the
client has a wish to criticize the therapist, even if the client's put-down has
much truth to it. Some therapists are young and some are old. Some are
tall and some are short. Some are handsome and some are ugly. Some are
beautiful and some are unattractive. What is crucial for both therapist and
client to get in touch with is the danger that is being warded off by the
client when he uses some realistic characteristic of the therapist in the
service of resistance.

Joan L. was assigned to another therapist at the same clinic where she
saw Mr. N. Similar to her reaction to Mr. N., she told her new therapist,
Mr. M., that he appeared too young and seemed inexperienced as well. Not
appearing defensive or attacking, Mr. M. inquired, "What bothers you
about having a therapist who seems young and inexperienced?" Joan replied, "What a stupid question!" and became silent. After about 20
seconds of silence, Mr. M. inquired, "I realize that you felt my question
was a stupid one, but could you tell me what was stupid about it?" Joan
went on to point out that, if Mr. M. were trained and experienced, he
would know what was stupid about his question. But inasmuch as he was
"an infant" in the profession, she would have to explain to him what the
issue was. "If you are young and inexperienced," said Joan with much
anger, "you won't be able to understand what my problems are all about
and you won't be able to help me with them. Now do you understand?"
The therapist said, "not quite," and went on to ask, "If I'm young and inexperienced what problems of yours won't I be able to help you with?"
Joan replied, "You're impossible" and another silence ensued.

After a 30-second silence, Joan said to Mr. M., "You're a persistent bastard, aren't you? You probably want to know about my sexual fantasies, my sexual experiences, and my sexual history" and glared at Mr. M. for several seconds. Mr. M. smiled and said, "I think you are also worried about how much of a voyeur I am!" Joan also grinned and said, "You're cute. I'm beginning to like you."

With much hesitation but with some determination in her voice, Joan went on to consider going into treatment with Mr. M. She was impressed that Mr. M. "knew how to avoid arguments and, you know, I do get into arguments with a lot of people." She also pointed out, "You never get defensive!"

Eventually, Joan did go into treatment with Mr. M. and was able to resolve many of her problems: her competition with and envy of men, her feelings of helplessness when dealing with angry thoughts and feelings, and her many sexual conflicts. Questions about the therapist's qualifications and attacks on his competence constitute one of the major resistances in the initial interviews. Most clients respond positively to a therapist who empathically tries to elicit the motives and feelings of discomfort that are behind the client's questions and criticisms.

Reluctance to Give Information

During the initial interviews, therapists want to get some data about the client's symptoms, ego functions, interpersonal problems, fantasies, memories, current living circumstances, job, and history. Although most clients are willing to answer the therapist's questions about their pasts and presents, some are reluctant to discuss certain facets of their lives. As we have suggested earlier in this chapter, entering psychotherapy is often experienced as being relegated to an ignoble, submissive position in which one has given up control. One way of restoring control is by withholding information from the therapist (Noble & Hamilton, 1983). In addition, exposing information can often be embarrassing, anxiety provoking, and shame inducing. While most candidates for psychotherapy recognize that giving information to the therapist will help them understand themselves and cope better, the degree of their discomfort is often so great that they cannot divulge pertinent data.

Inasmuch as refusal to give information to the clinician is an obvious form of resistance, its occurrence affords the therapist an excellent opportunity to demonstrate early in treatment how the phenomenon of resistance is addressed in psychotherapy. If the therapist responds sensitively, confidently, and empathically to the client's unwillingness to divulge information, this attitude will help the client feel less self-conscious and less anxious when the therapist later confronts him with embarrassing material. On the other hand, if the client feels pressured to divulge material, he will become progressively more uncomfortable with the therapist and may drop out of treatment.

Although very few clients respond well to being nagged or pressured, neither do most of them welcome a therapist who ignores the fact that they cannot reveal themselves. Said one dissatisfied client whose resistance was joined (Spotnitz, 1976), "When I told her [the therapist] that I found it difficult to talk about my sexual life and she said that 'sex was not too important,' I wondered about her competence, I thought she might be a liar, and I considered the possibility that she wasn't that eager to help me."

It would appear that the best stance that a therapist can take with clients who have difficulty revealing themselves is one that does not make them feel pressured to do so and that also recognizes that they feel in some imminent danger if they do present the data. In many ways, the mature therapist's demeanor in this situation can be likened to that of the loving parent who senses that his son or daughter is frightened of the dark. To ignore the child's phobia would be insensitive and irresponsible; to insist that the child confront the dark in one fell swoop would be callous. A middle position, which concomitantly empathizes with the child's feeling of terror and also recognizes that pressure will serve no useful purpose, is the most desirable attitude.

Harvey M., age 15, was referred to a mental health clinic by the courts because he had been convicted of stealing. In his intake interview with the social worker, he refused to discuss the details of his stealing. When the social worker, Ms. L., said that she couldn't help him with his problems unless he told her about the stealing, Harvey said to her, "Tough titty!" Apparently, Harvey's provocativeness angered Ms. L., and she then said to him, "Look, if you don't tell me what's been happening to you, you'll be sent away to an institution!" Harvey then stormed out of the office and refused to have anything further to do with Ms. L.

A few weeks later, Harvey was interviewed by Dr. K. in the same clinic. When the issue of Harvey's stealing came up in the session, Dr. K. assumed the position that it didn't matter if Harvey refused to talk about the stealing. To Dr. K., Harvey said, "You are using a gimmick, and you are full of shit. You know damn well you want to find out about the stealing. Cut the crap." When Dr. K. stated vehemently, "It really doesn't matter!" Harvey left the interview, never to return.

Most clients, particularly teenagers, are extremely wary of people they feel are not on the level with them. In the above example, Harvey was able to detect that Dr. K. was manipulating him, and therefore his suspiciousness became intensified and he had to abandon Dr. K. and the clinic.

Harvey was eventually seen by a private practitioner, Dr. J. Again the issue of Harvey's not wanting to talk about his stealing came up. Dr. J., not wishing to pressure Harvey to reveal the information and not wishing to ignore the matter either, told Harvey, "I realize you don't want to tell me about the stealing and I certainly don't want you to feel pressured to do so, but could you tell me what bothers you when you think of telling me about it?" Harvey responded, "It's a private matter, and I'll be god-damned if I'm going to let you feel like a big shot who knows all my business! I know about guys like you. You are in this business to put people down. I'm not going to be put down by you! I'll put you down instead!"

Dr. J. told Harvey that now he could see why Harvey didn't want to tell him too much. He asked, "Am I right in saying that the less you tell me the stronger you feel, and the more you tell me the stronger you make me?" Harvey then said, "You got my number, Brother." Realizing that he had divulged something about himself, Harvey retracted and pointing a finger at Dr. J. warned, "But that's all you're going to find out about me! You won that round, but no more!"

Dr. J. empathized with Harvey's plight. He said that apparently for some time Harvey had been worried about people taking away his power; consequently, he had to be a very private person. Feeling understood, Harvey was now able to talk to the therapist. Harvey told Dr. J. that he had been in power struggles all his life—with parents, with teachers, and with therapists. Eventually, he was able to go into treatment with Dr. J. to find out how come he was so prone to get into one-upmanship fracases.

Most people who come into psychotherapy have secrets (Fine, 1982; Greenson, 1967). The dynamics of secrets are complicated (we will have more to say about secrets in Chapter 5), and usually it takes much time for the therapist to understand their etiology and an even longer time for the client to discuss them in therapy. The sensitive therapist is neither lax about attending to the client's secrets nor does he pressure the client to reveal them. What is important for both therapist and client to realize is that, when a client has difficulty revealing material, he feels in danger and it is the dangerous situation that should be understood and eventually mastered by the client.

Requests for Advice and Interpretations

Inasmuch as psychotherapy involves paying a professional expert a sum of money for a limited period of time, usually 45 minutes, it should not appear too farfetched for the client to anticipate receiving some counsel or clarification on his problems when the first interview is near termination. Many clients and beginning therapists fail to appreciate the proven fact that people feel and function better when they are given the opportunity to talk to an attentive, empathetic, and quiet listener (Fine, 1982; Freud, 1913; Greenson, 1967; Strean, 1979). If clients have a good hearing from a therapist who listens and does not bombard them with interpretations, clarifications, reassurances, or questions, they usually leave the interview feeling more relaxed and self-confident. As one client reflected, "For the last three sessions, you've hardly said a word to me. But as long as I know that you are listening, I like myself more, I feel more hopeful, and I like people better. I really like doing most of the talking. Where else can it be like this?"

It is sometimes overlooked by clinicians that, by the time candidates for psychotherapy summon up the courage to make an appointment with a therapist, they already have tried many other alternatives. They have discussed their conflicts with relatives and friends; they have listened to the advice of physicians and clergymen; they have gone on vacations; they have participated in various forms of recreation; they have read books and experimented with self-analysis. The reason the candidate for psychotherapy is in the clinician's office is because all these previous attempts failed. Usually relatives and friends have not listened but have advised; often clergymen and physicians have not empathized but have prescribed; and in most instances, the beneficial results from vacations, recreation, books, and self-analysis are temporary and superficial. Consequently, by the time the candidate for psychotherapy arrives at the therapist's office he wants and should receive something different—an opportunity to talk at great length about himself to a caring, attentive listener.

Although most prospective clients welcome speaking their minds to a "dynamically inactive professional" (Fine, 1982), others feel that this is not enough and in their first or second interviews ask the therapist for some advice or interpretations.

It is very important for the therapist to keep in mind that all client requests have their unique meanings. If requests are gratified by the therapist rather than understood by both client and clinician, the anxiety that evoked them is not confronted, the conflict that is being expressed is not mastered, the autonomy that the client fears is not considered, and the resistance that is being demonstrated is not resolved.

Many individuals who seek psychotherapy are frightened of their own assertiveness and unconsciously view expressions of normal aggression as onslaughts on the therapist and others (Jaffe, 1983). Terrified of their own autonomy and independence, they turn the practitioner into an omnipotent giant who, they hope, will give them all the answers.

One of the most powerful resistances throughout the entire course of psychotherapy is the client's wish to have the therapist serve as an omnipotent parent (Freud, 1937a). When the therapist gratifies the client's request for advice or for an interpretation, he is unwittingly interfering with the client's psychological growth. Although dependent clients frequently resent the therapist when they do not get their requests gratified pronto, like indulged children they do profit from the limits imposed on them because they feel a certain pride when they can exercise their own ego functions. Then they do not need an omnipotent parent as much, and consequently, they like themselves more.

If clinicians do not comply with their clients' requests for advice or for some other form of intervention, they demonstrate their confidence in their clients' resources, and eventually most clients feel reassured by this. Of perhaps more importance, when the clinician does not gratify the client's wishes, the client, feeling frustrated, aggresses toward the therapist. It can be very anxiety reducing for the client when he sees that the therapist is not crushed or wiped out by his hostility.

Many therapists worry that if they do not give the client some diagnostic impression or some direction, particularly in the first interview, the client will feel deprived and not return for more treatment. They fail to appreciate that clients benefit, first and foremost, from talking and not so much from advice and counsel. They also fail to recognize that most clients welcome a therapist's attitude of "Let's see what you are feeling, now that you are asking me what to do." In the long run, most clients are suspicious of someone who appears to know it all. They would rather resent but grow with a therapist who examines rather than advises.

Adele N., a divorced woman in her late forties, consulted Dr. I. because she was having difficulties on her job. A high school teacher, Adele found herself in power struggles with her colleagues and superiors. In addition, she was experiencing quite a bit of difficulty with her students, who "often talk back to me."

Prior to consulting Dr. I., Adele had been in psychotherapy with several therapists—psychologists, psychiatrists, social workers, and psychoanalysts. In all these contacts, she presented herself as an extremely depressed woman who needed much support or else she would have to commit suicide. Actually, she had made several suicidal gestures and was able to succeed in alarming several of her therapists. Often they responded to her panic by hospitalizing her or prescribing medication.

What became quite apparent to Dr. I. in his first interview with Adele was how frightened Adele was of her own autonomy, independence, and aggression. Terrified of being an adult, she clung to a fantasy that she could have an enduring symbiosis with her omnipotent therapist. To gratify her symbiotic yearnings, she constantly asked her therapists for support, advice, and interpretations. When these demands were not gratified, she would threaten suicide and call the therapists at their homes. She was frequently successful in manipulating therapists to give her extra therapy sessions and to make home visits. In sum, Adele was able to succeed in getting her therapists either to gratify her requests or to be alarmed by her panic when they did not indulge her. As a result, she did not grow from any of her therapeutic experiences. Her fantasy of being a little baby united with a perfect mother in a Garden of Eden remained very much alive.

Toward the end of her first interview with Dr. I., after Adele had talked a great deal about her past and present, with the therapist saying almost nothing, Adele asked Dr. I., "So what do you think of all of this? Do you agree that I'm being victimized by the principal, by the teachers, and by the students?" Dr. I. responded, "What are you feeling right now?" To this Adele became furious, had a powerful temper tantrum, and told Dr. I. that he was a "cold, heartless, rigid, narcissistic Freudian" who did "not know what compassion is all about." She then got up to leave and said, "You want me out of here, don't you?" When Dr. I. suggested to Adele that it might be a good idea to understand better what was making her so angry, she sat down and proceeded to villify him some more. Although it was the end of the session, Adele refused to leave. Dr. I. told her, "We have to stop" and offered her another appointment, which Adele refused to accept. She said she would never come back to see "a pompous ass" like Dr. I. appeared to be.

Adele called within 1 day after her consultation and made another appointment with Dr. I. After discharging a great deal of anger and calling him "stupid" several times, she became more composed. She said, "I have to give the devil his due. When you seemed to be unaffected by my threats and unmoved by my demands, I began to feel more confidence in you."

Adele stayed in treatment with Dr. I. for several years. She continued to make many demands for advice, reassurance, interpretations, home visits, and proclamations of Dr. I.'s love. Dr. I. always assumed the same posture with Adele whenever she became demanding and tried to investigate with her what her symbiotic yearnings were all about. The more Adele was not indulged, the more she learned to cope with frustration. The more Dr. I. was not manipulated by her hostile temper tantrums, the more Adele could maturely assert herself.

After 3 years of therapy in which she was seen three times a week, Adele's suicidal gestures stopped, her interpersonal problems were lessened, and her self-esteem rose.

The more the clinician views clients' requests for advice and counsel as signs of resistance, the more clients have an opportunity to grow. Although it can be anxiety provoking for the therapist, particularly in the first interview, to frustrate clients' demands, most clients, after expressing some hostility, do benefit from the therapist's neutral, equidistant attitude (A. Freud, 1946). When the practitioner gratifies the client's request, it is usually because he is frightened of being disliked and the object of the client's scorn. However, the more that clients are given the opportunity to examine what they are feeling, thinking, and fantasizing when they make requests, the more they can become autonomous, independent, self-confident, and self-approving.

Fighting the Ground Rules of Psychotherapy

A way that many clients express their initial resistance to psychotherapy is by fighting the ground rules. This may take the form of asking for more than the allotted 45 or 50 minutes appointment time, requesting a reduced fee, or insisting on some form of environmental intervention, such as the therapist calling a spouse, boss, or in-law. The client's resistance to adapting to ground rules, like all resistances, must be investigated (Langs, 1973).

As we have suggested several times, many individuals experience entering psychotherapy as submitting to an arbitrary authority. Consequently, just as children defy their parents when they feel that unfair rules and regulations are being imposed on them, many clients resent seeing a therapist at a fixed appointment time, are adamant about paying a fee that appears too high, and feel demeaned when they have to talk about their feelings, fantasies, memories, and dreams while the therapist says next to nothing about events in his life.

Many therapists, like many parents, feel very uncomfortable in their role as authorities. Under the guise of providing an atmosphere of equality, they may quickly submit to the client's wish to lower the fee, lengthen or shorten the session, intervene in the client's environment, or provide information about their own feelings and fantasies. They fail to see the client's behavior as a manifestation of resistance and therefore do not help the client get in touch with what bothers him when he is asked to abide by some therapeutic ground rules.

Usually, but not always, when a client asks for a reduction in fee, cannot agree on a regular appointment time, or needs to know how the therapist is feeling, the client is experiencing some discomfort about the therapy and the therapist. This discomfort should be exposed. Occasionally, however, a candidate for psychotherapy really cannot afford the therapist's fee, and the therapist may modify his fee arrangements without any deleterious effect on the therapy. Although therapists need to be flexible about their fees and time schedules, even in cases where it is clear that the client has a very limited income or a difficult work schedule, a request to alter the fee schedule, the appointment time, or some other ground rule should always be subjected to examination by client and therapist.

Morton O., a single man in his early thirties, sought psychotherapy because he was in frequent disputes with bosses and had been fired from three jobs in the last 4 years. In his first appointment with the therapist, Dr. H., Morton pointed out that he always resented authority and found it difficult to conform to rules and regulations in school, college, and virtually everywhere.

Toward the end of his first interview when Morton and Dr. H. discussed the fee, the two ran into difficulty with each other. Morton told Dr. H. that his rates were exorbitant and that his schedule was extremely rigid. On reviewing Morton's income and expenses, it became quite clear that Morton could afford Dr. H.'s fee but just "could not be a part of something ridiculous and arbitrary." And when it came to working out a mutually convenient appointment time, Morton told Dr. H. that he would "be damned if I'm going to arrange my schedule to suit you." Inasmuch as the time was drawing to a close, Dr. H. suggested that Morton may wish to return for another interview to discuss the fee and appointment time further. Morton broke out in a tirade and exclaimed, "First of all, I deeply resent being cut off in the middle of a sentence. Just because you want to end the appointment doesn't mean that I'm ready to do so. Second of all, you want me to come back here at your convenience and pay you so that we can figure out a fee that will satisfy you. Look man, I think this business of yours may be all right for you, but it is not O.K. with me." Dr. H. told Morton that he realized that Morton had a lot of questions about him and the therapy and that he seemed to resent what appeared to be arbitrary rules. However, if Morton wished, they could meet again. Morton said, "How about right now? Why can't we meet right now?" When Dr. H. said, "We do have to stop," Morton said, "I'll stop, but I don't want to see you ever again."

Morton called Dr. H. 2 weeks after their first appointment and requested another consultation. During the interview, he told Dr. H. that he had been fired from his job and that he could come to see Dr. H. "at any time" inasmuch as he was unemployed. However, Morton went on to say that, because he was unemployed, he did not have any money so he would not be able to afford Dr. H.'s fee of $60 a session. Although Morton had substantial savings, he did not want to use any of it to pay for therapy. Here Dr. H. suggested that Morton may wish to postpone going into treatment until he got a job, or possibly he could find a low-cost clinic that would see him for a fee that would be acceptable to him. Morton responded with a furious attack on Dr. H., "I thought I'd give you a second chance, but I see that you are a money-hungry bastard! You want me to go to a clinic if I can't afford your fee, and you say that you care about people! You are a crook!" As Morton got up to leave, quite a bit ahead of the time the session would have been over, Dr. H. said, "Before you fire me as your therapist, I would like to be paid for these two sessions." Morton sat down and remarked, "You are a persistent bastard, aren't you? You really want your money and that's it. Here I am unemployed, broke, in the middle of all kinds of troubles, I don't have a therapist, and all you care about is getting paid! Well, screw you!" and he left without paying.

After a 3-week interval, Morton called Dr. H. again. He now had a job and one with flexible hours, and he wanted to see if he could work out "some arrangement" with Dr. H. Dr. H. told Morton that they could arrange an appointment to find out if they could work out "some arrangement," but before an appointment could be scheduled, Morton's balance of $120 would have to be paid. To this, Morton slammed down the phone.

A week after the phone call, Dr. H. received a check for $120 in the mail from Morton, and a couple of days later Morton called to make another appointment. In his third appointment, Morton was much more subdued and commented, "You remember when I told you at our first appointment that I have a lot of fights with bosses and other people in authority? Well, I seem to have been doing the same thing with you!" Morton went on to say that he really wanted to find out why rules and regulations upset him so much, because everywhere he went he was "in trouble with the rules of the road." He also pointed out that he liked the way Dr. H. dealt with him, "You don't let me get away with anything but you keep your cool. You know I'm a rebel, but don't seem to get angry about it!"

Morton eventually went into therapy with Dr. II. His major resistance, refusal to adapt to rules, was something that took several years to resolve. Morton experienced being cooperative in a very overdetermined neurotic way. He saw it as anal submission, homosexual yielding, and oral dependency, and he needed time to work out all these issues in his treatment.

Most clients who defy the therapist are people who constantly test limits in all relationships, particularly in their relationships with authorities. In working with these clients, the therapist should recognize that the rebelliousness covers up feelings of vulnerability, weakness, and humiliation. If the therapist neither submits to the client's manipulation nor responds with anger to his provocativeness, the defiant client, most of the time, will enter therapy.

Unrealistic Expectations

Although most individuals who enter psychotherapy recognize that the role of client involves hard work—keeping appointments; paying fees; saying everything that comes to mind; examining embarrassing fantasies, childish wishes, and ugly memories; dealing with sexual and aggressive transference feelings, to name just a few—it is the rare client who does not harbor unrealistic fantasies about the therapy and therapist. Often these unrealistic fantasies emerge in the first few interviews.

We have already suggested what some of the unrealistic expectations of clients are. Many candidates for psychotherapy hope that they will be united with a symbiotic mother (Stone, 1973). Others yearn for an omnipotent parent who will give the answers to life's perplexing questions. Some anticipate that the therapist will intervene in their environments and straighten out those who oppose them. Most clients hope that they will receive reassurance and reinforcement so that their self-esteems will rise quickly and that they will be given the necessary confidence to go out into the world and be loved and admired by everybody.

The unrealistic fantasies that we have just enumerated may be regarded as id resistances—childish wishes that clients try to gratify despite their realization that what they want cannot be attained. Because they persist in trying to be kings and queens, gods and goddesses, lords and ladies, many prospective clients are very depressed and angry because they feel deprived of the love, admiration, brilliance, and riches that they believe are somehow within their reach. They hope the therapist will lead them to the Promised Land.

Coping with clients' id resistances is not an easy task for most therapists, particularly when these resistances appear in the early interviews. When a prospective client has finally summoned up enough courage to call a therapist and bravely tells the clinician that he wants to enter therapy so that he can find a lover, achieve fame, or attain popularity, the therapist has to be very tactful and skillful in responding. If the therapist tells the prospective client that what he seeks cannot be provided, the client may react by feeling so let down that feelings of depression and despondency become intensified, and the wish to forget about being in treatment becomes very powerful. On the other hand, if the therapist promises something that cannot be delivered, the client will eventually feel teased, possibly feel destroyed, and may even become suicidal.

When the client verbalizes unrealistic wishes in the early interviews, the therapist should neither tell the client that the fantasies are unrealistic nor tell him that they can be gratified. Rather when the client presents hopes and expectations that seem farfetched, these fantasies should be explored and the motives that propel them should be understood.

Susan P., a single woman in her twenties, sought therapy because she wanted "to find a man" and felt her therapist could help her do so. She pointed out in her consultation with Dr. G. that she had attended all kinds of parties and gatherings but was not able "to get the man of my dreams." Susan also told Dr. G. that it was her understanding that he would be able to provide her with the proper techniques to get her man.

Dr. G. asked Susan, "Could you tell me about the kind of man that you are looking for?" Susan went on to describe her ideal: "He should be about 6 feet tall, 160 pounds, very handsome, very rich, very warm, very sexual, and very kind. He should be very intelligent and very worldly. He should be a combination of strength, wisdom, and beauty." After a silence, Susan asked, "Do you think my expectations are too high?" Dr. G. asked, "Is that what comes to mind, now?" Susan responded, "Well, sometimes I think that what I'm looking for doesn't exist. I can honestly say that no one I've ever met has approached my dream."

After another silence, during which Susan was eyeing Dr. G., a man whose height and weight came close to the height and weight of her ideal man, Susan blurted out, "I get the impression that you are the type of man I'm looking for. Are you?" Here Dr. G. asked, "Do I appear like the guy who can fill the bill?" Susan said, "I'm not really sure, but I'd like to find out."

In her second interview, Susan was feeling quite euphoric. "I really don't know you, but I think I could make it with you." Dr. G. then encouraged Susan to discuss her fantasies about their living together.

Susan described a blissful existence—"a perfect house with a perfect relationship between us, happy children, great sex, etc." As Susan discussed her fantasies, slowly and subtly she began to appear depressed. When Dr. G. mentioned this to her, Susan said that she was very frightened that, if she and Dr. G. lived together, after a while he would abandon her.

On exploring Susan's fear of being abandoned by Dr. G., client and therapist began to understand the dynamics behind it. Susan slowly uncovered a deep and unresolved oedipal conflict. As she herself stated it, "Daddy was my true love. As a child I secretly wished that he could be mine. When he and Mommy got divorced and I was about 10, I thought I could have him. But he married Shirley, and I guess I have felt abandoned ever since."

It did not take Susan too long to realize that the man she was yearning for was her father who, she felt, abandoned her. However, it took her many years of intensive therapy to resolve her resistance to accepting the fact that her father could not be her lover. She continued to look for father figures, often tried to make Dr. G. her father, and had to work very hard to overcome her resistances.

When a prospective client presents unrealistic fantasies about therapy and the therapist, it is important for the therapist to look at these id resistances much the same way he would view a client's dream. A fantasy, like a dream, contains hidden wishes that should be understood by client and therapist and eventually overcome by the client. If the therapist neither rejects nor promises when the client brings out his fantasies, the client, as in the case of Susan, can begin to appreciate the why's and wherefore's of unrealistic expectations.

COMMON MISTAKES OF THERAPISTS IN RESOLVING RESISTANCES IN THE INITIAL INTERVIEWS

Overzealousness

One of the countertransference problems that particularly beginning therapists show as they conduct their initial interviews with applicants for psychotherapy is an overeagerness to turn applicants into clients and to begin the therapeutic work right away. Although clients usually welcome a clinician who is pleased to work with them, they are often suspicious of those who seem too eager to treat them.

When therapists feel very eager to treat a prospective client, this is a countertransference reaction that needs to be analyzed. Often overeagerness is a manifestation of the therapist's unresolved rescue fantasies. The prospective client may unconsciously represent a parent or sibling whom the practitioner is trying to rescue from another parent or relative. Sometimes the prospective client reminds the therapist of himself, and the therapist wants to take care of the client the way he wished that someone had taken care of him. Therapists often wish for their clients to be the loving parents they never had. Sometimes they want to compete with other therapists, even their own, and demonstrate that they can achieve faster and better therapeutic results.

Dr. F., a therapist in his early thirties, had just started his private practice. He was eager for referrals and therefore was very pleased when he received a phone call asking for his help. The caller, a man in his middle forties, Jack Q., made a very significant slip over the phone. Consciously, Jack wanted to say, "I'm desperately in need of help!" but instead said, "I'm desperately in need of trouble." Dr. F. heard the slip and said to himself that he was probably dealing with a depressed masochist who was "desperately in need of trouble."

Over the phone Jack told Dr. F. that he was obsessing over the idea that his wife was having an extramarital affair. Jack had no proof of the affair, but he could not stop himself from constantly ruminating about it. Dr. F., who had suffered from obsessions himself and learned that what creates obsessions are forbidden wishes, became very eager to help Jack. He was saying to himself, "I'll show him that unconsciously he wants his wife to have an affair, and he'll be cured." To Jack he said, "I have some time today. Come in!"

Jack, despite his statement that he was "desperate," was not able to arrange an appointment with Dr. F. for several days. When he did come in for his first interview, he looked very despondent and agitated. He told Dr. F. about his obsession and mentioned that he was losing sleep and could not function too well on his job. Dr. F. empathized with Jack's plight and told him that he should start treatment three times a week right away "so that we can get to the bottom of this." When Jack said that he couldn't afford to pay for such frequent treatment, Dr. F. said, "Pay me whatever you can!"

Although Jack presented his history cooperatively and seemed to answer questions about his sex life with ease, he never returned for more appointments.

A therapist's overzealousness rarely, if ever, helps a client resolve his initial resistances to treatment. In the above case, the therapist was aware of the fact that his client had an unconscious wish to punish himself and to suffer, but he did not respond well to his client's conflict. Because Jack's suffering was something he unconsciously wanted, the therapist's optimistic statement about helping Jack only compounded Jack's resistances. Furthermore, if a client is obsessed about his wife having an affair, then the client probably unconsciously wants his wife to have an affair, and Dr. F. was aware of this important dynamic in Jack. What Dr. F. did not consider was that Jack was going to resist giving up the obsession. Consequently, when Dr. F. promised to relieve him of "the extramarital obsession," Jack did not want Dr. F. to be his therapist.

If therapists genuinely accept that resistance is a necessary component of therapy, that it protects the individual from real and imaginary dangers, then they can truly appreciate how frightening it is for a prospective client to be face to face with a clinician who is too eager to help.

Overactivity

Throughout this chapter we have reiterated that the most expeditious way for a therapist to help a client resolve initial resistances to therapy is to provide the client with an opportunity to talk. When clients hear themselves freely associate in the presence of an attentive listener, slowly they become sensitive to their wishes for punishment (superego resistances); they start to achieve a dim awareness of their childish fantasies (id resistances); they get an inkling of how they cope with danger by projecting, identifying with the aggressor, etc. (ego resistances); they become motivated to consider how dimensions of their neurotic functioning may offer them some gratification (epinosic gains); and they usually get in touch with fantasies, feelings, and irrational notions about the therapist (transference resistances).

Although most clinicians would not disagree with the notion that the best way to help clients is to provide a safe atmosphere in which they can freely associate, many therapists do not practice what they preach. In their eagerness to convince their clients that they are competent, many therapists present interpretations, clarifications, and confrontations in the first interview. Few clients, however, are impressed.

Aside from the important fact that it is the rare therapist who can be sure of a dynamic formulation after one interview, the therapist's overactivity inevitably induces anxiety in the client, who feels he has to work hard to keep up with his partner in therapy. Furthermore, most clients who seek psychotherapy are intelligent, sophisticated people and become quite wary of the clinician who appears to know so much, so fast. Finally, when the therapist is very active, particularly in initial interviews, the client is apt to feel seduced, punished, or attacked. Uncomfortable with these feelings, the client may wish to leave treatment.

Ms. E., a therapist in a mental hygiene clinic, felt very empathic toward her consultee Rachel R., an 18-year-old college student. In her first interview with Ms. E., Rachel brought out how depressed she felt, how much she missed home, how terribly difficult it was to concentrate on her studies, and how impossible it was to have a social life at the university.

When Ms. E. asked Rachel for her history, it turned out that Rachel was an only child who lived in a small town and got much attention and affection from her parents, extended family, and friends. On hearing this, Ms. E. told Rachel that she was having a great deal of difficulty at the university because the atmosphere was so different from that at home. At home everybody knew her and loved her, and here she did not get very much nurturing. This was making her very angry, Ms. E. told Rachel, but because she did not feel free to discharge her anger, she was turning her anger inward. This was causing Rachel's depression, and her depression sapped her energy so she could not study or relate to others.

Rachel told Ms. E. that her explanations were very informative and helpful, and she made another appointment to discuss her problems further.

Rachel canceled her next two appointments, saying she was ill. When Ms. E. got in touch with Rachel over the phone, it turned out that Rachel had gone to see another therapist. When Ms. E. asked Rachel what went wrong between them, Rachel responded, "To tell you the truth, I got a very upset stomach after our interview. I also kept having nightmares for several days. In the nightmares, some woman was forcing me to eat apples, and if I didn't eat the apples, she would throw them at me and hurt me."

The above illustration demonstrates how a well-meaning therapist who empathizes deeply with her client unwittingly can destroy the treatment. From Rachel's phone conversation with Ms. E., it was quite clear that the therapist's presentation of many interpretations made Rachel feel sick and angry, and she had to go somewhere else to be nurtured.

When therapists find themselves talking a great deal at any time, but particularly during the early interviews, they should examine their feelings closely. Often they are overidentified with the client, as appeared to be true in the above case, or else they may be feeling angry toward the client, competitive with him, or some other emotion that they are not mastering too well.

Praise and Criticism

When therapists empathically attend to their clients' productions and hear about the traumas they have experienced and the pains they have endured, it is extremely tempting to express sorrow for their clients' plights and offer praise for their endurance. It is also tempting to criticize those clients who demean and hurt others but are very self-righteous about their own sadism. Being first and foremost a human being, the clinician has values about "good" and "bad" behavior; consequently, he is going to admire some clients and disdain others.

One of the most difficult tasks in becoming a therapist is suspending judgment so that one can assess a client objectively and not contaminate diagnostic impressions and therapeutic interventions with one's own ethical imperatives. If therapists impose their own values on their clients' productions, the resolution of resistances will be hampered severely. Whenever clients sense that the practitioner feels that their behavior or attitudes are either good or bad, they no longer feel safe to be themselves in the treatment situation. Either they will work hard to get the therapist's approval and struggle valiantly to avoid disapproval, or if they are in a negative transference, they might unconsciously arrange to say and do those things that activate the therapist's criticism.

When therapists praise or criticize their clients, particularly in the first sessions, clients do not receive a proper perspective on how resistances are to be addressed. For example, if a client during his first interview points out how he refrained from telling off his psychotic mother, and the therapist praises him for his self-control, later in treatment the client will not feel as free to examine his resistances against aggression or how he uses aggression as a resistance. The therapist erroneously has given him a model for coping. By the same token, if another client brags about the way she told off her inept husband, who has not been employed for several months, and the therapist criticizes her for this, again the therapist has interfered with the process of resolving the client's resistances inasmuch as the wife's unconscious wishes to live and argue with an inept husband have been sidetracked.

If clients are praised for their achievements and condemned for their failures, particularly if this is done early in treatment, they are being invited, albeit unwittingly, to participate in a structured parent–child relationship rather than being welcomed into a partnership where their resistances will be understood and, it is hoped, resolved.

Barbara T., a married woman in her middle forties, sought treatment for several reasons. She suffered from a severe depression and had psychosomatic problems, severe sexual problems, nightmares, and very poor self-esteem. In her first interview with Dr. D., in which she described her psychotic mother who beat her and her alcoholic father who shunned her, Dr. D. praised her for her "survival ability." Although Barbara did not seem to react to Dr. D.'s praise, near the end of the interview she said, "I take it that it was good never to yell at my parents. I had read that it was a good idea, but I'm glad you confirmed my point of view."

As is clear in the above case, when the therapist praises or condemns, the client cannot examine his resistances with much freedom. Barbara seemed to have strong resistances against the expression of her own murderous fantasies. By rigorously defending against her hateful impulses, she had to pay the enormous price of being very depressed, having many somatic difficulties, and suffering from sexual problems. When her therapist praised her for surviving, he was unaware that he was reinforcing Barbara's resistances and was oblivious to his helping her maintain her severe neurotic difficulties, something that consciously he did not want to do.

Prematurely Announcing the Ground Rules

As we have already pointed out, to work effectively, psychotherapy requires disciplined behavior on the part of both parties. The therapist must keep appointments on time, listen carefully, understand deeply, confront tactfully, and interpret sensitively. He must be aware constantly of the client's resistances and their meaning, and stay alert to his own counter-resistances. These are just a few of the therapist's responsibilities.

Clients, as we know, also have rules to follow. They have appointments to keep and fees to pay. They are asked to say everything that comes to their minds and are required to adapt to many frustrating aspects of the therapeutic encounter.

Many practitioners feel an inner compulsion or a pressing obligation to present all the ground rules of therapy to their clients during the first session. Therapists will tell their prospective clients that they must pay for missed appointments, even when they go on vacations, and that fees should be paid at the last session of the month. Some clinicians, during the first session, will advise their clients that they should not make important decisions during the course of therapy and that changes of jobs, spouses, and residences are proscribed.

When the therapist announces rules and regulations during the first session, he can create the impression that the rules are more important than the client's welfare. Then the practitioner emerges as more of a disciplinarian than an enabler and sets a tone that can alienate the client. Individuals who seek therapy are eager to be understood and helped. When rules and regulations are announced to them, their resistances to therapy and the therapist become exacerbated because the latter tends to appear rigid and insufficiently caring.

What practitioners often overlook is that they have plenty of time to tell their clients about their policies. Sooner or later many clients inquire about them. Sometimes policies never become an issue. However, what seems to create the best atmosphere for therapy is when ground rules are discussed when they pertain to what is currently happening in the treatment. If, for example, a client misses a session and the fee policy has not been discussed yet, the therapist can say, "We have not discussed my policy on fees. I do charge for missed appointments. Inasmuch as we have not discussed it, I will not charge you for yesterday's missed session." Each client will react to this approach in his idiosyncratic manner. Some will experience it as an act of love, and some will experience it as an expression of hatred. But this stance does avoid the problem of announcing rules and regulations early in treatment, when most clients do not want to hear about them.

Usually when therapists announce ground rules in the first session, they are suffering from unrecognized countertransference problems. As is true with most compulsive activity, this is an attempt to cope with some anxiety. They may be worried about being exploited or cheated. They may be frightened that their authority will be usurped. They may be finding it easier to talk than to listen.

Mr. C. had listened to his consultee discuss many problems for about 30 minutes. The prospective client, Harold U., a 30-year-old single man, had been getting some relief as he discussed his feelings connected with the recent death of his father. He was clearly feeling close to the therapist while Mr. C. listened to Harold very attentively. However, the atmosphere of the interview changed dramatically when Mr. C. said, "Before we stop, I'd like to tell you some of my policies." Mr. C. went on to tell Harold his rules about fees when appointments were missed, rules about vacations taken when the therapist was working, and a host of other regulations. Although Harold tried to interrupt Mr. C. several times while the latter was presenting the rules, Mr. C. went on talking about his policies. Harold finally blurted out, "I think you care more about money than you care about your patients" and left Mr. C.'s office, never to return.

Harold went to see another therapist, Ms. B. Alert to what had transpired between Harold and Mr. C., Ms. B. did not discuss fee arrangements with Harold and waited for him to bring it up, which he did in his second interview. Because Harold felt understood by Ms. B. and not pressured to listen to her ground rules, they worked out a mutually satisfactory fee arrangement and a mutually convenient schedule of appointments.

It is very therapeutic for many prospective clients who are preoccupied with their troubles to have a consultation with a therapist who does not discuss any of the rules or regulations of therapy. Feeling listened to and nurtured, these clients by the second or third interview may feel more amenable to discussing certain rules. If therapists are too eager to present ground rules in the first session, resistances are intensified and client dropout is more possible.

Promises! Promises!

Particularly when candidates for psychotherapy have experienced unsatisfactory results with other helpers—parents, teachers, physicians, and other therapists—clinicians often feel a desire to tell clients in their first interviews that their experiences with them will be more rewarding. Feeling competitive with the previous helpers and desirous of getting the clients' confidence and appreciation, they point out without saying it directly that they are superior to their clients' parents, teachers, or therapists. Therefore, they should be trusted and loved.

If clients, during their first interviews, point out that their previous therapists were inactive, some therapists promise that they will be active. If clients complain that significant others were cold, some therapists promise to be warm. Therapists who make such promises want the client to realize that they can do it better.

When therapists promise to deliver something, they fail to realize that they are compounding their clients' resistances and interfering with the therapeutic process. There are many reasons why promising clients good therapeutic results is contrary to sound psychotherapy. First of all, no therapist can be sure in a first interview just what will transpire in a therapeutic relationship. Consequently, promising a client that he will get something is unrealistic. Second, individuals who seek psychotherapy have often been disappointed by broken promises and therefore become very distrustful of those who make promises. Third, and perhaps most important in the resolution of resistances, when therapists promise to behave differently from parents, previous therapists, and others, they set up an atmosphere that makes it difficult for the client to examine his own role in interpersonal relationships. Although parents can be cruel and previous therapists can be insensitive, clients mature the most when they are helped to face their own unique transference resistances, forbidden id wishes, punitive superego voices, and ego defenses. As we discussed in Chapter 2, even when the therapist behaves differently from the clients' parents, certain resistances are bypassed. What is particularly avoided is an examination of the client's internalized voices and an investigation of the client's id wishes that his superego repudiates and his ego opposes. Understanding this struggle is the essence of therapy, and the therapist's promise rarely helps enrich this understanding.

Bob W., a man in his early thirties, found commuting 100 miles to his therapist very tedious, and he was in a phase of his therapy in which he was feeling discouraged. Without discussing it with his therapist, Dr. A., he arranged a consultation with Mrs. Z., whose office was nearby Bob's home.

When Bob told Mrs. Z. that, in addition to finding his commute to Dr. A. difficult, he was annoyed that Dr. A. never gave him any advice, Mrs. Z. reacted very strongly. She told Bob that part of a therapeutic contract involved getting advice and that Bob was entitled to receive it. Although Bob was initially appreciative of Mrs. Z.'s comments, he began to feel uncomfortable with her but did not know why. Although he arranged another appointment with Mrs. Z., he did not keep it.

On discussing his appointment with Mrs. Z., Bob told Dr. A. that her promise of advice, although initially attractive, became upsetting to him. "I kind of felt engulfed and seduced by her," said Bob. "Furthermore, I felt disloyal to you, and she made the feeling of disloyalty stronger. But the main thing I've been working on here is my fear of being independent. If I have some resistance to being independent, and she promises me that she'll give me advice, how will I get better?"

Not only do a therapist's promises tend to compound a client's resistances to autonomy, but when the therapist promises to be different from the client's parents or previous therapists, he raises other difficulties. As we saw in the case of Bob W., when a client listens to his parents or therapist being attacked, he feels disloyal toward them. Feeling that he is betraying them, he finds it difficult to examine his own mixed feelings toward them and his neurotic conflicts become sustained.

Clients present many resistances to getting involved in treatment; some of these resistances become quite apparent in their first interview. The sensitive, empathic, and skilled therapist recognizes that all candidates for psychotherapy feel some danger when they become clients. The therapist also knows that the best way to help the client feel in less jeopardy is to spend most of the time trying to help the client speak his mind. In speaking his mind, the client should realize that the therapist neither praises nor condemns resistive behavior, but wants to make it safe for the client to resist. When the client feels that it is safe to resist, he can embark on a journey with the therapist to learn about the dynamic meaning and the etiology of his resistances.

CHAPTER 4

The First
Treatment Crisis:
Wishes to Flee the Treatment
and Other Impasses

If therapist and client have weathered the storms of the initial interviews and the early resistances to treatment have been worked out, the client usually moves into a positive transference. Most experienced clinicians have noted that the client who has been the recipient of attentive, empathic, listening enters into a phase of therapy that has been called "the honeymoon" (Fine, 1982). This therapeutic honeymoon usually begins around the third or fourth month of treatment and can last for several months and even up to a year or more.

During the therapeutic honeymoon, clients feel a sense of optimism, have many insights, and discover dimensions of their psyches that until now have been repressed. There are several reasons for their positive state of mind. First of all, unlike most relationships in which clients have been involved, in the therapeutic encounter all the attention is on them. When they are with their therapists, clients do not have to be concerned with other people's dilemmas, anxieties, and exhortations. This kind of relationship induces in most clients a feeling of importance and raises their self-esteem. Second, when clients unburden themselves and discuss embarrassing moments, shameful episodes, and infantile fantasies, the sensitive therapist does not judge or criticize them; he listens and tries to understand. Most clients feel very relieved when the anticipated punishment is not forthcoming. When guilt-ridden, self-effacing individuals who expect retribution, condemnation, and attack for their real or imagined transgressions receive in interview after interview warmth, kindness, and empathy instead, they begin to feel liberated and their self-images improve. They start to like themselves more, and consequently, they appreciate and like other people more. As they show increased warmth toward others, they are received more positively, and in response to other people's high regard, they feel that they are more desirable individuals. Finally, as clients feel less guilt and more self-worth, hope is rekindled in them and they start to esteem the therapist and value the therapy.

Inasmuch as the honeymoon phase is ubiquitous, many short-term therapists have contended that clients get the most out of treatment during the first several months. They then conclude that all therapy should be limited to several months (Eysenk, 1952; Freeman, 1981; Hepworth, 1979). What the advocates of short-term therapy tend to overlook, however, is that the therapeutic honeymoon, like all honeymoons, is a short-term affair. Like lovers who are ecstatic in a romance but cannot sustain their manic state for too long, clients in therapy cannot sustain their intense positive transferences toward their therapists forever.

Toward the end of a honeymoon, lovers frequently replace positive feelings with negative ones. Clients do the same thing: they shift their feelings toward their therapists after the therapeutic honeymoon has ended. The first treatment crisis (Fine, 1982; Glover, 1955) is characterized by a negative transference, and many clients threaten to leave treatment at this time. This crisis is caused by many factors and takes many forms. Just as lovers after a honeymoon are required to accept the hard fact that their partners cannot meet all their needs, many clients become furious with their therapists who have not supplied them with sufficient relief, self-confidence, and admiration. On the other side of the coin, just as some lovers cannot tolerate the pleasures of being loved and given to consistently and have to provoke arguments to relieve themselves of guilt, there are some clients who cannot tolerate their therapists' nonjudgmental, caring attitudes and seek to provoke the therapists into punishing them. Furthermore, just as children are shocked when adults do not reprimand them for their sexual preoccupations and aggressive fantasies, many clients are shocked that their therapists, who are often experienced as parental figures, do not reprimand them for their id productions in therapy.

Although some clients will leave therapy during the first treatment crisis regardless of the therapist's activity, if therapists can accept the first crisis as an unalterable fact of therapeutic life, they can help most of their clients resolve this first major expression of resistance, and treatment can go on productively. In this chapter, we look at the many manifestations of the first treatment crisis, assess the dynamics of clients' resistances at this phase of therapy, and examine the role of the therapist as he attends to the therapeutic impasses that transpire during the first treatment crisis.

EXPRESSIONS OF THE FIRST TREATMENT CRISIS

Therapist is Not Omnipotent

As we have suggested in earlier chapters, virtually all clients in psychotherapy unconsciously yearn for an omnipotent parent who will rescue them from their dilemmas, protect them from their enemies, and deliver them to a Garden of Eden (Freud, 1937a). Clients further hope that they will no longer feel frustrated, never feel deprived again, and always enjoy a blissful existence. As the therapist devotes so much of himself to the client's psychological welfare, these childish fantasies are stimulated and many clients dream of being adopted and then treasured by their therapists. Sooner or later, hopes get punctured and the client begins to question the value of the therapy and the expertise of the therapist.

It is important for the practitioner to realize that, when clients feel disappointed that the therapist is not the omnipotent and omniscient parent that they hoped they would have, they usually do not voice their resentments directly; they express fault with the therapy and the therapist in indirect, often subtle, ways. They may complain that sessions are too short, that the fees are too costly, that the therapist is too quiet, or that the appointment schedule is too inconvenient (Greenson, 1967).

When therapists hear their clients' complaints, some tend to become defensive. They may remind their clients that the fees are really quite reasonable or that the appointment schedule is eminently fair. If therapists do become defensive, clients feel misunderstood and become even more vituperative. Then therapeutic impasses grow stronger, and clients may abruptly terminate the treatment. Other practitioners, on hearing their clients' criticisms, cope with their anxieties differently. They try to modify their behavior and become more talkative or extend the therapeutic sessions and hope that this will dissipate their clients' negative feelings. When clients are indulged, it does not help them, either. They feel guilty for having been manipulative and also contemptuous of the therapist, whom they experience as having become too vulnerable. They may leave treatment, too (Fenichel, 1945).

It is absolutely crucial for therapists during the first treatment crisis not to defend themselves or apologize. They should continue to help their clients express all their criticisms of the therapy. When clients observe, over time, that their therapists neither praise nor condemn them for their attacks, but continue to listen empathically, most clients renew their positive feelings toward the therapist and begin to examine the dynamic meaning of their criticisms. As we have noted, the client's expression of hostility toward the therapist is usually accompanied by a feeling of relief, and as Fine has suggested, "the therapist, by adopting a neutral, relatively passive role offers (the client) no real cause for anger. Hence, when this feeling does come up he or she is in a position to trace the anger to its childhood roots or to explain it in terms of present-day dynamics" (Fine, 1982, p. 140).

Joan Z., a married woman in her early forties, came to treatment because of sexual problems. Unable to be orgastic with her husband, she felt depressed and suffered from low self-esteem. During her first 3 months of treatment with her male therapist, Dr. A., she made a lot of progress. She felt less antagonistic toward her husband and others, became less depressed, and began to like herself more. However, after a therapeutic honeymoon that extended into the fifth month of her three-times-a-week treatment, she began to feel very disappointed with her therapy and her therapist. She felt that he did not like her very much, did not appreciate her sufficiently as a sexual woman, and seemed bored with her. When Joan told Dr. A. that she thought it might be a good idea for her to switch to a woman therapist because Dr. A. could not really empathize with her wish for closeness with him and, in addition, seemed to squelch her attempts to be more intimate, Dr. A. asked Joan what about his behavior gave her these impressions. Belligerently Joan declared, "You hardly ever smile at me, you never praise me, all you do is listen." When Dr. A. remained silent, Joan said, "Don't just sit there! Defend yourself! Argue with me! Tell me that I'm wrong or that I'm right!" After another silence, Joan went on, "You have a fear of intimacy. You are terrified to get involved with me." Realizing that Joan was projecting her own fear of intimacy onto him, Dr. A. asked Joan what she thought his fears of intimacy were all about.

Joan began to analyze Dr. A. "You are afraid of being dominated and demeaned. You probably had a mother who bossed you around. You are a coward," she stated triumphantly and sarcastically. As Dr. A. encouraged Joan to talk more about her perceptions of him, she became more self-observant. In one of her dreams at this time, she had Dr. A. trying to embrace her, but she rejected him. When Dr. A. asked Joan what thoughts she had about her rejecting his embraces, she began to associate to her "sexy father" whose "hairy chest" and "suave demeanor" irritated her. Because Dr. A. was neither defensive nor offensive, Joan could begin to become aware of the childhood roots of her sexual problems. She later realized that her dissatisfaction with her husband and with Dr. A. emanated, in large part, from her very ambivalent feelings toward her father. As she recalled more memories that involved her father, her first treatment crisis slowly dissolved. In one of her sessions, around the tenth month of treatment, Joan reflected, "I wanted a perfect daddy who would love me perfectly and admire me all the time. I hated his guts for treating me as just a nice daughter. Although he loved mommy, he could have said once in a while, 'I'll be your perfect man, and you'll be my perfect lady.' The son of a bitch never said that."

Although some clients, like Joan, handle their frustrated yearnings by direct attacks on the therapist, other clients who really are feeling a lot of hostility toward the therapist are frightened of their own rage and attack themselves. The therapist should not be lulled into thinking that the masochistic behavior these clients show is just self-loathing (W. Reich, 1949). These clients are angry at the therapist and need help in bringing their anger to consciousness. They are furious at the practitioner for not being a perfect, powerful parent, but take the position that it is their fault because they are not better sons or daughters.

Richard Y., a graduate student in his midtwenties, was being seen by Ms. B. in a mental health center. Richard's difficulty was that he could not concentrate and absorb what he was studying. In addition, he was feeling lonely and socially isolated, having just left home for the first time in his life.

Richard did quite well for the first 2 months of treatment. He welcomed Ms. B. into his life with open arms inasmuch as he had been so lonely. Experiencing himself as the recipient of much love and concern, he soon became able to master his work at school and tried attending a few socials on campus.

Although Richard was improving in most areas of life, during his third month of treatment he expressed concern that he was only getting B's in his schoolwork and had not yet acquired a girl friend for himself. The therapist, not realizing that Richard was showing manifestations of his first treatment crisis and was turning aggression really aimed at Ms. B. against himself, began to reassure Richard. She told him that he was away from home for the first time and that he should not expect so much from himself. While Richard acknowledged that the therapist had a point, nonetheless, he continued his self-attacks. Again, Ms. B. reassured him, and again Richard berated himself and said that maybe he should become a graduate school dropout!

In supervision Ms. B. learned that Richard's complaints about school were really a displacement of his dissatisfactions about the therapy and that his attacks on himself were really disguised attacks on her. She also realized that her attempts to reassure Richard were keeping his aggression toward her from becoming conscious.

Ms. B. shifted her stance. When Richard resumed his self-abnegation, Ms. B. asked him what he thought was standing in his way of doing better. Surprised, Richard said, "You got me there!" and after a silence, "I guess this therapy confuses me." With help from Ms. B., he went on to say that he did not know how talking helped. He wanted something more. He wanted some praise from Ms. B., some recognition that he was better than most graduate students, and some statement from her that he was more interesting than her other clients.

As Richard vented some of his wrath directly at Ms. B. and as he saw that she maintained her neutrality, he began to consider some of the forces in his own childhood that were accounting for his dilemmas in therapy. "All my life, I received a lot of attention and affection from my parents, from my family, and from peers. Coming here to J. University has been a culture shock. I guess I really want you to be my loving mommy and loving daddy rolled into one!"

When clients project omnipotence onto the therapist, it is very important for the therapist not to fall into the trap of taking over their clients' burdens. Usually these clients' major defense in their interpersonal relationships has been to find some figure on whom they can unload their problems. This defense becomes a resistance in the therapeutic situation, and to resolve it, therapists must have faith in their clients' own capacities and leave most of life's responsibilities to them. Although initially clients will protest that the task of self-initiative (Erikson, 1950) is overwhelming, they gradually learn that they can carry many of their own burdens by themselves (Fine, 1982; Menninger, 1973). If their dependency wishes are gratified by the therapist, they cannot mature.

Client Suggests a New Therapeutic Modality

In this day and age, when many different therapeutic modalities are popular, clients understandably wonder about participating in them. Many clients after being in one-to-one treatment for a few months suggest to the therapist that maybe they should consider conjoint marital counseling, family treatment, or group therapy, either in addition to or in lieu of the therapy they are already receiving. Because therapists also wonder about certain advantages of therapies other than the kind they are conducting, it is quite easy for them to agree with a client who says, "My treatment will be accelerated if we bring my wife (husband) here; let's face it, I have marital problems, so the marriage should be treated." A therapist can also be convinced by a client's statement such as the following: "One of the things that I've always wanted to do is to improve my interpersonal relationships. I think group therapy will help me more than this treatment does."

Besides suggesting that the therapeutic modality should be changed, some clients after a few months of treatment point out that, in addition to their psychotherapy, it would be a good idea if they received tranquilizers or some other form of medication. As one client stated it, "I can go on trying to understand the reasons for my insomnia, but if I take medicine, it will help me faster."

It is axiomatic in dynamic psychotherapy that every request of every client should be explored. The reason for this is that, behind the manifest content of a logical request, as behind a dream, are latent fantasies that should be understood by both therapist and client. Hence, regardless of the merits of other modalities that the client is interested in, a request for a different modality should always be explored. When the request is examined, the therapist will ascertain, in almost every instance, that the client is in a state of resistance. Subtly the client is saying, "I'm dissatisfied with this treatment, and I have some questions about you." This dissatisfaction is an expression of the client's hostility toward the therapist and should be viewed as part of the first treatment crisis. When the therapist complies with the client's request and modifies or switches the therapy, aggressive fantasies toward the therapist are squelched, transference fantasies are ignored, neurotic conflicts are maintained, and resistances go unresolved.

When therapists are not confident of the treatment that they are offering, they can rationalize modifications in it. They can point out that they are not omnipotent, so it would be a good idea for the client to have two therapists and learn that no one person has all the answers. Or else, they can speak of "diluting an intense transference," which they believe will be in the client's best interest.

A joint willingness of client and therapist to change the therapeutic modality is almost always a sign of resistance and counterresistance. If clients are pleased with their therapy and therapists, and feel entitled to what they are getting, these changes would not be sought. Furthermore, if therapists believe that all behavior has meaning, they will investigate their clients' bids for modifying the treatment and, in all likelihood, will find out that their clients are masking negative transference feelings.

Shirley W., a woman in her early thirties, had been in treatment with Mr. C. for 6 months. She entered therapy when she became convinced that she was unable to sustain relationships with men. As soon as the interaction between her and a man became intimate, she withdrew.

In her treatment with Mr. C., after some initial resistances were resolved, she moved into a positive transference and told Mr. C. that, in contrast to her previous relationships with men, she felt understood and appreciated by Mr. C. As treatment progressed and Shirley was feeling more comfortable with men on the job and in her social life, she suggested to Mr. C. that she drop one of the two sessions per week that she had with him and start group therapy. Mr. C., aware that Shirley dropped her contacts with men when relationships became more intimate, suggested that "we explore your idea."

On hearing Mr. C.'s suggestion, Shirley became defensive and argumentative. She told Mr. C., "I don't see why you want to ask about it. Just accept my idea! If you question my idea, I feel you are questioning me." After a silence, Shirley became more belligerent and said, "You think that you are a big shot and the only one who can help me. Well, you are wrong, and I'm going to prove it." She went on to say that Mr. C. was just like her father—"always controlling and always dominating."

As Shirley and Mr. C. continued to analyze her request for group therapy, Shirley brought in several dreams and fantasies in which she was at group sessions "getting along famously with guys" and gossiping about Mr. C.'s "rigid Freudian position." After a while, Mr. C. was able to interpret to Shirley that her desire to go into group therapy was motivated in part by a wish to make him jealous of the other men in her life and to weaken her relationship with him. Shirley told Mr. C. that his interpretation "had no foundation" and that he was "a jerk."

Because Mr. C. was able to maintain his composure, eventually Shirley was able to investigate her contempt of him. She realized how much she "loathed a one-to-one relationship," and because of this recognition, she continued to examine her conflicts with men in her treatment and did not go ahead with group therapy.

By viewing a client's wish to modify or change the treatment as a resistance, we are not at this time arguing for the superiority of any one therapeutic modality. If a client is in family treatment or conjoint marital counseling and wants to enter one-to-one treatment, the request should be investigated. Inevitably, client and therapist will learn that the client is feeling some resentment about the treatment in which he is presently engaged.

When the therapist, without exploring the client's request, acquiesces to the client's suggestion and agrees to modify the treatment, the client usually responds by resenting the therapist and questioning his competence. Although this reaction may be a transference reaction in large part, the practitioner in one way or another is acknowledging that he cannot cope with the client's resistances (Langs, 1981).

Nathan V., a man in his mid forties, was in treatment with Ms. D. He had been in therapy because of potency problems in his marriage and conflicts emerging from his involvement in an extramarital affair. He had been doing reasonably well in his therapy and was beginning to feel closer to his wife, when during the eighth month of therapy, Nathan requested some marital counseling that would involve Nathan's wife, Rena, and himself, in conjoint treatment with Ms. D. Ms. D. thought that the idea was "splendid" and agreed to see Nathan and Rena together in one session per week and Nathan alone for another session.

Although at first, Nathan liked the new treatment arrangement, he began to feel impatient with it after about 6 weeks. In his sessions alone with Ms. D., he pointed out that his marital problems were all caused by Rena and that "she should be the patient, not me. She's the sick one." As Ms. D. listened to Nathan's complaints, she realized eventually that they were really complaints about her. In one session, when Nathan said, "I want a woman who will stand by my side come hell or high water," Ms. D. was able to sense that Nathan felt abandoned by her. Ms. D. suggested that seeing him with his wife, although he wanted this arrangement, nonetheless made Nathan feel abandoned by his therapist. Nathan replied, "Yes, I guess I felt I was too much for you and that I'm too much for any woman!" Although Ms. D. tried to help Nathan feel less rejected by her, he left treatment prematurely.

Some clients and some therapists maintain that certain symptoms of the client should be treated separately. As a result, there are clients in psychotherapy who are being treated for most of their problems, but certain conflicts are brought to a different therapist. When therapists send their clients to a marital therapist or a diet specialist or a vocational counselor, they have lost their objectivity. They have failed to appreciate that a marital conflict, for example, is no different from any other neurotic conflict. The client here is unable to face infantile wishes, superego commands, and maladaptive ego defenses that exist in his marital interaction. If the therapist recognizes that all chronic marital complaints are really unconscious wishes, then these unconscious wishes should come out in the therapy. Nathan, in the above example, had to come to grips with the fact that unconsciously he wanted to be impotent with Rena—it was safer than being potent with her. Potency frightened him. Furthermore, if the therapist does not take sides in a marital conflict, he will soon discover that the chronic marital complaint will be expressed in the client's major resistance—the transference. Nathan could not bear feeling potent with Ms. D. either and had to weaken their relationship. Conjoint marital counseling reinforced his conflicts with women. He could not tolerate being alone with one woman for too long.

If therapists find themselves ready to acquiesce when the first treatment crisis manifests itself by the client's wish to change the therapeutic modality, they should ask themselves what negative feelings of the client and what anxious feelings in themselves they do not want to face.

Fear of Intimacy

As we have seen, for many clients an intimate relationship is terrifying. Although clients defend against recognizing it, very often their neurotic conflicts as manifested in marriage, in parent–child interaction, on the job, or in social transactions are expressions of their dread of intimacy. For many people, intimacy conjures up fantasies that they will be eaten up, controlled, or dominated, or have their freedom and individuality taken away from them. Invariably, the fear of intimacy constitutes one of the major causes of the first treatment crisis.

While clients often react positively to the new intimacy that a psychotherapeutic relationship provides, sooner or later they begin to question it (Fine, 1982). The empathic listening of the therapist eventually stirs up dependency wishes, which create anxiety. Fears of homosexual submission, forbidden incestuous fantasies, and other immature cravings can turn an enthusiastic and well-motivated client into one who is apathetic and resistive.

Although all clients involved in psychotherapy have childish wishes for a symbiotic relationship and want to be impulsive, to regress, and to be passive, most clients resist acknowledging these fantasies. Particularly when these fantasies become part of the transference relationship with the therapist, most clients cringe and want to flee from treatment. As is true with most resistive behavior, clients do not say that they are terrified of the intimate relationship with the therapist. On the contrary, clients point out that the therapist is too hungry for contact, too obsessed with sexual material, or too intrusive. They state that they would like more feedback rather than have the therapist sit back silently while they suffer with unacceptable thoughts that the therapist is forcing them to verbalize (Schafer, 1983).

Sarah U., a 19-year-old college student, was in therapy with a woman therapist, Dr. E., in a college mental health clinic. In treatment Sarah spoke of her professors as "too authoritarian," her roommates as "too snobbish," and the college curriculum as "too dogmatic." She ascribed her insomnia, lack of appetite, and depression to "the lousy climate" of the college she was attending.

After 2 months of treatment in which she used her sessions for catharsis and brought out her resentment toward those with whom she was in contact at the college, Sarah felt a lot better and her symptoms diminished. Although she had nothing much to say about her therapy or her therapist during the 2 months of twice-a-week treatment, in her third month she began arriving at her sessions late, canceled one or two of them, and had little to say about anything in her life when she met with Dr. E.

On noting her resistant behavior, Dr. E. asked Sarah, "What are you feeling toward me these days?" Although at first Sarah averred that she had no feelings toward Dr. E., with encouragement Sarah was able to point out that she thought there was something "peculiar" about Dr. E.'s manner. Subjecting herself to examination, Dr. E. learned that Sarah had some thoughts that maybe Dr. E. was a lesbian.

Sarah's profound discomfort and intense embarrassment were quite visible as she talked about her fear that Dr. E. would sexually seduce her. When Dr. E. asked Sarah how she thought this was going to happen, Sarah, with some hesitation, talked about how at the end of an interview Dr. E. was going to grab her, undress her, and overpower her. With Dr. E. maintaining a quiet and cool demeanor, eventually Sarah was able to say that she had entertained homosexual fantasies from the start of treatment and had them at other times in her life, too. Sarah was able to bring in dreams where women about Dr. E.'s age were having sexual play with her. As client and therapist reviewed Sarah's fears, fantasies, and dreams, Sarah could eventually accept the interpretation that she projected her own homosexual wishes onto other women and then had to stay away from these women because she was afraid that she would act out her sexual wishes. As Sarah talked more freely about her sexual wishes, her treatment crisis dissolved.

In working with a client's fear of homosexuality, the therapist has to feel comfortable with this very charged issue. Some therapists because of their own anxiety become too reassuring, whereas others become too evasive. It is important for the client to feel safe in looking at forbidden homosexual fantasies, and this can best be achieved when the therapist's resistance to facing homosexual fantasies is at a minimum. Then he can feel free to be the object of homosexual fantasies or the object of scorn for having them.

Fear of Aggression

Most clients in psychotherapy have trouble with their aggression. Many cannot differentiate between normal, healthy assertiveness and abnormal, pathological violence. To disagree, criticize, or object is for many clients tantamount to being murderous. One of the main reasons for this confusion is that some clients harbor unconscious murderous fantasies toward people with whom they disagree or of whom they are critical. Consequently, when they assert themselves, they worry about how antagonistic and violent they may become.

In the therapeutic situation, because clients are encouraged to say everything that comes into their minds, inevitably they are going to have some critical thoughts toward the therapist. They may dislike the therapist's office, they may abhor the therapist's attire, they may hate the therapist's speech, or they may reject his complete demeanor. Because clients often perceive the therapist as a parent, they cannot easily accept these hostile feelings. They worry about retaliation, retribution, loss of love, or even being thrown out of treatment. Fearful of their angry fantasies, they repress them and become depressed.

One fairly common manifestation of the first treatment crisis is a moderate to severe depression in the client. When therapists observe this depression, it may activate anxiety in them. On seeing that the client, after feeling better for a while, starts to appear more apathetic, hopeless, and discouraged than he did when treatment first began, therapists may question their own competence and lose their own objectivity. Worried that the client will become suicidal, want to be hospitalized, or threaten to see another therapist, many therapists, out of their own desperation, become too active. By their overactivity, they may exacerbate their clients' symptoms instead of helping them get some relief from their depression.

When clients observe their therapists abruptly prescribing drugs, recommending more treatment sessions, or making many interpretations, they become quite frightened. They ask themselves, "If my therapist is very worried about me, and he must be if he is doing all that work, then I must be quite crazy!"

Not only can the therapist's overactivity cause many clients to question their own sanity, but therapeutic overactivity can rarely, if ever, resolve the resistances that sustain a depression. A depression evolves, as we have pointed out, when clients do not feel free to assert themselves because they are very frightened that they will become too violent. Consequently, they squelch their hostility, turn it against themselves, and become depressed. If the therapist is very giving to these clients in the sessions and becomes very busy in their clients' behalves outside of the sessions, the clients' negative transferences cannot be resolved because they are not being provided with an opportunity to discharge their hostility. It is asking too much from any client to express rage toward the therapist when the latter is an all-giving dispenser of drugs, advice, and interpretations.

A very common error therapists make during a first treatment crisis when the client is depressed and not voicing resentment is to encourage and even pressure the client to ventilate hostility. At first blush, this seems to be an eminently desirable plan. A clinician can reason as follows: "The client is miserable and depressed because he is holding back hostility. So, I'll encourage the client to release the hostility, and all will be well." What is overlooked here is what we know about resistances. The client's depression is used as a resistance against the expression of hostility because the client experiences the ventilation of hostility as something dangerous. The client would not be depressed in the first place unless he was so terribly frightened of hostile thoughts toward the therapist. Therefore, when the therapist encourages or pressures a depressed client to ventilate hostility, the client can only experience this activity of the therapist as cruel seduction or tormenting sadism. He feels like a frightened little child who is being pressured to fight a big bully.

When the practitioner notes that a client is depressed and it becomes clear that the depression is being used to ward off hostile thoughts toward the therapist, the practitioner should work with the client's fear of expressing criticism toward the therapist. The therapist should try to maintain an equidistant attitude (A. Freud, 1946) toward the client's conflict and point out to the client: "You are very frightened of your anger toward me. If you express it, you worry what will happen to me and what I will think of you. So you hold back your anger and are depressed." When clients feel that their therapists are relating to their complete psyches and not to just parts of them, they feel well understood. Then they can usually go on to speak their minds to their therapists. However, if they feel pressured or encouraged to discharge what they believe their therapists want to hear, they become more defensive and then may want to leave treatment. Most clients, particularly when depressed, need a hypothetical interpretation similar to the one mentioned above. It relates to the entire conflict of the client. Reference to the anger relates to the client's *id* wish; comments about the client's fear of the therapist's censure relate to *superego* commands; and the statement about the client's holding back relates to the *ego* and its defenses.

Matt T., a man in his early fifties, was in treatment with Dr. F., a psychiatrist. Matt sought treatment because he found it difficult to assert himself on the job, in his marriage, and in relationships with friends. An intelligent research scientist, Matt easily became intimidated by people, stammered and stuttered, and then withdrew from the interpersonal situation. In his withdrawals, he often became depressed and had suicidal fantasies.

At the beginning of his treatment, Matt became intrigued with Dr. F.'s observation that Matt was afraid of showing off his intelligence and that that accounted for his feeling intimidated by so many people. Matt began to speak more forcefully, vigorously, and confidently. His stuttering and stammering diminished a great deal, and he began to feel much more pleasure on the job and in his interpersonal relationships.

As treatment moved on, Matt became aware of competitive fantasies that had been repressed during most of his life. As he started to realize, during his sixth month of therapy, that he harbored many wishes to wipe out both father figures and sibling figures, Matt became quite depressed. His stammering and stuttering returned, his self-confidence diminished, and he began to feel suicidal again.

When Dr. F prescribed some medication for his depression, Matt complied with his psychiatrist's directives. However, the medication did not relieve Matt's depression. Instead, it made him feel jittery and tense. A short while after this, Matt asked, "Do you think I'm just one of those patients who can't be cured?" Dr. F., not noting the latent negative feelings that were being expressed toward him, reassured Matt and told him that he would get better soon. He had done well up until recently. All he needed was to come and visit Dr. F. three times a week instead of twice a week. Again, Matt complied with Dr. F.'s prescription and began to see his therapist three times a week. Now Matt began to become profoundly depressed. He was convinced that the increased frequency of his appointments was arranged "because I am falling apart."

Dr. F., feeling increasingly anxious by Matt's deteriorating condition, sought psychoanalytic consultation on his work with Matt. He learned from his consultant that Matt was acting out in his therapy his competition with father and sibling figures. Matt was viewing Dr. F. as a competitor and unconsciously was trying to defeat him. By getting worse, he was showing that Dr. F. was not such a competent therapist after all.

Dr. F. was buoyed by his consultation and immediately used the information in his work with Matt. He told Matt that their work got sidetracked after they had discussed Matt's competition with men. Matt agreed that it was after that he had been going downhill. Here Dr. F. interpreted, "You see, Matt, you are also competitive with me. You are not getting well because you want to defeat me." Matt vehemently denied Dr. F.'s interpretation and told him that, although he respected Dr. F. and valued his professional opinion, Matt would be working against himself if he were to compete with Dr. F. Feeling frustrated, Dr. F. became more active with Matt and told him, "You've got to fight it out with me and feel free to compete with me." The more Dr. F. encouraged Matt to compete with him and air his hostility, the more resistant Matt became. He denied his competition and hostility more and more, and became very depressed. Dr. F., in his discouragement about the therapy and anger toward Matt for not getting better, accused Matt of being stubborn and having a negative therapeutic reaction (Freud, 1923a). Soon after, Matt quit treatment and went to another therapist.

From the above case, we see how resistances can never be bypassed. Patiently, client and therapist must study what the therapeutic impasse is all about and determine together what it is that the client dreads. It is more important for client and therapist to understand the nature of the client's fears than it is to encourage the client to express frightening thoughts and feelings. As we saw in the case of Matt, when he was pushed to voice his hostility, he became more resistant and depressed. This is usually what happens to most clients when they are pressured rather than understood. It is particularly likely to occur when a depressed client is encouraged to ventilate hostility. Not only is the depressed client terrified of hostility, he is also trying to defeat the therapist. If the therapist wants the client to voice rage, the client will probably do the opposite and become more depressed.

Therapist as Superego

We have repeatedly seen how the client makes the therapist into a superego. This phenomenon has been observed by virtually every writer who has examined the psychotherapeutic process in depth (O. Fenichel, 1945; Fine, 1982; A. Freud, 1946; Freud, 1926; Greenson, 1967; W. Reich, 1949; Schafer, 1983) and accounts for the client's constant readiness to be criticized, demeaned, or rejected by the therapist. It also explains why the client frequently wants reassurance, praise, and approval from the therapist. If reassured, praised, and approved, most clients feel less guilty.

As therapy moves on, it is the rare client who does not anticipate at some time some negative response from the therapist. Particularly when the client discharges murderous wishes and sexual urges, he cannot believe that the therapist is consistently nonjudgmental and nonpunitive. "How can she still approve of me when I told her I hated her, hated my mother, hated my wife, and hated every other woman?" a male client may ask after 6 months of therapy. A female client may wonder, "I told him that he is a male chauvinist, a dope, and a nonsexual bore—how can he still want to see me?"

Another one of the major factors that precipitate the first treatment crisis is the client's unconscious wish for superego punishment. Convinced that they are being demeaned, criticized, and rejected for their sexual and aggressive wishes, most clients sooner or later aggress toward the therapist because he appears "so cold, withdrawn, critical, and nonsupportive." If the therapist does not react defensively or offensively to these attacks, this can be a very important turning point in the therapy.

Many clients learn that it is they, not other people, who are their own worst enemies when they see that, upon criticizing their therapists for being unempathic or uncaring, their therapists continue to be interested in them and concerned about them. Consequently, as we have reiterated constantly, when the therapist is being attacked, it is crucial that he not respond in kind (Schafer, 1983). If the client feels accepted for whatever his thoughts are, his own superego will diminish in its punitiveness. Furthermore, it is important during the first treatment crisis for therapists to keep in mind that they are being attacked because they are being experienced as unloving. The last thing they want to do is become punitive.

When therapists are experienced as punitive superegos, not only are clients angry at them for being so critical, but clients want to get rid of these punitive characters for being so controlling. Many clients say during the first treatment crisis, "If I didn't have you to contend with, I'd be liberated. I could have sex, be aggressive, and do everything I want, and I wouldn't have to account to you." If clients are convinced that life would be a lot easier if they did not have to account to their therapists, it may be inferred that these clients have succeeded in projecting their own superegos onto their therapists and expect their therapists to punish them in the same way they have been punishing themselves most of their lives.

When clients are convinced that leaving treatment will provide them with more autonomy, it is very tempting to point out to them that they will be taking their problems and their own superegos with them. However, such an interpretation will usually make them feel more controlled and more judged. It should be remembered that the client is trying to provoke a fight with the therapist and prove that, indeed, the therapist is attempting to curb the client's freedom. Consequently, warnings about not leaving treatment can compound resistances, with the client ending up convinced that the therapist wants to order him around.

When the client contends that the therapist is a punitive judge from whom the client must flee, the client's wish to leave treatment and his perception of the therapist must be given serious attention. The client should be asked what the therapist is doing that gives the client the impression that he is being negatively evaluated. In considering this question, many clients are able to see their own projections quite readily. Others are not able to do so and need more time to tell the therapist what the latter is against and why he is against it. As clients observe that the therapist does not reprimand them or become defensive, they can more ably differentiate between their own introjects and the reality of the therapist's attitude (Strachey, 1934). When they start to believe that the therapist is not such a difficult taskmaster, they become less rough on themselves.

Debbie S., a single woman in her middle twenties, was in treatment with a male psychologist, Dr. G. During her first 4 months of twice-a-week therapy, Debbie had been making a lot of progress. The product of a very repressive background in which both parents were fanatically religious and very authoritarian, Debbie used her therapy to vent much resentment about her "rigid parents." As she did so, she became much less depressed and began enjoying her job as an elementary school teacher much more.

Although Debbie had made no reference to Dr. G., during her fifth month of treatment, sessions began to become replete with comments about how much Debbie was convinced that Dr. G. felt very critical of her. Debbie told Dr. G. that she had the impression that he thought she was too aggressive, complained too much, and had nothing pleasant to say. When Dr. G. asked Debbie what gave her that impression, Debbie said, "It's nothing that you have said. It's in your attitude." When Dr. G. remained silent, Debbie went on to say, "I think you've been polite and courteous, but I know you hate me."

On trying to answer Dr. G. about why he hated her, Debbie pointed out, "Nobody likes to hear someone rant and rave. For the first few months of treatment, I did it toward my parents and now I've put you on the spot. I guess you hate me for my aggressive thoughts and deeds." Debbie at this point threatened to leave treatment, feeling that she was "shackled" by the therapist and that life would be better without him. She said, "I can't stand being with someone who hates me."

As Dr. G. maintained his calm interest in Debbie, she slowly could start to see how she was making him her "authoritarian and rigid parents" and her own authoritarian and rigid superego. As she started to see some of the differences between her own internalized voices and the therapist's realistic attitude, she began to feel less oppressed in her therapy and more comfortable in looking at some of her own aggressive and sexual wishes. She needed several months of consistently telling Dr. G. that he hated her for her aggression and of consistently seeing that all Dr. G. did was try to understand her without being defensive or offensive.

Sometimes, as in the case of Debbie, it is tempting for the therapist to point out quite early that the client is making him the punitive parent. But this gets the therapist off the hook too quickly. Usually when clients are permitted to complain about the therapist and the therapist listens empathically, clients begin to recall memories of their parents and see on their own that they are distorting the therapist. It is only after clients repeatedly criticize the therapist for being too much of a superego and do not connect this to their own introjects is it appropriate for the therapist to show clients how the past is being recapitulated in the transference.

Fear of Change

Most clients in psychotherapy have some notions about how they should turn out when treatment ends. What they should be like is different from what they fantasize they would like to be. The latter usually pertains to id wishes—to be omnipotent, to be omniscient, to be beautiful, to be rich, to be sexual, and to be admirable. On the other hand, what clients think they should be like relates to what they believe is appropriate behavior. This involves such ethical commands as "Thou shalt love thy neighbor as thyself" and come from that part of the psychic structure known as "the ego ideal" (Freud, 1923a).

Clients have a tendency to project their ego ideals onto the therapist and believe that the therapist is working overtime to force them to control their narcissism and intensify their altruism. Clients will quote Freud, who extolled work and love, and tell the therapist that he is trying to make them work harder and love more. They may even quote the Bible and tell the therapist that he wants them to suffer.

Because clients typically project their ego ideals onto the therapist, they tend to view change, not as something that they can bring about for themselves with the help of the therapist, but as something that will be done to them. Consequently, they begin to worry about being out of control, losing their identities, and relinquishing their wholeness. They fear being intruded upon, controlled, or ultimately having to merge with the therapist. A common fear is that therapeutic change will require them to give up a valuable part of their selves. Instead of finding comfort with the expectation that they will gain something positive from therapy, they worry that they will lose something dear. As many clients say, "I'm worried that I'll lose my mind."

Sometimes what the client projects onto the therapist actually mirrors the therapist's goals for the client. Clients angrily point out that their therapists want them to assert themselves more, enjoy sexual pleasure more, and to empathize with others more. Because therapists may in fact hope that the therapy will achieve these results, they may become defensive and try to convince their clients that the treatment goals are laudable and desirable. This attitude, of course, will strengthen resistances and cause clients to feel more pressured.

When clients fear change, even if the change seems attainable and praiseworthy, it is important for them to recognize that the pressure to change is coming from within themselves. When clients are helped to get in touch with their own internal voices, they can evaluate the merits of these internalized commands and decide for themselves what they want to do about their own life-styles. They will not profit from a therapist telling them what they should strive for.

In this day and age, when practitioners are confronted with clients with different life-styles (e.g., advocates of gay rights and women's liberation, one-parent families, unmarried couples, swingers, switchers), this issue becomes very pertinent. Experienced clinicians have noted over and over again that clients who have unconventional life-styles tend to believe that their therapists want to make them conform. This belief comes from the clients' ego ideal, which gets projected onto their therapists.

Because many therapists consciously or unconsciously feel uncomfortable with a client's deviant status, they may become too ingratiating or self-protective when the client accuses them of trying to impose their values on him. Actually, what is happening dynamically is that these clients are feeling ambivalent about their current modus vivendi but are resisting change. The part of themselves that wants to change is usually unconscious; it gets ascribed to the therapist, and the therapist, in their minds, becomes the taskmaster. If therapists understand that this is what is happening during the first treatment crisis, they can be more objective and helpful. They should keep in mind that clients who have deviant social statuses are always flirting with changing them. When they are in treatment, this wish gets stronger but more frightening.

In this regard, the first treatment crisis of homosexual clients is often arduous. These clients are usually convinced that the therapist is trying to make them heterosexual, and many therapists feel the need to reassure their clients that they are not. Therapists often fail to appreciate that when homosexual clients are accusing their therapists of trying to remake them sexually, these clients are going through their first treatment crisis and expressing a resistance against their own emerging heterosexual wishes.

When accused by homosexual clients of trying to make them heterosexual, therapists can handle their own anxieties by forgetting about the dynamics of resistance and instead telling their clients that homosexuality is a legitimate way of life that should never be condemned.

Joe R., age 30, was in treatment with a male therapist, Dr. H. Joe had been in therapy for 2 months without telling Dr. H. that he was homosexual. As he began to feel more comfortable with Dr. H., during his third month of once-a-week treatment, Joe told Dr. H. that he was gay. Dr. H. did not wait for Joe to talk further about his being gay and how he felt about it, nor did he do what was particularly crucial at this time, find out why Joe had resisted telling Dr. H. about his sexual preferences. Instead, Dr. H. stated, "You are a human being like everybody else, and you should not feel ashamed of your sexuality."

Joe went on to say that he knew he "was different," that perhaps his "homosexuality was caused by a neurosis," and that maybe the therapist was "going overboard to be kind." The more Joe questioned his homosexuality, the more Dr. H. reassured him. Consequently, Joe felt misunderstood and left treatment prematurely.

What we learn from the case of Joe is that the homosexual client has latent doubts about his sexual orientation. These doubts emerge during the first treatment crisis. They need to be ventilated and explored. As we saw in Joe's case, when he was excessively reassured by his therapist, he became quite suspicious of him and left treatment.

Competition—Fear of Cooperation

In the process of growing up, no child is exempt from feeling competitive. Children vie with the parent of the same sex for the love of the parent of the opposite sex. When the going gets rough, they compete with the parent of the opposite sex for the love of the parent of the same sex. All children compete with siblings and want to be their parents' favorite child (Freud, 1905a). Inevitably, these competitive wishes emerge in the transference relationship with the therapist.

One of the paradoxical aspects of psychotherapy is that the therapist who has the capacity to help clients enhance their psychosocial functioning is concomitantly hated for this capacity. Many clients after feeling better during the honeymoon stage of treatment turn against the therapist because the latter has demonstrated, at least in the client's mind, so much power. As one client stated, "It is true that you have helped me very much, but I envy your capacity to do so. I have had to borrow from your strength because I don't have that strength within myself."

When clients feel envious and competitive, they dread cooperating with the therapist. "I'm not going to let you have any further influence on me," said a woman after 4 months of treatment. She went on, "It makes you feel too powerful, and I resent you for that. I'm going to defeat your attempts at helping me."

When therapists observe their clients battling them during the first treatment crisis, it is important for therapists to keep in mind that, in one way or another, clients are protesting that they have been helped. Feeling that their therapists are high-and-mighty parents, clients have to try to reduce their helpers' powers. Two common countertransference problems can emerge at this time. Some therapists respond by feeling attacked personally and engage in a subtle counterattack. They point out to their clients that they are distorting their therapists' activity and that the therapists are being misjudged. Sometimes accurate interpretations are made, such as pointing out to clients that they are confusing their therapists with their parents. However, when clients feel that their therapists are defending themselves, they attack all the more.

The other countertransference response that is common at this time is for therapists to withdraw in the face of the battle and feel defeated.

Clients love and hate the therapist for this, and feeling confused, they may leave treatment without realizing that they are upset because they were not helped to recognize and discuss their ambivalence toward the therapist.

Inasmuch as it is inevitable that clients will compete with them, practitioners have to master their own competitive wishes. As was pointed out in Chapters 1 and 2, a therapist can help a client only as far as the therapist has matured. If the therapist has not resolved resistances to cooperation and is still actively or passively competing with parents or his own therapist, the practitioner will either join the client in a competitive duel or refrain from intervening. When a client resists cooperating with the therapist, it is the therapist's task to help the client face what is dangerous about cooperating.

Ann P., a woman in her early thirties, was being seen in a child guidance clinic in connection with her son, Steven, age 8. Steven, a passive and effeminate youngster, was being treated for phobias, compulsions, and social withdrawal. Ann was seen on a weekly basis by a social worker, Mrs. I., who was trying to help her better understand her relationship with Steven. Mrs. I. was also Steven's therapist.

The relationship between Ann and Mrs. I. was going quite well for the first 3 months of treatment. Ann was able to acquire insight into her subtle pattern of demeaning and controlling Steven. On becoming aware of her hostility toward her son, Ann examined the roots of it and was able to feel more loving toward Steven and to act more permissively with him. Fairly soon after Ann had shown improvement in her functioning and attitudes, she started to come late for her interviews with Mrs. I. and canceled a couple of appointments. When Mrs. I. took note of Ann's resistive behavior, Ann denied that it had any meaning. When Mrs. I. persisted in trying to have Ann explore the meaning of her absences and cancellations, Ann exclaimed, "I truly resent this psychological perspective of always trying to find meaning to one's behavior. Accidents do happen, illnesses do occur, and alarm clocks can stop working." When the therapist was silent, Ann objected and said, "If you really have a point to make, make it or I'm leaving." Here, Mrs. I. said, "Apparently you are so angry at me, you feel like dumping me." Ann went on to tell Mrs. I. that she could not tolerate "all these psychological explorations" and found herself feeling like "an ant under a microscope, always being scrutinized."

As Mrs. I. continued to be relatively quiet and to listen empathically to Ann's criticisms of both the psychotherapy and herself, Ann slowly began to become more introspective. "Somehow you remind me of my older brother (who was a teacher), and I feel that both of you think you are superior to me and are contemptuous of me." Ann brought out how she felt less bright, less capable, and less insightful than both her brother and Mrs. I.

The more Mrs. I. permitted Ann to compete with her and deride her, the more cooperative Ann became. Eventually, Ann could see how her denigration of Steven was an unconscious attempt to make him feel the same way that she felt next to her brother.

When a client is busily demeaning the therapist, it is important for the practitioner to permit the client to do so. Practitioners sometimes forget that the resistance to cooperation is best overcome when the client feels free to voice uncooperative and hostile attitudes toward the therapist. On feeling safe to be themselves in the therapy, clients can move on to study their resistances to treatment. When the therapist reacts personally to the client's provocation and tries to show the client that his attitude is unrealistic, the client always wins the competition by terminating treatment.

Jim O., age 15, was in treatment in a mental health clinic for his antisocial behavior. He was referred to Dr. J., a psychologist, to increase his understanding of his thievery, his drug addiction, and his breaking and entering. After resolving several initial resistances to therapy, Jim began to like Dr. J. He said in the twentieth interview of his once-a-week treatment, "You are like an old man to me. Sometimes I wish you could be my dad!"

Not too long after Jim had complimented Dr. J., he began to cancel appointments, arrive late, and resume his antisocial activity. When Dr. J. asked about Jim's resistive behavior and pointed out how it paralleled Jim's rebellious activity on the outside, Jim became outraged and said, "You don't know what you're talking about. I don't have to take anything from anybody! You are not going to tell me how to live." Dr. J. said that Jim was angry at him because he was confusing him with all the other authority figures in his life who weren't understanding of him. Jim responded that Dr. J.'s ideas were "a lot of bullshit" and that Dr. J. didn't "know the score." Again Dr. J. quickly answered that Jim was refusing to let himself be helped because he was viewing Dr. J. unrealistically. The more Dr. J. tried to point out reality to Jim, the more indignant Jim became. Soon Jim left treatment.

As was mentioned in Chapter 2, when a client is in a negative transference, regardless of how correct the therapist's interpretations are, the client will oppose them. This is what happened in Jim's treatment. He needed time to deride Dr. J. and compete with him. Had Dr. J. withheld his interpretations for a while and let Jim talk about his hatred, Jim may have been able to resolve his resistances to cooperating and not leave treatment prematurely.

Fear of Symbiosis

Wishing to merge with mother is a normal stage in child development (Mahler, 1968). In the first year of life, when infants feel very helpless, they want their mothers to gratify their bodily needs and their psychological wishes. When adults enter treatment, they usually feel quite helpless. Thus, the wish for merger gets rekindled, and unconsciously, they want to be one with the practitioner.

Very rarely is the wish for symbiosis with the therapist accepted unequivocally; most clients feel ambivalent about it. On the one hand, they want their therapists to open up their hearts and tie an umbilical cord around them. On the other hand, most clients are ashamed of these desires and feel humiliated that they perceive their therapists as so big and giving while they view themselves as so small and needy. To resist experiencing their symbiotic wishes, and to deny their feelings of smallness and passivity, many clients adopt a pseudoaggressive defense and say to their therapists, in effect, "Who needs you?" At this time they may wish to cut down the frequency of their appointments, or they may want to leave treatment altogether.

When clients begin to feel uncomfortable with their symbiotic wishes, they may become very argumentative and quite hostile. They may question the validity of the therapeutic process and accuse the therapist of fostering too much dependency. They may speak of the virtues of short-term treatment and attack the practitioner for conducting an enterprise that seems so questionable.

As we have suggested, it is sometimes difficult for therapists to cope with clients who for several months have been pleasant and cooperative and who then suddenly become vituperative and attacking. Yet this shift in attitude is par for the course of therapy, and practitioners have to accept the fact that if they are going to help their clients mature they cannot always be the recipients of love and the objects of admiration. Instead, they have to listen carefully to their clients' attacks and help them see what is frightening them.

Helen N., a married woman in her early forties, sought therapy because she was quite depressed. She was getting very little satisfaction from her marriage, found it difficult to cope with her teenage daughters, and was in continual arguments with her colleagues at work and her friends in the community.

After 4 months of treatment with Dr. K., a male psychologist, her depression lifted, and she was enjoying her relationships with family, friends, and colleagues a lot more. Because she was functioning so much better, she suggested to Dr. K. that she be seen once a week instead of twice a week. As Dr. K. listened to Helen's arguments to lessen the frequency of their appointments, he found them quite convincing. However, he neither agreed nor disagreed with her, but maintained his neutral attitude. Dr. K.'s noncommital stance frustrated Helen. She became very angry at him and said, "Why the hell don't you agree with me? You just sit there and let me stew. Why don't you support my wish for more independence?" Dr. K. pointed out to Helen that apparently she wanted his permission and support to cut down the frequency of her sessions. "What are you feeling when you want me to agree with you?" he asked. Helen said that his comment made her feel like leaving the treatment right now, and she was silent for the rest of the session.

In subsequent sessions, Helen tried to provoke and demean Dr. K. by telling him that he was very unhelpful and unsupportive. He reminded her of her mother who was "too engulfing" and "too controlling." As Helen talked more about her "overprotective" and "powerful" mother, who always made her so insignificant, eventually Dr. K. was able to interpret to Helen that she was feeling so angry at him because, like her mother, he made her feel like such a helpless little girl. Although Helen fought Dr. K.'s interpretation to some extent, she was also able to reveal how "small" and "dependent" she felt in all her relationships. As she described many episodes in her life that made her feel childlike, Dr. K. was able to show her that she had a wish that terrified her and that wish was to be a little girl with big adults. Again, Helen fought the interpretation, but because Dr. K. maintained a quiet but interested stance, Helen could slowly acknowledge her childish wishes. As she gained some understanding and mastery of her symbiotic wishes, she felt stronger and her first treatment crisis was resolved.

Like the client's wish to alter the modality of treatment, the client's wish to reduce the frequency of appointments should generally be regarded as a resistance. This is particularly true when the client's request to reduce the frequency of appointments comes up during the first few months of therapy. If therapists do not appreciate that the client's request is a sign of resistance, they are not likely to explore the client's wishes and possible anxieties, but instead might support the request. Even if the therapist is convinced that the client's desire to reduce the number of sessions is a sign of increased autonomy, the practitioner should not reject or support the client's proposal. If the client is truly feeling more independent, then he will not need the therapist's support and can make the decision on his own.

When clients are able to get the therapist's approval to cut down the number of sessions, they later feel rejected. Sometimes they view the therapist's acquiescence as a sign that the therapist does not consider the treatment that important or that the therapist is weak and vulnerable. These thoughts often make the client want to quit treatment.

Bob M., a 22-year-old college student, was in treatment at a college counseling center. He was referred for counseling by the college health service because his symptoms seemed to be psychological in origin. He suffered from insomnia, had gastrointestinal problems, and was quite depressed. From the beginning of treatment, Bob responded very positively to his therapist, Ms. L. Within 2½ months of twice-a-week treatment, his symptoms virtually disappeared. After expressing his profound gratitude to Ms. L., Bob suggested that he reduce the frequency of his sessions from twice a week to once a week. Feeling elated by Bob's progress, Ms. L. quickly agreed with Bob's proposal and started to see Bob on a weekly basis.

After a few weeks of feeling euphoric, Bob again began to experience symptoms. Although he made no direct reference to his therapist, he used his sessions to talk about people who "let me down." When Ms. L. finally got the message and told Bob that she thought he was including her among those people, it was too late. Bob stated vehemently that depending on anybody was a waste of time. Despite Ms. L.'s efforts to stop him, Bob left treatment.

What is instructive about Bob's case is that a therapist can become too elated about a client's progress and lose his objectivity. Ms. L. was too pleased with Bob and with herself; consequently, she did not see Bob's desire to lessen the frequency of his appointments as a sign of resistance. Bob felt misunderstood by Ms. L. and left treatment.

Acting Out

In our discussion of the first treatment crisis, most of the examples of resistance have been clearly directed at the therapist. Another form of resistance that can constitute part of the first treatment crisis is when the client does not express the resistance directly in the treatment sessions but acts it out with someone on the outside. Frequently therapists do not recognize that intensified battles with a spouse are really a displacement of anger toward the therapist. Similarly, fracases with bosses, disputes with peers, or tempestuous sexual affairs might all be manifestations of disguised transference reactions.

The reason that this is often difficult to recognize is that, while the client is fighting it out with others, he is usually feeling positively and behaving cooperatively with the therapist. However, it is precisely because the client is frightened to reveal certain erotic, angry, or dependent fantasies toward the therapist that he does act out.

Acting out the transference probably takes place with every client to some extent. Freud took the position that the client's actions are substitutes for memories:

> The patient does not remember anything of what he has forgotten and repressed, but acts it out. He reproduces it not as a memory but as an action, he repeats it, without, of course, knowing that he is repeating it. . . . The patient does not say that he remembers that he used to be defiant and critical towards his parents' authority, instead, as the analysis proceeds, the transference becomes hostile or unduly intense and . . . remembering at once gives way to acting out. (1914b, p. 150)

Since Freud's conceptualizations of acting out were formulated, psychoanalysts and therapists have used the term to denote any time a client uses substitutes as targets of feelings or fantasies aroused toward the clinician that the client does not feel secure enough to verbalize in the therapist's office (Sandler, et al., 1973).

Once the therapist has recognized that certain actions of the client are really displaced transference responses, the therapeutic goal is to help the client understand the meaning of the fantasies or feelings that are being acted out. As is true with helping the client with any resistance, the clinician must try to determine what danger the client sees in verbalizing the transference feelings directly. Is the client afraid of loss of love? Is the client afraid the therapist will abandon him? Is the client afraid of retribution? Knowing the danger helps the clinician relate more confidently to the client.

An expedient method of locating the danger for the client is to observe closely his interaction with those with whom he is acting out. For example, if a man is arguing intensely with his wife and admonishing her for withholding sex, the therapist can infer, from his understanding that a chronic marital complaint is an unconscious wish, that intimacy with the wife is the danger. If intimacy with the wife is threatening, it can be further inferred that the man is afraid of feeling intimate with the therapist.

In order to help the client see that his acting out with his wife is a disguised transference response, the therapist must not take sides in the marital dispute. Most clients want the therapist to support them in their struggles. When the therapist does not, he becomes the recipient of the clients' anger. As the anger is investigated, clients and therapists invariably discover that it is a defense against intimacy.

During her sixth month of treatment, Gertrude M., a married woman in her late thirties, became increasingly involved in severe marital disputes. She kept telling her male therapist, Dr. N., that her husband was threatened by her desires for intimacy and that she couldn't tolerate his apathetic attitude any longer. As she began thinking of divorce or of having an extramarital affair, she tried to get Dr. N. to support her. When Dr. N. did not take a position regarding Gertrude's wish to have an affair, Gertrude slowly began to get irritated with Dr. N. "You are supposed to help me get better? Shouldn't I try something else?" she asked belligerently. When Dr. N. pointed out to Gertrude that she was having mixed feelings about moving away from her husband and therefore wanted Dr. N. to give her some direction, Gertrude's fury grew more intense. She told Dr. N. that he was an apathetic man, afraid of closeness, and probably turned off by sex.

When it became clear to Dr. N. that Gertrude's complaints about her husband and about her therapist were identical, he asked her, "What do you make of the fact that you have an apathetic husband and an apathetic therapist?" Gertrude responded by saying that she was beginning to realize that she didn't have a problem with sex or with being close. "It's all of you men! You are scared of me!" she concluded. On being asked what men were frightened of, Gertrude responded by recalling memories of her father, who always kept at a distance from her and who did not respond to her femininity. She realized that she interpreted her father's apathy and withdrawal as indicative of something being wrong with her own sexual wishes. As Gertrude became more aware of the sexual fantasies toward her father that she was trying to disown, she gained some appreciation of the fact that she was frightened to feel sexual toward her husband and Dr. N. When she could accept her own fears of intimacy a little more, her acting out diminished.

Acting out was regarded by Freud as a particular manifestation of resistance that could have undesirable consequences for the patient or the progress of his treatment. Because of this, it appears to have been a natural step for his followers to apply it more to behavior that is "undesirable" in a general sense than to other forms of behavior. Carried to its extreme, any socially or morally undesirable behavior is labeled "acting out" by some (Sandler et al., 1973). However, Helene Deutsch (1966) has pointed out that, to some extent, we are all acting out, because nobody is free of regressive trends, repressed strivings, and childish fantasies. It is crucial for the practitioner to be as nonjudgmental and empathetic as possible when helping clients who are acting out. Otherwise, clients will feel criticized and this resistance will not be resolved.

Fear of Regression

As we pointed out in Chapter 3, clients rarely show only one form of resistance. The man or woman who acts out might also be frightened of symbiotic fantasies toward the therapist, and the person who wants to change the therapeutic modality might also be angry at the practitioner for not being omnipotent.

A very common form of resistance that may accompany other resistances around the time of the first treatment crisis is the client's fear of regression. This fear is expressed in a number of ways: "I'm losing my mind"; "I'm afraid you are turning me into a child"; "You are making me a homosexual"; "I'm afraid I'm going to run around the room, break your furniture, and hurt you"; "I've got to get away from here. I'm going to hug you, kiss you, and then rape you"; and so on.

The client's fear of regression should not really come as a surprise to the informed clinician. When an individual is given the opportunity to say whatever comes to mind to a nonjudgmental, caring listener, it is inevitable that he will want to gratify childish wishes. Feeling cared for and loved, the client often reasons, "Alas, I have found the perfect parent. How wonderful! I would like to curl up on my wonderful parent's lap and regress. I want to satisfy all my demands, and since this perfect parent is omnipotent, I have the right to be furious when I do not get what I want when I want it."

Although clients have strong desires to regress, most of them have to deny these wishes. It is frequently humiliating for an adult to feel like a baby. The desire to be a passive and helpless infant in the arms of a strong adult usually conflicts with the client's wish to be an autonomous and strong adult. In the treatment situation, when childish wishes rise to the surface, clients often need to repudiate them. Fearing that they might go out of control and act out in the sessions, clients work overtime to get the therapist to place some limits on them or to do something that will interrupt the regression.

The client's fear of regressing can often activate fears in the therapist. Clinicians who have not mastered their own desires to regress worry that they will have a demanding baby on their hands who will engulf and weaken them. To counteract this possibility, clinicians may do many things—offer advice, prescribe medication, or bombard the client with interpretations. When clinicians behave this way, their clients usually sense the therapists' apprehension and become even more concerned that they might be losing their minds or that they are deteriorating.

In working with clients who fear regression, the practitioner must keep in mind that clients really desire the thing that they fear, even though this desire is unconscious. Because clients deeply wish what they deeply fear, practitioners must be able to demonstrate that they feel comfortable with their clients' primitive wishes and are prepared to talk about them without being anxious. It is only when the client senses that the therapist is not frightened to discuss such impulses as oral incorporative wishes, symbiotic desires, homosexual cravings, or sadistic fantasies that the client can face these impulses in himself. Consequently, the attitude that the therapist must have with the client who fears regression is: "You are very frightened of your wish to eat me up (or have sex with me, or hit me, etc.), and you fear that if we talk about it, you'll do it."

The inability to distinguish between wishes and actions emanates from childhood. Most, if not all, children feel that thinking about something is equivalent to acting on it. This is why children who have secret sexual or hostile wishes often develop phobias of animals, burglars, or thieves. These figures are stand-ins for parents who children fear will punish them for all their "horrible" thoughts.

To adults in psychotherapy, telling their therapists about their "horrible thoughts" is experienced as if they were children revealing their "crimes" to parents. This is why it is necessary for the therapist to have a calm, warm, empathic demeanor while helping clients talk about their regressed wishes.

Michael K., a man in his mid twenties, was in therapy with Dr. O., a woman therapist. During his seventh month of therapy, Michael told Dr. O. that he was feeling increasingly uncomfortable in his treatment sessions. Exploration revealed that Michael was afraid to reveal to Dr. O. his erotic fantasies about her. When Dr. O. asked Michael what he was worried would happen if he did talk about his erotic fantasies, Michael said, "If you knew what they were, you'd hate me." When Dr. O. replied, "You are afraid you'll threaten me with your fantasies and I'll cope with my vulnerability by getting angry," Michael replied, "You sound pretty nice and reassuring, but I'm not sure." Michael was apparently uncertain about his possible impact on Dr. O. He was worried that maybe he'd "floor her." When Dr. O. repeated, "Floor me," Michael was able to tell Dr. O. that he would like to throw her on the floor, "and bang away at you." On seeing that Dr. O. was unperturbed by his sexual and sadistic fantasies, he asked her, "Are you frightened of me?" She answered, "Should I be?" Michael told Dr. O. that it was one thing to talk about all these wishes, but he could really get off his chair and "bang away" at Dr. O. "Then what?" asked Dr. O. Michael talked about smashing Dr. O.'s head off, eating it up, slugging her in the body, raping her, and then chopping her into bits.

The more Dr. O. listened attentively and helped Michael explore his fantasies, the less anxious he became. After several weeks of this, Michael said, "If I can believe you won't reject me or you won't get frightened of me when I tell you all these evil things, I'll get through this and be alive and well."

It is quite clear from the above case that, if the therapist is not frightened of the client's primitive wishes, the client's dread of them lessens. In order to help clients resolve their fears of regressive fantasies, the therapist must demonstrate that he welcomes them and is not going to be "floored" by them. The clinician should also keep in mind that a regression in therapy will go no further than anything previously experienced in the client's life. If a client has never been severely regressed, a severe regression in therapy is unlikely.

Client Wants a Consultation with Another Therapist

From our discussion of the first treatment crisis, it is quite clear that this is a time when clients are quite hostile toward their therapists. They are furious because their therapists are not omnipotent, angry that their therapists appear to be punitive superego figures, and irritated that many of their fantasies are being punctured. Regardless of how resistance is expressed, clients during the first treatment crisis are characteristically in a negative transference.

Fairly frequently during the first treatment crisis a client will suggest to the therapist that he should get "a second opinion." Irritated at the therapist and dissatisfied that therapist and client are at a stalemate, the client wonders if another expert can either explain the dynamics of the current therapeutic impasse or determine that the client is in the wrong hands. This suggestion of the client's can upset the therapist, and in many instances, this is precisely what the client wants to do.

There is probably no therapist in practice who welcomes hearing that the client wants a second opinion. Many clinicians at this time feel attacked, accused, and accosted. Some respond angrily and defensively, and prohibit their clients from seeing another expert. To justify their prohibition, they may interpret their clients' wishes as acting out. Or they may feel so crushed and frightened of their own anger that they sit back passively and either do nothing or tell their clients that indeed it may be a good idea to see a consultant.

If the clinician recognizes that the client's wish for a consultation with another therapist is a resistance, then the clinician will neither prohibit nor endorse a consultation. Rather the practitioner will attempt to help the client understand his motives for wanting a consultation. When clients see that the therapist's attitude is one of trying to understand rather than reacting positively or negatively, most of them begin to identify with the therapist's stance and to explore their own motives. Some clients, however, do go ahead with a consultation.

If the client does have a consultation, it is important for the therapist once again, to take a calm, investigative attitude to ascertain what material the client brings to the sessions. In many ways, the therapist can look at a client's report of a consultation the same way he views other reports when the client quotes the opinions of family and friends about the treatment. Clients invariably use the opinions of others to buttress their own positions. If they think the therapist is cold and distant, they may very well quote a consultant who thinks so. If they think that the therapist is too intrusive, they will find another person to agree with that point of view. The therapist should recognize that when a client quotes somebody else's opinion about the therapist, this opinion is almost always the client's opinion of the therapist at the time, and that is what should be investigated in the therapy.

A wish for a second opinion is an attempt to belittle the therapist. The task of the therapist at this time is to help the client determine and understand what is going on in the therapy that poses a danger for him.

Sandra D., a 35-year-old single woman, had been in treatment for about 8 months when she told her male therapist, Dr. B., that she wanted "a second opinion." She told Dr. B. that she was experiencing him as much too pressuring, critical, and confronting. She further contended that Dr. B. imposed too many of his own ideas on her, did not support her enough, and seemed too preoccupied with sex. When Dr. B. listened attentively to Sandra's complaints but did not say anything, Sandra furiously remarked, "This is typical of what I mean. I am all upset right now and you don't give a damn. All you want me to do is suffer." Dr. B. responded here and said that Sandra experienced him as very cruel. He asked her if she had any ideas about why he might be this way? Sandra stated, "That's your makeup. You are sick. You need a therapist!"

In subsequent sessions, Sandra went on to criticize and condemn Dr. B. some more. She asked in one session, "Do you have any objections if I see a consultant?" When Dr. B. asked, "Would you like me to object?," Sandra said, "Yes, you stupid bastard. At least once, I'd get some emotion from you. You dry, stupid prick!" A dream of Sandra's at this time was revealing. She dreamed that she was in Rome and saw two men. One was a priest who looked like the therapist. He was trying to have sex with Sandra but was clumsy and inept. Another man was nearby and he and

Sandra had "great sex." After Sandra pointed out that the priest was Dr. B., who knew nothing about sex, and that the other man was the future consultant, who could give her a good time, Dr. B. said, "I guess you feel I don't know how to turn you on. Another man can!" Sandra triumphantly agreed.

In another dream Sandra was undressed, and again Dr. B. was a clumsy sex partner. Sandra pointed ou, "My dreams tell me that I should see a consultant because you don't know anything." Dr. B. said, "Your dreams also show you are frightened of your sexual fantasies toward me. You make me into somebody who can't help you sexually." Sandra said, "That's a crock of shit" and went on to demean and villify Dr. B. some more. After a couple of sessions in which Sandra threatened again to see a consultant, Dr. B. said, "Are you aware that lately every time I come up with something, you want to knock it down?" Sandra retorted, "There you go with that Freudian shit, again. You want me to talk about sex. You want to force me into it, don't you?"

Dr. B. told Sandra that the impasse between them was quite clear. She felt furious that Dr. B. was insisting that she talk about sex. Sandra agreed and told Dr. B. that he reminded her of her father, who always insisted on his own point of view. "That's why I want another point of view, not yours. I do want to belittle you. I wanted to do that with my father," Sandra remarked insightfully.

As Sandra talked more about her "authoritarian" father who seemed so much like Dr. B., she became less vituperative. When she compared Dr. B. and her father and criticized both of them, Dr. B. was silently accepting. The more he listened, the more Sandra could examine her transference feelings. The treatment crisis ended when Sandra said, "I guess I wanted you to be the father I could attack and show up. You weathered the storm nicely."

The client's wish for a consultation with another therapist, as the case above reveals, almost always indicates that a resistance is operating and almost always suggests that the client is in the throes of a negative transference. The more the therapist listens empathically to the client's complaints about the therapy and tries to ascertain, with the client's participation, what is currently dangerous in the therapy, the greater is the possibility that the client will forgo a consultation with another professional. If the client does go ahead and have a consultation, the therapist should listen carefully to the client's reports and bear in mind that, when the client quotes somebody else, the opinions quoted probably mirror the client's own, whether these opinions are about the therapist or somebody else.

Client Leaves Treatment

As we have implied throughout this chapter, if therapists are prepared for the first treatment crisis, they will make the appropriate efforts to help their clients resolve it. However, as Fine (1982) has pointed out, no therapist should be blind to the fact that some clients will leave treatment no matter what the therapist does. No one has yet succeeded in curing all the people who come for help.

Some clients have a powerful conviction that all helping people are not to be trusted. Regardless of how understanding, skilled, and empathic their therapists are, they have to be rejected. Such people are so terrified of their own dependency wishes that to rely on a therapist feels intensely humiliating to them. Therefore, they often leave treatment prematurely. Then there are clients whose resistance to cooperating is so great that, when they enter treatment, they feel like children who must surrender their bodies and souls to the therapist. These individuals have to protect themselves by defeating their therapists. Further, some clients are so petrified of their sexual fantasies that the intimacy implicit in psychotherapy appears overwhelming to them. These clients often have to flee the treatment, too.

There are also some individuals whose ego functions are so weak that the requirements of a psychotherapeutic relationship are overwhelming to them. For example, there are some men and women whose frustration tolerance is so limited that they cannot cope with time-limited sessions, cannot wait between sessions to see the therapist, and cannot share the therapist with other clients. These clients, like fragile children, want instant gratification and cannot take "no" for an answer. When they cannot get the therapist to give them what they want immediately, they leave treatment.

Sam C., age 50, was seen in a family agency for help with his alcoholism. The product of a broken home, Sam never had any close relationships with anybody. He described himself to his social worker, Mrs. H., as "a loner" and he said that no one could be trusted. After 2½ months of treatment in which he improved a great deal—he took a new job that paid well, reduced his alcohol intake, and made some new friends—Sam wanted to quit treatment. When Mrs. H. asked what bothered Sam about their work, Sam brought out that he was getting "sick and tired of depending" on someone else and that he wanted to try it alone. When Mrs. H. asked Sam what was it about depending on her that upset him, Sam asked impatiently, "What do you want to be, my mother? Do you want to adopt me? Do you want to live with me?" Without waiting for Mrs. H.'s response, he told her that this was going to be their last appointment, that he did not want to discuss their relationship any further, and left the office. Attempts on Mrs. H.'s part to get Sam back into her office yielded no response from him. Phone calls to Sam after this last appointment also got nowhere. Sam insisted that he had to "go it alone."

As we saw in the case of Sam, when dependency wishes are strong and mistrust is powerful, it is extremely difficult to help the client stay in treatment. When Sam asked "What do you want to be, my mother?" he was revealing his secret wish to have Mrs. H. be his mother. This wish was as strong in him as it was unacceptable to him. Because of his enormous distrust and low frustration tolerance, Sam had to flee treatment rather than talk about his wishes.

Although it is rarely easy to accept a client's leaving treatment prematurely, the level of distrust of some clients, the degree of insatiability in others, and the terror in still others causes them to defeat the best made treatment plans of competent clinicians.

COMMON MISTAKES OF THERAPISTS DURING THE FIRST TREATMENT CRISIS

Throughout this chapter we have alluded to many countertransference problems that are triggered in the therapist during the first treatment crisis. In our case vignettes and discussions, we have shown how a client's negative transference can induce negative feelings in the therapist toward the client. Therapists may become very anxious and angry when the client wants to have a consultation with another professional, to switch to another treatment modality, or to quit treatment altogether. Therapists may feel threatened and frightened when the client is in the middle of a powerful regression or about to act out in a self-destructive manner. When therapists feel anxious, angry, frightened, or threatened, they may make mistakes that interfere with the resolution of the first treatment crisis. In this section, we discuss some of these common mistakes.

Therapist Gives Advice

Usually when the therapist is frightened that the client will regress too much or is angry at the client for not progressing enough, he offers advice. Advice giving is almost always a manifestation of an unresolved countertransference problem. The therapist has lost faith in the client's capacity for autonomy, has lost confidence in his own capacity to help the client understand resistances, and in most instances, has not been understanding what psychological dangers the client has been fearing. Advice is usually given clients when they are involved in chronically unhappy marriages, in difficult job situations, or in other kinds of interpersonal difficulties with family and friends in which they feel helpless, tortured, ambivalent, and conflicted.

As we have noted several times in the chapter, when clients complain repetitively to their therapists about how unhappy they are in relationships, it is extremely important for both therapists and clients to understand that clients derive unconscious gratification from this. That is why advice rarely works. If an individual is in an unhappy marriage, an unhappy love affair, or a frustrating job and the therapist advises the client to leave the unhappy situation, the therapist is overlooking the fact that few individuals leave a situation from which they are deriving gratification. Also, if a client is given advice on how to get along better with a person with whom he is fighting, the advice will probably be subtly rejected because the client unconsciously wants the fight to continue.

There are still other reasons why advice has untherapeutic effects. When clients persist in complaining to their therapists about their unhappy interpersonal situations, they are almost always in a latent negative transference. As we discussed earlier in this chapter, the depressed and the suicidal client are unconsciously fighting the therapist. When they or any other unhappy, helpless clients are given advice, the advice has to be defeated because the clients have unconscious wishes to render the therapist ineffective. Further, as Langs (1973) has pointed out, most clients respond to direct advice with some degree of mistrust. They feel manipulated and wonder why the therapist's objectivity and neutrality have disappeared. They also get frightened of passive and submissive wishes in themselves that advice from the therapist can arouse.

In adopting an advice-giving role, the therapist takes a risk. How can the therapist be so sure that the advice is correct? The client legitimately wonders, "Why does my therapist have to play God?" and the client's fantasies regarding omnipotence will determine his reaction to the advice. Either the client will remain in treatment for many years, passively surrendering to the therapist but not getting along well with others, or the client will quit treatment because the therapist is perceived as too arrogant and dominating.

Ronald R., a man in his thirties, was in treatment with Dr. H., a male therapist. Repeatedly Ronald complained to Dr. H. about how his wife was critical, dominating, and asexual. Dr. H. eventually told Ronald that he was not assertive enough and that he was too submissive with his wife. Ronald went home and tried to heed Dr. H.'s advice. Returning to sessions, he told Dr. H., "Things have gotten worse. The fighting is ferocious." Dr. H. gave more advice, and Ronald again tried to follow it. Eventually Ronald's wife left him and Ronald left treatment with Dr. H.

In the above case, Ronald's complaints about his wife and his requests for advice masked his negative transference. Because he wanted to defeat Dr. H., he arranged unconsciously to defeat Dr. H.'s advice. Commenting on the limitations of advice giving, Langs has said:

> The therapist need not tell a patient to modify his life situation or realities, thereby depriving him of his autonomy, ingenuity, self-criticism, and capacity for change. He need not promote passivity and helplessness, inadequate functioning, and a poor and disturbed self-image—all of which the patient, unfortunately, will later exploit, and which will haunt the therapist. The therapist need only interpret to the patient, and confront him with what he sees and understands; he can and should expect the patient to then act according to the insights he attains. In so doing, the patient grows and matures. . . . Direct advice and manipulation are generally to be avoided in insight psychotherapy. (1973, pp. 549–550)

Therapist Gives Reassurance

When a client continues to suffer, keeps getting further depressed, and feels that nothing is going to happen, many therapists begin to question their own competence and, in their anxiety, start to reassure the client that all will be well quite soon. Sometimes the therapist's reassurance is coupled with interpretations designed to alter the client's attitude right away.

Giving reassurance rarely works for the same reason that giving advice rarely works. When clients continue to suffer and be depressed, unconsciously they want it that way. Consequently, if therapists try to talk their clients out of something that their clients unconsciously desire, attempts to reassure them are bound to backfire. Second, as we have suggested repeatedly, when clients constantly tell the therapist that their depression is worsening or that their lives are deteriorating, they are in a negative transference. If clients are in a negative transference, they will have to show the therapist that the reassurance offered was the "wrong medicine" that made matters worse instead of better. Finally, as Langs (1973) has suggested, providing clients with reassurance strips them of their autonomy and self-respect. Feeling angry at being demeaned, they have to defeat the therapy and the therapist. As Edinburg, Zinberg, and Kelman (1975) have suggested in *Clinical Interviewing and Counseling:*

A counselor may be tempted to offer someone afraid of death the hope of an afterlife, or to point out the advantages of democracy or freedom to a member of a totalitarian gang. However, such information, no matter how well meant, puts the counselor in the position of being an omniscient, preaching, paternalistic figure and prevents the development of a working relationship. (p. 26)

Therapist Denies that Resistance Exists

As we have seen repeatedly, resistances during the first treatment crisis are usually accompanied by hostile feelings toward the practitioner. Some practitioners are so frightened by their clients' destructive wishes and so terrified of their own murderous fantasies, that they have a compulsive need to try to create and maintain positive transference and countertransference relationships with their clients. When the client arrives late for sessions, they can distort the meaning of this behavior and call it a sign of increased autonomy and declining dependency, or if the client does not pay fees, these therapists can label the client's behavior "appropriate testing."

Usually those therapists who wish to disregard the reality of resistances and to forget that a first treatment crisis is par for the course have not faced these issues in their own personal therapy. As we have reiterated, a therapist can help his clients resolve only as much as he has resolved.

Dr. W., a prominent psychotherapist, frequently bragged to colleagues: "I have never once had the negative transference. All my patients love me and I love them." It turned out that Dr. W. had a relationship with his own therapist where they both lauded each other in every session. This prevented Dr. W. from maturing, and he could not help his clients to do so in any significant way.

When therapists refuse to accept the reality of resistance or of the first treatment crisis, their clients suffer. Diagnostic assessments are blurred, treatment plans are misdirected, and clients feel they are with a professional that does not understand them. The first treatment crisis, if accepted as par for the course and taken seriously by both therapist and client, can lead to a deepening working relationship. This deepened relationship can help client and therapist resolve future resistances in the treatment, which are inevitable.

CHAPTER 5

The Middle Phase:
Refusals to Comply with Basic Requests

When the first treatment crisis is resolved, the relationship between client and therapist usually deepens. As is true with any two individuals who are involved in an impasse, when angers are discharged and misunderstandings are clarified, loving feelings reemerge. However, the therapy encounter, like any other interpersonal relationship, is not confined to one crisis. Even after a major impasse has been worked through, resistances and counterresistances reappear. Therapists have to assess constantly the meaning of their clients' resistive behavior and to determine how to help them overcome their resistances.

Many of the client resistances that we have reviewed in Chapters 3 and 4 reappear during the middle phases of treatment, albeit in a disguised form. Clients continue to fear intimacy; they persevere in their quest for an omnipotent parent; they persist in questioning the validity of the treatment; and they flirt often with the possibility of changing the treatment modality.

In examining client resistances during the middle phase of treatment, we shall use the categories developed by Reuben Fine (1982) in which he divides resistances into those where clients refuse to comply with basic requests (e.g., refusing to talk, constantly arriving late for sessions, absenting themselves from sessions), and those that are expressed more subtly (e.g., somatizing, excessively complying with the therapist's instructions, reacting ambivalently to interpretations).

In this chapter we focus exclusively on those resistances that involve the client's refusal to cooperate with requests, and in Chapter 6 we will discuss those resistances that are expressed more subtly. As was true in previous chapters, we try to understand the dangers that clients are defending against when they resist, we examine the therapist's countertransference problems, and we discuss those therapeutic procedures that seem pertinent in resolving specific resistances.

Client Wants to Keep Secrets from the Therapist*

In virtually all psychotherapeutic relationships, clients are requested to say everything that comes to mind. Yet the client's conscious withholding of material is a resistance that has confronted every practitioner on numerous occasions. While most clients recognize that, in order to be helped, they must present their thoughts, feelings, and fantasies freely, many of them do conceal their associations because they fear how the therapist might react or what the therapist might do. This fear usually involves a projection of the client's critical superego onto the therapist, who is unconsciously perceived as a disapproving figure (Fine, 1982; Freud, 1912a).

In Chapter 1 we referred to the "Rat Man" as the first example in the psychotherapeutic literature of a client who consciously withheld material from the therapist (Freud, 1909). The patient, a man in his twenties treated by Freud early in his therapeutic career, concealed for some time his suspicion that Freud was related to another individual named Freud who lived in Budapest and had committed one of the most notorious crimes of that day. The "Rat Man" held back his hostility to Freud because he was frightened of his therapist's possible retaliation.

Freud's "Rat Man" is typical of the many clients who consciously withhold material from the therapist because they feel that the information will be either self-damaging or offensive to the therapist. Often, withheld material has a sexual implication, but almost any kind of material may be concealed if it appears unacceptable to the client's superego.

What is most important in dynamically oriented psychotherapy is not the client's secret as such but the psychological factors that make the client hold on to the secret with tenacity. Furthermore, in working with clients who have conscious secrets, it is crucial for the therapist to convey to the client that it is less important to divulge the secret itself than it is for the client and therapist to determine what frightens and inhibits the client so much that he must withhold the secret. This is in line with a general principle in psychotherapy that we mentioned several times in Chapter 2: Interpret resistance before content (Fenichel, 1945; Glover, 1955; W. Reich, 1949).

As we have already implied, consciously withholding material from the therapist can have many different meanings. Some clients withhold material because they do not want to risk appearing too clever. Others hold back facts, fantasies, or dreams because they are worried about sexually stimulating the clinician or being sexually stimulated by him. To many clients, sharing a secret with the therapist is experienced as a confession of a forbidden sexual act. Greenson has stated:

* Parts of this section are drawn from an article by the author, "The Patient Who Would Not Tell His Name," *Psychoanalytic Quarterly, 53,* pp. 410–420.

In general, secrets are related to secretions. They always have some anal or urethral connotation, and are considered shameful and loathsome, or its opposite, that is, very valuable and to be hoarded and protected. Secrets are also connected to the parents' secret sexual activities, which now the patient repeats via identification and which the patient does in revenge in the transference situation. In addition to all of this, secrecy and confession are always involved with problems of exhibitionism, scoptophilia, and teasing. The secret is inevitably involved in the transference situation as a special form of resistance. (1967, p. 133)

Keeping secrets from the therapist frequently provokes countertransference reactions in the practitioner. However, if such reactions are subjected to self-analysis, they can often be used in understanding the client's conflicts. When the therapist feels that he is being teased, provoked, sadistically tortured, castrated, mutilated, or defeated by the client's secretiveness, the therapist may learn later that these reactions are responses that the client is consciously or unconsciously trying to induce in the therapist. While the clinician's idiosyncratic feelings and fantasies are material for private perusal, as we have already suggested, the therapist can use countertransference signals in conjunction with other clues as a guide to a better understanding the clinical material (Blum, 1983).

The following case is presented in detail because it involves a client who kept many secrets from his therapist. The vignette offers an opportunity to understand the complex dynamics in a client's keeping secrets from the therapist and suggests pertinent therapeutic procedures than can help clients resolve the resistances that comprise the conscious withholding of secrets.

In the case illustration that we will review, one of the secrets that the client withheld from the therapist was his name. He did not tell the therapist his name until after a year and a half of four-times-a-week, psychoanalytically oriented treatment had elapsed.

The client, whom we shall call Mr. A., was 36 years old and sought treatment for many reasons. He had just been fired from his job as a salesman and was feeling so depressed that he could not feel sufficient motivation to seek another job. In addition, Mr. A. had been suffering from many symptoms for several years. He was plagued by constant insomnia, had peptic ulcers and other gastrointestinal complaints, and suffered from many phobias—subways, bridges, small rooms, and cars. He was frequently impotent with his wife, and he felt that there "had always been a big distance between us during our 10-year marriage." Mr. A. also reported that he could not feel comfortable with his son, age 8, and with his daughter, age 5; he had "little to do with them." Although he almost always was a good student, Mr. A. constantly found himself in low-paying jobs and derived little satisfaction from them. "Most of my life," said Mr. A. in his first interview, "I've been a depressed loner."

Regarding his history, Mr. A. was the oldest of two children; he had a sister 2 years younger than himself. Father was described as a hard-working owner of a restaurant, who had little to do with the client. Mr. A. stated that, although his father had little to do with him, he felt pressured and criticized by him on frequent occasions. Father died when the client was 14 years old. Mr. A.'s mother was described as alternately seductive and punitive. He envied his sister who "got all the attention."

At the end of Mr. A.'s first interview, during which he appeared defer-ential, compliant, and very depressed, he pointed out that he would not be able to be in treatment with the therapist "if you *insist* that I give you my name." When the therapist asked him why he was concerned about the therapist knowing his name, Mr. A. responded with some irritation, "The F.B.I. frequently makes checkups on people, and if they find out that I was in treatment, I'd never get a job." Again he asked, "Are you going to *insist* on knowing my name?" The therapist pointed out Mr. A's use of the word *insist* on at least two occasions, and Mr. A. responded, "I'm told that psychoanalysts and psychotherapists are very insistent people and I'm wary of them." The therapist suggested that Mr. A. may wish to have an-other consultation with him so that they could discuss further Mr. A.'s doubts about the therapist and about treatment.

In Mr. A.'s second interview, he started the session by telling the thera-pist that he was pleased that "you didn't *insist* on getting my name, so I'll try you for a while." When the therapist remained silent, Mr. A. went on to say that he was now worried that the therapist would *insist* that he use the couch. After a brief silence, Mr. A. pointed out that he was feeling an acute back pain that was causing him enormous distress and that he had to sit in an upright position or he would pass out. His associations enabled the therapist to offer the interpretation that Mr. A. was very worried that the therapist would dominate and control him by insisting that he give his name and also that he lie on the couch. The interpretation partially re-lieved Mr. A.'s back pain, and he ended the second session by saying, "I think that we can work something out together. You are not that insistent." But the client had to warn the therapist that, although the therapist's fee was acceptable, he would rather pay him in cash so that the therapist would not see his signature on the checks.

Although Mr. A. eventually did use the couch, he sat up for 20 sessions. During this time, he spoke of his insecurity on jobs and pointed out that he frequently viewed employers the way he had been experiencing the therapist—as people who *insisted* on dominating and controlling him.

Mr. A. seemed to derive some benefit from an interpretation that the bosses appeared to be reminiscent of his "pressuring" father and soon was able to begin job interviews. He eventually took a job as an office manager.

When Mr. A. was on the job about 2 weeks, he reported that once again he found himself in arguments and power struggles with superiors. Although he could now recognize that these interpersonal problems emerged from within himself, because the identical phenomenon had also occurred with his father and with the therapist, he felt helpless to do anything about them. Here the therapist suggested that Mr. A. might want to consider using the couch in order to understand better what was unconsciously contributing to his problems with bosses and to his other conflicts.

Although Mr. A. went to the couch quite compliantly, within two or three sessions, he became very suspicious of the therapist's motives. He thought that the therapist preferred Mr. A. to be on the couch so that the therapist could be in a "one-upmanship" position with Mr. A. whereby the therapist could see Mr. A. but Mr. A. could not see the therapist. Mr. A. was "so glad" he had not given the therapist his name because he was now convinced that the therapist would give it to government agents and get paid for doing so. His paranoid fantasies consumed the therapy for about 2 months, during which he vehemently described the therapist as an opportunist, a manipulator, a sadist, and probably a homosexual. In his sixth month of treatment, Mr. A. had a dream in which the therapist was yelling at him for not paying him enough money and for not being more productive in the treatment. In the dream the therapist was again "insisting" that Mr. A. tell more fantasies, more dreams, and more associations. Shortly after the session in which Mr. A. discussed this dream, the therapist commented that Mr. A. felt that the therapist wanted him to be his slave, much like he felt he had to be with his father. The client agreed with the interpretation and then told the therapist that he was convinced that the therapist was involved in psychotherapeutic work so that he could be a slave master and sadistically torment his clients.

As Mr. A. investigated the therapist's motives in becoming a tormenting slave master, he said that the therapist was "basically a homosexual" who was trying "to fool the world by acting as a heterosexual." Mr. A. told the therapist in his eighth month of therapy, "You are essentially a passive man who wants to be fucked up the ass, but are scared to admit it." When asked why he thought the therapist was frightened to acknowledge his homosexuality, Mr. A. pointed out, "You like to tease and fool the world. Maybe if you tease somebody long enough, they will rape you in anger— that's what you really want."

Concomitant with Mr. A.'s using his therapy sessions to investigate the therapist's homosexuality, he told the therapist how much better his own life was becoming. He was sexually potent with his wife, he was not engaged in struggles with his bosses, and his relationship with his children was much better. The only thing that bothered him about this was that he was convinced that the therapist must be suffering with envy inasmuch as he was a celibate with a homesexual problem while Mr. A. was enjoying so much sexual pleasure with his wife. Furthermore, Mr. A. felt that, as he was achieving pleasure from his work, the therapist also felt envious because he did not seem too happy in his work.

Mr. A. could "empathize" with the therapist's plight because, just as the therapist was very jealous of Mr. A.'s enjoyable sexual relationship with his wife, Mr. A. could remember feeling the same way about his parents' sexual relationship. And just as the therapist envied Mr. A.'s success in his job, he could remember when he was a boy and envied his father's popularity and business acumen. For several sessions, Mr. A. mocked the therapist, denigrated him, and was contemptuous of him. In one of his dreams during this period, he made the therapist a pig with glasses on, trying in vain to do work, but emerging as a failure. In another dream, he made the therapist a catcher on a homosexual baseball team. When the therapist asked why a catcher, Mr. A. answered that the therapist wanted "to sniff the batters' asses and touch their genitals when nobody was looking."

As Mr. A. projected his homosexual wishes onto the therapist and saw that he did not react argumentatively or defensively, he slowly began to identify with the therapist's attitude and started to look at his own homosexual fantasies. While tentative and frightened at first, he began to talk of his interest in boys' penises when he was a high school student and showered after gym. When the therapist asked Mr. A. to try to recall his fantasies when he was in the showers with other boys he associated to performing fellatio and having anal intercourse with the other boys. He then proceeded to tell the therapist that, ever since he was a student in high school, he "kept a secret from the world." The secret was that he was unable to urinate or defecate in public toilets. This inhibition caused him a great deal of embarrassment and difficulty. Therapy revealed that major etiological factors contributing to his phobia about urinating and defecating in restrooms were strong homosexual wishes to have fellatio and anal intercourse with the men in the restrooms.

As Mr. A. examined his homosexual fantasies with less terror, he could eventually allow himself to discuss them in his transference relationship. After having several dreams and fantasies in which the therapist was "insisting" on having anal intercourse with him, he acknowledged his own wish to have the therapist "insist" on having sex with him. He told the therapist a joke he had heard several years ago in which a man says to a young woman, "So help me, I'll rape you!" and the woman replies "So rape me, I'll help you!" After telling the joke he was able to point out his identification with the woman who was being raped.

During Mr. A.'s 270th treatment session, which occurred after a little over a year and a half of therapy, Mr. A. brought in a dream in which the therapist was raping him unmercifully. In the middle of anxiously and embarrassedly telling the therapist his dream, he began to giggle. When his giggling subsided, the therapist asked him what he was thinking and feeling while he was giggling. With a note of triumph he said, "You broke the hymen, my name is————." Sounding relieved, he went on to say how much he had enjoyed teasing the therapist, but he concluded, "Enough is enough." It should be mentioned that the client's last name was the same as a slang term used for the female genital.

After several sessions during which Mr. A. expressed a feeling of well-being because now he could tell the therapist his name, he had a dream in which he was a teacher discussing with his students the derivation of the word *secret*. Associations to the dream helped Mr. A. make his own interpretation. He pointed out the similarity between the words *secret* and *secretion* and thought that the dream was his way of making two more "confessions" and revealing "two more secrets." One "confession" was that Mr. A. masturbated two or three times a day and enjoyed "secreting a lot of sperm." He had held back talking about his compulsive masturbation because it involved raping men and being raped by them, and this was "too shameful and too embarrassing to talk about." "However," Mr. A. pointed out, "when I started to fantasy raping you and being raped by you, sucking you and being sucked by you, I thought it was time to talk about it in therapy." Mr. A. also acknowledged that, although his guilt, shame, and embarrassment made him hold back from examining his compulsive masturbation, holding back information made him feel powerful. He could tease the therapist the way he was teased by his parents, who both walked around in the nude but "never gave me very much, always holding back on me."

The other confession that Mr. A. could now make was that he had been an excellent student in college but abruptly quit as soon as the possibility of earning his degree became a reality. Therapy revealed that Mr. A. resisted talking about his academic successes because he was very frightened that the therapist would be envious and then reject him. He often thought that his achievements in school activated envy and rage in his father, and therefore it was something that had to be subdued or avoided altogether.

During the middle of the third year of Mr. A.'s therapy, further understanding emerged as to why he had to keep his intellectual capacities and achievements a secret. Succeeding academically or on the job was an oedipal victory that made him feel intensely guilty for "being too murderous and too sexual." He pointed out that, around the age of 14, when he was having many incestuous fantasies toward his mother and his sister as well as many "combative and murderous fantasies" toward his father, his father did die suddenly. A dream during this phase of treatment revealed what Mr. A. called his "biggest, deepest, and worst secret." He dreamed that his sister and mother were putting on bathrobes over their nude bodies while his father was lying on the floor dying. Mr. A. was very "apologetic" as he looked at his dead father in the dream, but he could sense a "note of glee" in himself at the same time.

As Mr. A. got more in touch with his profound guilt about believing he had killed his father and "took over" his mother and sister, he felt more comfortable about returning to college and completing his studies. Although he did complete his work, he had considerable resistance to giving up his low-paying job and bettering himself. Although Mr. A. speculated that he was afraid to become the therapist's equal, which did sound like a possibility, further treatment showed that another secret was at work. This secret, however, was less conscious. Dreams and fantasies of Mr. A. showed that he believed that, if he were successful on the job and in life, it would mean that he had completed his treatment successfully. "This," pointed out Mr. A. to the therapist, "would give you too much satisfaction. I don't want you to feel too smug."

Mr. A.'s last year of treatment consisted primarily of examining the secret pleasure he derived in defeating the therapist by not getting better. As he became more aware of his strong oedipal wishes to defeat the therapist and of his deep homosexual yearning to hold on to a father figure, he could eventually terminate treatment and move on to a successful career.

While working with Mr. A., the therapist analyzed several countertransference reactions, which helped him better understand the clinical material and relate to the client with more empathy. A few times during the therapy, particularly during the early phases, the therapist felt irritated and teased by Mr. A. and occasionally fantasied "insisting" that he tell the therapist his name, thus complying with Mr. A.'s own fantasy to be forced into submission (i.e., raped). In contrast to his treatment of any other client, the therapist found himself talking a great deal about the case of Mr. A. with colleagues. As the therapist analyzed his wish to discuss Mr. A. with colleagues, he got in touch with a fantasy—if he talked about the client enough, maybe someone would know Mr. A. and tell the therapist his real name. This preoccupation with Mr. A. certainly complied with Mr. A.'s own wish to tease the therapist and to have a father who was very concerned about him.

It should also be mentioned that, as the therapist became frustrated about not knowing Mr. A.'s secrets, he occasionally observed paranoid reactions in himself, wondering "Who was this man, really?" A few of his colleagues also became somewhat paranoid when he discussed the case with them and wondered about the "possible dangers" in treating Mr. A. These paranoid reactions in the therapist and his colleagues were again something Mr. A. unconsciously wished to happen (i.e., the therapist should suffer and feel in danger as he did).

Finally, Mr. A.'s secretiveness, teasing, and preoccupation with sexual matters kept the therapist very alert with him, almost always on his toes. This posture was one that Mr. A. craved because it gratified several wishes for him: He enjoyed teasing the therapist because he was getting sadistic gratification tormenting him rather than suffering himself; he had a parental figure giving him enormous attention; he gratified himself sexually by having a father figure constantly stimulated by him.

The dynamics of Mr. A.'s secretiveness become quite clear if we recall his dreams, fantasies, and transference reactions. Like most clients who keep secrets from their therapists, Mr. A. projected his critical superego onto the therapist and feared his disapproval (Fine, 1982; Freud, 1912a). However, as the clinical material demonstrates, Mr. A.'s secretiveness encompassed many other motives, and these motives seem to provide valuable suggestions as to why clients withhold material from their therapists.

Mr. A. enjoyed teasing his therapist. In effect, he was playing a popular childhood game, "I've Got a Secret, but I Won't Tell." By teasing his therapist, Mr. A. could place him in a passive, dependent position and sadistically torment him—a position he very much feared for himself but one he unconsciously wished for, too. In teasing the therapist, Mr. A. could move from his traditional position of victim to that of victor, from passive object to powerful director. Instead of the therapist being his tormentor, the therapist would be his slave. By teasing the therapist, Mr. A. could experience a sense of grandiosity and not feel castrated and humiliated.

One of the most important motives in Mr. A.'s keeping his name a secret was an unconscious wish that the therapist rape him. From the first session to the 270th, Mr. A. was extremely preoccupied with his fear that the therapist would "insist" on Mr. A. revealing his name (and using the couch). Mr. A.'s fear about the therapist's insistence masked his strong unconscious wish to be raped. When he could face his wish to be raped, to be a woman who would lose her virginity, he could reveal his name.

Mr. A.'s notions about the similarity between the words *secret* and *secretion* seem quite ingenious. They parallel the notion of Greenson (1967), who concluded that confessing a secret was like confessing unacceptable sexual wishes.

For Mr. A., keeping secrets was in many ways keeping his sexual fantasies hidden. Not only did he have to hide his wish to be a virgin woman and to be raped, and not only did he have to keep his compulsive mastur-bation a secret, but Mr. A. was also holding back his incestuous wishes and oedipal desires. Mr. A.'s secret murderous wishes coupled with his incestuous wishes (i.e., his oedipal conflict) seem to explain his wish to keep secret his academic accomplishments and intellectual potential. Doing well academically or professionally was unconsciously equated in Mr. A.'s mind with destroying father and seducing mother and sister. These wishes were Mr. A.'s "deepest, darkest, and worst secrets."

Finally, Mr. A. had to keep his negative therapeutic reaction (Freud, 1923a) a secret. He could not terminate treatment successfully until he could understand the dynamics of his secret wish to defeat his therapist and to deprive his therapist of the gratification of helping him.

The therapist's activity with Mr. A. suggests some means of helping a client who resists by withholding secrets. At no time did the therapist try to get Mr. A. to divulge his name. Rather, the therapist constantly con-veyed the attitude: "It is dangerous to tell me your name and to tell me other secrets as well. Don't worry about telling me your secrets. Let's concentrate on what frightens you so much about telling them to me." Feeling understood by the therapist, Mr. A. could stay in treatment. How-ever, what emerged as powerful dangers for Mr. A. were the possibilities of facing his homosexual fantasies and acknowledging his desire to be raped.

Mr. A. projected his forbidden sexual fantasies onto the therapist, and the therapist tried his best to encourage Mr. A. to do so. As the client saw that the therapist could face "his homosexual fantasies" and "desires to be raped," eventually Mr. A. could identify with the therapist's nondefensive, self-examining attitude, and he began to explore his own terrifying fantasies.

As Greenson has pointed out:

> The analysis of a secret is a very rewarding, although difficult (experi-ence). . . . However, it is important to realize that it is an error to use coercion, threats, or pleadings to get the patient to tell his secret. . . . The analytic attitude is that we shall attempt to analyze secrets as we would any other form of resistance. We are just as determined and just as pa-tient. We may be aware that a patient has a conscious secret, but we know that it is the unconscious factors that have to be analyzed before the patient can reveal the secret. (1967, pp. 130–133)

Persistent Lateness

The reasons that clients persistently arrive late for appointments are many and varied. Consequently, it is very important for therapists to encourage their clients to explore in depth what bothers them about coming to appointments on time before any definitive conclusions are drawn or any dynamic interpretations are made.

Some clients arrive late for appointments because they are full of mistrust and anger toward the therapist. They feel that the therapist is interested primarily in making money and has no real compassion for them. Other clients experience punctuality as yielding and submitting, and they worry that, by arriving on time, they might be surrendering their own powers to the therapist. Also there are clients who are so frightened of their warm and sexual feelings toward the therapist that they arrive late to maintain a distance. They do not want their therapy to become too important a feature in their lives, and they do not want the therapist to think that he is that important to them.

Therapists often react to their clients' lateness with anxiety. They worry that their clients may be planning to quit treatment; they begin to question their own competence; they wonder if they are unloved; and they feel hurt and angry because they believe they are being disparaged. When therapists respond personally to their clients' lateness, they can become punitive and admonish their clients for their "improper" behavior by telling them that they *should* arrive on time for their appointments. Some practitioners have gone so far as to threaten to stop the treatment if their clients continue to be late. Although these therapists use rationalizations to justify their threats, they are usually acting out revenge toward their clients.

In contrast to the therapists who respond punitively to their clients' lateness are those who become indulgent. They do not explore their clients' motives for coming late; they often make up the time that has been lost; or they may even offer make up appointments. Fearing their clients' permanent departure, they need to placate them.

When therapists respond either punitively or indulgently to their clients' lateness, they do not help them come to grips with what is motivating their resistive behavior. Those clients who are punished often react with fury and may quit the therapy altogether. Others get into a futile power struggle with their therapists. And those clients who are treated permissively often respond with guilt to their therapists' overgenerosity, or they may become very contemptuous of their therapists for an attitude that appears too obsequious.

Nothing seems to help clients resolve their resistances to arriving on time for appointments better than a neutral, empathic attitude that conveys to clients the following message: "I'm not going to tell you how to behave. But let's see if we can understand what bothers or frightens you when you do come late."

Dick B., age 31, had been in twice-a-week therapy with Dr. Z., a male therapist, for about a year. Although he had been coming to all of his sessions promptly, he began a pattern of arriving 10–15 minutes late for them. When Dr. Z. confronted him with his lateness, Dick could not think of any reasons to account for his behavior. Further exploration prompted Dick to say, "I guess treatment isn't as important to me as it used to be. I'm not as depressed, my sex life has improved, and I'm doing well on the job. Maybe I'm near termination!" As Dr. Z. reflected on Dick's associations, it became clear to him that Dick's lateness began when he was feeling and functioning better. He also realized that Dick's lateness expressed some anxiety about his improvement. Consequently, Dr. Z. said to Dick, "It appears that your lateness began when you started to feel and function better. Let's see what that means to you."

As Dick began to think about his improved psychological status, he had many associations to it. He realized that in so many ways he was doing a lot better than his father ever did, and he felt guilty about that. He also wondered if Dr. Z. resented his improvement because, as Dick pointed out, "No man is exempt from competition or jealousy." Finally, Dick realized, "When I feel good, I start to feel cocky and look down on people, and I think that bothers me."

As it became clearer to both Dr. Z. and to Dick that the client's persistent lateness expressed both his anxiety about competitive feelings and his anxiety about success, these issues received center stage in the therapy. The more Dick was able to talk about his competitive fantasies toward his father and toward Dr. Z., the more his persistent lateness subsided.

Although Dick is typical of many clients who come late for sessions, other clients use their lateness to ward off feelings of intimacy toward the therapist that appear dangerous to them.

Sally C., age 35, was a single woman who had been in twice-a-week treatment with a male therapist, Dr. Y. She sought treatment primarily because she was unable to sustain relationships with men. After her honeymoon phase of treatment ended, she experienced a treatment crisis during which she felt that Dr. Y. did not like her and found her "repulsive." When her thoughts about her therapist's negative reactions toward her were investigated, it became clear that Sally was reexperiencing her sibling rivalry toward her two sisters and brother. Just as she was convinced that her parents preferred her siblings to her, she was equally convinced that Dr. Y. preferred all his clients over her. After Sally ventilated her rage toward Dr. Y. and became aware of how she was recapitulating her past with him, her treatment crisis subsided and she became more positive toward Dr. Y.

At the beginning of Sally's second year of treatment, although she told Dr. Y. how much better she was feeling and how much he was helping her, she began to arrive around 20 minutes late for her sessions. When it was obvious to Dr. Y. that Sally's lateness was becoming a characteristic pattern, he asked her what she thought was going on between them that accounted for it. Sally, an elementary school teacher, told Dr. Y. that several of her students needed extra attention and she was spending time with them after school, "trying to help them feel more accepted." As Dr. Y. listened carefully to Sally's associations, it became apparent to him that Sally was giving her students what she wanted from him—namely, extra time and attention. Dr. Y. said to Sally, "You seem to find it easier to give to your students than to take from me!" Sally gasped after hearing Dr. Y.'s interpretation and told him that the idea of taking from him filled her with "horror."

As therapist and client explored what dangers Sally thought there were in taking from him, it became quite apparent that she entertained many pregenital fantasies toward him that terrified her. When Sally felt safer, she was able to talk about merging with Dr. Y., swimming around in his stomach, and never leaving him. Her symbiotic wishes were so frightening to her that she coped with them by trying to keep at a distance from Dr. Y. As Sally was helped to verbalize her symbiotic fantasies in her treatment sessions, her lateness diminished appreciably.

As we have suggested already, many clients view treatment as if they were submitting to a powerful and arbitrary parental figure. Resentful of what they experience as ruthless domination by their therapists, these clients act out their rage and revenge by continually coming late for their appointments. Although most of them explain their lateness by pointing to certain priority things that must be done at the office or at home, some consciously and purposively arrive late for sessions and say that they are doing this to avoid feeling that they are submitting to their therapists' wishes. They derive sadistic gratification from keeping their therapists waiting, and they appear similar to children who get pleasure from knowing their parents are worried about their whereabouts.

When clients consciously or unconsciously try to provoke their therapists into power struggles by coming late for appointments, it is important for therapists to do nothing but interpret their clients' forbidden desires and strong anxieties, and not be drawn into fracases with them. As soon as therapists find themselves in arguments with their clients, they have ceased working on their clients' resistances and instead have been successfully drawn into a power struggle. Although therapists who participate in disputes with their clients may win arguments, they often lose clients.

Marvin D., a 19-year-old college student, was in treatment with Ms. T. at a college mental health clinic. He was referred to the clinic by guidance personnel because his grades were so low that he was in danger of flunking out.

Seen on a weekly basis by Ms. T., Marvin spent the first couple of months ranting and raving about the college personnel. He described the professors as dogmatic, the dormitory administrators as contemptible, and the students as spineless. When Ms. T. patiently and empathically listened to Marvin's complaints without much comment, Marvin seemed to derive benefit from his contacts with her. His grades improved, his attacks on those around him lessened, and his self-esteem rose.

Soon after client and therapist took note of Marvin's improvement, Marvin started to come late for his appointments. When Ms. T. asked him about this, Marvin was evasive at first. On being encouraged to think more about why he was coming late, Marvin told Ms. T. that he resented her questions and saw them as "an invasion of my privacy." He went on to tell her that the appointment schedule seemed to be more for her convenience than for his, and furthermore, she probably was learning more from him than he was learning from her.

Moving away from her quiet, reflective posture that had governed her demeanor in treatment up until now, Ms. T. told Marvin, "Until now you have been cooperative, and that's why you've gotten something out of this. Now, you are rebelling and it's going to affect your life in a negative way." Marvin told Ms. T. that, until now, she had been a cooperative therapist, but now she was becoming a tyrannical parent "just like everybody else on this college campus seems to be." When Ms. T. told Marvin that he was distorting her intentions, he told her that she was distorting his. A power struggle ensued, and Marvin left treatment prematurely.

Whenever a client makes derogatory statements about significant others, as Marvin did in the case above, the therapist can be quite assured that sooner or later he will be the recipient of the client's hostility in one form or another. Just as it was helpful to Marvin when Ms. T. patiently listened to his criticisms about college personnel and did not censure him for his remarks, it would have been particularly helpful to him if she had maintained a similar attitude when Marvin demeaned her.

It is often much easier for therapists to maintain their neutrality when the client attacks others; they may lose it, though, when they are the victims of attack. Had Ms. T. recognized that Marvin's criticisms of school personnel were also criticisms of her, she might have been better prepared for his lateness, and had she permitted Marvin to voice his criticisms of her, which his lateness expressed, he may have been able to understand and master his lifelong battle with all authorities. However, inasmuch as Ms. T. argued with him, Marvin had to defeat her by leaving treatment.

It is hardly ever helpful to clients to tell them that their lateness should cease and desist. Also, it is hardly ever helpful to argue with them about anything. If clients are habitually late, usually the therapist can be of most assistance in resolving this resistance by encouraging them to think about what is bothersome about the therapy and what is irritating about the therapist. When clients voice what is irritating or upsetting to them, the enabling practitioner listens and does not argue, understands and does not criticize. With this therapeutic posture, the clinician stands the best chance of helping clients resolve the problems that their lateness expresses.

Persistent Cancellations

Clients can resist treatment by finding reasons to absent themselves from sessions. Although illnesses, deaths, and important business and professional engagements do occur, when clients cancel appointments persistently, most likely they are experiencing a great deal of anxiety in connection with the therapeutic encounter and therefore feel compelled to avoid it.

Very often the reasons for cancelling appointments are similar to those for arriving late for sessions. Some clients have to avoid their therapists because they are terrified of their sexual and aggressive fantasies toward them. Other clients tend to cancel appointments because they anticipate rejection from their therapists. And still other clients experience their therapists as powerful parents, and one way of reducing their therapists' power is to have little to do with them. This can be done most effectively by not coming to sessions.

Usually clients who habitually absent themselves from interviews feel much more frightened of treatment than those who are habitually late. Absence from interviews implies a desire for complete avoidance; lateness, on the other hand, suggests some ambivalence toward the therapist and the therapy, because when the client is late for interviews, he is absent from some of and present at some of the session.

Therapists' policies about cancellations vary considerably. Some practitioners do not charge for missed appointments and try to find alternate times for clients who cancel. Other therapists charge for all missed appointments and never offer alternate times. Like some physicians, there are therapists who do not charge for canceled appointments if their clients notify them 24 hours in advance. Then there are practitioners who charge half of their usual fee when a cancellation occurs. There are other types of arrangements, too. Different policies are formulated by different therapists who have different needs, anxieties, therapeutic philosophies, and kinds of clienteles.

When persistent cancellations occur, the therapist should try first and foremost to help the client express what frightens, angers, or upsets him about the therapy and the therapist. However, both clients and therapists tend to feel much more comfortable when there is some agreement made between them for handling cancellations.

Although there are some exceptions to the rule, such as those whose jobs require them to be out of town on occasion, most clients in the long run profit the most from their therapy when they are charged the full fee when they cancel appointments. Charging clients for missed sessions has the effect of focusing squarely on their transference reactions (Fine, 1982). Feelings toward the therapist that are being expressed by cancellations have a better chance of being discharged in treatment sessions if the therapist does not indulge the client. Second, if practitioners do not charge for missed appointments, clients can interpret this policy as condoning their absences. Third, when therapists do not charge for missed appointments, they can appear to have no needs of their own, like omnipotent parents. This gives clients a false sense of reality and may even help them maintain some of their own grandiose fantasies. Finally, it can be helpful to clients in overcoming their resistances to accepting reality to note that their therapists are not that dissimilar from landlords who charge rent regardless of whether or not their tenants are in the apartment, or from academic institutions that charge tuition whether or not students attend classes.

Unless therapists genuinely believe that charging for canceled sessions is truly in the best interests of the client and will really help in resolving resistances, they probably should not use this policy. However, they will have to accept that some of their clients will be somewhat suspicious of them and wonder about their leniency.

Susan E., a single woman in her early thirties, was in treatment with Dr. S., a male psychologist. She sought therapy for depression, lack of sexual desire, and job dissatisfaction. From the very beginning, treatment had not been easy for Susan. She felt that Dr. S. was seeing her only to make money, and she questioned the value of talking about herself, particularly about her dreams, fantasies, and personal history. Despite her complaints, she stayed in treatment and did not miss one session for close to a year.

As Susan began to look for a new job during her second year of treatment, she canceled several appointments with Dr. S. Dr. S. did not question the fact that Susan arranged for her job interviews at times when she had regularly scheduled appointments with him. Rather, he encouraged her to "better herself" by looking for a job that would pay her more money and give her more satisfaction. At first, Susan was pleased with Dr. S.'s attitude about cancellations, but she slowly began to question his overpermissiveness. In describing a potential employer, she seemed to be referring to Dr. S. indirectly when he said, "At first he seemed like a nice guy. But after a while, I got the impression that people could walk all over him and I don't want a boss like that." A little later, referring to another potential employer, she remarked, "He seemed to be somewhat masochistic. He was overconcerned about pleasing me and did not talk very much about what I could do or should do on the job."

When Dr. S. could, he offered Susan alternate times for her regularly scheduled appointments. However, most of the time she refused them, saying that the times offered were inconvenient for her. When she did come to appointments, she often arrived late and related to Dr. S. rather superficially. When Dr. S. commented on Susan's lateness and changed way of relating to him, Susan smiled in relief. She said, "I wondered when you were going to bring it up. If you don't take care of yourself and try to make a decent living, how can I allow myself to do the same?" She spent several interviews deriding Dr. S. and referred to him as "a puppy dog," "a Casper Milquetoast," and "a masochist." She concluded, "When you make your job less important to you than you make my job, I lose respect for you."

Susan's response to the way Dr. S. handled cancellations is quite instructive. We learn that when the therapist does not charge for missed sessions, the client is likely to feel that the therapist does not value the therapy enough and does not take sufficient care of himself. The therapist's lax policy can create guilt in the client, because the client is not being confronted with the hostility that is being acted out. While therapists have to remain flexible about their fee policies, they also have to keep in mind that their clients' persistent cancellations almost always express resistance. The resistance must be confronted, and it seems to stand a better chance of resolution in the transference relationship if the therapist not only explores the client's motives but also charges for missed sessions.

Prolonged Silences

As we suggested in our discussion of keeping secrets from the therapist, although most clients recognize that, in order to mature they need to talk, many feel quite reluctant to do so. As in most interpersonal events, when clients do not talk to their therapists, the silence can have many possible meanings. By not talking, a client may be acting out defiance toward the practitioner. As one client stated, "I know you are in this business to listen. I'll fix you 'good' by depriving you of what you really want." A client's silence may also express a wish to resist by becoming very passive. Said another client, "I feel like doing absolutely nothing here. I hate to work. If *you* want to talk, it is O.K."

Frequently sexual and aggressive fantasies seem so dangerous to some clients that they cope with their terror by becoming speechless. Occasionally clients may be convinced that their therapists are not interested in their productions. By being silent, they can determine if the therapist will become sufficiently concerned to ask them to talk. Declared a client, "I'll be silent so that eventually you might say, 'What comes to your mind?' Then I'll hear your voice, and I'll know that you care."

As with any resistance, it is important for the practitioner to help the client understand that it is crucial for therapist and client to ascertain the nature of the dangers that maintain the client's silence. Although most clinicians accept this axiom, their clients' silences can arouse intense countertransference problems in them. Some therapists react to prolonged silences of their clients with irritation or boredom. Feeling that they are being wiped out by these clients, they retaliate by becoming very silent themselves (Greenson, 1967). Other practitioners respond to prolonged silences with feelings of helplessness and hopelessness. Feeling very discouraged, they believe that nothing they say will be effective (Fenichel, 1945) and give up. Some therapists feel so indignant toward their clients' seeming disrespect and uncooperativeness that they handle their hostility by commanding their clients to speak.

One way that therapists can be helpful to clients who resist by prolonged silence is to ascertain what talking means to these clients. For some, talking is equivalent to revealing parts of themselves that are embarrassing and that should be kept hidden. For others, talking is experienced as a form of submission; hence, they protect themselves from being dominated by maintaining their silence. Sometimes speaking is associated with forbidden sexual pleasure, and therefore some clients have to inhibit their speech in the same way that they have to inhibit their sexuality.

After therapists have determined what speech unconsciously means to their silent clients, they should try to reduce their clients' sense of threat and enhance their sense of safety in the therapy.

The following case, presented in detail, demonstrates the unconscious meaning that talking has for many silent clients and also suggests some ways of helping these clients resolve their resistances.

Rhoda F., was a 21-year-old married woman who sought psychotherapy because of severe sexual frigidity, phobias, work inhibitions, several psychosomatic complaints, tics, and tremors.

When Rhoda was 8 years old, her mother died of cancer after a long and painful illness. Father, an acute alcoholic, was unemployed frequently. Consequently, Rhoda took over all the domestic chores, including the care of several younger siblings. Although a capable student, Rhoda was verbally inhibited in class and frequently broke out in hives when called upon by her teachers to speak. Her social life was meager, and from early child-hood through her teens, she spent much of her time in fantasy.

As the client's anamnesis unfolded, it became apparent that Rhoda viewed her mother as someone who always sought a parasitic and sym-biotic relationship, mostly with her but with the other members of the family as well. Describing her mother as "engulfing" and "hurtful," Rhoda intensely feared contact with her. Yet she also entertained fantasies of blissful merger with her mother. Father was experienced as "overstimu-lating," "overhungry," "demanding," and "slovenly." Like mother, he seemed to remove himself emotionally from Rhoda when it came to meet-ing any of her maturational needs. He alternated between violent-tempered alcoholic bouts and periods of withdrawal.

Rhoda's ego functions were seriously impaired. Constantly over-whelmed by sadistic fantasies, she had superficial relationships with peo-ple. She also had to deal constantly with terrifying fantasies of being attacked.

Rhoda came to treatment a few months after marrying a neighbor who was described as very shy, inhibited, and unaggressive. The client related to her male therapist, Dr. R., with intense verbal inhibition and with much embarrassment. In her treatment sessions, she frequently blushed and often broke out with hives. On the very few occasions that she was able to utter a few words, there was a strong submissive quality in her demeanor.

Rhoda presented her problems and salient life history in her first couple of interviews but then found it difficult to proceed further. She responded to interpretations of her anxiety in the transference either with quiet sub-missiveness or with silent withdrawal and missed several appointments.

Any verbal activity, whether it was Rhoda or Dr. R. talking, tended to exacerbate her symptoms. Even a couple of words from either of them brought on hives, blushing, and nausea. When it became obvious that helping Rhoda to talk only made her feel worse, Dr. R. thought that maybe what Rhoda needed was an experience where she could feel safe in not feeling compelled to produce. Consequently, he said to Rhoda, "I think it is too upsetting for you to talk. How would you feel if we both were quiet for a while and then see what happens? If you feel like talking at any time, I'll be glad to listen to you." Rhoda silently nodded to Dr. R.'s suggestion, and as if to test him, remained absolutely silent for the rest of the session.

During the next 3 months of twice-a-week therapy except for Dr. R. greeting Rhoda with a nod, reminding her when each session was termi-nated, and thanking her for her monthly check, both parties maintained a mutual silence. Rhoda gradually became more relaxed, less apprehensive, and her blushing and hives disappeared.

At the end of the 3 months, Dr. R. asked Rhoda how she was experiencing the therapy. Rhoda replied quickly and said, "Fine." When asked what was fine about the therapy, Rhoda said that she could never recall an experience "with anyone where I didn't feel forced to *put out* for them. Here it is very different, and I'd like it to continue." Because the silence appeared to be having a remedial effect on Rhoda, Dr. R. accepted the client's prescription, and the mutual silence continued for several more weeks.

Rhoda broke the silence during the fifth month of treatment to report that she had sex with her husband the past week and "it worked." She went on to say that, although she was having sex, she felt that she had "defied" the therapist. Exploration revealed that Rhoda was experiencing Dr. R. as "a lazy good-for-nothing" who didn't care about her welfare and didn't want her to have any pleasure from life. She said with much anger, "You are lazy just like my drunken father."

With Rhoda now willing to talk, Dr. R. encouraged her to look at her hostile feelings toward him. She likened the therapist more and more to her father, who wanted Rhoda to cater to him, submit to him, and indulge him. Her verbal aggression continued for about a month, during which time Rhoda was symptom free, felt freer in all her relationships, enrolled in an evening college course, and was promoted from a stenographer to assistant office manager at work.

When Rhoda's husband ascribed her marked improvement to her treatment and wanted Dr. R.'s help for himself, the client retreated into silence again. When investigative questions went unanswered and interpretations of Rhoda's defiance and negativism induced the return of past symptoms, Dr. R. and Rhoda were silent again for several more sessions.

Rhoda interrupted the second mutual silence by asking, "How can I beat you? By talking or being quiet?" When Dr. R. asked why it was so important to defeat him, Rhoda talked of her wish to defeat anybody who had control over her. She associated to both of her parents, who she felt exploited her; thus, she could not trust the therapist, who might do the same.

The treatment turned more and more to a mutual investigation of Rhoda's transference reactions, resistances, fantasies, and history, with the client freely associating to her wishes to defeat and rebel.

Silence can be an overdetermined reaction, as it was in Rhoda's case. By not talking to the therapist, Rhoda could control him, manipulate him, and render him impotent, thus placing the therapist in the same psychological position that she had been in with her parents and significant others. Furthermore, by maintaining her silence, Rhoda could feel triumphant inasmuch as she could experience, for the first time in her life, a power over somebody who was asking something of her that she did not want to give.

By not insisting that she talk, the therapist enabled Rhoda to feel safer with him and understood by him. This increased her self-esteem and her self-confidence substantially. As a result, she was able to move toward an examination of her lifelong rebellious wishes and defiant fantasies.

Often the persistently silent client is trying to defeat the therapist's efforts. If the therapist does not react with impatience or with punishment, but instead views the silence as an inevitable and understandable resistance that protects the client from danger, the persistent silence usually can be overcome.

Persistent Demands on the Therapist

During the middle phase of psychotherapy, when the relationship between client and therapist deepens, other psychological events also occur. The client, experiencing the uniqueness of the confidential therapeutic relationship, where all attention is focused on him, begins to experience more intense fantasies, more powerful id wishes, and more punitive superego commands. The client's dreams suggest more primitive and childlike desires, and the client's transference reactions reveal more complex problems. All these psychological events induce considerable anxiety in the client.

One of the ways that clients cope with their anxieties during the middle phase of treatment is by fighting the demands placed on them in their role as clients and instead placing demands on their therapists. Although this form of resistance is used during other phases of therapy, it is very common during the middle phase. Instead of answering their therapists' questions about their own feelings, thoughts, and reactions, clients ask about the therapist's feelings, thoughts, and reactions. Instead of interacting with the therapist only in the consultation room, clients want to talk to their therapists over the telephone between sessions. Sometimes they demand to see the therapist in a setting outside of the therapist's office, such as in a restaurant. In lieu of 45- or 50-minute appointments, clients try to prolong their sessions by several minutes or may ask for double sessions. These and other demands of clients suggest that the frustrating aspects of psychotherapy are very upsetting to them and that therefore they want to alter the arrangements.

As we have suggested in previous chapters, many therapists have considerable difficulty coping with their clients' demands. They usually prefer to ask the questions rather than to answer them. They want to hear fantasies rather than to report them. They would rather direct the therapy than be directed. As clients try to engage them in role reversals, therapists may resent feeling controlled and become uncomfortable as they fear that their private lives are being invaded.

We have also pointed out in previous chapters that two types of countertransference problems are quite common when therapists are confronted with their clients' demands. One response is to gratify their clients by answering their questions and yielding to their requests. The other reaction is to respond mechanically to their clients with a cold, stereotypic retort, such as, "Why do you ask?" or "Why do you need me to do this?" Some therapists even go as far as forbidding their clients to ask questions or make requests, and justify their stance by calling it "good for the treatment." To repeat, neither of these responses helps resolve resistances. If clients are gratified, they remain indulged children who will not be able to cope with frustration. If they are coldly and mechanically treated, they become so furious that they cannot cooperate with the therapist and might leave treatment altogether.

In Chapter 3, we discussed the dynamics of clients who ask the therapist personal questions and suggested some technical procedures to help them resolve this form of resistance. During the middle phase of treatment, personal questions are posed to the therapist again, but they are of a different nature. In the beginning phase of treatment, clients' questions usually revolve around one of their major concerns, the therapist's qualifications. As treatment moves on and clients talk about their marriages, sexual lives, rages, and other intimate issues, their questions usually involve concerns about these issues. However, the same principle that we discussed in Chapter 3 still holds: The clinician should always attempt to ascertain the latent meaning of the client's questions and help the client appreciate their significance.

When a client asks if the therapist is married, for example, the client may wish to use the therapist as a role model for his own marriage; the client may wish to expose immaturity or lack of sophistication on the therapist's part, thereby indicating resentment and fear of the helping situation; the client may be having loving and sexual fantasies about the therapist; or the client may be competing with the therapist and attempting to place him in the position of interviewee. Because these and other possible motives may be behind questions, it is rarely helpful to answer them directly.

To eventually help the client resolve resistances, it is important to relate such questions to the ongoing sessions. For example, when an adolescent boy had been talking about "hating all adults over 35" and then asked his social worker how old she was, the social worker directed the client's attention to this sequence of events and said, "I think you are wondering whether to hate me or not." The teenager was then able to look at his ambivalence toward his therapist and toward other adults.

As we have implied several times, no therapist interested in helping the client gain increased autonomy and higher self-esteem will worry too much about frustrating the client. No therapist need fear saying to a client, "We want to understand you better. Let's see if we can figure out why you asked me." Yet some clients do not take "no" for an answer. If they persist in asking questions and in wanting answers, the therapist interested in resolving resistances might say, "You are persisting in asking questions and in wanting answers. Let's see what is on your mind that might account for your persistence. We should get to your real concerns."

When clients see that the practitioner uses everything they say as grist for the therapeutic mill, they gain some conviction that the best way to help themselves is to explore the thoughts, feelings, and fantasies that propel their questions.

Oscar G., aged 40, a father attending a child guidance clinic asked Mr. Q., the social worker, if he was an athlete. When Mr. Q. replied, "I know athletics interest you, Mr. G. Would you like me to be an athlete?" Oscar responded, "Well, if you aren't, you must be some kind of fairy! Are you?" "You are wondering whether I'm gay," Mr. Q. responded. Oscar eventually went on to discuss his doubts about his own masculinity and his consequent discomfort with his sons. By not answering Oscar's questions directly, Mr. Q. could help Oscar face his own anxiety about his homosexual fantasies.

Personal questions, if explored fully, will tell us something more about the client. Whatever information a clinician reveals about himself usually has limited positive effect on the outcome of the therapy. Therefore questions such as these should be answered only under very rare circumstances.

Whether the client's questions are about the therapist's life or not, the same principle holds: Find out why the client is concerned with the issue at hand.

Requests for Phone Contact Between Sessions

Many clients find it difficult to be independent of their therapists between sessions. For some, their symbiotic longings are so strong, they feel convinced that they will not survive without contact with their therapists. Other clients harbor such murderous rage toward their therapists that they have to make phone calls to find out if the practitioner is still alive. Also, there are clients who feel so romantically attached to their therapists that they have to make phone calls to express their love. Finally, there are those clients who crave love so much that they feel compelled to call their therapists for reassurance and validation.

Inasmuch as the middle phase of treatment frequently provokes child-like yearnings in clients, the therapist can emerge as a parental figure whose warmth is craved and whose presence seems mandatory. Rarely are clients aware that they are seeking a merger with their therapists when they seek telephone contacts. On the contrary, they often arrange some crisis that needs immediate attention and are convinced that they cannot wait until their next session to discuss it. Instant help is needed for such things as a severe marital conflict, a job that seems in jeopardy, or a parent–child fracas that seems unresolvable. Also, some clients feel suicidal, over-whelmingly depressed, or intensely anxious and believe they must call their therapists or they will disintegrate and deteriorate.

When therapists receive a phone call from clients who are depressed or suicidal because their mates are ready to abandon them or their bosses are ready to fire them, it is very tempting to try to handle the crisis over the phone. The client appears in serious jeopardy, and the therapist feels an obligation to provide some relief.

It is important for the practitioner to keep in mind that crises rarely occur within a brief period of time. If the client is really in a difficult and perplexing situation, the therapist, in most instances, has already heard some details about it. Therefore, it is reasonable to hypothesize that, when a client calls a therapist between sessions, the client is trying to cope with feelings, fantasies, and anxieties that are not being discussed in regular sessions.

Like any other event between client and therapist, when a client calls a therapist, the practitioner should be aware that the call has unconscious meaning and also transference implications. Experienced clinicians have observed that it is only certain clients who wish to call their therapists be-tween sessions, and it is usually these clients who call habitually. This tends to suggest that in many instances, if not most, the client who wants phone contact with the therapist is using the calls as a resistance to avoid talking about such issues as dependency cravings, sexual longings, or ag-gressive fantasies.

When therapists find themselves receiving many phone calls from clients, it behooves them to examine their own countertransference feel-ings. Some therapists, to feel needed and important, subtly or even overtly encourage their clients to call them between sessions. Other therapists who feel anxious about their clients terminating or worried that they are not doing enough for their clients, may also encourage their clients to call them. As is true with any form of client resistance, therapists always have an obligation to examine their own possible roles in creating or sustaining it.

Despite alll these cautions, it is important to mention that real crises do occur in clients' lives. Sudden deaths do happen, illnesses do erupt, and serious accidents do take place. Therefore, no therapist can be absolutely certain when a client calls that the client is acting out a resistance and should be told immediately to wait until the next appointment to discuss what is on his mind.

When practitioners do receive phone calls from their clients, it would appear that the most helpful response is to listen to the client for a minute or two. If it is clear that the matter is not absolutely urgent, and most of the time it is not, the therapist can tell the client, "What is happening is very important, and I would like to try to help you with this. I'd like to discuss this with you in detail in our next session." Most clients can accept the frustration that is inherent in these remarks, particularly when they sense that the therapist is interested in their welfare and has a real desire to discuss the issue with them.

Some clients, however, will not accept the therapist's limiting the call to a minute or two and will rebel at the idea of waiting until their next appointment. If the therapist has some time available, it may be wise to tell these clients that they may have a session in the office before their next appointment. When clients reject this offer, the therapist can begin to think about how much the client is resisting having regular appointments and how much the client is seeking extratherapeutic gratification.

Mindy H., a single woman of 30, had been in treatment for about a year with Dr. P., a female therapist. Mindy sought treatment because she was suffering from many problems: depression, sexual conflicts, job dissatisfaction, and psychosomatic ailments. Her twice-a-week therapy had been helpful to her, and many of her symptoms had diminished in severity.

Because Mindy was so grateful to the therapist for the benefits that she derived from treatment, she began to have many loving feelings toward Dr. P. As her loving feelings grew, Mindy became interested in Dr. P.'s private life. When Dr. P. did not answer Mindy's questions regarding Dr. P.'s education, social life, and intellectual interests but turned them back to her with the suggestion that Mindy examine her own fantasies, Mindy began to become quite depressed. Concomitant with her depression, Mindy began to call Dr. P. between sessions. The phone calls were made for a variety of reasons: to change appointments, refer other patients, and ask if insurance forms could be filled out.

Although Dr. P. noted that Mindy's phone calls began when she started to become interested in the therapist's private life and was not getting her curiosity satisfied in the sessions, Dr. P. also noted that Mindy made no reference to her phone calls during her sessions. Therefore, Dr. P. decided to ask Mindy about the calls.

At first, Mindy justified her calls by terming them "legitimate requests." However when Dr. P. asked her why she preferred to make her requests over the phone rather than in the office, Mindy became furious. She told Dr. P. what "a rigid therapist" she was and how much Dr. P. "shunned human contact." She told Dr. P. further that she was beginning to like her, but obviously Dr. P. "would not encourage a human friendship but just wanted a therapeutic relationship."

When it became clear to Dr. P. that Mindy's phone calls were an expression of her resistance to accepting the limitations of the therapy and that what Mindy really wanted was a friendship, Dr. P. told her, "I think you would rather have me as a friend than as your therapist." Mindy readily agreed and began to weep. She brought out strong yearnings for a mother figure and while doing so had many fantasies of being a baby rocked, hugged, and nourished. The more Mindy could talk about her yearnings, the less she had to make phone calls to her therapist. Furthermore, by talking about her desires for a mother and examining her anger at Dr. P. and at others for not gratifying these wishes, her depression subsided.

Although there are exceptions, most phone calls from clients, particularly from those who call the therapist habitually, should be regarded as signs of resistance. The client's phone call often reflects a desire to be taken care of by the therapist but can gratify other motives as well. The call can ward off hostile feelings toward the therapist, serve the purpose of trying to placate the therapist, and be used to discharge affects and thoughts that cannot be verbalized safely in the treatment situation.

Extratherapeutic Contacts

Most therapists discourage social contacts between clients and themselves. Rather than yield to their requests to have lunch with them or to attend a party together, most therapists prefer to help their clients investigate the fantasies and anxieties that motivate these requests. If clients persist and go on insisting that the therapist attend an engagement party, a wedding, a baptism, or a Bar Mitzvah, the therapist who is interested in helping clients resolve their resistances will tactfully say, "I really can't go" and will stress the importance of understanding what is going on in the client–therapist relationship and in the client's unconscious that prompts the request. As we have suggested several times, indulging clients' demands prevents them from strengthening their frustration tolerance and from strengthening such other ego functions as impulse control and object relations.

Despite the fact that many therapists try to conform to the model of the "abstinent, anonymous surgeon who is an opaque mirror for the client" (Freud, 1912a), many therapists are not able to practice what they preach. Just as Freud defined technique narrowly but maintained with his patients personal relationships that he took for granted and tended to exclude from the therapy (Lipton, 1977), many therapists show that they are really quite ambivalent about the role of the therapist.

If a conflict does exist between safeguarding the therapist's anonymity as opposed to the therapist emerging as a "real" person, it may become most apparent when therapist and client meet outside the consultation room. If the two parties are face to face at a professional meeting, in the theater, at the supermarket, or on the street, unconscious transference and countertransference fantasies may be activated, and unresolved conflicts of both parties may come to the fore.

One of the possible sources of tension in the extratherapeutic contact is that both client and therapist may wish to gratify exhibitionistic and voyeuristic wishes but concomitantly feel obliged to defend against this (Tarnower, 1966). A corollary of this is that both parties may also become frightened if they feel that the image they would like the other to maintain of them has a chance of being punctured. It is difficult, if not impossible, for a therapist to sustain a surgeon-like countenance when the client observes him outside his office.

Because treasured unconscious transference and countertransference positions risk being altered, because regressive wishes can be stimulated, and because new and different behaviors are often prescribed when the client is not in the therapist's office, the extratherapeutic contact can assume a phobic and neurotic quality for client or therapist. Particularly if client and therapist meet in the presence of others, both may fear that the confidentiality of their sessions is in danger of being violated. And even if they go unobserved, client and therapist may become unduly concerned about the injunction to avoid acting out. Finally, the parties are often caught unprepared, a situation that usually induces some anxiety.

The extratherapeutic contact has the potential of releasing hidden anxiety, thus provoking transference and countertransference fantasies and affects, such as primal scene conflicts, oedipal and homosexual desires, sadistic and masochistic urges, and oral incorporative yearnings. This may be why few therapists have reported on their outside contacts with clients. In any event, the dynamic meaning of these experiences for the client and therapist has been relatively unexplored and has tended to be shrouded in secrecy.

One of the few papers on this subject was written by Tarnower (1966). He discussed the phobic wish of some therapists and clients to avoid such contacts. He suggested that extratherapeutic meetings can provide important material for the therapy and that clients generally respond intensely to them. While the therapist may justify his wish to avoid this type of contact as an effort not to contaminate the transference, his avoidance may serve defensive purposes for him. Because extratherapeutic contacts may gratify a variety of transference and countertransference wishes, Tarnower concluded that these contacts must always be subjected to exploration.

In the paper "A Psychoanalyst's Anonymity: Fiddler behind the Couch," Katz (1978) wrote of his experiences with patients after they observed him play the leading role of Tevye in the Topeka Civic Theater's production of *Fiddler on the Roof*. Katz concluded that his patients' responses (which were intense) fell into the familiar categories of transference and resistance phenomena and could be managed without employing special techniques.

Whether or not therapists carefully try to avoid meeting their clients outside the consultation room, the extratherapeutic contact is for many a fact of life. Even in large communities, clients can meet their therapists at the theater, restaurants, concert hall, swimming pool, or supermarket. In smaller communities, they drive by each other's homes, meet in office buildings, at P.T.A. meetings, at social gatherings, in the park, or on the street. Mental health professionals in large and small communities meet their therapists as teachers in the classroom, in the audience of a lecture, on the podium at scientific meetings, or in journals and textbooks.

Inasmuch as the extratherapeutic contact is a clinical reality for many clients and therapists, it is incumbent upon both parties not to try to avoid or stimulate such contacts, but to investigate their dynamic meaning to the client when they do occur. If the extratherapeutic contact is viewed as an interpersonal experience that is not to be encouraged or discouraged but is to be thoroughly understood, it can then be used in the treatment to promote understanding of transference and countertransference phenomena, clarify resistances, and serve as a barometer of therapeutic progress.

When therapeutic neutrality is truly valued as an important dimension of treatment, the therapist will not prohibit or permit a specific action of the client; rather the therapist will try to understand it when it occurs. Consequently, the orientation toward extratherapeutic contact will be similar to the stance we have suggested regarding other interpersonal events that transpire between therapist and client (e.g., canceled appointments and telephone calls). The therapist will attempt to help the client associate to these events so that fantasies, dreams, history, and other dimensions of the client's psychic life will be revealed.

Inasmuch as there is a paucity of case examples of the extratherapeutic contact in the literature, a case illustration will be presented in detail. The case* is one of intensive psychoanalytically oriented therapy and is helpful

* This case is drawn from an article by the author, "Extraanalytic Contacts: Theoretical and Clinical Considerations," *Psychoanalytic Quarterly, 50*(3), pp. 238–259 (1981).

in pinpointing the many transference and countertransference factors involved in the extratherapeutic contact.

Jane was a single, 30-year-old teacher of emotionally disturbed children. She sought treatment because she suffered from severe bouts of depression, psychosomatic ailments, lack of work satisfaction, and poor interpersonal relationships, especially with men.

Her mother died a few months after she had given birth to Jane's brother, when Jane was 3 years old. The client viewed her life as enjoyable prior to that time. "Daddy and I were like lovers and buddies, and I was in heaven! Mother was sick most of the time, and I don't really remember her very much." For many years after her mother's death, Jane was described by her father and other relatives as "paralyzed, depressed, and green."

After a short period of resisting getting involved in treatment because she feared being overwhelmed by strong oral and symbiotic cravings, Jane moved eagerly into a four-times-a-week therapy. During the first 18 months of treatment, she became aware of feelings of guilt because she experienced herself as an oedipal victor. She also uncovered strong yearnings to be close to her mother. While looking at her wishes to merge symbiotically with her mother, Jane brought out a desire to attend a lecture that the therapist was giving for social workers and psychologists. "It is in a little over a week, and I'll need a 'yes' or 'no' answer because we won't have time to look at all my motives by then," Jane declared. When the therapist remained silent, Jane expressed indignation and irritation that he would not make the decision for her.

In a later session prior to the lecture, when the therapist interpreted her wish for permission or prohibition from him, Jane began to feel considerable anguish. With much hesitation and reluctance, she stated that the prospect of the extratherapeutic contact was stimulating wishes to eat various parts of the therapist's body—arms, legs, penis, etc. While she associated to some of her cannibalistic fantasies toward him, she cried, felt uncomfortable, was nauseated, and became "very disgusted" with herself.

The cannibalistic fantasies that were stimulated by the idea of seeing the therapist in a face-to-face encounter made Jane feel so guilty and ashamed that she began to wonder whether she should attend the lecture. She began to experience herself as an "oddball" and said, "Everybody there will know I'm a hungry and peculiar baby who wants to gobble you up." Although Jane continued to have her misgivings, she anticipated attending the lecture with more excitement than guilt. Yet her ambivalence and teasing continued. She pointed out at the session before the lecture,

"I'm going, I think. You haven't stopped me like some therapists do—but then again, you haven't approved of the idea, either. I'll take my chances about how much I'll be improper and look peculiar."

At the lecture, the therapist noticed that Jane was animatedly taking notes. Part of his recording after the lecture stated: "Jane was eager to get everything that she heard on paper. She seemed to value what I said, and I feel she experienced the lecture as if she were at her mother's breast, taking in everything she could." With regard to his own reactions, the therapist recorded: "I enjoyed seeing Jane, and I really got to feel how pleasureful it must be for a mother to feed an infant. For me, the lecture gratified my countertransference wish to be the mother that Jane yearns for."

Jane came in excitedly to the sessions following the lecture and said: "You became a real person for me, rather than some distant figure. I saw you smile, clean your glasses, and a whole lot of stuff that I never get to see. It was great—but I was too stimulated. I had fantasies of sucking in each and every one of your words. I wrote down everything you said so I could go over it again and again. At the lecture and later when I went over your work, I had fantasies of first sucking in your words, then eating up your tongue, and then later your whole head, and then your body. I remember at one point in the lecture feeling that your penis was like a big breast covering me snugly." She pointed out that she wanted to "hold on to every one of your words and never let them go away." Later, she said, "If I didn't busy myself writing, I was afraid that I might come up to the podium, grab you, and devastate you. I was, and still am, so scared of my crazy appetite."

Toward the end of the session, Jane reported a dream: "I found my mother in a kitchen of a building. As I looked at her, I wanted to hug her but was scared to do so." Jane had several associations to the dream. The building appeared very similar to the one where the therapist lectured. Just as she felt very conflicted about hugging and eventually devouring the therapist, so did she feel very frightened about her wishes to incorporate her mother. "I was so scared of gobbling you up; and in the dream—I guess— if I let myself go, I'd rip my mother apart. You seemed so near yet so far—oh, just like I made my mother in the dream! But if I don't keep you far away, God knows what I'll do to you."

In subsequent sessions, Jane's excitement slowly moved to depression. She referred to the extratherapeutic contact as the therapist's "holding out a carrot" and felt that the whole situation "was a tease." She admonished the therapist for not stopping her from going to the lecture and reflected, "All you did was make me think I could have a close relationship with a good parent, and then you let me down." Her depression eventually turned to strong rage. In the transference, she experienced the therapist as the mother "who promises but doesn't deliver and may as well be dead."

As Jane's treatment continued, she moved back and forth between her wish to merge with her mother, her hatred of her mother for dying, and her oedipal competition and guilt. By the third year of treatment, she was dealing with phallic issues and her competition with father, brother, and the therapist (whom she was experiencing as father and brother in the transference). During the third year of treatment, she became aware of a panel discussion in which the therapist would be participating and stated that she was planning to attend. She dreamed that she was chairman of a panel discussion, and the therapist was a young boy who flubbed his lines. In Jane's associations to her dream, she said that she would like to feel like a boss to the therapist "instead of always feeling bossed around" by him. "I'd like to have you feel uncertain of yourself and be weak, like I often feel when I'm with you." She likened the therapist to her father, who always seemed so extraordinarily confident of himself. "You are smug and cocky just like he is," Jane stated angrily. She then had a fantasy of putting a rusty meat hook up the therapist's anus and castrating him by yanking off his penis and "chewing it up savagely." This was followed by another fantasy of both client and therapist being soldiers and of her shooting the therapist with two dozen bullets.

At the second extratherapeutic contact, the therapist thought he saw Jane in the audience, frowning, but he was not sure. After the panel discussion, he wrote, "Jane has been associating to her phallic wishes and phallic competition. The transference has been essentially negative. She experiences me as the father whom she would like to castrate and then hostilely incorporate his penis. I suspect that she will report negative feelings about my participation in this panel. . . . I felt somewhat vulnerable as I thought about Jane hearing me talk and had associations to my younger sister with whom I competed. I have to observe more carefully my own wishes to compete with Jane and whatever sense of threat I feel when with her."

Following the second contact, Jane entered her session in a rage. She bellowed, "You are a big exhibitionist! A 20-foot prick is what you are—always showing off! Why don't you keep quiet for a while? You take up too much room! You make too much noise! Your voice is too booming!" Later in the same session, Jane reported a dream in which she and the therapist were boxers in a ring, and she knocked him down for "a count of nine." Among her associations to the dream was one in which she likened the therapist to the boy who was valedictorian in her senior class at high school and whose academic average was .005 higher than hers. "I wanted to beat the shit out of him in the same way I want to beat the shit out of you. You are both cocky big heads who get all the laurels. I hated my brother for the same reason and my father, too, and all men who think because they got something dangling between their legs, they're somebody." When Jane associated to her knocking the therapist down for a count of nine, she thought of her wish to hurt him, make him suffer, and fight some more. "If I knock you out, the fight is over. I want you to suffer and suffer and suffer while I beat you and beat you and beat you." For several weeks she discussed her depreciation of her own vagina, her penis envy, and her overidealization of the men (particularly father, brother, and the therapist) whom she wished to castrate.

Toward the end of Jane's third year of treatment, she began to focus more directly on oedipal issues and had memories and fantasies of running off with father and having a baby with him. These rather classical oedipal fantasies were recapitulated in her transference relationship. Around this time, she mentioned that she had heard from a colleague in an organization to which she belonged that the therapist would be addressing that organization the following week. Jane told him that she felt very differently from how she did prior to the last encounter. She fantasied walking off with the therapist after the lecture and going to a hotel. Furthermore, she had a wish to exhibit the affair to the audience and "beat them all to the punch." She was further able to talk about how she was repeating with the therapist her fairly strong conviction that she really did murder her mother and capture her father. In the session preceding the lecture, she slipped and said, "I'm looking forward to marrying you—I mean meeting you—at the conference."

At the third extratherapeutic contact, the therapist did not see Jane in the audience but knew she was there. He wrote: "Lately Jane has been talking about oedipal issues. She is freer to express and analyze her sexual fantasies about her father and about me. She is looking at her competition with her mother with less trepidation. Perhaps this extratherapeutic contact will provoke more sexual fantasies about father and me." With regard to his own countertransference feelings, the therapist wrote, "When I was giving my paper, a couple of times I was really reading to Jane and felt like a lover reading poetry and trying to seduce his woman. The extratherapeutic contact really brings my unconscious and preconscious libidinal wishes toward Jane to the surface!"

In the session that followed the lecture, Jane reported that she spent much of her time and energy at the presentation looking for and at the therapist's wife. She recalled memories of looking for her mother after her mother died. She had fantasies of merging with the therapist's wife and for the next five sessions came to her appointments dressed in green—the color of his wife's attire at the meeting. In a dream, reported one session later, Jane was in a cave looking for a woman with whom she could have oral sex.

In Jane's associations to her dream, she thought the woman in the dream was the therapist's wife, and she went on to describe how she wanted to take his place with his wife. She likened his wife's appearance to her mother's appearance and had several fantasies of having mutual masturbation and cunnilingus with the therapist's wife. To the cave, Jane associated a house, then a stomach, and then a whole body. She had wishes to merge with the therapist's wife and went back and forth between being a man with his wife, a little girl with her, or a mother herself, with his wife being her young daughter.

Jane's associations to the dream, which had a negative oedipal and homosexual theme, helped the therapist to recognize some of his own counterresistance problems. In many ways, he was resisting confronting Jane's wish to take his place with his wife. By overemphasizing and concentrating too much on her oedipal fantasies about him, the therapist diminished in his mind her desire to compete with him.

During Jane's fourth year of treatment, she went deeper into her oedipal fantasies and also dealt with many homosexual fantasies about her mother and the therapist's wife. Occasionally, she would use the oedipal position to defend against the inverted oedipal position, and vice versa. As she discussed these fantasies in depth, her external life changed. She became a supervisor on her job, dated men with regularity, and felt much less depressed. In this period, Jane and the therapist had an "accidental" extratherapeutic contact. They met at the theater. Jane and the therapist exchanged smiles and "Hi's," and Jane commented that the play was "very moving." The therapist recorded: "Jane has been intensely involved with many oedipal issues, particularly incest and murder. My hunch is that this extratherapeutic contact will intensify some of these wishes. . . . When I saw Jane with a man at the theater, I felt like a proud papa attending the wedding of his daughter. I also felt some narcissistic satisfaction in realizing how much Jane has progressed in her treatment."

At the following session, Jane reported a dream in which the therapist's wife and Jane's male companion were killed in a car accident, and she and the therapist arranged a liaison with the expectation that they would be married. Jane's associations exposed a wish to wipe out the therapist's wife and be his wife. She resented her male companion for not being a perfect lover and omnipotent human, as she currently imagined the therapist to be. She then recalled some memories from early childhood when she did acrobatics and gymnastics with her father and was sexually stimulated by him. At those times, she would fantasy being father's "queen" and would wish her mother had died. Jane then spent several sessions having fantasies of first wiping her mother out and then having sex with father, feeling guilty about it, and then merging with mother. After feeling too engulfed by mother, she would repeat the same sequence of fantasies.

About 3 weeks after Jane's last extratherapeutic contact she began to recall resenting her parents' sexual relationship. She had had fantasies of getting in between them in bed and shoving her mother onto the floor. She realized that she briefly fantasied doing this to the therapist's wife when she saw her at the theater with him. The parallel between Jane's reactions to seeing the therapist and his wife at the theater and her childhood reactions to her parents' sexual relationship was apparent.

During Jane's fifth and sixth years of treatment, she continued to work on many preoedipal and oedipal themes. She had fantasies of being in mother's body and was in conflict over whether to stay in or break out and kill mother. In addition, she expressed oedipal fantasies similar to those noted above and competitive, phallic fantasies in which she would wrestle and castrate father, brother, or the therapist. In Jane's seventh year of treatment, she attended a panel discussion in which one of her supervisors and the therapist participated. The therapist recorded, "Jane is much more individuated and is enjoying her work and love relationships. She is relaxed much of the time. That's the way she seemed today. Maybe she'll respond to the lecture with less infantile transference fantasies. . . . I experienced Jane as a colleague—an equal of mine. Most of the time I forgot she was in treatment with me. I think she is getting ready (and so am I) for termination."

After this meeting, Jane mentioned in her next session that she was struck by the fact that she saw the therapist and her supervisor as "real people who are competent but not gigantic, imperfect but far from ineffective, sexual but not Superman or Batwoman."

The sequence of Jane's reactions to her extratherapeutic contacts suggests that she perceived her therapist in line with her current transference position and her unique constellation of resistances. Each of the contacts provided material for the therapy and induced an intense response on her part. It would appear that the extratherapeutic contacts enhanced Jane's treatment and did not contaminate it.

Therapists often ask whether extratherapeutic contact is valuable to the treatment or whether it creates hazards. Is it part of the therapy that needs to be worked with or is it a necessary evil? Whether an extratherapeutic contact is viewed as valuable or hazardous depends to a large extent on how the therapist feels about meeting the client outside of the consultation room. If the therapist is anxious that treasured transference and countertransference positions will be altered, worried that he cannot contain regressive wishes in the client or in himself, is uncomfortable in departing from the anonymous, neutral role, then the therapist will, in all probability, find reasons to explain why the meeting should be avoided.

The extratherapeutic contact usually intensifies the current transference position; one of its values, therefore, is to aid therapist and client in further understanding how the client is experiencing the therapist. Also, the therapist has the opportunity of increasing his understanding of current countertransference reactions.

On the other hand, extratherapeutic contacts may serve to lessen the possibility that the therapist will be a fantasy object, particularly if they occur early in treatment. For instance, in Jane's case, she did say, "You are holding out a carrot. . . . You are a tease." Some clients may have to deal with more frustration than they can bear.

Yet the extratherapeutic contact is a fact of life for many therapists and clients. It has values and potential hazards, as do such other departures from routine as cancellations by the therapist, vacations of the therapist, gossip about the therapist, and the therapist raising fees. The best means of using extratherapeutic contacts constructively is by subjecting them to therapeutic exploration. As Greenson (1967) has suggested, whatever the source, whether picked up in the consultation room or from an extratherapeutic contact, knowledge about the therapist is usually the vehicle for unconscious fantasy and must become the subject matter in therapy.

Reluctance to Pay Fees

In almost all therapeutic encounters, clients pay therapists fees. Usually the fee is arrived at by mutual agreement between clients and therapists whereby clients pay what they can afford and therapists receive what they feel they deserve. Providing that the arrangement is satisfactory to both parties, when clients do not pay their bills at the time agreed, usually the last session of the month, the nonpayment in most instances can be regarded as a resistance.

The reasons clients delay paying their bills, as with most resistive behaviors, are complex and varied. Those clients who have strong wishes to be cared for feel angry at paying a fee. They believe they are paying a price to be loved, and like children who want to be loved unconditionally, they experience fees as totally unnecessary and as a bothersome imposition; it punctures their narcissism and threatens their omnipotent fantasies. There are also clients who view the therapist as an arbitrary parent, and paying him a fee can be experienced as "putting out" and "working hard" for someone who is not putting out or working hard enough for them. Clients also can view paying fees in sexual terms. Many of them dream or fantasy that the therapist is a prostitute and that paying the practitioner a fee is like paying for sex. One client said in this regard, "You humiliate me and derogate me by charging me. It's like paying for 'a fix' or getting charged for 'a blow job.' "

Therapists can be uncomfortable about asking for money and about receiving it. In their overidentification with clients, they can feel like indifferent prostitutes, arbitrary parents, or unloving friends. When therapists do not feel confident about themselves, they are prone to accept their clients' arguments that fees are too high and burdensome.

As we know, every complaint from a client that is chronic and persistent is usually, if not always, a product of wishes, defenses, and superego injunctions. Therefore, as with any other form of resistance, the meaning of the nonpayment of fees should be well understood by both client and therapist.

Most clients usually respond positively to an empathic attitude of the therapist's that conveys the notion that "Sure I like to get paid on time, but more important, let's try to understand what you are feeling toward me that makes you reluctant to pay me?"

Although most clients who are delinquent in paying fees usually resume payments when they feel understood rather than reprimanded, some cannot resolve their resistances and continue to withhold payments. Most of the time, they have rationalizations for doing so, such as the rent must be paid or an uncooperative spouse is overspending the money that is set aside for the client's therapy.

When a client does not respond to an understanding therapeutic attitude and continues to withhold payment of fees, the therapist should point out to the client that treatment will stop at a specified date if fees are not paid. This intervention is necessary, not just to protect the practitioner's income, but to help the client cope better with his acting out. It also helps the client with reality testing, because the therapist says, in effect: "I am not an omnipotent parent who will indulge you, nor can I permit you to exploit me."

If therapists continue to treat clients who accumulate debts, they are not helping these individuals because they are reinforcing the clients' infantilism. When clients are placed in this unrealistic psychological position, they inevitably want more and more childish wishes gratified. Eventually, they will have to be turned down, and like children who feel that they have a legitimate right to be treated as royalty, they feel furious and desperate when they are dethroned.

Just as it is a disservice to clients' treatment and a hindrance to their psychological growth to permit them to accumulate debts, it is also ill-advised to charge them lower fees than they can afford. Although it is difficult to ascertain just what an affordable fee is, most therapists have some ideas about typical fees for different income groups in the geographical area in which they work. When clients are charged less than a reasonable fee, like those who accumulate debts, they feel like special children whose narcissism must be indulged. An interesting observation made by experienced therapists is that those clients who are charged low fees are often those who accumulate debts.

Janet I., a divorced woman in her late thirties, sought help for depression, poor interpersonal relationships, job dissatisfaction, and an inability to get along with her 5-year-old daughter, Diane, whom she found difficult to limit.

At her initial consultation with Ms. K., her therapist, Janet brought out that she could not afford Ms. K.'s usual fee of $40 per session. Without exploring Janet's financial situation, Ms. K. lowered the fee to $30, for which Janet was very grateful.

Much of Janet's treatment was focused on her inability to limit Diane's demands. "When the child wants something, I can't say 'no'," remarked Janet over and over again. While Ms. K. gave Janet advice on how to deal with her daughter, Janet was unable to follow through on it.

Ms. K. did not realize that Janet was not able to limit Diane because Ms. K. was not limiting Janet but indulging her instead. By allowing Janet to pay a low fee without exploring Janet's economic situation and by giving her advice without examining the feelings that propelled her requests for advice, Ms. K. was treating Janet as if she were a needy child. This did not help Janet cope with Diane's childish wishes, nor with her own.

Although Janet paid her monthly fees promptly for the first 2 months of treatment, she began to accumulate a debt. Although Ms. K. ignored this at first, she did bring the debt to Janet's attention when 3 months' worth of unpaid fees had piled up. Janet reacted furiously to Ms. K.'s neutral statement: "You are having difficulty paying me." Janet told Ms. K. that she was "not understanding," "not humane," and "much too selfish." She further brought out that Ms. K. gave her the impression that at first she was "very understanding but now you seem so cold and so cruel." Ms. K.'s attempts to resolve the impasse were unsuccessful, and Janet quit therapy prematurely.

Not paying fees is a resistance that can express a variety of emotions. As with the handling of any other resistance, the therapist should approach this with understanding and empathy. If the client does not respond positively, the therapist is forced to become firm and limiting. Otherwise, as we saw in the case of Janet, a therapeutic impasse occurs and the client may leave treatment in anger.

Not paying fees is a clear example of the client's refusal to comply with basic requests of the therapist. Though difficult to handle at times, it is a clearer form of resistance than are the subtle resistances to which we will turn in Chapter 6.

CHAPTER 6

The Middle Phase Continued: Subtle Resistances

In Chapter 5, we discussed the psychodynamics and the technical handling of those behaviors that appear to be obvious resistances (e.g., lateness to appointments, cancellation of sessions, consultations with other therapists, and demands to alter the treatment modality). In this chapter, we examine the dynamics and the treatment of those resistances that are not readily apparent either to client or to therapist. Very often, therapists and clients note that, although the client attends all sessions, arrives on time, speaks freely, pays the therapist's fees cooperatively, and seems to have positive feelings toward the practitioner, the client nevertheless does not make any therapeutic progress. When this occurs, the therapist has to think of which subtle resistances are at work and how they are protecting the client.

Client is Compliant

Every experienced clinician has worked with a type of client who initially appears as a joy to treat but who ends up frustrating and exasperating the therapist. This client characteristically moves into a therapeutic relationship very readily and cooperatively. He verbalizes wishes, feelings, and anxieties with ease and accepts interpretations with gratitude. Never does this client arrive late for appointments, cancel sessions, or have an unpaid bill. Yet this same client, who sought therapy because of dissatisfaction with a low-paying job, an unrewarding marriage, or a poor social life, continues to mention that these presenting problems never improve. When the therapist realizes that this very cooperative client stays fixed in a poor job or cannot leave an unrewarding marriage, he starts to feel some impatience and irritation toward the client. The therapist feels like a frustrated parent, whose loved son or daughter is not succeeding in school or in social relationships.

Although clinicians usually find feelings of impatience and irritability toward their clients difficult to cope with, these countertransference reac-

224

tions can be profitably used in doing therapy. When therapists find that they are beginning to feel annoyed with their "cooperative" clients who do not get better, usually they can hypothesize that these seemingly compliant individuals are trying unconsciously to defeat the therapist.

Compliant clients are usually dominated by punitive superegos; hence, they feel very obligated to submit to most therapeutic requirements. However, like children who feel they must surrender to their all-powerful parents, these clients secretly resent their therapists and rebel against them by not using the therapy constructively. They appear like some of the clients identified by Abraham, whom we referred to in Chapter 2, who "grudge the physician any remark that refers to the external progress of their (therapy) or to its data. In their opinion he ought not to have supplied any contribution to the treatment" (Abraham, 1960, p. 307).

Although most clinicians do not at first realize it, the consistently compliant client is really quite defiant. He is reminiscent of the toddler who willingly sits on the potty and tries hard to defecate in order to please the parent, but despite persistent efforts, the child never produces. When the parent becomes exasperated and takes the child off the potty, the youngster acts out his secret rebelliousness and has "an accident" by messing up the floor with feces. Compliant clients come to sessions regularly, but like compliant toddlers, they resent it. It is as if they experience their appointments with their therapists as orders to go to the bathroom and to produce for their authoritarian and arbitrary therapist.

The compliant client is usually quite masochistic, and as most clinicians know, masochistic individuals have many sadistic fantasies. As Theodor Reik described them in his book *Masochism in Modern Man* (1941), the lambskin they wear hides a wolf. Their yielding always includes defiance, and their submissiveness always contains some opposition. Beneath their softness is hardness; behind their obsequiousness, rebellion is concealed. Through their defeated position, they gain a secret victory.

If the therapist can cope with his irritation with the compliant client and try to make it safe for this client to express defiant feelings and rebellious fantasies toward the practitioner, treatment can be a very productive experience. However, it usually necessitates some care on the therapist's part not to be too gratifying. If the therapist is too gratifying, the compliant client will never disagree.

Saul A., 45, was a capable and successful business executive but found himself doubting his capacities, feeling inferior to his colleagues and depressed by the fact that "I can never like myself for too long." Saul was also disturbed about his relationship with his wife of 16 years, who "alternates between warmth, indifference, and constantly putting me down." For many years, he had fantasies about getting a divorce, but he found it "very painful to think about what it would be like living without Virginia [his wife] and the kids." One of the factors precipitating Saul's wish to enter therapy was a growing ambivalence about his 2-year affair with Ruth, a married woman in his community whom he was seeing several times a week. Saul was worried that Virginia would find out about the affair and decide to leave him.

Saul described his parents as "strict disciplinarians." If he was not first in his class or the outstanding performer on the ball field, or if he did not "say the right thing at the right time," Saul got a tongue lashing. His parents frequently compared him unfavorably with other children whose performance was more to their taste. "Once I got all A's except for one B, and my younger sister got all A's and the whole family ridiculed me."

Saul graduated with honors from an Ivy League college and had his choice of several jobs. Women liked him, but he was particularly attracted to Virginia "because she had both feet on the ground, seemed to know the rules of the road, and wouldn't take crap from anybody."

Rather early in treatment, Saul was able to understand how Virginia was an externalization of his "ego ideal"; that is, he too would have liked to have been in the position of "not taking crap from anyone." Saul idealized Virginia, who seemed to enjoy her dominant position with her husband—telling him what to do, what not to do, and in general making him "toe the line." Virginia was clearly a parental figure for Saul. He craved her approval but rarely felt that he deserved it. After about 4 years of marriage, Saul began to feel some resentment toward Virginia for her controlling attitude and behavior. However, when he asserted himself, he would soon become frightened of his aggression and intimidated by his wife's counterarguments.

In his transference relationship with his male therapist, Dr. W., Saul assumed the role of the hard-working son. He conscientiously reported dreams, fantasies, and history; he always accepted Dr. W.'s interpretations, cooperatively answered his questions, came for his appointments on time, paid his bills promptly, and was very deferential in his attitude toward Dr. W.

Despite Saul's cooperativeness, he recognized himself that he was not making any progress toward resolving his ambivalence about his affair and he did not feel any increased comfort in his marriage. When Dr. W. suggested that maybe Saul felt some dissatisfaction with the therapy or therapist, Saul responded by praising Dr. W. for his "warmth, understanding, and kindness." However, when Dr. W. told Saul that Saul had a marked tendency to praise people without acknowledging any of his resentments, in his characteristic manner Saul complied with Dr. W.'s interpretation and said, "That is quite true" and produced loads of material to validate

Dr. W.'s notions. As a matter of fact, Saul told Dr. W. that he was "brilliant," offered "sharp insights," and was "truly helpful." To this Dr. W. said, "You work hard to be a good boy, and you also work hard to give people what you think they want to hear." Although Saul chuckled on hearing Dr. W.'s interpretation, he did say, "In a paradoxical way, you educated me to something. I realize that I'm always licking ass and never standing up to you and not standing up to anybody else."

Despite the fact that Saul maintained his compliant stance, he began to see that, similar to his relationship with Virginia, he found it difficult to verbalize his anger toward Dr. W. because he was very fearful that his therapist "would retaliate unmercifully." In the eleventh month of his three-times-a-week therapy, Saul dreamed that he was about to yell at a male figure who clearly represented the therapist, but before he could get out any words, Saul lost his voice. In another dream, a nightmare that kept him awake for hours afterward, he saw Dr. W. about to fall off a building and get killed. Saul tried to convince himself in the dream that it was not Dr. W. who was in danger but some stranger.

As Saul associated in his dreams, he could feel for the first time in many years how much pent up rage was in him. As he saw that he could aggress toward Dr. W. and that Dr. W. maintained his neutrality and did not counterattack, Saul was able slowly to give up his compliant defense.

Saul is typical of many masochistic clients who come for psychotherapy. Initially, they are unaware of the tremendous sadism buried beneath their self-effacing and debasing mien. Psychologically, they are like submissive children who are trying to please and extract love from a therapist whom they experience as strict and dominating; when the love they desire is not forthcoming, repressed rage begins to seek expression.

Many times a client's compliant defense is not addressed in the treatment. When this occurs, the client leaves treatment in a loved and beloved transference, and the client's latent resentment is never addressed in the client–therapist relationship. This client feels better for a short while but has to seek out a second therapist.

Mary Ann B. came for more therapy after a 2-year respite from her previous treatment, which lasted for 5 years at a mental health clinic. When Mary Ann was 23 years of age and entered her first therapy, she was suffering from migraine headaches, depression, intense sadomasochistic battles with men, frequent promiscuity, stuttering, and limited job satisfaction. A high school graduate, she seemed much brighter than her limited formal education would imply. Although physically very attractive, she described herself as feeling unappealing, stupid, and not very engaging.

At the time of her second therapy, Mary Ann was 30 years of age and had just become separated from her second husband. She described both of her husbands as bright, dominating, successful businessmen with whom she was passionately in love at first, but grew to resent their domination and sadism. She compared her husbands to her father, with whom she had a very close relationship that had many erotic overtones. From the ages of 4 through 12, Mary Ann was awakened nightly by her father, brought to the bathroom to urinate, and was wiped by him always. Mother was a quiet person, who seemed very much in the background.

When Mary Ann sought treatment a second time, she was in a state of active self-hate and depression. She described her previous therapist, a male, as "wonderfully warm, good-looking, patient, kind, and supportive." Because this therapist was the finest man she had ever met, she was convinced of his competence and therefore found it quite difficult to explain that, within 3 months after the therapy had ended "successfully," all the symptoms that she began treatment with had returned.

As Mary Ann described her first therapeutic encounter, it became quite clear that a constant, mildly erotic transference maintained itself throughout her 5 years of treatment. The therapist's interpretations, as much as could be gathered, centered around Mary Ann's fear of her aggression toward men that had developed because she had constantly felt intimidated by her father. Although no part of her aggression emerged in the transference with her first therapist, Mary Ann was helped to assert herself more with men and was able to separate from her husband without too much conflict. During her first treatment, her depression had lifted, her stuttering had diminished, her self-esteem had been strengthened, and she went on to a better job. Although part of her frigidity remained, therapist and client felt that termination was in order.

As mentioned, Mary Ann's symptoms and interpersonal problems returned a few months after termination. Although she tried "to do it alone," she began to feel the need for more therapy quite keenly after a while. She did not want to go back to her first therapist because "something must have gone wrong."

Within 6 months after she began her second treatment, Mary Ann did become involved in a rather stormy negative transference with her male therapist, Dr. V., who handled the therapy much differently than his predecessor had. When Mary Ann's questions about her therapist's life were turned back to her and her own fantasies were requested, when her pleas for advice about how to handle boyfriends were frustrated and her own thoughts were sought, Mary Ann brought out many sadistic fantasies toward Dr. V. She wanted to take an ax and hit him over the head, saw off his legs, and castrate him. She contrasted Dr. V. with her first therapist and said, "He never let me feel empty or vulnerable. He was always there. You feel so separate and never part of me."

Following her fantasies and dreams of castrating Dr. V., Mary Ann's transference became erotic and quite positive. However, when she was able to fantasy having an affair with Dr. V., during the eighth month of her two-times-a-week therapy, the sexual encounters that she pictured took place in jungles. Dr. V. would be chasing her and attempting to subdue her, rape her, and then beat her up unmercifully. In her fantasies, Mary Ann had to pay a price for a crime—that at 4 years old she stole her father's penis. This penis was of enormous size; it extended from the bottom of her toes through her mouth. Because Mary Ann believed that she had part of Dr. V.'s penis in her mouth, she was able to understand for the first time in her life why she stammered and stuttered. Further treatment, which involved a continued examination of her sadistic fantasies toward her father and Dr. V., resolved her sexual problems and diminished many of her interpersonal conflicts.

The treatment of Mary Ann clearly demonstrates that beneath Mary Ann's compliant facade were strong phallic-aggressive fantasies, oral incorporative wishes of a sadistic nature, and intense penis envy. Because her first therapist "supported" her, answered her questions, and gave her advice, she felt attached to him symbiotically as if his penis were always part of her. With her second therapist, when her requests and demands were subjected to investigation, the ensuing frustration released her phallic aggression and her wish to castrate. Furthermore, when her expressions of erotic wishes were not met with reassurance, as they were in her first therapeutic encounter, she could finally experience a fantasy that had been with her most of her life and had seriously interfered with her adaptation: She had stolen her father's phallus.

Although there are many dimensions of Mary Ann's treatment that have not been discussed, we have enough information to demonstrate how the compliant transference can be used defensively to protect the client from expressing and the therapist from hearing the client's sadistic and negative transference fantasies. From this case we realize once more that, if the therapist is too friendly and supportive, the therapist can deprive the client of the opportunity to dissent. It seems quite apparent that a protective and supportive approach, frequently advocated by many therapists (K. Adler, 1967; Blanck & Blanck, 1979), turns the therapist into a gratifying parent. The result is that the client is forced to idealize the therapist. This offers both client and therapist a passive form of narcissistic joy, but the client's negative fantasies go underground only to reappear in the form of symptomatology after separation and termination (Nagelberg, 1959; Strean, 1982).

When the client is psychologically required to suppress and disguise hostile reactions to frustration, the resistance against feeling and expressing the hateful parts of the psyche is, of course, maintained. Yet when the client is helped to discharge hostile fantasies, the ego is freed of its excessive destructiveness and the creative parts of the personality are made available for healthier productivity (Nagelberg, 1959).

Client Refers Other Clients

A common occurrence in psychotherapy that has been shrouded in secrecy and neglected in the literature is the client's referral of other individuals to the therapist for treatment (Strean & Blatt, 1976). Although many therapists accept referrals from clients without investigating their clients' motives for making the referral, others consistently reject referrals, contending that to accept them would be to join with clients in a subtle form of acting out (Langs, 1974). We believe that neither of these approaches is constructive. Rather, what is crucial is helping clients get in touch with the motives that propel their wish to refer other clients, particularly when the referral may be a manifestation of resistance.

Clients make referrals to their therapists for a variety of reasons. A referral may be an expression of love, such as when the client feels grateful to the therapist for help received and wants to express thanks in the form of a gift. A referral may be made when a client wants a friend or a relative to be the recipient of the same kind of competent help that he has received. Sometimes a referral is made to placate and ingratiate the therapist. Particularly if a client is unable to tolerate angry feelings toward the practitioner, he can deny them by performing "good deeds." Occasionally, a referral may be used by the client as a form of extratherapeutic contact with the therapist. As one client said to his therapist, "I feel like your colleague when I speak to you over the phone and talk about sending you a patient." Often many unconscious motives coalesce when a client makes a referral, and feelings of love and hatred can be expressed at the same time.

The referral, like all interpersonal events that transpire between client and therapist, is a product of unconscious desires, superego mandates, and ego defenses. Inevitably the wish to refer emanates from transference fantasies, and very frequently the client's desire to refer induces countertransference fantasies in the therapist. Therefore, when a client makes a referral to the practitioner, the action should be considered grist for the therapeutic mill. As with the extratherapeutic contact, which we discussed in Chapter 5, the sensitive clinician neither condones nor rejects referrals. Rather, the clinician studies the action with the client so that resistances can be uncovered and transference issues can be clarified. If the client's wish to refer is dismissed or accepted without being examined, many dynamic issues that are pertinent to the client's therapy go underground.

It is particularly important for client and therapist to recognize when referrals are used in the service of resistance; this is likely to be the case when the client refers habitually. It should be noted parenthetically that a client's reluctance to refer someone may also be a sign of resistance, but this issue is difficult to address unless the client brings it up in sessions. Usually, when clients constantly refrain from making referrals, they wish to keep the therapist all to themselves and to be loved exclusively.

Although there are many motives for making a referral, one theme that has been noted quite frequently by researchers is that the person who is selected for referral often symbolically represents a part of the client that he resists facing in his own treatment (Strean & Blatt, 1976). When clients resist facing such issues as dependency strivings, hostile fantasies, or sexual desires, they can project these wishes onto relatives, friends, or colleagues, and then want their therapists to treat these people. Said one client to her therapist, "My brother has difficulties with sex. Since this has never been a problem of mine, I don't know how to help him with this. I'm sure you can help him." In effect, the client's wish to refer her brother was her way of getting rid of her own sexual conflict and have her brother treated for it instead.

Peggy C., a 28-year-old attractive woman, sought treatment for sexual problems, poor interpersonal relationships, especially with men, and job dissatisfaction. In her transference relationship with her therapist, Peggy perceived him as a "benign parental figure" whose very utterance made her "feel stronger." The therapist, Dr. S., emerged in Peggy's dreams as an omnipotent mother with a very big penis who would give Peggy this appendage, or one similar to it, some day.

While Peggy was in the throes of her "phallic-mother" transference, she suggested to some of her women friends that they should get treatment from Dr. S. When Peggy described her friends as "women who couldn't accept their own womanhood," who were "masculine" and were "ball breakers," Dr. S. asked her how she felt about these women and why he would be a good person to treat them. Peggy responded, "They will identify with you and feel like better persons." When this thought was investigated further, Peggy brought out her tremendous contempt for women and her admiration of men and wish to be one, and eventually she realized that she was "seeing herself through" (i.e., identifying with) the friends she wished to refer to Dr. S.

By investigating Peggy's wish to refer her friends to him, Dr. S. was able to help Peggy resolve a resistance. Peggy's wish to refer clients to Dr. S. was her way of warding off examination of her own self-contempt and idealization of men.

Somewhat related to the dynamic constellation we have just discussed is another common motive that is involved in client referrals. Frequently, clients come close to resolving a conflict in treatment and then attempt to adapt to a new way of life. In this new position, increased comfort is coupled with a wish to regress to the older, habitual ways of handling anxiety. To convince themselves and their therapists that they are making progress, they refer a prospective client "who is as I *used* to be" and whom the therapist can help. In this situation, clients frequently feel like older siblings of the referred party, and despite their overt concern for the relative, friend or colleague, they also demonstrate some latent rivalry and subtle contempt toward them. These clients, by their referral, seem to be saying, "It's not my problem anymore. It is the other person's."

Norman D., age 35, sought treatment for depression, temper tantrums, impotence with his wife ("but success with others"), insomnia, dissatisfaction with his job, chronic masturbation, and various psychosomatic complaints. He appeared to handle a great deal of his passivity and latent homosexuality by Don Juan behavior.

In treatment Norman formed an inverted oedipal transference with his male therapist, Dr. R. He attempted to identify strongly with Dr. R. and extolled him constantly while passively submitting to him in his dreams and fantasies. Because of his implicit fears of Dr. R., Norman dropped his extramarital affair within a few months after treatment began, thinking that was what Dr. R. expected of him. Like an obedient son, he committed himself to be "a full-time husband because that is only fitting and proper." At the same time this was occurring, Norman attempted to refer male clients to Dr. R. He described them as "guys who are as I used to be—always running around."

When Dr. R. explored Norman's desire to refer male clients to him, what became exposed was the client's fear that the therapist would punish him for not being a one-woman man, for his wish to continue his affairs, and for his desire to be the therapist's special "son" who would be superior to the clients he wished to refer.

As we implied earlier in this discussion, therapists have to be keenly aware of their own feelings about accepting referrals from clients. If they are unduly concerned about receiving referrals in order to buttress their income or enhance their self-images, they may be too ready to accept referrals without sufficiently exploring the client's transference reactions and other salient issues. On the other hand, if they are too ready to reject referrals, their clients will sense this, and again dynamic issues that feed the clients' resistances will not be addressed.

Referral is a universal practice in psychotherapy. Whether practitioners work in clinics, social agencies, or private practice, they have to confront this issue constantly. Therefore, it behooves them to be aware of the dynamics in a client's referring another individual for psychotherapy so that transference problems can be clarified and resistances can be resolved.

Dreams and Fantasies Used in the Service of Resistance

Although clients in therapy, particularly those involved in psychodynamically oriented treatment, are encouraged to discuss their dreams and fantasies, this material can also be used in the service of resistance. When clients find aspects of their day-to-day living too painful to confront or too embarrassing to reveal, they can resist facing these issues by constantly focusing on dreams and fantasies. If clients are frightened to examine upsetting realities in marriage, on the job, or elsewhere, their anxiety can be somewhat reduced by focusing exclusively on their internal lives. For example, a client who cannot tolerate his anger toward a boss may bring to his therapy sessions one dream after another that deals with father figures punishing him, but he may not be able to associate his dreams with the real job conflict he is experiencing. Similarly, a woman may be having real interpersonal conflicts with her husband, but because she experiences much pain in facing these conflicts, she may fill her therapeutic hours with fantasies of the perfect man and not be aware of the relationship of these fantasies to her real conflicts.

If a therapist is intrigued with fantasies and dreams and has a preference for this kind of material, it will not be too difficult for the therapist to overlook the fact that the fantasies and dreams are being used as a resistance. Fenichel (1945) gave an excellent illustration of this in his report on a patient in analysis who brought in many dreams that involved the patient's drinking milk. Questions, confrontations, and interpretations of the analyst were to no avail because an important reality issue was being overlooked. The patient was giving all his money to his analyst, and as a result, he was economically impoverished. Because he could not feel safe in sharing this fact with the analyst, his resistance took the form of dreaming every night about milk, but suffering every day because he could not satisfy his real hunger.

In contrast to therapists who prefer to hear fantasies and dreams from their clients are those clinicians who would rather listen to real events of their clients' lives. When these practitioners are deluged by symbolic material, they feel frustrated and may react with irritation. This may take the form of not listening to their clients' fantasies and dreams, and they may tell clients to focus on their real lives instead. Such a stance overlooks the fact that dreams and fantasies are being used as a protection against pain and danger. As we know now, if clients sense that their resistances are not being respected, they feel even more threatened and may leave treatment.

As we have been stressing throughout this book, the sensitive therapist, who is appreciative of the complex dynamics of resistance, remains alert to all dimensions of the client's life—internal and external. He recognizes that external realities can be used by clients as a resistance against discussing internal realities and vice versa. Consequently, when the therapist has enough data to be convinced that an aspect of the client's life is being avoided in therapy, he should share this finding with the client in a tactful and empathic manner. How is this notion carried out in practice?

When clients avoid reality issues and concentrate on fantasies and dreams, their fantasies and dreams usually offer clues to what is being avoided. If a client dreams about milk constantly and does not discuss real-life issues at all, the therapist can hypothesize that the client is in reality hungry. If a female client fantasies about romantic men but does not refer to the men in her life, it can be reasonably inferred that she is suffering in her day-to-day relationships with men. And if a man consistently dreams about battles with father figures and avoids discussing real transactions with men, again the therapist can legitimately wonder about the pain that the client is experiencing with men in his daily life.

On hearing dreams and fantasies with the same theme but no references to the realities of the clients' lives, the therapist can wonder out loud: "You've been dreaming a lot lately about milk. Are you missing out on something in your daily life?" Or "You've been fantasying a lot lately about desirable men. How are the men in your life treating you?" These questions, when asked tactfully and in an empathic manner, usually help most clients talk about the painful realities in their lives. However, some clients may continue to resist discussing the real issues in their lives and want to keep them a secret. Then the therapist can use the technical procedures that we discussed in Chapter 5 for dealing with clients who use secrets as a way to resist.

Joyce E., a 19-year-old college student, was in treatment with Ms. Q. because she was failing several of her courses, was very depressed, and had a poor social life. Ms. Q.'s quiet, nonjudgmental attitude helped Joyce feel and function better in school and in her social life.

After about 4 months of weekly therapy, in which the client continued to report on how much she had been helped in the treatment, she brought in dreams in which she was loving and being loved by Ms. Q. Explorations of Joyce's homosexual fantasies, interpretations of her maternal transference, and confrontations of her preoedipal yearnings were all accepted by

Joyce with gratitude, and she brought in more material to confirm the correctness of Ms. Q.'s interventions. However, the same kinds of dreams continued to be reported by Joyce.

It was not until Ms. Q. began to question what was going on in Joyce's daily transactions with women that the meaning of her persistent dreams became clearer. When Joyce was confronted with the question, "How are your relationships with the women in your life going?," she turned red with embarrassment and became very silent. On Ms. Q.'s taking note of how much her question upset Joyce, she was able to state eventually that she was sexually attracted to a woman professor, had many erotic fantasies toward her, but was afraid that Ms. Q. would react punitively if she heard "how much of a lesbian I am."

Joyce E.'s continual preoccupation with dreams served as a resistance to protect her in therapy. By focusing exclusively on her dreams, she could avoid discussing a real relationship that upset her. Joyce's transference fantasies, although offering a clue to what really distressed her, also served as a resistance to protect her against facing her real feelings toward her female professor.

Client Overemphasizes Reality Issues

One of the most common and most persistent resistances in psychotherapy is the client's overemphasis on reality issues (Fine, 1982; Strean, 1979). Many clients maintain a conviction that they are victims of realistic circumstances and continually point out to their therapists that, if these external circumstances were different, they would be happier human beings. Husbands blame their wives for their misery, and unhappy wives are sure that they are the victims of their neurotic husbands. Children are convinced that they would have much more joy in life if they had different parents, and angry parents frequently point out that they were not blessed with kind and considerate children. Bosses project their difficulties onto their employees and vice versa. It seems that it is very difficult for most clients to take responsibility for their problems, and this is one of the main reasons that neurotic misery is difficult to overcome; many people, if not most, do not realize that they write a major portion of their own interpersonal scripts.

Many clinicians, particularly those who work in clinics and social agencies, are confronted daily with clients who ask for advice on how to manipulate their relationships. "How shall I deal with my tyrannical boss?" "What can I do about my alcoholic husband?" "Why does my wife always nag me?" "How can I improve my sex life?" These are typical of the questions that so many clients ask of their therapists. All these queries, it should be noted, ignore the contribution of fantasies, dreams, wishes, superego mandates, anxiety, defenses, and history to the client's conflicts. Rather these questions all imply that problems can be resolved by manipulating one's environment.

Many therapists can be seduced into the belief that the source of all the client's difficulties lies in the environment. Many practitioners have advised clients to get divorced because the clients appear to be the victims of abusive spouses. A similar type of intervention has often been used with the unhappy employee who is advised to leave the job in order to get away from an impossible boss. When a therapist offers this kind of advice, he is usually too identified with the complaining client and thus too hostile toward significant others in the client's environment. He has forgotten an important facet of psychodynamic theory, that regardless of what significant others do, clients bear some responsibility for their troubles and only by looking into themselves can they enjoy happier lives (Fine, 1982).

When a clinician tries to manipulate a client's environment without understanding the client's dynamics first, there is a strong likelihood that treatment results will be quite limited. There are several reasons for this. First, when clients are having difficulty in their interpersonal relationships, they are usually deriving unconscious gratification from their difficulty. As we have pointed out several times, underneath every chronic marital complaint and every chronic parental complaint are unconscious wishes. Consequently, when a client is advised to divorce a spouse or to place a child in an institution, this approach will usually backfire because the client really wants the very thing about which he is complaining. Second, when the therapist attempts to manipulate the client's environment, the client is treated like an indulged child and therefore cannot grow. Finally, clients seem to be able to sense intuitively when they are not receiving appropriate help. If they receive advice on how to manipulate their environments, they become suspicious of their therapists and may drop out of treatment (Langs, 1974).

Beginning therapists usually need to see for themselves the futility of giving advice and of manipulating their clients' environments. Only after noting what happens in a clinical situation can they begin to alter their approach.

Sally F., a married woman in her midthirties, was seeing Mr. P., a young social worker in a social agency, for marital counseling. After Sally spent several sessions making derogatory remarks about her husband, Mr. P. told Sally he thought that she should leave her husband. Astonished, Sally said that she "had never thought of that." She quickly defended herself and said, "I don't have the money!" Mr. P. told Sally that he would help her find the money. Although Sally was grateful to Mr. P. for his "kindness and consideration," she rejected his offer of help and left treatment.

All clients need an opportunity to talk about fantasies and other intrapsychic variables that contribute to their real problems. However, although it is important for the therapist to help the client get in touch with what motives propel real-life problems, it is equally important for the client to have an empathic ear while discussing these issues. Some therapists are too quick to focus on their clients' intrapsychic lives while they are in agony about a relationship with a spouse, upset about a child, or distressed about a boss. Only when clients feel they are not being judged, rushed, or criticized can they begin to assume responsibility for their interpersonal problems and the other dilemmas that occur in reality. If they are pushed too quickly to look at their own roles in their interpersonal conflicts, they feel blamed and criticized and may leave treatment. However, if they get a nonjudgmental, quiet ear, they may eventually see how in many ways they are writing their own scripts.

Ronald G., a 22-year-old college student, was in treatment because college officials accused him of selling drugs on campus. Although he denied that he had anything to do with drugs, when he was given the choice of going into therapy or leaving college, he chose the therapy.

Ronald spent several weeks in his once-a-week therapy talking nonstop about his "lousy dorm," "horrible professors," and "crazy classmates." When his therapist, Ms. O., asked for more information about these, it became quite clear that Ronald could not take any responsibility for his interpersonal difficulties. However, he did compare the professors to his "engulfing" and "overprotective" parents and raged about how all adults belittled him.

When Ms. O. realized in the sixth month of treatment that much of Ronald's contempt toward others was his way of defending himself against feelings of weakness, smallness, and vulnerability, she said to Ronald, "When you are with your profs, you get the feeling that you are back home again with your parents, don't you? Then you feel small and hate it." Ronald acknowledged that Ms. O.'s interpretation was correct and gave many examples from his daily life to corroborate it.

In Ronald's eighth month of therapy, he said to Ms. O., "I'm glad you took your time in showing me how I screwed up. If you did it fast, I would have quit."

What clinicians sometimes forget is that when clients focus exclusively on reality, they are terrified of revealing their fantasies, wishes, and anxieties. Usually these clients are also frightened of intimate feelings toward their therapists and worry that they will be trapped into a powerful dependent relationship or be seduced into a humiliating sexual position. That is why these clients require much patient listening before the therapist can show them how their intrapsychic lives contribute heavily to their day-to-day problems.

A very common resistance is the client's persistent complaint that he is physically unattractive. Many men spend many hours of therapy lamenting about their small builds, and even more men complain about the smallness of their penises. Often women clients bemoan their sad fates because they are sure they are not attractive enough. Usually these men and women have received a great deal of reassurance from others, but this helps them for only brief periods of time inasmuch as their convictions about their unattractiveness are very strong.

Just as complaints about others mask unconscious wishes, complaints about oneself are also used for defensive purposes. When a male client complains that his penis is too small, the therapist knows that the client's conscious fretting serves the unconscious purpose of gratifying his *wish* to have a small penis—a large one would frighten him. Similarly, when a female client talks about her "poor" physical appearance, the therapist realizes that, despite the client's conscious pain, she wants to feel unattractive; if she thought she were pretty or sexy, she would be upset.

Inasmuch as clients distort reality to protect themselves from experiencing specific wishes and guilts, there is only one approach that will help them—namely, an examination of the feelings, fantasies, and memories that cause them anixety.

Tom H., age 35, was in therapy with Dr. N., a male therapist. He sought therapy for an acute depression, lack of confidence, poor self-esteem, and a barren social life. During the course of his therapy, Tom became preoccupied with the fact that he had a small penis. Although Dr. N. tried to help him talk about his sexual feelings and memories, Tom insisted that his penis was too small and that he needed medical attention. During his ninth month of twice-a-week psychotherapy, he said, "We can talk about feelings, thoughts, memories, and all that junk, but it is not going to change the size of my penis. I'm going to see an M.D. for this, not a head-doctor, like you!"

Tom consulted about six physicians, and all assured him that the size of his penis was adequate. However, this did not satisfy him, and he persisted in consulting more and more physicians. Finally, one doctor injected him with testosterone, a male hormone. Within a few days Tom exclaimed,

"My penis has grown and you, Dr. N., are all wrong!" Tom began dating some women and felt euphoric for about 6 weeks. Then one day he came into a session and in a dejected manner said, "My penis has shrunk again, and I need more testosterone." When he went back to the doctor who gave him the testosterone, the doctor told him that his problem was psychological, but Tom did not believe him and got testosterone from another physician.

During the course of Tom's travels to physicians, he began to have dreams with homosexual themes. It became clear to Dr. N. that Tom was receiving homosexual gratification from the injections he was getting from the physician, and Dr. N. further realized that homosexual gratification was something he was looking for from him. When Tom brought in a dream in which he made Dr. N. (who was a psychologist) a medical doctor who was injecting him in the anus, Dr. N. could make the interpretation that his client was looking to be anally penetrated by him. After some protests, Tom spent several weeks recalling childhood memories of having sex play with older boys; most of the sex play consisted of mutual masturbation.

As Tom examined some of his masturbating experiences with older boys, he reminded himself that he always thought that the older boys' penises were much bigger than his own. Soon he was able to recall how small he felt next to his father. As Tom got in touch with fantasies and memories of surpassing his father and "cutting him down," he was able eventually to understand that, by telling himself that his penis was small, he could resist facing his intense competition with his father and other older men.

Reuben Fine has stated:

From the analysis of the reality resistances, it is gradually brought out that the patient's concept of reality is always distorted to some extent; loss of contact with reality can scarcely be maintained as a criterion of a disturbance because it occurs in every case. The differences are primarily matters of degree. . . . The therapeutic process helps to provide the person not only with new insights into his inner life, but also with new ways of perceiving the outer world. This is particularly true of the people in his life who, before therapy, are viewed as happy gods and are gradually made into unhappy mortals as he overcomes his blind spots. (1982, p. 172)

The Negative Therapeutic Reaction

Toward the end of his career, Freud (1926) discovered the *negative therapeutic reaction*. By this term, Freud referred to the many patients who could verbalize all the interpretations given to them but still maintained their symptoms. He reasoned that there must be some force within these patients that prevents their using the insights gained. Freud identified this force as the superego.

When clients resist getting better, their superegos are restraining them from enjoying pleasure. The superego, which is the internalized voices of the parents, forbids the client to enjoy life. Many a client will say, "If my parents heard me talking about sex or aggression in these sessions, they would be furious." Very often after a client has verbalized a thought that is unacceptable to the superego, the client will fantasy that the therapist is upset and ready to throw him out of treatment, thus making the therapist a punitive superego.

Since Freud's discovery, much has been learned about the negative therapeutic reaction. In addition to experiencing superego pressure, the client with the negative reaction to therapy is also trying to defeat the therapist in a subtle manner. By calling attention to the fact that he never improves from treatment, the client is demeaning the clinician and not permitting the therapist to have any influence. Although an oversimplification, it can be stated that the client gets better through positive feelings toward the therapist and is made worse by negative ones. When clients insist that they will never get better, they are unconsciously discharging anger toward their therapists (Fine, 1982).

The negative therapeutic reaction, like virtually all the client's responses, has its roots in childhood. When children feel restricted, frustrated, or neglected, they respond with revenge. They may refuse to eat, to go to the toilet, or to go to school. Just as many capable children defy their parents by not succeeding academically, many capable adults take revenge on their therapists by refusing to get better.

Needs to defeat parents spring from many sources; consequently, there are many possible sources for the negative therapeutic reaction. Clients may be acting out childish competition with their therapists. They may be angry that infantile fantasies of omnipotence are not being gratified by the therapist or that the therapist is not an omnipotent parental figure. Clients can react negatively to sexual frustration, to denial of dependency gratification, or to the therapist's neutrality and relative anonymity.

In helping clients resolve their negative therapeutic reactions, it is important for the therapist to keep in mind that the clients' repressed rage should be verbally released in the therapy sessions. When clients see that their therapists do not react in kind (Schafer, 1983) but are nonjudgmental and accepting, clients eventually identify with their therapists' attitude and the punitiveness of their superegos diminishes.

After being in treatment once a week for 2 years, Kaye I., age 44, told her therapist, Dr. M., a woman of about the same age, that she still could not enjoy sex. Kaye pointed out to Dr. M. that she was aware of her competition with her mother, her adoration of her father, her sibling rivalry, her punitive toilet training, and her wishes to be a little girl, but her frigidity still continued.

As Dr. M. carefully listened to Kaye's enumeration of complaints, she noted the sarcasm in Kaye's voice and called this to her attention. Surprised, Kaye said that she had "no malice" toward Dr. M. and she couldn't understand why Dr. M. was "attacking" her. When Dr. M. was silent, Kaye tearfully brought out that she thought Dr. M. disliked her and wanted her to end the treatment. When Dr. M. did not confirm or deny Kaye's assessment, eventually Kaye could discharge some of her anger. She told Dr. M. that she was "a cold therapist," "an insensitive woman," and "a taskmaster." She compared Dr. M. to both of her parents, who "never wanted me to enjoy a thing."

The more Kaye felt free to ventilate rage toward Dr. M. and toward her parents, the better she felt. When she noted that she derived more sexual pleasure in her life after she had vented her anger in therapy, she realized that her resistance to functioning better had a lot to do with her wish to defeat Dr. M. in the same way she wanted to defeat her parents.

Concomitant with the negative therapeutic reaction are usually feelings of hopelessness. Although the client is unconsciously fighting the therapist, consciously he feels that "nothing seems to help. This is my fate." On hearing their clients speak of enormous pessimism, many therapists are inclined to change the therapeutic modality. Instead of trying to understand the forces that maintain their clients' resistances, they offer advice, prescribe drugs, or manipulate their clients' environment. All these procedures are bound to fail because clients who feel hopeless are unconsciously at war with their therapists and want them defeated. Many times clients who are in the throes of a negative therapeutic reaction secretly hope that their therapists will depart from the standard technique. Then they can prove that "everything you try does not work."

One dimension of the negative therapeutic reaction often overlooked is that the client may unconsciously be trying to get the therapist to gratify some unrealistic childhood wish and is angry that the hoped-for gratification is not forthcoming. This phenomenon is frequently seen among college dropouts who resent the fact that they are not the omnipotent children that they thought they were prior to entering college (Strean, 1982). These clients need much help in shedding some of their grandiose fantasies.

Joe J., 19 years old, was in treatment with Dr. L., a male psychologist. He was referred for therapy because he had failed most of his courses in his freshman year at college. Joe was directed by college officials to take a year off and get treatment. If Dr. L. advised the college that Joe was psychologically able to return the next year, he could do so.

Besides his failure in college, Joe was daydreaming incessantly, attending porno films daily, and masturbating compulsively; he was also taking drugs and was very depressed. Joe's relationships with people consisted of weekly chats with his father, who gave him a handsome allowance of $150 a week, and with some call girls and prostitutes. Joe mentioned early in treatment that he was teacher's pet in grammar school and in high school, but now that he was in a large metropolitan university where he got lost in the crowd, he had little desire to study. Joe's history reflected that he had succeeded in getting to be many people's "favorite."

After presenting salient features of his life, Joe attempted to manipulate Dr. L. by assuring him that, if the therapist wrote a letter right away, Joe could return to college and "all would be well." When Dr. L. asked Joe how either of them could be sure that Joe could do the work well, instead of answering the question, Joe became sullen and depressed. With mild exasperation he said, "I don't think this therapy will work."

After expressing his pessimism about the therapy, Joe became silent. When he saw that Dr. L. remained silent too, Joe attacked the therapist by saying that Dr. L. was supposed to help people but instead seemed like an army sergeant. He pointed out that, if he were the therapist, he would have written a letter a long time ago. The attacks on Dr. L. continued without retaliation until Joe saw that he could not intimidate the therapist nor induce much guilt in him.

Joe then moved to a new tactic. He told Dr. L. that he thought that the therapist did not like him and it made him "feel lousy." As a matter of fact, Joe was getting very depressed from the treatment and was using more drugs. Joe asked, "Aren't you worried about me?" He then reported a dream in which he was lying in a hospital bed suffering and crying and the medical attendant was merely studying him. When Dr. L. remarked that Joe wanted to be pitied and fussed over rather than understood, Joe went on another tirade. He told Dr. L. that he was "a cold stiff," "a sadist," and "a nonhumanist." He looked at a picture of Freud in Dr. L.'s office and said, "If he were alive, he'd be ashamed of you."

The client pointed out over and over again that he was much brighter than the therapist, his professors, and his parents, and he was sure he could do college work. He talked about his successes in high school, where he never had to study. During his third month of therapy, Joe had several dreams of wanting to be back there. When Dr. L. told Joe that his wish to be back in high school defended against his doubts about succeeding in college, Joe tried to debate this issue with the therapist, and in an attempt to prove Dr. L. wrong, he took a part-time job, enrolled in a community college, and took three courses.

The client did reasonably well on the job as well as in the courses, but a month later he was depressed again. He threatened to quit college, the job, and therapy. Joe mentioned that in all three places he felt very unappreciated and again blasted Dr. L. for his unsympathetic attitude. Here the therapist pointed out that it was quite clear that Joe would have an extremely hard time making it in college or in any job because, like a child, he seemed more interested in being admired than in anything else. Shortly after this, Joe had a dream in which he was happily gazing in a mirror when a worker from a moving company altered the mirror so that Joe looked less handsome. The client was able to interpret the dream himself, "I guess you won't let me happily gaze at myself and be a baby. You want movement."

After 9 months of twice-a-week therapy, Joe was able to acknowledge for the first time that therapy was having its impact. He recalled that all his life he was given to by everybody, and he had loved it and had not realized that "as you get older you do have some responsibilities, I guess." He went on to examine more seriously his relationships with adults and with peers and presented one vignette after another to substantiate the notion that he had never considered alternatives other than that he be His Majesty, the Prince. With his increased ability to renounce some of his egocentrism, narcissism, and omnipotence, Joe was able to finish a successful semester at the community college and continue his job. He returned to the university and got A's and B's in his courses. From a near recluse, he began to date girls; from a contemptuous student, he began to enjoy his professors and his courses; and from a depressed boy he became a rather spontaneous and warm young adult.

At the time of a follow-up interview several years after his 2 years of treatment had ended, Joe had received his doctorate in philosophy, was happily married, and was about to teach in a well-known university.

There are myriad factors that can contribute to the negative therapeutic reaction. One common theme is the client's unconscious wish to defeat the therapist. In order to resolve this resistance, the client needs a therapeutic atmosphere that makes it safe to release hostility and a therapeutic relationship that stimulates the client to uncover the frustrated childish wishes that create rage.

Client Intellectualizes

A subtle resistance that many clients use in treatment is intellectualization. The client rarely talks about hurt, rarely considers anger, and rarely allows sexual feelings into consciousness. Instead, the client focuses exclusively on ideas and concepts. To cry, aggress, love, or hate induces feelings of vulnerabiliy in the client; consequently, he protects himself from feeling weak by appearing like a strong intellectual.

Intellectualizing clients often frustrate their therapists. Clinicians usually like to deal with emotion, and when they meet with clients who keep affects out of interpersonal dialogues, they may feel deprived and become irritated. Sometimes it is difficult for therapists to recognize that intellectualizing clients are anxious, frightened people who need to resist in the way they do to avoid feeling demeaned. When therapists get in tune with the fragile component of these clients, they can be of much help to them.

Mabel K., a 35-year-old single woman, was a college professor in treatment with a female therapist, Dr. J. Mabel sought therapy because she felt "a vacuum" in her interpersonal life "a void" in her love life, and "lacunae" in her "overall adjustment." From the very beginning of her treatment, Mabel related to her therapist as if the latter were a member of a seminar. Mabel sermonized, pontificated, and left little room for Dr. J. to say anything. When Dr. J. tried to ask a question or make a comment, Mabel interrupted her and initiated a new "lecture series."

After 4 months of therapy, Dr. J. began to feel bored, sleepy, irritated, and helpless when she was with Mabel. At first, Dr. J. questioned her own competency and wondered what she was doing incorrectly that caused her client to intellectualize so much. On examining her doubts further, Dr. J. realized that she had little opportunity to affect Mabel deleteriously because she was given little opportunity by her client to talk. The more Dr. J. reflected on her own feelings, the more she could see that Mabel wanted to maintain distance between them, lest Mabel feel within herself what she was inducing in Dr. J.

Understanding her client better, Dr. J. during the fifth month of treatment interrupted one of Mabel's monologues and asked, "What are you feeling toward me as you discuss this?" For the first time in her therapy, Mabel was quiet and obviously upset by Dr. J.'s question. After a minute of silence, Mabel said, "I guess I never think much about you. Are you somebody who subscribes to the notion of transference?" Dr. J. replied, "I subscribe to the notion that when two human beings get together they have feelings toward each other." Mabel said, "That's a dimension of interpersonal interaction that I haven't considered too fully."

As Dr. J. patiently but consistently helped Mabel recognize that she was terrified to feel anything toward her therapist, Mabel began to take risks and voice some hurt and anger. As she recalled that when she was a child emotional spontaneity was extremely limited in her family, Mabel could begin to feel for the first time in her life some yearnings to be caressed and loved. She also started to feel some anger for not having emotionally responsive parents.

Although Mabel's treatment lasted several years, the more Dr. J. felt free to focus on the fact that Mabel was leaving her out of the treatment relationship, the more Mabel was able to experience her feelings in and out of therapy.

As we saw in the above case, when the therapist studied her own feelings in the treatment encounter, she could better empathize with her client's psychological state of vulnerability and eventually help her resolve her defensive use of intellectualization. Intellectualizing clients, like most clients, are frequently able to overcome their defensiveness when the therapist is free to help them examine their activity and inactivity in the transference relationship.

Client Emotes Excessively

Whereas some clients are frightened of their emotions and defend against becoming aware of them by intellectualizing, others are frightened of their thoughts and resist by rarely thinking about who they are and why they behave the way they do. Although psychotherapy should be essentially an emotional experience, as we have noted repeatedly, one of its goals is to provide clients with self-awareness. There are some clients, and some therapists as well, who believe that treatment should be a cathartic process and nothing else. Consequently, they take the position that each therapeutic hour should be one in which the client ventilates anger, discharges sexual wishes, cries, and yells. Adherents of this position fail to realize that clients' ego functions—judgment, reality testing, frustration tolerance, interpersonal relations, etc.—will be strengthened only if they gain some mastery over their emotions and achieve some understanding of them.

Clinicians sometimes overlook that clients who emote excessively, even if they appear very distressed, are receiving pleasure from their emotional outpourings. Their exhibitionistic wishes may be gratified or their masochistic urges may be satisfied. These clients frequently appear like little children who believe that the source of all their difficulties is outside of themselves, and as they discharge their emotions, they hope that their therapists will take pity on them and rescue them.

Such clients can induce a variety of countertransference reactions. If the therapist is one who values the discharge of emotions unaccompanied by understanding, then he might derive some vicarious gratification by identifying with the client. When this is the case, the therapist may encourage the client, however subtly, to continue his rantings and ravings. On the other hand, many therapists resent clients who show a tendency toward emotional excesses. Inasmuch as therapists, to be productive and constructive with their clients, must constantly monitor their discharge of emotion, they may be envious of clients who spend their time in therapy discharging their emotions.

As we have discussed in previous chapters, all resistive behavior implies that the client feels in danger. One of Freud's earliest findings was that a resistance is constructed to ward off "unbearable ideas" (Breuer, J. and S. Freud, 1893–1895). Clients who emote excessively dread facing the idea that they are immature children who are frightened to grow up. They also dread confronting such material as omnipotent fantasies, dependency strivings, murderous impulses, and childlike sexual urges. In working with clients who emote excessively, it is necessary to help them look at their feelings rather than just discharge emotions (Fine, 1982).

The clients we are discussing usually find the therapist's suggestion to reflect on their feelings very distasteful. A male client, when he was asked by his therapist to see if he could better understand why he was having one temper tantrum after another in his therapy, said, "You are interrupting my orgasm. You cruel bastard!" Stated a woman who was asked by her therapist about the possible meaning of her constant crying jags in and out of therapy, "You have no concern about me, and you show no care for me."

When therapists work with hyperemotive clients, they can be of much help to them in resolving this form of resistance if they view themselves as parental surrogates who are trying to wean overindulged children. With this paradigm in mind, the therapist warmly but firmly frustrates the client's acting out in sessions, listens patiently and empathically to the client's inevitable anger, never censures the client for his fury, but never retracts from the position that the client's emotional excesses should be examined in treatment.

Harvey K., age 45, entered treatment with Mr. G. because he was upset about the ending of his third marriage and depressed about being fired from his third job in 4 years. From the beginning of his three-times-a-week therapy, Harvey used his sessions to vent his anger at bosses, wives, relatives, friends, and the therapist. There was never a dull or a silent moment in any of his sessions; Harvey yelled, cried, and swore. Occasionally, Mr. G. tried to say something, but he was always summarily dismissed by Harvey.

After Mr. G. saw that Harvey's rantings went on unabated for 4 months, Mr. G. said, "Let me stop you for a minute. I think you should start to consider what makes you feel in a rage all the time!" Harvey looked at Mr. G. and said, "You no good mother fucker! You don't know how to do therapy." Then he got up to leave. As he was half way out the door, Mr. G. said, "I think it might be a good idea to stay and see what upsets you so much when you don't get what you want." Harvey returned but spent the rest of the session telling Mr. G. how he was trying to force Harvey to submit to him and be overpowered by him.

Harvey came 20 minutes late for his next session and proceeded once again to tell Mr. G. what a poor therapist he was. After listening to Harvey's yelling and screaming for 15 minutes, Mr. G. interrupted him and asked, "Do you have any thoughts about why you arranged to be late today?" "There you go again, always trying to understand my motives, you bastard," Harvey exclaimed. He went on to tell Mr. G. that he was not interested in discussing his motives. He knew what was best for him and that Mr. G. "would have to show more flexibility."

Although Harvey's tirades continued for another month, occasionally Mr. G. would try to investigate with him what set off his anger. When Harvey saw that Mr. G. was not intimidated by his outbursts, Harvey's level of intense emotionality diminished somewhat. By the eighth month of treatment, he was able to answer Mr. G. when he asked, "What thoughts do you have about your enormous reluctance to examine your motives?" Harvey said somewhat reflectively, "I guess I always have to be boss. If I'm not, I feel like I'm your slave."

When Harvey recognized that when he wasn't a tyrannical boss he felt like a slave, treatment took a major turn for the better. He got in touch with passive wishes, dependent yearnings, and homosexual strivings— thoughts that had tortured and terrified him for many years. Over time Harvey could appreciate how his intense emotionality served as a resistance against dreaded thoughts.

The client who is intensely emotional can be very trying on the therapist. If the therapist keeps in mind that the client's emotional outbursts are used to ward off frightening thoughts, it is easier to relate therapeutically to the client. Furthermore, if the therapist can feel comfortable in the role of a parental surrogate patiently weaning his child, the resistance has a chance of being resolved.

Somatization

Many clients in psychotherapy have physical ailments. Some of these, such as migraine headaches, insomnia, asthma, and back pain, have a psychogenic basis; others, such as appendicitis, cancer, and pneumonia, may be entirely organic.

It is always important in working with clients who have bodily ailments to make sure that they receive the appropriate medical examinations before psychotherapy is initiated. This enables the therapist to cope better with major resistances of clients who somatize. Some clients who have physical ailments that are psychologically caused insist that their problems are of an organic etiology. Other clients whose bodily ailments are organically caused insist that their maladies are of a psychological origin. When therapists are clear about the facts, they are more able to help those clients who resist by not accepting the medical attention they need and also those who resist by not facing the psychological factors that propel their physical maladies.

For the many clients who like to believe their physical ailments are of a psychological origin when they really are not, the therapist's task is to help them understand better what the ailment means to them and why they fear medical therapy. Often these clients distort the meaning of their maladies because their ailments are experienced as a blow to their narcissism and a puncturing of their fantasies of omnipotence. When these issues are addressed in psychotherapy, such clients may be able to go and get the medical attention they need.

Henry L., age 50, was in therapy with Dr. F., a male psychotherapist. Although Henry had made a lot of progress over the 6 years of his three-times-a-week psychotherapy, he never felt free to discuss a prostate problem that for the past several years had caused him a lot of pain. One day the problem was so agonizing, he had to be rushed to a hospital by ambulance. When he was dismissed from the hospital later in the day with the recommendation that he get further tests, he ignored the advice and went for his usual therapy session.

Interestingly, the excruciating pain that Henry was experiencing for many hours diminished while he was in his therapist's office. This convinced Henry that his prostate problem was psychosomatic and that he did not need surgery.

Further work helped both Dr. F. and Henry realize that the client was using massive denial and self-hypnosis to avoid facing the possibility of surgery. The thought of surgery activated fears of dependency wishes, blows to his narcissism, and a puncturing of his omnipotent fantasies. The surgery also would take Henry away from his therapist, to whom he was very attached, and away from his work, to which he was also very committed.

As Henry was able to get in touch with the many issues that induced strong feelings of vulnerability in him, he was able to face the surgery with less terror.

Many clients use psychosomatic ailments as a resistance. Rather than verbalize their rage, they develop such symptoms as migraine headaches or back pains. Rather than face their separation anxieties, they develop an acute case of asthma, and rather than confront their dependency wishes and passive fantasies, they develop an ulcer. When unacceptable wishes and overwhelming anxieties are converted into psychosomatic symptoms, this is always an unconscious process. Consequently, clients who suffer from psychosomatic symptoms often find it difficult to take responsibility for their plights. Instead, they believe their ailments are imposed on them.

Individuals with psychosomatic problems frequently resent being referred to a psychotherapist. When their physicians prescribe psychotherapy, they may feel abandoned, rejected, and misunderstood. Said one man who was referred to a psychologist for pruritis ani (itchy anus): "It hurts down there [pointing to his anus] not up here [pointing to his head] and I don't belong here. I've been seeing that doctor for years, and now he sends me to the wrong place. I don't need a shrink!" Stated a woman at her initial consultation with a therapist: "I really thought my doctor was helping me with my peptic ulcer. When he sent me to you, I felt horrible. He thinks I'm crazy and that the ulcer is all in my mind."

In working with clients who have somatic illnesses of a psychogenic origin, the therapist should allow these individuals time to vent their outrage about being cast into the position of "a sick patient with psychological problems." When they see that the therapist accepts their anger and does not try to convince them that their problems are signs of craziness, after some time, they may consider the possibility of participating in a psychotherapeutic encounter.

A real difficulty in working with individuals who have psychosomatic problems is that they derive considerable secondary gain from their ailments. The client with an ulcer unconsciously relishes the ministrations of a physician; the client with migraine headaches feels less guilty after experiencing much pain; and the client with gastrointestinal disorders receives masochistic gratification on fretting over a bland diet.

As we have already suggested, it is only by having a therapist who is extremely patient and nonjudgmental that clients with psychosomatic problems can feel some comfort. When they note that the therapist does not depreciate their real pains, does not discuss psychodynamics they do not want to hear, and is not intolerant of their deep suspiciousness, they can involve themselves in psychotherapy.

When clients with psychosomatic problems feel genuinely accepted, they do begin, albeit cautiously, to discuss aspects of their interpersonal and intrapsychic lives. On feeling safer with their therapists, they can release anger, dependency wishes, and sexual desires. As these clients discuss their real feelings with an empathic therapist, it is common for them to somatize less. Usually they do not see the connection between their release of emotions and the diminution of their symptoms. Stated one client after discharging some hostility over a period of several sessions, "I haven't had a migraine for the last several weeks. Maybe I'm getting more sleep!" Another client with ulcers who had spoken to her therapist about deep dependency wishes for a number of sessions said, "I haven't had any ulcer attacks for a number of weeks. It must be the milk I'm drinking."

It is not necessary for the therapist to point out that the psychotherapy is "the cure" when clients point out that they are feeling better. This is for the clients to discover by themselves. If the therapist extols the therapy, clients feel controlled and demeaned and may go into a negative therapeutic reaction. However, when clients begin to note the positive effects of their therapy and to understand the relationship between discharging their affects and feeling better, the therapist can use these discoveries when the clients somatize again. Often clients with gastrointestinal problems who have begun to see the relationship between their bodily ailments and their psychological conflicts will respond positively when the therapist says, "Let's see what you can't stomach these days." Similarly, clients with migraine headaches may be able to look into themselves when asked, "What thoughts are giving you a headache?"

Bob R. was a 15-year-old boy who had been referred to Dr. G., a male psychologist, because he was suffering from asthma. Bob protested the referral and in his initial consultation told Dr. G. that psychotherapy was ridiculous, that Dr. G. looked like a zombie, and that all that Bob needed was medication. When Dr. G. verbalized how manipulated and angry Bob felt, the client said, "Don't give me that sweet talk. All you want is my money." He went on to say that "shrinks" were stupid people who should be hospitalized and that he wondered if Dr. G. had been in a mental hospital for "sad and depressed shrinks."

Dr. G. wondered to himself how "sad and depressed" Bob was feeling and sensed that Bob was projecting his own problems onto Dr. G. Therefore, he tried to help Bob discuss in more detail his perceptions of his therapist. Dr. G. asked, "Do you have any thoughts about what makes me sad and depressed?" Bob liked the question and answered, "See, you do need a psychologist" and began to tell Dr. G. about Dr. G.'s sick parents and how they gave him "a deep inferiority complex."

Inasmuch as Bob felt like a strong doctor with Dr. G. and experienced Dr. G. as "a sick patient," he could continue to come to therapy. As he felt less threatened by Dr. G., he could talk about his own life a little. He brought out some anger at his own "sick parents" and, in his sixth month of once-a-week therapy, confessed that at times he felt unloved.

During the first 6 months of his treatment, Bob did not have one asthma attack. Although he mentioned the fact, he saw no relationship between his symptom-free state and his therapy. However, when Dr. G. said he was going on a vacation, Bob had an attack right in the session. When Dr. G. asked Bob how he felt about not having therapy sessions for a while, Bob said, "I'm relieved. I hate coming here, and you do me no good."

After Dr. G. returned from his 2-week vacation, Bob used his sessions to knock the therapy and the therapist, but for the next 4 months was symptom free. When Dr. G. again mentioned that he would be going on another vacation, Bob had another asthma attack in the session. This time Bob said, "You are probably going to say I'm upset about your going away. Well, maybe you're right, you bastard! I hate to think of needing you, but I do." He cried and laughed as he sang, "I should care. I should let it upset me. I should care, and I do."

Because Bob could acknowledge his dependency wishes, he felt much better, and his asthma was completely cured in time.

Although clients with psychosomatic problems can be helped, there are some who are totally unwilling to accept any psychological interpretations of their symptoms. They continue to rely exclusively on physicians, and when psychotherapy begins to help them, they must oppose the therapy and the therapist.

Reuben Fine cites the following case:

> Melvin, a man of forty, originally suffered an acute anxiety attack for which he went to a physician, who could find nothing organically wrong and recommended psychotherapy. In therapy he was placed with a female therapist, toward whom he responded with a great many sexual reactions. This response corresponded to his life style: Melvin had gone through a long succession of women without any real gratification.
>
> Although he made considerable progress in therapy, at one point the therapist took a ten-week vacation. While she was away, Melvin began to consult a physician. Even though the physician told him over and over that he had nothing organically wrong (his symptom was persistent indigestion), he would not believe it. He eventually broke off therapy and resorted to further physiological treatments for his ailments. (1982, p. 186)

Client Cannot Grasp the Meaning of the Therapist's Remarks

The dialogue between client and therapist is hardly ever a completely rational one. Clients always experience their therapists' remarks through the lens of their current transference state. As we have already suggested several times, if clients are feeling positively toward their therapists, they will in all probability accept their therapists' interpretations and use them constructively. If they are in a negative transference, they will be inclined to disagree with their therapists' comments and oppose using them. Finally, if clients are feeling ambivalent toward their therapists, the therapist's comments most likely will be received ambivalently. Many a client in a positive transference has warmly applauded an incorrect interpretation, and many a client in a negative transference has rejected a correct interpretation.

If clinicians constantly keep in mind that transference is ever-present in the therapeutic relationship, they can better respond to those clients who rarely understand what the therapist is talking about or rarely agree with the content of the therapist's remarks. These clients are in a negative transference, and the negative transference is their major resistance. It is kept alive by clients because they are most uncomfortable when they co-operate with their therapists and are very frightened when they feel warmly toward them. Furthermore, many clients resent their therapists because the therapists are experts. One way of discharging their resentment and gratifying their competitive wishes is to fail to understand the therapists' remarks.

Those clients who habitually fail to grasp the meaning of their therapists' remarks are almost always unaware of their resentment and competition. They appear like young children in school who are striving valiantly to grasp the meaning of the material but just "can't seem to get it." They do not realize that they "can't get it" because they are fighting the learning process. Fear of dependency wishes, distrust of mentors, anger at being imposed upon, terror of sexual wishes are factors that interfere with learning at school and with learning in psychotherapy.

Because psychotherapy is a learning process, clients will relate to their therapists similarly to the ways they related to their teachers and their parents. Children who have been well fed, appropriately limited, and given solid sexual education usually make the best students. They are also the ones who can use therapy well. However, most individuals who seek therapy have not been the recipients of these nutrients and therefore will subtly fight learning in therapy.

Therapists, like parents, can react with impatience and irritation when clients do not incorporate their teachings. Some therapists, in response to their clients failure to grasp their comments, repeat the comments over and over again, only to find that the clients continue to resist. Other therapists give up and do not try to work with their clients' resistive behavior, and dread the time when their appointments come around. These counter-transference reactions can alert therapists to the fact that their clients are subtly fighting them.

When clinicians find that their comments are being rejected or misunderstood, they can tell themselves that their clients unconsciously want to reject them. Slowly, tactfully, and patiently, they must address the latent negative transference. A good way to begin is to ask these clients, "How do you feel right now?" Many will confess that they feel miles away from the therapist and the consultation room. This confession can lead therapist and client to explore how distant from others the client has felt during his whole lifetime. Later, the therapist can ask, "How do you feel toward me right now?" and see just how uncomfortable and tense the client feels.

As the clinician helps the client see that he fails to grasp material because he is uncomfortable with the clinician, the resistance has a chance of being resolved. It will not be resolved by repeating interpretations, admonishing the client to cooperate, or censuring the client's uncooperative behavior.

Sam J., age 40, was in twice-a-week therapy with Ms. B. for depression, sexual difficulties, and feelings of inferiority. After a honeymoon in which Sam felt and functioned better and praised Ms. B. for her help, he moved into a phase of treatment where he failed to understand Ms. B.'s questions and interpretations.

When Ms. B. repeated her questions or reframed her interpretations, Sam continued to point out that he felt "lost," "confused," and "dumb." Slowly it dawned on Ms. B. that Sam was fighting her. During the sixth month of treatment, when Sam was consistently saying that he felt "stupid" and "unable to get to the meaning" of Ms. B.'s comments, Ms. B. asked, "How are you feeling right now?" Sam brought out that he felt "miles apart" from Ms. B. When Ms. B. asked Sam what he thought was the cause of their being "miles apart," Sam brought out how he consistently felt the same way in his marriage, at work, and virtually everywhere. He also brought out that he felt "a big distance" from others as a child.

As Sam was able to talk about his childhood resentments and fears, he gradually began to feel that Ms. B. was his "friend" and began to overcome his resistances to her "teaching" him.

Failure to grasp the therapist's comments is often an overdetermined resistance. By not comprehending questions and not hearing interpretations, the client is maintaining a distance from the therapist. The client really feels like a misunderstood child but is afraid to admit it. Instead, he casts the therapist in the role of the person who is being misunderstood. This projection onto the therapist of the client's difficulty has to be understood by the therapist as an attempt on the client's part to avoid pain. When the therapist empathizes with the client's pain, the client's resistance may be resolved.

CHAPTER 7

Termination:
The Pain of Separation

Because psychotherapy inevitably activates pain, every client resists the process in direct and indirect ways. A minority of clients find therapy so intolerable that they terminate treatment prematurely, and a minority of therapists experience their work with some clients as so difficult that they encourage them, albeit unwittingly, to discontinue treatment. Yet the majority of client–therapist dyads survive the first treatment crisis and also resolve the resistances and counterresistances that emerge during the middle phases of therapy. It is sometimes overlooked that, throughout every treatment encounter, client and therapist are working toward the realization of treatment goals. Sooner or later they have to face the issue of terminating the therapeutic encounter.

Termination as an inevitable phase of the treatment process has received limited attention in the psychotherapeutic literature. Few writers have discussed this as a realistic goal of psychotherapy, and fewer have written about technical procedures that are applicable to the termination phase. Although every experienced clinician recognizes that most, if not all, clients resist termination and that most, if not all, therapists have their counterresistances to the process, the subject has received scant attention.

CRITERIA FOR TERMINATION

Regarding criteria for terminating psychotherapy, Freud in his paper "Analytic Therapy" (1917) referred to the neurotic individual's "return to health" in terms of "whether the subject is left with a sufficient amount of capacity for enjoyment and of efficiency" (p. 457). In effect, Freud took the position that an individual is ready to terminate psychotherapy when he can enjoy the realities and cope with the inevitable frustrations of work and love.

Endorsing Freud's notion about termination, Nunberg (1928) added that at termination the unconscious of the client should be more conscious and the client's ego should not have to expend as much energy in repressing. Hence, such ego functions as judgment, reality testing, and impulse control should be working well. Stated Nunberg, "The energies of the id become more mobile, the superego more tolerant, the ego freer of anxiety and the synthetic function of the ego is restored" (1928, p. 119).

One of the criteria on which most writers on the subject agree is that, before termination can be considered, neurotic symptoms should be relinquished. If the client has entered therapy with such symptoms as sexual inhibitions, phobias, compulsions, or obsessions, these symptoms should have subsided, and there should not be symptom substitution. Furthermore, most experts believe that the client should have some understanding about how and why the symptoms evolved; otherwise, there is the risk of rearousal of symptomatology after termination (Dewald, 1972; Firestein, 1978; Jones, 1936).

Firestein in his book *Termination in Psychoanalysis* (1978) points out that, in some cases, therapist and client will have to be satisfied with incomplete symptom subsidence, but the client should show a tolerance of the remaining symptoms. However, Firestein goes on to postulate some rather ambitious criteria for termination:

> Object relations, freed of transference distortions, have improved, along with the level of psychosexual functioning, the latter attaining "full genitality." Penis envy and castration anxiety have been mastered. The ego is strengthened by virtue of diminishing anachronistic countercathectic formations. The ability to distinguish between fantasy and reality has been sharpened. Acting out has been eliminated. The capacity to tolerate some measure of anxiety and to reduce other unpleasant affects has improved. The ability to tolerate delay of gratification is increased, and along with it there is a shift from autoplastic to alloplastic conflict solutions. Sublimations have been strengthened, and the capacity to experience pleasure without guilt or other notable inhibiting factors has improved. Working ability, under which so many aspects of ego functioning, libidinal and aggressive drive gratification are subsumed, has improved. (1978, p. 227)

Firestein (1978) adds that, in a group of some 30 published contributions that discuss termination, different authors may have emphasized one or another of the above items, but overall there is much agreement.

A few writers have attempted to point out that the person terminating psychotherapy is not going to be exempt from conflict for the remainder of his life. Hartmann (1964) has averred that "a healthy person must have the capacity to suffer and to be depressed" (p. 6). Aarons (1965), drawing heavily on Hartmann's work, has pointed out that in successful psychotherapy conflicts are resolved, but not eliminated, and are replaced by a choice of alternatives.

Regarding transference, most writers take the position that clients are ready for termination when they can perceive the therapist essentially as he really is, rather than as a distorted object who is a product of childish fantasies (Fine, 1982; Firestein, 1978; Jones, 1936). Ferenczi (1927) emphasized that the client at termination should have become "completely unruffled" by the therapist and be able to express emotions freely when with the therapist. Bridger (1950), who has endorsed Ferenczi's position, has suggested that, as an aid to determining the state of transference resolution, the therapist should assess the client's tolerance of intervals between sessions and over vacations. Firestein (1978) has pointed out that it is difficult to appraise the influence of important unfulfilled wishes that can persist during and after termination that propel the client's transference state. He also has suggested that it is never completely possible for the therapist to know precisely what the transference reverberations of termination will be before they actually occur. Firestein concludes, "A measure of approximation in the employment of the criterion of transference resolution is therefore inescapable. Transference resolution continues into the (posttherapeutic) period, a fact asserted by numerous (therapists)" (1978, p. 230).

A practical means of assessing a client's readiness to terminate psychotherapy is to determine how near he approximates "the analytic ideal" (Fine, 1982). This would mean that the client has reduced his hatred markedly and can love easily, and is able to communicate with a wide range of feelings, to be part of a family and of the society, to enjoy sex, to be creative, and to show an absence of neurotic symptoms. In addition, the client's ability to separate from the therapist without too much anxiety is also implied in Fine's criteria for termination.

SEPARATION ANXIETY

Although ending a relationship can be a joyful and positive experience, more often it is a painful, frightening, sad, and ambivalent affair. Separation can be particularly anxiety ridden for clients of psychotherapists. Usually a person enters therapy because he is having difficulty coping with himself and his environment and is under some kind of stress. The need for therapy, as well as the problems and the processes that produce the need, frequently induces feelings of vulnerability and other powerful emotions. If the client has found the therapist to be an empathic ally, separation will not be a matter-of-fact phenomenon but, like the loss of any other important person, it can generate a sense of helplessness and grief (Briar & Miller, 1971).

Separation from clients can be discomforting for therapists as well. They too have had an emotional investment in the process and in their clients' lives, and are not immune to feelings of loss and grief.

It may very well be that the superficial attention paid to this important event stems from the fact that termination conjures up painful associations for both therapist and client—memories of past rejection, abandonment, and loss. As Fox, Nelson, and Bolman (1969) have suggested, the gap in the literature appears to be a reflection of the therapist's defensive processes against the affects involved in termination—a sort of "institutionalized repression."

As much as therapists and clients wish to avoid confronting the end of their relationships, the feelings and ideas associated with separation, as with every other issue of importance in the client's life, must be expressed, understood, and mastered. If they are not, some of the gains of treatment will be lost, and clients will not receive the help they need in confronting future separations.

Inasmuch as termination conjures up painful emotions, many clients regress and manifest the very symptoms that they presented at their initial consultations. By reverting to the old symptoms, they are expressing a wish to begin treatment all over again instead of ending it. Annie Reich (1950) has observed that the revived symptomatology is a client's reaction to his awareness that childish wishes are not going to be gratified by the therapist. Saul (1958) has concluded that the reappearance of old symptoms is an expression of revenge. It is as if the client is saying, "See, you have had no effect on me!"

It would appear that under the impact of separation, with all the anxiety that it induces, clients, by unconsciously returning to the psychological state that existed at the beginning of treatment, are crying out for a parent to comfort them. Kohut (1971) has taken this point of view when he states that the client "recathects once more his demands for the incestuous transference objects before he finally resigns himself to the fact that they are indeed unobtainable" (p. 94).

In many ways, the anxiety that clients experience at termination can be likened to the way children feel at weaning. Having been the recipients of tender love, care, and nurturing, they are reluctant to give this up. Although clients, like children, do have an impulse to grow and relinquish old patterns, taking on new frustrations is never a simple matter. Just as children balk and have temper tantrums when they are weaned from the breast or the bottle, many clients respond to termination with intense anger. They resist termination because they resist the requirements of independence and autonomy. Their anger at this time is an expression of protest at being weaned from their therapist's benign breasts.

With loss comes mourning, and many experienced therapists have pointed out that the termination phase is reminiscent of a funeral. Depending on the quantity and quality of the losses that the client has experienced during his lifetime, the mourning at the loss of the therapist can be mild to severe.

Although every client reacts to termination in his idiosyncratic manner, no client is exempt from feeling separation anxiety. Even though clients enjoy the idea of "graduating" and feel pleasure about "a job well done," it is essential for the clinician to recognize that every client who faces termination has to cope with frustration. Hopes and fantasies are punctured, and real gratifications must be relinquished. That is why many clients at this time not only regress to less mature behavior and manifest old symptoms, but also are inclined to demean the therapy and the therapist, make derogatory remarks about the therapist's procedures, become skeptical about professional help, and explode with rage, anxiety, and sadness. The therapist must contend with these expressions of resistance without being badgered into postponing the termination (Firestein, 1978).

As we have suggested throughout this book, the client's relationship with the therapist stimulates dependency needs and wishes, transference reactions, revelation of secrets, embarrassing moments, exhilaration, sadness, and gladness. Consequently, saying good-bye to the therapist is never easy.

Fifteen-year-old Olive A. had seen her social worker, Ms. Y., weekly for about 9 months, and much progress had been made. Initially a socially isolated and depressed girl who was doing poorly in her academic work, Olive had begun to date, to feel more pleasure in her life, and to become more successful in her schoolwork. She used her relationship with Ms. Y. to talk about hostile and loving feelings toward her parents and other authority figures; she also talked about sexual anxieties, unpleasant memories, and traumatic episodes. In the course of these discussions, Olive felt angry with Ms. Y. at certain times and loving at others. Sometimes she felt well understood and at other times she referred to her therapist as a "ninny."

When Olive began demonstrating less conflict and more autonomy in her day-to-day activities and began to hint that she could "go it alone," Ms. Y. asked her how she felt about ending therapy. After an initial expression of exuberance, Olive declared that her "whole world is caving in." It took many interviews to help Olive express her rage at termination, her gratitude for being helped, and her ambivalence about coping alone. In some interviews, there was real despair in her voice and some of her initial problems returned. She talked about Ms. Y. as "the mother and father I've always wanted and the best friend I've ever had."

After 2 months of discussing termination, Olive suggested that the interviews be held every 2 weeks instead of weekly. Again, the longing for the relationship with Ms. Y., although lessened, was still present. It took 3 more months for Olive to feel comfortable with the idea of being "weaned," and even more work was necessary before she could genuinely welcome being independent.

In reviewing the case of Olive, it becomes apparent that, even in short-term therapy on a weekly basis, the client can have strong resistances to termination. Like many other clients, Olive had to work through her strong wish to maintain an attachment with a parental figure who was also "a best friend." In her termination phase, Olive regressed, her symptoms returned, and she felt acute anger. Consequently, many sessions were needed in order for Olive to resolve her separation anxiety.

When confronted by the client's wish to regress and by the revival of symptoms, beginning therapists feel quite disillusioned. They wonder about their competence, worry about their impact on the client, and start to question whether therapy helps anyone. It is extremely important for all clinicians to recognize that termination inevitably provokes regression and anxiety in clients, and their clients' anger, fears, and helplessness need ventilation. If clinicians do not recognize that anxiety is always present at termination, they will falsely reassure their clients, respond to them with anger, or do something else that is antitherapeutic.

The feelings that Olive experienced at the idea of termination were expressed quite directly. Often clients communicate their separation anxiety nonverbally, through lateness, new crises in their lives, somatic complaints, and unaccountable feelings of depression. The same procedures that we discussed in previous chapters for working with these forms of resistance are no less applicable at termination. Therapist and client have to sensitize themselves to the meaning of these resistances and to the dangers that the client is experiencing.

INDIVIDUALIZING SEPARATION

In order for it to be a positive experience, separation, like any other human event, must be individualized for each client. If therapists understand their individual clients well, they will be better able to anticipate the probable reactions to termination and govern their own behavior accordingly. For example, if clients during the course of therapy have shown many conflicts involving "trust versus mistrust" (Erikson, 1950), it is inevitable that the gains derived from the helping process will be both trusted and mistrusted. If clients were manifesting difficulties that made them doubt their abilities to manage their own lives, separation will probably rekindle "autonomy versus self-doubt" conflicts, and if the problems that emerged in treatment were primary oedipal conflicts, then oedipal issues will probably dominate the treatment process.

George B., age 26, had been in twice-a-week treatment with Dr. T., a female therapist, for close to 3 years. George entered treatment because of sexual difficulties, inability to sustain relationships with women, and depression.

During the course of his therapy, George discovered that what seemed to be in his way when he tried to achieve sexual and emotional pleasure with women was strong anxiety and guilt about his incestuous fantasies. All the young women he dated were involved in relationships with other men. George would become very excited about defeating the other men in his competition with them, but soon after he "triumphed," he lost interest in the women, became impotent with them, and terminated the relationships. George realized during the course of his therapy that he was acting out an oedipal conflict—competing with father for mother. He began to see that, as soon as he conquered the woman, he felt so guilty about his incestuous wishes and hostile-competitive urges that he had to castrate himself—that is, make himself impotent.

As George discussed his oedipal conflicts in therapy, he often made Dr. T. the object of his desires. He had frequent fantasies about the men in her life and often dreamed about killing them and winning Dr. T. During the course of his treatment, George gave up many of his destructive and competitive wishes toward men and was able to tone down many of his incestuous desires. In his third year of treatment, he met a young woman with whom he could sustain a warm relationship that was enjoyable sexually, and he was seriously thinking of marrying her.

As George found that he was liking himself more and saw that many of his conflicts were resolved, he initiated the idea of termination. When Dr. T. asked George to discuss how he felt about ending treatment, initially he was ecstatic, felt proud of himself, praised Dr. T., and thanked her profusely. However, about 3 weeks later, George was very depressed. He started to denounce therapy and felt that Dr. T. seduced him into believing that she could help him, but obviously she could not. When Dr. T. asked George how come he allowed himself to be seduced by her, George responded with intense affect: "I thought I could make it with you. I really thought that even though therapists aren't supposed to screw their patients, I'd be different. Now that we are talking about ending, I kind of feel my chances of hopping into the sack with you are ending."

George needed several months to discuss with Dr. T. how angry he was to remain "just a patient" and never be "a special guy" to her. His intense oedipal conflict, which had occupied center stage during much of his therapy, also was the most dominant theme during termination.

Just as separation means different things to different clients, it means different things to different therapists. As is true with clients at termination, therapists have many reactions—loss, anger, depression, sense of accomplishment, pleasure, etc. Furthermore, therapists find that various clients affect them differently; some clients will induce a wish to hold on, whereas others will activate a wish to let go. Some will stimulate a sense of failure, and others will stimulate a joyful feeling of mastery and success. For therapists to effect a positive termination experience for their clients, they have to be sensitive not only to their clients' feelings but also to their own feelings toward their clients.

Dr. S. had worked with Mary C., a 45-year-old woman, for over 4 years. During this time, he helped her resolve many marital conflicts, depressive feelings, and somatic problems. In the termination phase, Dr. S. found that he could not empathize with Mary's mourning and separation anxiety. Instead, he found himself looking forward to Mary's departure with pleasure. As he observed his gross insensitivity to her over and over again, Dr. S. felt obliged to examine his reactions quite carefully. As he did so, he realized that he was making Mary his sister whom he regarded as "a pest." Terminating treatment with Mary was like getting rid of his pesty sister. As Dr. S. was able to separate his own sibling rivalry from his treatment of Mary, he could more easily identify and empathize with Mary and help her through the termination process.

INTERVENTIONS AT TERMINATION

The specific interventions of therapists at termination are not very different from their activities at any other time during the psychotherapeutic process. Therapists will plan their activities on the basis of their assessment of the client, the client's level of maturation, the client's idiosyncratic resistances, and the meaning of termination to the client. If the prospect of termination has activated feelings of rejection, remorse, and mourning from the client's prior interpersonal relationships, the therapist needs to encourage the client to verbalize, discharge, and understand the meaning the client ascribed to earlier separations. As clients realize that their own anger and unrealistic fantasies might have been at work in past relationships and therefore may have caused them to experience separations very personally and punitively, they may come to appreciate how they are distorting their current experience with their therapists. Thus, the therapist can provide learning experiences for clients on the meaning of separation and loss, and help them lessen their resistance to these events (Siporin, 1975).

Therapists have to sensitize themselves first and later their clients to the mixed feelings that termination inevitably induces. Feelings of anger, depression, joy, exhilaration, and fear not only reflect how clients experience the therapist but suggest what termination and separation in general mean to them. When distortions are unraveled and clients begin to understand emotionally that "the end" is also the beginning, that life does not stop because a relationship has ended, and that they are not being personally rejected, new perceptions evolve, self-esteem rises, and they can face themselves and the world with added strength.

Th clinician's role in the termination process is largely governed by how clients are experiencing both termination and the therapist as they talk about it. For clients who distrust the gains they have made, the therapist offers opportunities to express feelings that the experience was worthless. As the therapist helps clients resolve their resistance against trusting help that has been offered by not censuring their clients when they demean the help and the helper, clients usually come to see themselves, their therapists, and the world a little more clearly. Similarly, if clients, despite the many gains they have made during therapy, fear being autonomous and insist on continuing to rely on the therapist, the therapist should help these clients verbalize their childish demands again so that they can reflect on their doubts concerning their autonomous capacities. As they do this, clients recall past sessions, reconsider old distortions, and eventually move on with more self-confidence.

Many therapists fear that at the termination phase clients will regress to where they were at the beginning of the treatment and stay there. This regression, which we have referred to throughout this chapter, seems to take place with most clients in most settings. If therapists recognize the regression as temporary and do not feel that all their work and their clients' has gone down the drain, therapists can help clients discharge their anxious feelings, empathize with their reluctance to be on their own, and help them understand the unique meaning separation has for them. With this understanding, the client can usually face independence with more certainty.

COMMON RESISTANCES DURING TERMINATION

Having recognized that each client responds to termination in his unique way, it is helpful for the clinician to become familiar with common resistances of clients during the ending phase. The resistances that we will discuss are shown by most clients at some time during the termination phase but are accentuated by some, depending on their unique histories, dynamics, transference reactions, and cluster of resistances that were confronted during the treatment process.

Client Fears Success

Many clients resist termination because ending therapy usually implies success. Although most individuals consciously want to master tasks, overcome obstacles, and enhance themselves, as we have discussed in earlier chapters, many clients are terrified by success and achievement, and therefore shun it.

Success as we have seen can mean the equivalent of defeating parents, subduing rivals, and destroying others. Although fantasies connected with success are usually unconscious, many clients consciously feel guilty and depressed without realizing that their despondent condition is a punishment for their destructive wishes that have been aroused by success. The doom and gloom that appears at termination is often an expression of the fear and terror that success arouses.

Many clients unconsciously view termination as a destructive triumph over their therapists. Recognizing that they may not need their therapists any longer, they worry if they are on the verge of defeating them and destroying them. To resist facing their hostile fantasies, many clients at termination arrange to weaken themselves by regressing to neurotic and childish ways of coping.

Bill D., age 40, had been in twice-a-week treatment with Dr. R., a male therapist, for 3 years. He was in treatment for sexual problems, marital conflicts, and psychosomatic ailments. One of the major traumas in Bill's life was his father's death when the client was 12 years old. At that time, Bill was entertaining many hostile and competitive fantasies toward his father, and when his father died, Bill felt very guilty. His therapy revealed that he thought that he had killed him.

Treatment with Dr. R. was very helpful to Bill. As he relived his hostile fantasies in his transference relationship and saw that Dr. R. remained alive, Bill was able to be more assertive, felt freer sexually, and his psychosomatic problems subsided. However, when Bill and Dr. R. began to discuss termination, all of Bill's presenting problems returned.

When Dr. R. suggested to Bill that perhaps the return of his symptoms had something to do with his feelings about ending treatment, Bill associated to his graduating high school and to his graduating college. He mentioned that, although all his friends and relatives appeared joyous at these times, he was very depressed. Further exploration led Bill to talk about his wish "to hold on to my teachers and not let them go." When Dr. R. asked Bill what came to his mind about not letting people go, he thought of the many dreams and fantasies he had about holding on to his father and never wanting to know that he was dead.

After Bill talked about wanting to hold on to his father, he was able to discuss his strong wish to hold on to Dr. R. He said, "If I let you go, I feel I've killed you!" The more Bill could focus on his wishes to kill Dr. R. and to kill his father, his symptoms abated. Inasmuch as these wishes were not new to Bill, he could use his past work in therapy to overcome his guilt over his destructive wishes and consider again why he felt he had to destroy in order to succeed.

While termination frequently provokes the client's resistance to succeed, a corollary of this is the client's resistance against seeing the therapist succeed. Many clients harbor considerable revenge toward their parents and do not want to provide them with the satisfaction of thinking they did a good job as parents. Rather, they would prefer seeing their parents fret over doing a poor job. This wish, as we discussed in previous chapters, can be transferred to the therapist and is a component of the negative therapeutic reaction (Freud, 1926).

When clients feel revengeful toward their parents, and most do to some extent, not only will they feel revengeful toward the therapist during many phases of the therapy, but they will feel particularly vindictive at termination. For the revengeful client, successful therapy and a peaceful good-bye to the therapist is like letting parents get away with murder. As one client said to his therapist, "If we terminate successfully, I'll feel I'm forgiving you for your mistakes. The hell with that!" The reader will recall the case of Mr. A., the client who would not give the therapist his name for a year and a half. Mr. A. spent most of his last year of treatment discussing his resistance to permitting his therapist to feel successful.

Dependency Conflicts

There are two major ways that dependency conflicts emerge during termination. Some clients, on recognizing that ending treatment means they will be on their own, try very hard to deny they have any feelings about leave-taking. As a result, many of their termination sessions are devoid of affect, as they try to keep a distance from their therapists. These clients emerge as similar to children who are trying valiantly not to cry, despite the fact that they feel very upset. Other clients, to whom we have already referred in this chapter, are so frightened to "cut the cord" they cannot talk about anything else other than how dreadful they feel about being on their own.

Both of these reactions can sometimes be seen in the same client at different times during the termination process.

The therapist's task with clients who deny their sad feelings is to help them get in touch with the danger they worry they will be in if they permit themselves to cry and mourn. Many of them mistakenly believe that, if they have successfully completed treatment, they should not cry and mourn. These clients need help in seeing that a mature adult can be sad, depressed, and mournful (Hartmann, 1964), without regressing to the level of a little child.

For those clients who dread autonomy, the therapist should help them become sensitized to what independence means to them. As we have suggested earlier in this chapter, for many clients being independent means that they are being rejected, hated, abandoned, and even killed. Sometimes these reactions are in response to feelings of guilt. In the following case, the client showed both reactions: a fear of her dependent feelings and a fear of her independent feelings.

Elaine E., a college student, age 20, had been in treatment on a weekly basis for about a year with Ms. P. at a university mental health clinic. At intake, Elaine was doing poorly in her college work, suffered from insomnia, had little self-confidence when she socialized with her peers, and was quite depressed.

Initially, treatment consisted of helping Elaine resolve her resistance to facing that she was missing home. After a couple of months of therapy, Elaine could permit herself to cry and talk about how she missed family dinners and longed for the parties with her friends. As Elaine was able to do this, her symptoms diminished and she felt and functioned better. Slowly she developed a strong, dependent transference toward Ms. P. and began to idealize her. As she brought out her wishes to be Ms. P.'s daughter, she began to identify with her more and more and thought seriously of becoming a therapist herself. This activated some competitive wishes toward Ms. P., which were resolved quite well.

As Elaine was feeling quite good about herself and coping nicely with her environment, she brought up the idea of termination. When Ms. P. asked her how she would feel about stopping treatment at the end of the academic year, Elaine was quite elated about the idea and for the next couple of sessions was in a euphoric mood. However, her manic state soon turned into a bland one and she began to have little to say in her sessions. She came late for appointments and canceled a couple of them, which had not been her pattern during most of the treatment. On trying to investigate the shift in Elaine's attitude, Ms. P. asked her what she thought was going on between them. Elaine, after a few defensive remarks, told her therapist that she guessed she had to have "a stiff upper lip" and be "a real woman" in front of Ms. P. When Ms. P. reminded Elaine that this was the way she coped with leaving home and starting college (i.e., denying her feelings), eventually Elaine was able to experience her sad and mournful feelings about ending treatment. She could tearfully tell Ms. P. how much she would miss her and long for her in the same way she had longed for her family and friends when she left home for college.

As Elaine brought out her strong dependence on Ms. P. and asked if she could see her socially after treatment was over, it became clear that Elaine was reexperiencing her wish to be Ms. P.'s daughter. She was encouraged to talk about these fantasies and the gratifications that she thought could be derived if she were adopted by Ms. P. As during the middle phases of her treatment, Elaine began to talk about her wishes to identify and compete with her therapist. Exploration revealed that, when Elaine wanted to be an adult, and Ms. P.'s equal, she became frightened of some of her destructive wishes toward Ms. P., which were similar to fantasies that she entertained toward her mother during childhood. Her regression to a dependent little girl, it became obvious, was used as a resistance against being autonomous.

The last few sessions of Elaine's therapy consisted of discussions about Elaine's fear of independence. She wanted to be but feared being "a wonder woman with no feelings." When this distortion was resolved, she could successfully terminate therapy.

Elaine's termination phase reveals a phenomenon that takes place with most clients. What was so apparent with Elaine is that she resisted termination in the same ways that she resisted aspects of the entire treatment process. At termination, she had to keep "a stiff upper lip," which was reminiscent of her stoic appearance at the beginning of treatment—a fight against her dependency wishes. When she allowed herself to cry and mourn at termination, this was a recapitulation of her strong wish to be her therapist's daughter, which showed itself earlier in treatment. During treatment and again at termination, it became clear that part of her desire to be a little girl was a resistance used to protect her from being "a wonder woman."

Because clients recapitulate at termination old patterns that were used earlier in the treatment process, both therapist and client can reflect on their earlier discoveries to help them resolve the resistances that emerge during the termination phase.

Punctured Fantasies

As we have pointed out throughout this book, although individuals seek therapy because they are dissatisfied with themselves, it is difficult for them to take responsibility for their unhappy lives. Husbands blame wives for their marital problems and vice versa; children blame their parents for their interpersonal difficulties and vice versa; and employers and employees do the same thing.

Although clients spend much time in therapy trying to overcome childish wishes, omnipotent fantasies, grandiose desires, and other unrealistic aspirations, termination usually reactivates these old wishes. Most individuals find it very difficult to relinquish yearnings to be the best looking, richest, smartest, most loved, and sexiest person in the world. Termination calls forth the awareness that these wishes have not been realized, and the therapist is often called to task for not performing an adequate job.

Usually, clients are not direct about this issue of punctured fantasies, and most of the time they are not consciously aware of why they are so indignant. They may compare themselves with other people who have been in therapy and state that, in contrast to others, they have been given "a raw deal" or have been "ripped off," while their friends and colleagues have better and happier lives. It usually takes some time for clients to recognize that their indignation is related to the puncturing of those omnipotent and grandiose fantasies that were discussed earlier in treatment.

When therapists do not feel guilty or helpless in the face of their clients' attacks, they can be of much help by asking their clients to consider what they were looking for from therapy. As clients are helped to explore their aspirations, they often do become more realistic about what therapy can and cannot do.

Freda F., aged 40, had been in treatment with Ms. M. for 3 years on a three-times-a-week basis. Freda had marital problems, conflicts with employers, psychosomatic ailments, and several phobias.

During the course of her treatment, Freda was able to get in touch with deep-seated rage that had been repressed most of her life. In discharging her rage, Freda became aware of her competition with men and also of her tremendous resentment toward her parents for seeming to favor her two younger brothers. Freda also learned in her therapy that one of the main factors contributing to her marital problems was her unconsciously relating to her husband as if he were a brother. This made Freda very competitive with her husband and made sex with him appear as if it were incest; hence, sex was avoided a great deal.

While working on her competition with men, Freda also became aware of her strong fantasies of omnipotence. In her fantasies, she wanted to kill anyone who seemed powerful because she wanted all the power for herself. She often compared herself to Hitler or Stalin and contended that she wanted to bomb the world because it never made her the center of attention for too long.

As Freda got more in touch with her intense grandiose fantasies, she started to experience them in her transference relationship with Ms. M. In her dreams she gave Ms. M. a penis and tried to rip it off her. She later realized that her image of Ms. M. was what she wanted to be, a phallic woman.

Freda made much progress in her therapy. Over time she began to appreciate the futility of wanting to be a man, and therefore her anger subsided appreciably. She also was able to link her own omnipotent fantasies to her desire to be a man and realized how much she was devaluing herself as a woman and overidealizing men.

As Freda felt and functioned better and found herself consistently feeling positive toward Ms. M., she suggested that she and Ms. M. consider termination of treatment. When Ms. M. showed interest in considering the possibility, Freda remarked that she was pleased to have finished a good job and was ready "to face the world on my own." When she asked Ms. M. if she agreed with the idea of termination and Ms. M. did not answer but instead encouraged Freda to discuss how she thought Ms. M. might feel, Freda exploded with rage. She bellowed, "I thought by now you could be a person and at least offer an opinion since it's near the end of treatment. All you do is sit there with your shit-eating grin and never give a thing."

Freda spent several weeks castigating Ms. M. for all the things that Ms. M. did not give her. Ms. M. never gave her personal opinions about anything, hardly ever praised her, and always made Freda feel like "a second-class citizen." After Freda ventilated her anger, Ms. M. asked Freda, "If you had your druthers, what would you have liked from me?" Freda, following some defensive remarks, pointed out that she wanted Ms. M. to turn her into "a perfect human being," one who was consistently admired, always praised, never disliked, very popular, never anxious, and never indecisive. As Freda continued to explore her aspirations, it became apparent that termination reactivated her strong infantile grandiosity and she was furious that Ms. M. did not turn her into a goddess. It took Freda several months to resolve her resistance to becoming "an ordinary mortal living in an imperfect world." It was difficult to give up her wish "to be a goddess who was out of this world."

The fantasies of omnipotence that we observed in the case of Freda exist to some extent in every client. Fantasies of being "out of this world" are replicas of the child's ideas of what it is like to be grown up. In children's minds, adults have none of the shortcomings and miseries of children. They do no wrong, have no limitations, and are free from anxiety. The client's assumption that perfect bliss characterizes the condition of a "well-therapized" person really expresses the client's longing for the happiness of babyhood (Schmideberg, 1938).

One of the tasks that confronts all clinicians at termination is to help their clients recognize that some of what they are looking for from therapy does not exist. In effect, clients need help in accepting that there is no Garden of Eden and that a fantasied Paradise Lost can never be regained. Clients also need help at termination (and throughout the therapy) in learning that they are "more like other people than otherwise" (Perry, 1982). For many clients, it is an insult to their narcissism to be like others.

Usually it is a sign that clients are getting ready to terminate treatment successfully when their ideas of "cure" become more realistic. Then they see and accept themselves as more like others; also, they can more easily accept limitations in themselves and in others. This, of course, means that these clients have had therapists who accept themselves as being very similar to others and to their clients.

As we pointed out at the beginning of this book, most clients enter treatment anticipating a magical fulfillment of their wishes. During most of the treatment process and particularly during the termination phase, the therapist is trying to help the client slowly come to grips with the fact that there is no such thing as magic (Weinshel, 1984).

As magical wishes and fantasies of omnipotence are toned down and the resistances to termination are resolved, client and therapist are ready to part company. But therapeutic work continues after the formal ending, because the client has learned a way to confront problems and overcome anxieties.

In successful therapy where major problems have been overcome and major resistances have been resolved, therapist and client retain a continuing fondness for each other even though their formal relationship has ended. They realize what Sigmund Freud said to Theodor Reik at their last meeting, "People who belong together do not have to be glued together" (Reik, 1948).

References

Aarons, Z. (1965). On analytic goals and criteria for termination, *Bulletin of the Philadelphia Association of Psychoanalysts, 15*, 97–109.

Abraham, K. (1919). A particular form of neurotic resistance against the psychoanalytic method. In *Selected papers on psychoanalysis.* New York: Basic Books, 1960.

Ackerman, N. (1958). *The psychodynamics of family life.* New York: Basic Books.

Adler, A. (1927). *The practice and theory of individual psychology.* New York: Harcourt.

Adler, G. (1967). Methods of treatment in analytical psychology. In B. Wolman (Ed.), *Psychoanalytic techniques.* New York: Basic Books.

Adler, K. (1967). Adler's individual psychology. In B. Wolman (Ed.), *Psychoanalytic techniques.* New York: Basic Books.

Alexander, F. (1948). *Fundamentals of psychoanalysis.* New York: W. W. Norton.

Alexander, F. (1956). *Psychoanalysis and psychotherapy.* New York: W. W. Norton.

Alexander, F. (1960). *The western mind in transition.* New York: Random House.

Alexander, F. (1961). *The scope of psychoanalysis.* New York: Basic Books.

Alexander, F. (1965). *Psychosomatic medicine: Its principles and application.* New York: W. W. Norton.

Arlow, J., & Brenner, C. (1964). *Psychoanalytic concepts and the structural theory.* New York: International Universities Press.

Balint, M. (1967). Sandor Ferenczi's technical experiments. In B. Wolman (Ed.), *Psychoanalytic techniques.* New York: Basic Books.

Bergler, E. (1969). *Selected papers of Edmund Bergler.* New York: Grune and Stratton.

Bergmann, M., & Hartman, F. (1976). *The evolution of psychoanalytic technique.* New York: Basic Books.

Bieber, I. (1962). *Homosexuality.* New York: Basic Books.

Blanck, G., & Blanck, R. (1974). *Ego psychology: Theory and practice.* New York: Columbia University Press.

Blanck, G., & Blanck, R. (1979). *Ego psychology II. Psychoanalytic developmental psychology.* New York: Columbia University Press.

Blum, H. (1983). The position and value of extratransference interpretation. *Journal of the American Psychoanalytic Association, 31,* No. 3, 587–618.

Boss, M., & Condrav, G. (1967). Existential psychoanalysis. In B. Wolman (Ed.), *Psychoanalytic techniques.* New York: Basic Books.

Brenner, C. (1959). The masochistic character, genesis and treatment. *Journal of the American Psychoanalytic Association, 7,* 197–226.

Brenner, C. (1966). The mechanism of repression. In R. Lowenstein (Ed.), *Psychoanalysis—A general psychology.* New York: International Universities Press.

Brenner, C. (1973). *An elementary textbook of psychoanalysis* (2nd ed.). New York: International Universities Press.

Brenner, C. (1974a). Some observations on depression, on nosology, on affects and on mourning. *Journal of Geriatric Psychiatry, 7,* 6–20.

Brenner, C. (1974b). On the nature and development of affects: A unified theory. *Psychoanalytic Quarterly, 43,* 532–556.

Brenner, C. (1976). *Psychoanalytic technique and psychic conflict.* New York: International Universities Press.

Brenner, C. (1979). Depressive affect, anxiety, and psychic conflict in the phallic–oedipal phase. *Psychoanalytic Quarterly, 48,* 177–197.

Brenner, C. (1982). *The mind in conflict.* New York: International Universities Press.

Breuer, J., & Freud, S. (1893–1895). Studies on hysteria. In J. Strachey (Ed.), *The standard edition of the complete psychological works of Sigmund Freud* (Vol. 2). London: Hogarth Press.

Briar, S., & Miller, H. (1971). *Problems and issues in social casework.* New York: Columbia University Press.

Bridger, H. (1950). Criteria for termination of an analysis. *International Journal of Psychoanalysis, 31,* 202–203.

Briehl, W. (1966). Wilhelm Reich: Character analysis. In F. Alexander, S. Eisenstein, & M. Grotjahn (Eds.), *Psychoanalytic pioneers.* New York: Basic Books.

Bychowski, G. (1952). *Psychotherapy of psychosis.* New York: Grune and Stratton.

Coles, R. (1970). *Erik H. Erikson: The growth of his work.* Boston: Little, Brown and Company.

Coltrera, J., & Ross, N. (1967). Freud's psychoanalytic technique. In B. Wolman Ed.), *Psychoanalytic techniques.* New York: Basic Books.

Deutsch, H. (1939). A discussion of certain forms of resistance. *International Journal of Psychoanalysis, 20,* 72–83.

Deutsch, H. (1966). Discussion remarks in *A developmental approach to problems of acting out* (E. Rexford, Ed.). Monographs of the American Academy of Child Psychiatry, No. 1.

Dewald, P. (1972). The clinical assessment of structural change. *Journal of American Psychoanalytic Association, 20,* 302–324.

Dickerson, M. (1981). *Social work practice with the mentally retarded.* New York: The Free Press.

Dyer, R. (1983). *Her father's daughter: The work of Anna Freud.* New York: Jason Aronson.

Edinburg, G., Zinberg, N., & Kelman, W. (1975). *Clinical interviewing and counseling.* New York: Appleton-Century Crofts.

Eisenstein, S. (1966). Otto Rank: The myth of the birth of the hero. In F. Alexander, S. Eisenstein, & M. Grotjahn (Eds.), *Psychoanalytic pioneers.* New York: Basic Books.

Ellis, A. (1962). *Reason and emotion in psychotherapy.* New York: Lyle Stuart, Inc.

Ellis, A. (1973a). Emotional education with groups of normal school children. In M. Mohesen (Ed.), *Counseling children in groups.* New York: Holt, Rinehart and Winston.

Ellis, A. (1973b). *Humanistic psychotherapy: The rational emotive approach.* New York: Julian Press.

Erikson, E. (1950). *Childhood and society.* New York: W. W. Norton.

Erikson, E. (1959). Identity and the life cycle. *Psychological issues.* New York: International Universities Press, vol. 1, no. 1.

Erikson, E. (1964). *Insight and responsibility.* New York: W. W. Norton.

Erikson, E. (1980). *On the generational cycle.* New York: W. W. Norton.

Eysenck, H. (1952). The Effects of Psychotherapy: An Evaluation. *Journal of Consulting Psychology.* Vol. 16: pp. 319–323.

Fenichel, O. (1938). Problems of psychoanalytic technique. In D. Brunswick (Ed.), *Problems of psychoanalytic technique.* New York: The Psychoanalytic Quarterly Press.

Fenichel, O. (1945). *The psychoanalytic theory of neurosis.* New York: W. W. Norton.

Fenichel, O. (1953). *The collected papers of Otto Fenichel* (H. Fenichel & D. Rapaport, Eds.). New York: W. W. Norton. First Series, 1953; second series, 1954.

Ferenczi, S. (1927). The Problem of Termination of Psychoanalysis. In: *Final Contributions to Psychoanalysis.* New York: Basic Books, 1955, pp. 77–86.

Ferenczi, S. (1950). *Sex in psychoanalysis.* (Ernest Jones, Trans.). New York: Basic Books.

Ferenczi, S. (1952). *Further contributions to the theory and technique of psychoanalysis* (J. Richman, Ed.). New York: Basic Books.

Ferenczi, S. (1955). *Final contributions to the problems and methods of psychoanalysis* (M. Balint, Ed.). New York: Basic Books.

Fine, R. (1962). *Freud: A critical re-evaluation of his theories.* New York: David McKay.

Fine, R. (1971). *The healing of the mind.* New York: David McKay.

Fine, R. (1975). *Psychoanalytic psychology.* New York: Jason Aronson.

Fine, R. (1979a). *The history of psychoanalysis.* New York: Columbia University Press.

Fine, R. (1979b). The love life of modern man. In G. Goldman & D. Milman (Eds.), *Modern man: The psychology and sexuality of the contemporary male.* Dubuque, Iowa: Kendall-Hunt Publishing Co.

Fine, R. (1979c). *The intimate hour.* Wayne, N.J.: Avery Publishing Group, Inc.

Fine, R. (1981). *The psychoanalytic vision.* New York: The Free Press.

Fine, R. (1982). *The healing of the mind* (2nd ed.). New York: The Free Press.

Firestein, S. (1978). *Termination in psychoanalysis.* New York: International Universities Press.

Ford, D. & Urban, H. (1965). *Systems of psychotherapy.* New York: John Wiley and Sons.

Fox, E., Nelson, M., & Bolman, W. (1969). The termination process: A neglected dimension in social work. *Social Work, 14*(4), pp. 53–63.

Freeman, D. 1981. *Marital Crisis and Short-Term Counseling.* New York: The Free Press.

Freeman, L., & Strean, H. (1981). *Freud and women.* New York: Ungar.

Freud, A. (1942a). What children say about war and death. *New Era in Home and School 23,* 185–189.

Freud, A., (1942b). Young Children in Wartime: A Year's Work in a Residential Nursery. Writings, III, pp. 142–211 (with Dorothy Brolingham).

Freud, A. (1946). *The ego and the mechanisms of defense.* New York: International Universities Press.

Freud, A. (1949). Some clinical remarks concerning the treatment of cases of male homosexuality. *International Journal of Psycho-Analysis 30,* 195. (Summary)

Freud, A. (1965). *Normality and pathology in childhood: Assessment of development.* New York: International Universities Press.

Freud, A. (1971). Child analysis as a subspecialty of psychoanalysis. In *The writings of Anna Freud* (Vol. 7), 189–203. New York: International Universities Press.

Freud, S. (1891). *On aphasia, a critical study.* New York: International Universities Press.

Freud, S. (1896). Further remarks on the neuro-psychoses of defense. In J. Strachey (Ed.), *The standard edition* (Vol. 3). London: Hogarth Press.

Freud, S. (1897). Abstracts of the scientific writings of Dr. Sigmund Freud, 1887–1897. In J. Strachey (Ed.), *The standard edition* (Vol. 3). London: Hogarth Press.

Freud, S. (1900). The interpretation of dreams. In J. Strachey (Ed.), *The standard edition* (Vols. 4 & 5). London: Hogarth Press.

Freud, S. (1904). Freud's psychoanalytic procedure. In J. Strachey (Ed.), *The standard edition* (Vol. 7). London: Hogarth Press.

Freud, S. (1905a). Fragment of an analysis of a case of hysteria. In J. Strachey (Ed.), *The standard edition* (Vol. 7). London: Hogarth Press.

Freud, S. (1905b). Three essays on the theory of sexuality. In J. Strachey (Ed.), *The standard edition* (Vol. 7). London: Hogarth Press.

Freud, S. (1909). Notes upon a case of obsessional neurosis. In J. Strachey (Ed.), *The standard edition* (Vol. 10). London: Hogarth Press.

Freud, S. (1910). Wild psychoanalysis. In J. Strachey (Ed.), *The standard edition* (Vol. 11). London: Hogarth Press.

Freud, S. (1911). The handling of dream interpretation in psychoanalysis. In J. Strachey (Ed.), *The standard edition* (Vol. 12). London: Hogarth Press.

Freud, S. (1912a). The dynamics of transference. In J. Strachey (Ed.), *The standard edition* (Vol. 12). London: Hogarth Press.

Freud, S. (1912b). Recommendations to physicians practising psychoanalysis. In J. Strachey (Ed.), *The standard edition* (Vol. 12). London: Hogarth Press.

Freud, S. (1913). On beginning the treatment. In J. Strachey (Ed.), *The standard edition* (Vol. 12). London: Hogarth Press.

Freud, S. (1914). Remembering, repeating and working through. In J. Strachey (Ed.), *The standard edition* (Vol. 12). London: Hogarth Press.

Freud, S. (1915). Observations on transference love. In J. Strachey (Ed.), *The standard edition* (Vol. 12). London: Hogarth Press.

Freud, S. (1916). Some character types met with in psychoanalytic work. In J. Strachey (Ed.), *The standard edition* (Vol. 16). London: Hogarth Press.

Freud, S. (1917). Analytic therapy. In J. Strachey (Ed.), *The standard edition* (Vol. 16). London: Hogarth Press.

Freud, S. (1919). Lines of advance in psychoanalytic therapy. In J. Strachey (Ed.), *The standard edition* (Vol. 17). London: Hogarth Press.

Freud, S. (1920). Beyond the pleasure principle. In J. Strachey (Ed.), *The standard edition* (Vol. 18). London: Hogarth Press.

Freud, S. (1923a). The ego and the id. In J. Strachey (Ed.), *The standard edition* (Vol. 19). London: Hogarth Press.

Freud, S. (1923b). Two encyclopedia articles. In J. Strachey (Ed.), *The standard edition* (Vol. 18). London: Hogarth Press.

Freud, S. (1925a). Negation. In J. Strachey (Ed.), *The standard edition* (Vol. 19). London: Hogarth Press.

Freud, S. (1925b). Preface to A. Aichorn's *Wayward youth*. In J. Strachey (Ed.), *The standard edition* (Vol. 19). London: Hogarth Press.

Freud, S. (1926). Inhibitions, symptoms, and anxiety. In J. Strachey (Ed.), *The standard edition* (Vol. 20). London: Hogarth Press.

Freud, S. (1936). A disturbance of memory on the Acropolis. In J. Strachey (Ed.), *The standard edition* (Vol. 22). London: Hogarth Press.

Freud, S. (1937a). Analysis terminable and interminable. In J. Strachey (Ed.), *The standard edition of the complete psychological works of Sigmund Freud* (Vol. 23). London: Hogarth Press.

Freud, S. (1937b). Construction in analysis. In J. Strachey (Ed.), *The standard edition of the complete psychological works of Sigmund Freud* (Vol. 23). London: Hogarth Press.

Frosch, J. (1983). *The psychotic process.* New York: International Universities Press.

Garrett, A. (1951). *Interviewing: Its principles and methods.* New York: Family Service Association of America.

Garrett, A. (1958). The Worker–Client Relationship. In H. Parad (Ed.), *Ego psychology and dynamic casework.* New York: Family Service Association of America.

Germain, C. (1982). The ecological approach. In discussion on "Resistance," *Practice Digest, 5*(1), 8–9.

Germain, C., & Gitterman, A. (1980). *The life model of social work practice.* New York: Columbia University Press.

Gill, M. (1982). *Analysis of transference* (Vol. 1). New York: International Universities Press.

Glasser, W. (1965). *Reality therapy.* New York: Harper & Row.

Glasser, W., & Zunin, L. (1973). Reality therapy. In R. Corsini (Ed.), *Current psychotherapies.* Itasca, Ill.: F. E. Peacock Publishers, Inc.

Glover, E. (1931). The therapeutic effect of inexact interpretation, *International Journal of Psychoanalysis, 12,* 397–441.

Glover, E. (1955). *The technique of psychoanalysis.* New York: International Universities Press.

Goldstein, A. (1973). Behavior therapy. In R. Corsini (Ed.), *Current psychotherapies.* Itasca, Ill.: F. E. Peacock Publishers, Inc.

Gray, P. (1973). Psychoanalytic technique and the ego's capacity for viewing intrapsychic activity. *Journal of the American Psychoanalytic Association, 21,* 474–495.

Greenson, R. (1953). On boredom. *Journal of the American Psychoanalytic Association, 1,* 7–21.

Greenson, R. (1958a). On screen defenses, screen hunger, and screen identity. *Journal of the American Psychoanalytic Association, 6,* 242–262.

Greenson, R. (1958b). Variations in classical psychoanalytic technique: An introduction. *International Journal of Psychoanalysis, 39,* 200–201.

Greenson, R. (1960). Empathy and its vicissitudes. *International Journal of Psychoanalysis, 41,* 418–424.

Greenson, R. (1961). On the silence and sounds of the analytic hour. *Journal of the American Psychoanalytic Association, 9,* 79–84.

Greenson, R. (1967). *The technique and practice of psychoanalysis.* New York: International Universities Press.

Greenson, R. (1978). *Explorations in psychoanalysis*. New York: International Universities Press.

Grotjahn, M. (1967). Franz Alexander—The Western mind in transition. In F. Alexander, S. Eisenstein, & H. Grotjahn (Eds.), *Psychoanalytic pioneers*. New York: Basic Books.

Haley, J. (1963). *Strategies of psychotherapy*. New York: Grune and Stratton.

Hamilton, G. (1951). *Theory and practice of social casework*. New York: Columbia University Press.

Hartmann, H. (1950). Comments on the psychoanalytic theory of the ego. In *The psychoanalytic study of the child* (Vol. 5). New York: International Universities Press.

Hartmann, H. (1958). *Ego psychology and the problem of adaptation*. New York: International Universities Press.

Hartmann, H. (1964). *Essays on ego psychology: Selected problems in psychoanalytic theory*. New York: International Universities Press.

Hepworth, D. (1979). Early Removal of Resistance in Task-Centered Casework. *Social casework*, Vol. 69, no. 7, pp. 317–322.

Horney, K. (1939). *New ways in psychoanalysis*. New York: W. W. Norton.

Horney, K. (1945). *Our inner conflicts*. New York: W. W. Norton.

Horney, K. (1950). *Neurosis and human growth*. New York: W. W. Norton.

Jaffe, D. (1983). Some relations between the negative oedipus complex and aggression in the male. *Journal of the American Psychoanalytic Association, 31*(4), 956–984.

Jones, E. (1936). The criterion of success in treatment. In *Papers on psychoanalysis*. Boston: Beacon Press.

Jones, E. (1953). *The life and work of Sigmund Freud, The formative years and the great discoveries* (Vol. 1). New York: Basic Books.

Jones, E. (1957). *The life and work of Sigmund Freud, The last phase* (Vol 3). New York: Basic Books.

Jung, C. (1956). *Two essays on analytic psychology*. New York: Meridian.

Jung, C. (1971). *Psychological types*. Princeton, N.J.: Princeton University Press.

Kaiser, H. (1976). Problems of technique. In M. Bergmann & F. Hartman (Eds.), *The evolution of psychoanalytic technique*. New York: Basic Books.

Katz, J. (1978). A psychoanalyst's anonymity: Fiddler behind the couch. *Bulletin of the Menninger Clinic, 42*, 520–524.

Kelman, H., & Vollmerhausen, J. (1967). On Horney's psychoanalytic techniques: Developments and perspectives. In B. Wolman (Ed.), *Psychoanalytic techniques*. New York: Basic Books.

Kempler, W. (1973). Gestalt therapy. In R. Corsini (Ed.), *Current psychotherapies*. Itasca, Ill.: F. E. Peacock Publishers, Inc.

Kernberg, O. (1976). *Object relations theory and clinical psychoanalysis.* New York: Jason Aronson.

Kesten, J. (1970). Learning through spite. In H. Strean (Ed.), *New approaches in child guidance.* Metuchen, N.J.: Scarecrow Press.

Kohut, H. (1971). *The analysis of the self.* New York: International Universities Press.

Kohut, H. (1977). *The restoration of the self.* New York: International Universities Press.

Kris, E. (1951). Ego psychology and interpretation in psychoanalytic therapy. *Psychoanalytic Quarterly, 20,* 15–30.

Langs, R. (1973). *The technique of psychoanalytic psychotherapy* (Vol. 1). New York: Jason Aronson.

Langs, R. (1974). *The technique of psychoanalytic psychotherapy* (Vol. 2). New York: Jason Aronson.

Langs, R. (1975). Therapeutic misalliances. *International Journal of Psychoanalytic Psychotherapy, 4,* 77–105.

Langs, R. (1976a). *The bipersonal field.* New York: Jason Aronson.

Langs, R. (1976b). *The therapeutic interaction.* New York: Jason Aronson.

Langs, R. (1979). *The therapeutic environment.* New York: Jason Aronson.

Langs, R. (1981). *Resistances and interventions.* New York: Jason Aronson.

Langs, R., & Stone, L. (1980). *The therapeutic experience and its setting.* New York: Jason Aronson.

Lipton, S. (1967). Later developments in Freud's technique (1920–1939). In B. Wolman (Ed.), *Psychoanalytic techniques.* New York: Basic Books.

Lipton, S. (1977). The advantages of Freud's technique as shown in his analysis of the rat man. *International Journal of Psychoanalysis, 60,* 215–216.

Loevinger, J. (1976). *Ego development.* San Francisco: Jossey-Bass.

Mahler, M. (1968). *On human symbiosis and the vicissitudes of individuation.* New York: International Universities Press.

Meador, B., & Rogers, C. (1973). Client-centered therapy. In R. Corsini (Ed.), *Current psychotherapies.* Itasca, Ill.: F. E. Peacock, Publishers.

Menninger, K. (1942). *Love against hate.* New York: Harcourt.

Menninger, K. (1963). *The vital balance.* New York: Viking.

Menninger, K. (1973). *Theory of psychoanalytic technique* (2nd ed.). New York: Basic Books.

Nagelberg, L. (1959). The meaning of help in psychotherapy. *The Psychoanalytic Review, 46*(4), 50–63.

Nelson, M. (1968). *Roles and paradigms in psychotherapy.* New York: Grune and Stratton.

Neubauer, P. (1983). Anna Freud's legacy. *Psychoanalytic Quarterly, 52*(4), 507–513.

Noble, D., & Hamilton, A. (1983). Coping and complying: A challenge in health care. *Social Work, 28*(6), 462–466.

Novey, R. (1983). Otto Rank: Beginnings, endings, and current experience. *Journal of the American Psychoanalytic Association, 31*(4), 985–1002.

Nunberg, H. (1928). *Practice and theory of psychoanalysis.* New York: Nervous and Mental Disease Publishing Company.

Perry, H. (1982). *Psychiatrist of America. The life of Harry Stack Sullivan.* Cambridge, Mass.: Harvard University Press.

Pumpian-Mindlin, E. (1966). Anna Freud and Erik H. Erikson—Contributions to the theory and practice of psychoanalysis and psychotherapy. In F. Alexander, S. Eisenstein, & M. Grotjahn (Eds.), *Psychoanalytic pioneers.* New York: Basic Books.

Rank, O. (1907). *Der Kuenstler.* Vienna: Heller.

Rank, O. (1909). *The myth of the birth of the hero.* Leipzig and Vienna: Deuticke.

Rank, O. (1912). *The incest motif in poetry and saga.* Leipzig and Vienna: Deuticke.

Rank, O. (1924). *The trauma of birth.* New York: Harcourt Brace and Company.

Rank, O. (1932). *Art and the artist.* New York: Alfred A. Knopf.

Rank, O. (1945). *Will therapy and truth and reality.* New York: Alfred A. Knopf.

Rank, O., & Ferenczi, S. (1924). *The development of psychoanalysis.* Leipzig and Vienna: Zurich International Press.

Reich, A. (1950). On the termination of analysis. In A. Reich (Ed.), *Psychoanalytic contributions.* New York: International Universities Press.

Reich, W. (1945). *The sexual revolution.* New York: Orgone Institute Press.

Reich, W. (1946). *The mass psychology of fascism.* New York: Orgone Institute Press.

Reich, W. (1948). *Listen, little man.* New York: Orgone Institute Press.

Reich, W. (1949). *Character analysis* (3rd ed.). New York: Orgone Institute Press.

Reik, T. (1941). *Masochism in modern man.* New York: Grove Press.

Reik, T. (1948). *Listening with the third ear.* New York: Farrar, Strauss.

Rogers, C. (1954). *Psychotherapy and personality change.* Chicago: University of Chicago Press.

Sandler, J., Dare, C., & Holder, A. (1973). *The patient and the analyst: The basis of the psychoanalytic process.* New York: International Universities Press.

Saul, L. (1958). *Technique and practice of psychoanalysis.* Philadelphia: Lippincott.

Schafer, R. (1976). *A new language for psychoanalysis.* New Haven and London: Yale University Press.

Schafer, R. (1983). *The analytic attitude*. New York: Basic Books.

Schmideberg, M. (1938). After the analysis. *Psychoanalytic Quarterly, 7,* 122–142.

Siporin, M. (1975). *Introduction to social work practice*. New York: Macmillan.

Socarides, C. (1978). *Homosexuality*. New York: Jason Aronson.

Spotnitz, H. (1969). *Modern psychoanalysis of the schizophrenic patient: Theory of the technique*. New York: Grune and Stratton.

Spotnitz, H. (1976). *Psychotherapy of preoedipal disorders*. New York: Jason Aronson.

Spotnitz, H., & Meadow, P. (1976). *Treatment of the narcissistic neuroses*. New York: Manhattan Center for Advanced Psychoanalytic Studies.

Stamm, I. (1959). Ego psychology in the emerging theoretical base of casework. In A. Kahn (Ed.), *Issues in American social work*. New York: Columbia University Press.

Sterba, R. (1953). Clinical and therapeutic aspects of character resistance. *Psychoanalytic Quarterly, 22,* 1–20.

Stone, L. (1951). Psychoanalysis and brief psychotherapy. *Psychoanalytic Quarterly, 20,* 215–236.

Stone, L. (1961). *The psychoanalytic situation: An examination of its development and essential nature*. New York: International Universities Press.

Stone, L. (1966). The psychoanalytic situation and transference: Postscript to an earlier communication. *Journal of the American Psychoanalytic Association, 15,* 3–58.

Stone, L. (1971). Reflections on the psychoanalytic concept of aggression. *Psychoanalytic Quarterly, 40,* 195–244.

Stone, L. (1973). On resistance to the psychoanalytic process. In B. Rubinstein (Ed.), *Psychoanalysis and contemporary science*. New York: Macmillan.

Strachey, J. (1934). The nature of the therapeutic action of psychoanalysis. *International Journal of Psychoanalysis, 15,* 127–159.

Strean, H. (1975). *Personality theory and social work practice*. Metuchen, N.J.: The Scarecrow Press.

Strean, H. (1978). *Clinical social work*. New York: The Free Press.

Strean, H. (1979). *Psychoanalytic theory and social work practice*. New York: The Free Press.

Strean, H. (1980). *The extramarital affair*. New York: The Free Press.

Strean, H. (1982). *Controversy in psychotherapy*. Metuchen, N.J.: The Scarecrow Press.

Strean, H. (1983). *The sexual dimension*. New York: The Free Press.

Strean, H., & Blatt, A. (1976). Some psychodynamics in referring a patient for psychotherapy. In H. Strean (Ed.), *Current Issues in Psychotherapy*. Metuchen, N.J.: The Scarecrow Press.

Sullivan, H. (1953). *The interpersonal theory of psychiatry.* New York: W. W. Norton.

Sullivan, H. (1954). *The psychiatric interview.* New York: W. W. Norton.

Sundel, M. (1982). *Behavior modification in the human services.* Beverly Hills: Prentice-Hall, Inc.

Szasz, T. (1957). On the experiences of the analyst in the psychoanalytic situation: A contribution to the theory of psychoanalytic treatment. *Journal of the American Psychoanalytic Association, 4,* 197–223.

Tarnower, W. (1966). Extra-analytic contacts between the psychoanalyst and the patient. *Psychoanalytic Quarterly, 35,* 399–415.

Weinshel, E. (1984). Some observations on the psychoanalytic process. *Psychoanalytic Quarterly, 52,* 63–92.

Whitmont, E., & Kaufman, G. (1973). Analytical psychotherapy. In R. Corsini (Ed.), *Current psychotherapies.* Itasca, Ill.: F. E. Peacock Publishers, Inc.

Wolman, B. (1972). *Handbook of child psychoanalysis.* New York: Van Nostrand Reinhold Company.

Wolpe, J. (1958). *Psychotherapy by reciprocal inhibition.* Stanford: Stanford University Press.

Wyss, D. (1973). *Psychoanalytic schools.* New York: Jason Aronson.

Author Index

Subject Index

Acting out, 25, 30
  in first treatment crisis, 173-175
  Freud, S. on, 174, 175
Active technique, Ferenczi on, 60, 62-64
Advice-giving:
  as mistake of therapist during first treatment crisis, 182-184
  request for, during first interview, 131-135
Aggression, fear of as expression of first treatment crisis, 159-163
Alterations of ego, as obstacle to success in psychotherapy, 10-11
"Analysis Terminable and Interminable" (Freud, S.), 10, 59, 69
Analyst, *see* Therapist
Analytic Attitude, The (Schafer), 101
Analytic honeymoon, 149-150
  Fine on, 92-93
  see also First treatment crisis
Analytic ideal, 92
  Fine on, 32
  termination and, 256
"Analytic Therapy" (Freud, S.), 254
Analyzability, Freud, S. on, 51
Anxiety, 13
  Brenner on, 33
  free-floating, 15
  Freud, A. on, 13-14
  instinctual, 13-14
  moral, 14
  real or objective, 13
  of separation at termination, 256-259
Appointments:
  cancellations

first interview, 117-119
  in middle phase, 200-202
  persistent lateness to, 2, 195-200
  resistance to time of, 135-137
Archaic fantasy object, Strachey on, 82
Artist, The (Rank), 69
Autonomy *vs.* shame and doubt, Erikson on, 19
Auxiliary superego, Strachey on, 82-83

Beginning treatment, *see* Initial resistances
"Beginning the Treatment, On" (Freud, S.), 56
Behavior therapy, resistance and, 108-109
Birth trauma, Rank on, 67, 69
Blockage, Horney on, 41
Bodily changes, during therapeutic session, *see* Change, in body during therapeutic session

Cancellations of appointments, *see* Appointments
Cathartic method, Breuer on, 45-46
Change:
  in body during therapeutic session, 61
  fear of in first treatment crisis, 165-168
Character analysis:
  Kaiser on, 77
  Reich on, 14, 74-75, 76
Character resistances, 36
  Reich on, 14-16, 74-76
Clarification, Greenson on, 89, 91
Client-centered therapy, resistance and, 42, 109
Collected Papers (Fenichel), 79